Studies in Theology and Sexuality, 3

Marriage after Modernity

Christian Marriage in Postmodern Times

Published by Sheffield Academic Press Ltd
Mansion House
19 Kingfield Road
Sheffield S11 9AS
England

Printed on acid-free paper in Great Britain
by Bookcraft Ltd
Midsomer Norton, Bath

British Library Cataloguing in Publication Data

A catalogue record for this book is available
from the British Library

ISBN   1-85075-944-8
       1-85075-948-0 pbk

CONTENTS

ACKNOWLEDGMENTS

This book could never have emerged without the help of many people. I thank the electors of the Alan Richardson Memorial Fellowship for their confidence in my proposal, in 1995, to undertake *Marriage after Modernity*. The Fellowship gave me an invaluable term of research leave in the Department of Theology, Durham, England. I thank all the members of that department for their warm welcome, for their company and their erudition. Conversations in particular with Stephen Barton, Ann Loades, Alan Suggate and David Brown helped me. I thank Judy Turner and John Hurst at Van Mildert College, not only for their hospitality but for their interest in and enthusiasm for the project. Above all I thank Phyllis Richardson for making the Fellowship possible. Her kind hospitality and deep interest in the book, during and since my stay in Durham, are greatly appreciated.

I thank Elizabeth Stuart for offering me a contract for the book on behalf of Sheffield Academic Press almost as soon as she had heard of it. I thank my colleagues in the Department of Theology and Philosophy at the University College of St Mark and St John—Caroline Major, Lisa Isherwood, Marian Carter, Jim Little, Will Large, Paul Grosch and Allen Brent—for helping to make the department an academic environment where teaching *and* research are valued, and where undergraduate and postgraduate students alike are inspired and supported. I thank Virginia Ramey Mollenkott, Gerard Loughlin and Elizabeth Stuart for reading the completed draft and making helpful suggestions. Most of all thanks are due to Grace, partner in marriage for thirty-two years. For her, marriage is a practice and she is superb at it. I have learned more about marriage from her than books can tell me.

Adrian Thatcher
July, 1998

Chapter 1

MARRIAGE, METHOD AND MODERNITY

1. *Christian Marriage*

The purpose of this book is first to offer an unreserved commendation of Christian marriage at a time when it is widely disparaged and disowned; and secondly to contribute to a renewed vision for Christian marriage at a time of unprecedented social change.

Marriage is a universal institution which, theologically speaking, is given with creation itself (Gen. 2.24; Mk 10.6-8; Mt. 19.4-6). It is written into the way things are. The marriage relationship is an 'eminently human love', a love which brings together 'the human and the divine'.[1] Partners in marriage are capable of being simultaneously mediators and recipients of that relational love of God which led to the world being created and restored through Christ. For most Christians, East and West, marriage is held to be a sacrament, a *locus* of divine love and grace, which come from beyond the couple themselves and potentially endows their relationship with a non-natural bond of permanent and deepening affection.

This view of marriage as created and uniquely blessed by God will not be recognized by many married and post-married people, whether inside or outside the Christian Church. In every century the theology of marriage has probably not matched the experience of marriage, especially the experience of wives. No account of Christian marriage can hope to be credible which does not acknowledge the gap between high-sounding assertions about the God-given purposes of marriage, its sacramentality, and so on, and the historical lived reality of marriage which may actually have served quite different ends, for example, securing legitimate heirs to property and controlling reproduction,

---

1.   *Gaudium et spes: Pastoral Constitution on the Church in the Modern World*, §49. See, e.g., Austin Flannery OP, *Vatican Council II: The Conciliar and Post Conciliar Documents* (Leominster: Fowler Wright, rev. edn, 1988), p. 952.

while imprisoning wives in permanent legal, moral and domestic subordination to their husbands. Many accounts of holy matrimony merely provide, in Rosemary Haughton's telling phrase, 'a theology of marriage shattered by experience'.[2] A credible Christian theology of marriage will never lose sight of real marriages, and it will seek to speak about, and on behalf of, both partners.

Marriage is frequently discovered to be a violent, loveless institution, and increasingly it is delayed, avoided and terminated. Fewer people are marrying. In the USA there were over 1.1 million marriages in 1990 representing 9.8 marriages per 1000 population. This is only slightly down from the figure of 10.6 marriages per 1000 population for 1980 and 1970.[3] However the provisional figure for 1995 showed a fall to 8.9 marriages per 1000 population,[4] while the number of people avoiding marriage altogether was forecast to double, to 12%.[5] In England and Wales, there were fewer first marriages in 1992 than in 1892, even though the population grew by three quarters during the intervening century.[6] There is now a divorce for every two marriages, and Britain has the highest divorce rate in the European Union.[7] In 1996 a US Government agency calculated the likelihood of a new marriage ending in divorce or anulment at 43%.[8] About 80% of all people marrying in the 1990s will have cohabited first.[9] Research on the enduring effects on

2.   Rosemary Haughton, 'The Meaning of Marriage in Women's New Consciousness', in William P. Roberts (ed.), *Commitment to Partnership: Explorations of the Theology of Marriage* (New York: Paulist Press, 1987), pp. 141-54 (149). For a sustained treatment of marriage which *does* take (North American) experience seriously, see Evelyn Eaton Whitehead and James D. Whitehead, *Marrying Well: Stages on the Journey of Christian Marriage* (New York: Image Books, 1983).

3.   US Census Bureau, *Current Population Survey Reports* (March 1998), based on *Monthly Vital Statistics Reports* (43.12, Supp.), July, 1995.

4.   US Census Bureau, *Statistical Abstract of the United States 1997* (Washington, DC: Hoover's Business Press, 1997), p. 109.

5.   *Statistical Abstract*, p. 112.

6.   Robert Whelan, 'Editor's Introduction', in *idem* (ed.), *Just a Piece of Paper? Divorce Reform and the Undermining of Marriage* (London: Institute of Economic Affairs Health and Welfare Unit, 1995), pp. 1-2.

7.   Whelan (ed.), *Just a Piece of Paper?*, p. 6.

8.   Centres for Disease Control and Prevention (CDC), 1998.

9.   Report of a Working Party of the Board for Social Responsibility, *Something to Celebrate: Valuing Families in Church and Society* (London: Church House Publishing, 1995), p. 34.

children of divorce in Britain and the United States is horrifying.[10] Traditional marriage in every century is now seen to have been shaped in part by patriarchal attitudes and practices. The extent of contemporary violence and abuse in domestic households is only beginning to become evident.[11] Romantic, or companionate marriage, in which most Western societies have heavily invested, has created too many burdens and expectations and so encouraged its own demise. A credible theology of marriage will require a tough-minded vision of holy love which includes romance, companionship and long-term commitment. It will ask why the gap between thought and experience was ever allowed to grow so wide, and it will seek to restore the theological understanding of marriage and the actual experience of marriage into a living unity. It will assume the equality of partners before each other and before God, and therefore take issue with the subordination of women to men assumed in some New Testament texts.[12] There are *theological* reasons for regarding marriage as a partnership of equals—without minimizing the genuine differences between them, and in advance of mutually agreed gender roles. These will be explored and commended.

An adequate theology of marriage can probably never be written. The breadth of theological knowledge required, spanning biblical studies, historical theology, church history, contemporary theology and Christian ethics, is matched by the breadth of social history, sociology, social theory and law which all contribute to the understanding of marriage as a historical, theological, social and legal institution. But even this demanding breadth of field is eclipsed by the daunting problems of interpretation which press themselves on any theological inquiry into this topic. The method and principles of interpretation adopted in this book are coterminous with it and best understood by

10. Patricia Morgan, 'Conflict and Divorce: Like a Horse and Carriage?', in Whelan (ed.), *Just a Piece of Paper?*, pp. 19-35; The National Commission on Children, *Beyond Rhetoric: A New American Agenda for Children and Families* (Washington, DC: US Government Printing Office, 1991).

11. See Pamela Cooper-White, *The Cry of Tamar: Violence Against Women and the Church's Response* (Minneapolis: Fortress Press, 1995).

12. James Dunn deals with the question 'How can a twentieth-century European wife hear the command to be subject to her husband in everything (Eph. 5.24) as the word of God?'. See his 'The Household Rules of the New Testament', in Stephen C. Barton (ed.), *The Family in Theological Perspective* (Edinburgh: T. & T. Clark, 1996), pp. 43-64 (61).

reading it. But that does not absolve the author (indeed *any* theological author) from declaring his or her working presuppositions, so this will be attempted next. Since hermeneutical problems (problems of inter-pretation and meaning) appear to be circular, I will do little more than stipulate my own operating assumptions.

2. *Method*

That I am English, married, heterosexual, middle-aged, middle-class and an Anglican layman, may all be safely inferred from what follows. But the business of handling theological sources and the method of arguing from them towards suggestions, proposals and conclusions is less straightforward. I shall use six principles: loyalty to Jesus Christ, to the Bible, to tradition, to experience, to culture and to the people of God. These principles are uncontroversial, yet as soon as one begins to spell them out, controversy is inevitable.

a. *Loyalty to Jesus Christ*
A Christian theologian should seek above all to be faithful to the revelation of the one triune God, as that has been given in Christ, medi-ated through the Spirit and received by the Church. The reign or king-dom of God proclaimed by Jesus reverses worldly norms and expecta-tions and creates a body of people who must love their enemies (Mt. 5.44), sit down to eat with sinners (Mk 2.16; Mt. 11.19), treat each other as equals (Mk 10.35-45), and discern the hungry, thirsty, refu-gees, the unclothed, the sick, prisoners, as the sisters and brothers of Christ (Mt. 25.31-46). Marriage was not a priority among the first Christians. Members of the early churches believed themselves to be 'in Christ' (e.g. 2 Cor. 5.17), and this meant membership of a body of people whose new identity was given them by the crucified and risen Christ (e.g. Rom. 6.3-11), and whose human nature was transformed by God's Spirit (Rom. 8.1-17).

A Christian theologian will therefore wish to remain faithful to Jesus Christ. What other reason can there be for persisting with the attempt to speak the language of a rejuvenated and relevant theology to our con-temporaries in church, academy and world, *unless* it were to remain faithful to Christ? The academy is increasingly sceptical about the coherence of *any* theological truth-claims, and the effort involved in seeking to engage with the 'post-Christian',[13] secular world would surely be excessive if there were no ultimate driving passion to communicate the gospel. Seeking to remain faithful to Jesus Christ indicates that the ultimate theological loyalty is to the transforming power of the Trinitarian God, and not to anything else, such as the detached, intellectual and androcentric theology of the European Enlightenment. Seeking to remain faithful to Jesus Christ means that no other theological source has the claim on us that Christ has, whether this be Bible, creed, tradition or church. Seeking to remain faithful to Jesus Christ assumes continuity with all previous generations of Christians.

b. *Loyalty to the Bible: The Symphonic Imperative*
The witness of the scriptures is to Jesus Christ (Jn. 5.39).[14] From the wealth of literature on biblical interpretation, two questions of Stephen Barton are particularly appropriate for anyone embarking on a theology of marriage which takes the Bible with unconditional seriousness. Addressing the issue of human sexuality specifically, he inquires whether,

> Instead of asking, is the Bible good news for human sexuality?, the question we should be asking is much more of the kind, what sort of people ought we to be and become, so that we are enabled to read the Bible in ways which are life-giving in the area of gender and sexuality?
>
> What if the Bible is more like the text of a Shakespearean play or the score of a Beethoven symphony, where true interpretation involves corporate performance and practical enactment, and where the meaning of the text or score will vary to some degree from one performance to another depending on the identity of the performers and the circumstances of the performance?[15]

13. The term is used to suggest that, in Western societies, most people were once aware of their Christian heritage, whereas now they are unaware of it and do not practice the Christian faith. See Vigen Guroian, *Ethics After Christendom: Toward an Ecclesial Christian Ethic* (Grand Rapids: Eerdmans, 1994).

14. A detailed hermeneutic (i.e. method of interpretation) for biblical teaching about sexuality and gender is offered in my *Liberating Sex: A Christian Sexual Theology* (London: SPCK, 1993), Chapter 2, and my (co-authored with Elizabeth Stuart) *People of Passion: What the Churches Teach About Sex* (London: Cassell, 1997), Chapter 10. See also the criticisms of Rowan Williams in his review of *Liberating Sex* in *Theology*, 98.781 (1995), pp. 3-24 (71): and of Stephen C. Barton, 'Biblical Hermeneutics and the Family', in *idem* (ed.), *The Family*, pp. 6-10.

15. Stephen C. Barton, 'Is the Bible Good News for Human Sexuality?

There are several advantages in letting one's use of the Bible be shaped by these two questions. Attempts to do so will be called 'the symphonic imperative'. We are reminded that there have been, and remain ways of reading the Bible which are *not* life-giving, where discrimination against women, children, slaves, Jews and people of colour has been authorized and normalized, ostensibly by the highest religious authority available to Christians, the very word of God itself. Instead of the beautiful symphony, there has sometimes been a cacophony, as the players have not performed the score as a whole, or have allowed one instrument to drown out all the others, or not allowed the conductor to conduct the performance. These questions remind us that Bible-reading is inseparable from activities and performance among the community of readers. From the point of view of the symphonic imperative it is not the Bible but the community of readers who constitute the problem. The symphonic imperative is the obligation to make music with all Christians, interpreting the score of the Bible to make the glad sound of God's unconditional love.

The symphonic imperative does not dispense with the need for the highest critical and scholarly standards when interpreting the biblical texts. However there is a mountain of scholarly material about the sayings of Jesus and Paul on marriage (below, Chapter 3), and particularly on divorce (below, Chapter 8), and when commentators are divided about what conclusions may be drawn from them the symphonic imperative can be a useful arbiter. The challenge to the community of readers to interpret the Bible in life-giving ways is particularly appropriate to the theology of marriage. First, there are difficult biblical texts about marriage which *prima facie* are *not* life-giving. We will come (below, 3.1.1) to biblical texts which, for example, deploy the metaphor of marriage so as to justify violence against women and to stereotype them as whores deserving punishment. What kind of performance is appropriate as these chilling texts are read? As Renita Weems insists,

> Any discussion about such texts … must address the matter of the metaphor's effects on marginalized readers, especially those against whom it polemicizes. In short, what does it do to those who have been actually raped and battered, or who live daily with the threat of being raped and

Reflections on Method in Biblical Interpretation', in Adrian Thatcher and Elizabeth Stuart (eds.), *Christian Perspectives on Sexuality and Gender* (Leominster: Gracewing; Grand Rapids: Eerdmans, 1996), pp. 4-13 (6).

battered, to read sacred texts that justify rape and luxuriate obscenely in every detail of a woman's humiliation?[16]

Other texts unmistakeably support women's subordination to men (below, 3.2) and it is possible that the surface meaning of some of the sayings of Jesus about divorce have been used to confine wives in impossible marriages. But the symphonic imperative predisposes us towards settling for the interpretation which enhances people's lives.

The key to the interpretation of several of the New Testament texts is to be found in their immediate context: for example, the Pharisees' attempt to trick Jesus into affirming a contentious position over divorce (Mk 10.2; Mt. 19.3), Paul's expectation of the imminent return of Christ[17] (1 Cor. 7.29-34), or the early church's need to demonstrate to its pagan neighbours that it did not wish to overthrow the patriarchal family.[18] These urgent demands determined to no small extent the solutions given in the Scriptures. Today's community of readers addresses very different questions about marriage and family life when it seeks to arrive at 'the mind of Christ' and to proclaim afresh the Good News.

c. *Loyalty to Tradition: The Witness to Other-Regarding Love*
One of the hardest problems for theology is how to handle the past. In particular, how is the wisdom of past generations to be disentangled from the androcentric world-view which distorts it? Marriage practices of former generations, very different from our own, give rise to the pressing question 'Once we admit that certain of our Christian predecessors may, because of the cultural discontinuities which separate them from us, be *strangers* to us, we have to ask the question: how do we understand a stranger?'[19] The Church of England report on marriage, *Marriage and the Church's Task* (1978), tried to deal with theological and historical change by distinguishing between the unchanging substance of faith and its changing, historical expression. Raising the proper question of how loyalty to Christ and the Church's traditions is achievable in the present, the authors say,

16. Renita J. Weems, *Battered Love: Marriage, Sex and Violence in the Hebrew Prophets* (Minneapolis: Augsburg–Fortress, 1995), p. 8.

17. Thatcher and Stuart, *Christian Perspectives*, pp. 17-18.

18. Dunn, 'The Household Rules', p. 61.

19. Nicholas Lash, *Change in Focus: A Study of Doctrinal Change and Continuity* (London: Sheed & Ward, 1973), p. 173.

> ...it is required of Christians, if they wish within this living tradition to
> be loyal to what has come to them from the past and also responsive to
> what confronts them in the present, to discriminate as carefully as possi-
> ble between the substance and its expression, the unchanging and the
> changing. They may neither accept nor reject without reflection and
> discernment the movements of social and cultural change, for these are
> neither necessarily identical with nor necessarily opposed to the provi-
> dential will of God.[20]

The authors also think the interpretation of the Bible may be guided by
distinguishing between the eternal significance and the merely temporal
manifestation of its essential message. 'The witness of the New Testament comes to us from a specific cultural context, and we are constrained to keep in mind the distinction between that which is of
permanent and that which is of only transient value and significance.'[21]

The authors of this report have identified the problem of the complex
tension between current and former versions of living faith within a
single historical tradition, but have stumbled over how to deal with it.
A later Anglican report, *An Honourable Estate* (1988), honestly raises
the question of how the tradition is to be 'deployed by the Church in
the changing social context of its mission', but does not provide an
answer.[22] The authors say there is 'an acceptance on our part the
Church is always having to interpret its given tradition in the social
context', and that 'the rooting of our doctrine in creation reminds us of
the continual need to be sensitive and creative in interpreting the experience of marriage for all who enter into it. We cannot escape the
dialectic between the tradition and our history'.[23]

It may be optimistic to hope that Christians can discern either in
doctrine or in marriage an unchanging substance or core which can then
be contrasted with peripheral, transient or insubstantial developments
or versions of the core. A similar hope is found in a semi-official
Roman Catholic work justifying the ever-growing practice of annulment (below, 8.3) in that church. Ralph Brown, having just announced
some of the momentous changes to marriage brought about at Vatican

20. Report of the General Synod Marriage Commission, *Marriage and the
Church's Task* (The Lichfield Report) (London: CIO Publishing, 1978), p. 32, §83.

21. *Marriage and the Church's Task*, p. 39, §102.

22. Report of a Working Party established by the Standing Committee of the
General Synod of the Church of England, *An Honourable Estate* (GS801; London:
Church House Publishing, 1988), p. 13, §42.

23. *An Honourable Estate*, p. 13, §42.

II, then says in the same paragraph, 'We need to appreciate that while at the heart of the work of the Church's Courts is the fact that *marriage is an unchanging reality*, society's perception of this reality does change'.[24] ('Society's perception' of marriage means those psychological and psychiatric fields which are very useful to the marriage tribunals.) But the unchanging substance or 'unchanging reality' is not going to be identified so easily.

There is an implication that basic meanings are somehow fixed, trans-temporal yet accessible to believers from within the flux of history; while there are changing, transient expressions of those meanings which for each new generation will vary. One might conceivably regard the creeds of the Church as the unchanging core, at least of its doctrine, but within the changing historical tradition each new generation will interpret the creeds differently and may disagree over what constitutes the overall interpretative task. One might say the unchanging core of marriage is the lifelong union of one man with one woman. But this would tell us nothing about which version of marriage as a historical institution was to be preferred, nor what its purposes are, nor about the permitted ages of entry, possibilities of exit, freedom of parties to marry (or re-marry), the quality of the relationship which marriage might be expected to engender, and so on. Since Christianity is a historical faith, its meanings can only ever be grasped historically. While Christians can thankfully grasp that God's revelation comes from beyond history, they may not be able to distinguish between the eternal core and the transient options within the whole. There is an unintended Platonizing in *Marriage and the Church's Task*. The studiously neutral attitude towards social and cultural change may also suggest that the possibility of discerning the promptings of the Spirit of God outside the churches and their memberships, may have been overlooked.

A more promising way of handling tradition may be to reaffirm loyalty to Jesus Christ and to apply the symphonic imperative to tradition just as Barton has applied it to Scripture. This would enable us to hold several elements in tension. Loyalty to Christ would be sharply distinguished from a generalized loyalty to 'what has come to us from the past' since much of this will be simply unserviceable. Loyalty to Christ entitles us to suppose (with Anthony Thiselton) 'that all that

---

24. Ralph Brown, *Marriage Annulment in the Catholic Church* (Bury St Edmunds: Kevin Mayhew, 3rd edn, 1990), p. 13 (emphasis added).

Christian traditions claim about love, and about God as self-imparting Trinity, might be true'.[25] We would be under no illusion that much of the tradition would be strange to us and that certain emphases or parts of it would be unacceptable, in particular, the pervasive androcentrism with its negative or subordinationist attitude to women. The symphonic imperative is compromised because music cannot be made with it. Patriarchy compromises the witness of tradition to divine love, and we are right ever to be suspicious of its manipulative influence. But divine love is not manipulative. As Thiselton continues,

> If love ... serves your interests as being my own (not my own as yours), what reason could there be for one who loves like that to use manipulation, or for the other to suspect it? A love in which a self genuinely *gives* itself to the Other *in the interests of the Other* dissolves the acids of suspicion and deception.[26]

This 'suspicion and deception' has a subject and an object. Its subject is the 'postmodern self' and the object is any system of beliefs which we consciously allow to influence us. The subject may have come to the disabling conclusion that all claims to universal truth are fraudulent, and all 'temporal narratives' by which we might choose to live are no more than 'a wish-fulfilment deceptively projected by the self, or, still worse, a manipulative construct which serves the power-interests of those who suggest it'.[27] Insofar as another self is capable of being reached at all, it is genuine love which serves the other's interests that can do it. This point about the love which serves the other's interests has several applications in a Christian theology of marriage.

First, Christianity is a faith witnessing to a God whose own being is given through Christ, in the interests of others. This is the meaning of the cross of Christ and the communion of the Persons within the Trinity. Secondly, inasmuch as the tradition reflects the interests of interest groups, and not the interests of everyone, beginning with the marginalized and vulnerable, correction will be needed. Thirdly, the uncompromising claim made for Christian marriage is that, by means of it, the other-regarding love of God is incarnated and exemplified in the world, and that no other relationship is so positively charged. This claim will receive microscopic investigation in later chapters, and it

25. Anthony Thiselton, *Interpreting God and the Postmodern Self: On Meaning, Manipulation and Promise* (Edinburgh: T. & T. Clark, 1995), p. 160.

26. Thiselton, *Interpreting God*, p. 160 (author's emphasis).

27. Thiselton, *Interpreting God*, p. 160.

will become apparent that marriage has no monopoly on incarnating the divine love. But fourthly, it is clear that marriage has itself often functioned as a manipulative construct to serve patriarchal interests, and descriptions of marriage which co-opt and incorporate incarnational and Trinitarian meanings will be peculiarly capable of serving the power-interests of those who promote them. A Christian theology of marriage will therefore seek to affirm genuinely other-regarding love, as opposed to the manipulative love which serves the interests of one partner only.

A careful study of Christian marriage actually assists with a partial resolution of the theological problem of handling tradition. Marriage is most obviously a historical institution which has changed through time. Indeed it may be misleading to continue to use the single substantive term 'marriage' as if there were a single, common, nuptial experience which can be discerned through history. If theologians are able to glimpse something of the historical interaction between theological understandings of marriage and the social and cultural contexts where these understandings are implemented, they may be better equipped to understand their own context, and the imaginative interaction with it which is required of them now.

d. *Loyalty to Experience: Listening to Silenced Voices*
Revelation, Scripture and tradition have been usefully combined with experience, reason and culture in statements of sources or 'formative factors' of theology.[28] But experience and culture have acquired new significance in recent theology, and a theology of marriage will appropriate both.

One immediate imperative is to listen to the silenced voices of the past. A book about marriage will attend to the experiences of people whose lives have been and are affected by the institution of marriage. Yet a top-down exposition of marriage has rarely listened to experience. It is necessary to listen to those whose lives have been enriched and impoverished by marriage. That will include listening to wives locked into a patriarchal institution (below, 2.1.e-f); working-class and peasant couples whose nuptial arrangements have probably never been controlled by the church and yet which have shown much good, human, common, caring sense; women and men coerced into an institution for

28. See, e.g., John Macquarrie, *Principles of Christian Theology* (London: SCM Press, 1966), p. 4.

which they were clearly unsuited; celibate people w   e demonstrated that marriage is inessential for a fulfilled life;   sbian and
gay people whose deep human needs have not and ar   net by heterosexual marriage; and partners whose marriages h   e thrived and
whose children have been loved. Taking seriously the symphonic
imperative requires that *all* the people of God be given the opportunity
to be heard.[29]

The priority due to experience is the main characteristic of 'sexual
theology'. According to James Nelson, sexual theology is to be distinguished from the theology of sexuality.[30] The latter concerns itself with
the Bible and tradition as these deal with sexual questions. These
findings are then applied to contemporary sexual dilemmas and problems. But sexual theology begins with our experience as embodied,
sexual beings. It prompts us to ask 'What does our experience as
human sexual beings tell us about how we read the Scripture, interpret
the tradition, and attempt to live out the meanings of the gospel? The
movement must be in both directions, not only in one.'[31] Beginning
with experience is more likely to guarantee that connections are made
between tradition and contemporary life.

The importance of experience may be contrasted with the treatment
of experience in several church documents. In *Familiaris consortio*
Christian spouses and parents are urged to offer 'their unique and
irreplaceable contribution to the elaboration of an authentic evangelical
discernment in the various situations and cultures in which men and
women live their marriage and their family life'.[32] They are said to be
'qualified for this role by their charism or special gift, the gift of the
sacrament of matrimony'. This seems a promising recognition of the
contribution which experience can make to theology, but it makes little
difference to the 'theology from above' which this document provides,
and takes little heed of the difficulties experienced by Catholic

29. 'In order for a biblical performance to be truly communal all the performers
must have a voice. All "legitimate voices" must be heard.' See Thatcher and Stuart,
People of Passion, pp. 262-63.

30. James B. Nelson, *The Intimate Connection: Male Sexuality, Masculine Spirituality* (Philadelphia: Westminster Press, 1988; London: SPCK, 1992), pp. 115-16:
idem, *Body Theology* (Louisville, KY: Westminster/John Knox Press, 1992),
pp. 21-24.

31. Nelson, *Body Theology*, p. 21.

32. John Paul II, *Familiaris consortio* (On the Family) (Vatican City: Vatican
Press, 1981), section 8, 'Evangelical Discernment'.

Christians with some Catholic doctrine. The church will continue 'to examine and authoritatively judge the genuineness' of the 'expressions' of lay opinion and 'educate the faithful' where necessary. In *Marriage and the Church's Task*, the section devoted to 'Marriage and Human Experience' operates entirely on the level of theory![33] It is a good example of the genre of theology of marriage shattered by experience. Experience, in the sense of how people find something, or test something out for themselves, or acquire real experimental knowledge of something, is absent, and this deprives the writers of an important theological source. The authors rightly identified 'the continual need to be sensitive and creative in interpreting the experience of marriage for all who enter into it' but failed to notice the ambiguity of the experience of marriage and its importance as a theological source.

e. *Loyalty to Culture: Discerning the Spirit*
The cultural situation or social location is a formative factor of theology in two ways. Cultural questions largely determine the content of theological answers,[34] and 'whoever controls the questions to a considerable extent also controls the answers'.[35] A theology of marriage must be careful to register the actual questions raised by whoever is affected by the institution of marriage. Speaking of oppressed groups Hodgson writes

> It is precisely the questions that have risen out of the situation of these groups that have brought to light new meanings hidden in ancient texts, as well as aspects of human experience and existence that have not been thought about before.[36]

It is not suggested that people whose lives are affected positively or negatively by marriage should be automatically numbered among the oppressed. It *is* suggested that a theology of marriage should hear and respond to their questions, and this volume must be firmly judged by the criterion whether it has done so.

33. *Marriage and the Church's Task*, pp. 32-39, §§84-101.

34. Paul Tillich's 'method of correlation' was, of course, famously built on this assumption, although he more usually spoke of *existential* questions and theological answers. See his *Systematic Theology* (3 vols.; Digswell Place: Nisbet, 1957), II, pp. 14-18.

35. Peter Hodgson, *Winds of the Spirit: A Constructive Christian Theology* (London: SCM Press, 1994), p. 25.

36. Hodgson, *Winds of the Spirit*, p. 25.

Secondly, the renewed confidence among theologians in the doctrine of the Trinity has led to the expectation that God the Spirit may be found more widely and pervasively than either Roman Catholic or Protestant theology has hitherto suspected. Theology itself operates in a global, pluralistic context and this context has led Christians to discern the work of the Spirit outside the beliefs and practices of Christianity. Christian Trinitarianism, says Gavin D'Costa, 'discloses loving relationship as the proper mode of being', and makes the love of one's neighbour 'an imperative for all Christians'.[37] Just as we might expect evidence of the work of God the Spirit among the non-Christian religions, we may also expect evidence of her, blowing where she wills (Jn 3.8), enabling loving relationships to become the norm between human beings.

Christian theologians often offer negative criticism of the wider culture, without stopping to offer appreciation of it.[38] *Marriage and the Church's Task* is helpful here. Clearly embarrassed by the injunction to wives to 'be subject to your husbands as though to the Lord' (Eph. 5.22), they say

> The writer ... accepted without question the authority of husbands over wives, just as he accepted without question the right of masters to own slaves. Both ideas were *part and parcel of the prevailing culture of the day*. Christians of other cultures, however, are not bound by their regard for Scripture to accept either. Some indeed would claim, as would most of us, that the historical processes ... by which ideas of authority and subordination in marriage have been largely superseded by expectations of sharing and equality, reflect the movement of the Holy Spirit no less than did the abolition of slavery. They can see nothing in nature or in revelation which gives to husbands an unalterable and indisputable right to the obedience of their wives.[39]

There is both negative and positive criticism in the theological verdict reached here. On the one hand, subordination of women to men is conveniently rejected as belonging to the secular culture of the time, with no admission of the contribution of biblical thought to patriarchal marriage. On the other hand, the Holy Spirit is conveniently invoked as

37. Gavin D'Costa, 'Christ, the Trinity, and Religious Plurality', in *idem* (ed.), *Christian Uniqueness Reconsidered: The Myth of a Pluralistic Theology of Religions* (Maryknoll, NY: Orbis Books, 1990), p. 19.

38. On the importance of Christians understanding culture, see *Familiaris consortio*, section 4, 'The Need to Understand the Situation'.

39. *Marriage and the Church's Task*, p. 130, §47 (emphasis added).

the inspiration for changes to marriage which are historical and cultural (that is not to say that Christians had no involvement with them), because the authors believe these changes are consistent with the gospel. While the subordination of women to men cannot be so easily excused, the authors are right to make judgments of this kind. It will be necessary to look positively as well as critically at marriage as a contemporary cultural institution. Loyalty to culture means openness to the possibility that the inspiration of the Holy Spirit may be discerned beyond the confines of the churches. Opposition to historical changes, when it is appropriate, must be grounded in the gospel, not in mere fondness for the *status quo ante*.

f. *Loyalty to the People of God*

There are several traditions of Christian theology, each with its built-in attitudes to what is to count as authoritative. The *Catechism of the Catholic Church* holds 'The task of giving an authentic interpretation of the Word of God, whether in its written form or in the form of Tradition, has been entrusted to the living teaching office of the Church alone', while 'the faithful' are to 'receive with docility the teachings and directives that their pastors give them in different forms'.[40] But it is widely known that many Roman Catholic theologians do not believe the Vatican exercises a monopoly on the formulation, interpretation and communication of Christian truth, just as millions of Roman Catholics do not receive with docility their church's teaching on sexual questions. Evidence accumulates that young people are leaving the Roman Catholic Church because of the negative impact of its unrevised attitude to birth control, premarital sex and homosexuality.[41] Probably fewer than 10 per cent of English people believe that the churches provide adequate answers to the moral problems of the individual or of family life.[42] While there is considerable growth in those churches which offer

40. *Catechism of the Catholic Church* (London: Geoffrey Chapman, 1994), p. 26, §§85, 86.

41. See 'Catholicism and Young People: Some Ethical Considerations', paper read by Káren North at the British Sociological Association Sociology of Religion Conference, Bristol, April 1997. For the judgment of English Catholics on the teaching of their church on birth control, and the way it was reinforced in 1968, see Michael P. Hornsby-Smith, *Roman Catholic Beliefs in England* (Cambridge: Cambridge University Press, 1991), p. 83.

42. Based on a 500 questionnaire survey in a middle-class area of Southampton,

moral absolutes and simple certainties, there is also, more significantly,
a strongly perceived lack of connection beyond the churches between
the lives of vast numbers of people and Christian teaching. The
resources of Bible and tradition are not being accessed by them, and
their lives are being impoverished as a result. The traditions of faith and
theology are far too important to be left to the traditionalists in the
churches. An imaginative reclamation and redistribution of the wealth
of the past is needed.

The notions both of a community of Bible readers and a historical
community of Christians who have sought to bear witness to the other-
regarding love of God in Jesus Christ have already been found useful.
Contemporary theology only makes sense if there is a contemporary
community of Christian people to whose ultimate judgment theologians
must submit their work. That is why theology is 'a practice of the
Christian community', and 'a constructive activity that requires critical
interpretations and practical appropriations of faith's language about
God in the context of contemporary cultural challenges and their theological implications'.[43] The six principles discussed in this chapter give
some indication of how the activity might work and how it will work in
this book. Theology exists for the whole people of God almost all of
whom are neither theologians nor clergy.

The concept of 'the people of God', however, has blurred edges.
Theology written only for academics and church-going Christians
would inevitably be insular. Since marriage is a human institution, a
theology of marriage must engage with marriage as it exists inside and
outside the churches. When theology engages with secular realities it
speaks not *to* the people of God but on their behalf. Much of the book
has this dual character. It will contribute to internal dialogue (below,
2.1) within the faith about all aspects of marriage, but it will also
engage with marriage as a human reality.[44] Indeed since marriage is a
way of experiencing the grace of God, a theology of marriage which
engages with it as a human reality cannot but be an evangelistic enterprise. It will point to the grace of God, perhaps not yet discerned, at the
heart of human relationships.

England, reported by Rob Hirst to the British Sociological Association Sociology
of Religion Conference, Bristol, April 1997.

   43. Hodgson, *Winds of the Spirit*, p. 10.

   44. Edward Schillebeeckx's term. See his *Marriage: Human Reality and Saving
Mystery* (London: Sheed and Ward, 1965).

There was once a time when Protestant theology divided itself into liberal and conservative factions and theologians devoted precious energy to defining themselves against opponents. This is an irritating and debilitating way of doing theology for several reasons. First, the imperative of the Church's mission renders the indulgent airing of past divisions largely irrelevant. A world indifferent to the gospel will not be choosy about which residual tradition of Christianity communicates the Good News. Secondly, a century of ecumenism has enabled a confident interchange of theological ideas across the divisions of Christendom. For Protestants this is just as well, for almost all contemporary theological work on marriage has been done by Roman Catholics. Wherever a theologian stands, she or he will need to learn from other theological and ecclesiastical perspectives.

Thirdly, the old theological map simply fails to register the most important contours and features of the contemporary terrain. Feminist theology, liberation theology, and lesbian and gay theology have made a permanent contribution to contemporary theology and changed it forever. The living presence in the world of non-Christian religious traditions makes all Christian theology which fails in a generous neighbourly estimation of them arrogant and imperialistic. And fourthly, the imperative of Christian communication in a post-Christian world imposes new priorities and tasks which in a previous, less sceptical age did not emerge. A theology of marriage represents just such a task. The crisis in which marriage stands today demands a theological response which is neither partial nor partisan but which seeks to listen to and learn from the various theological sources and traditions.

3. Modernity

The book is called *Marriage after Modernity* because 'after modernity' suggests a push beyond the ambiguous legacy of modernity. The term 'modernity', says David Lyon, 'refers to the social order that emerged following the Enlightenment'. It is

> all about the massive changes that took place at many levels from the mid-sixteenth century onward, changes signalled by the shifts that uprooted agricultural workers and transformed them into mobile industrial urbanites. Modernity questions all conventional ways of doing things, substituting authorities of its own, based in science, economic

growth, democracy or law. And it unsettles the self; if identity is given
in traditional society, in modernity it is constructed.[45]

Theologians appear to have three reasons for talking about postmodernity. First, they think there is, or has been, something called
'modernity'. Secondly, modernity is coming, or has come, to an end.
And thirdly, the ending of modernity represents an opportunity for
something else, perhaps a new beginning for Christian thought and
practice. Since marriage is a historical and social institution it is
enmeshed in the changes signified by the transition from modernity to
postmodernity. 'After Modernity' assumes that we can identify the
main features of 'modernity' and look forward to something different.
It conveys a sense of fast-moving change which presents faith and
theology with outstanding opportunities for imaginative communication
inside and outside the churches.[46] But the term 'modernity' has multiple, contested meanings, so it is necessary to be more specific about
how it will be used in this book.

a. *Postmodernity*

Hans Küng uses 'postmodern' 'as a heuristic term for discovering what
distinguishes our era of history from those which have gone before'.[47]
For Küng, one of the 'central problem areas' facing the postmodern era
is the relationship between men and women. He asks,

> So for postmodernity, instead of discriminatory male privileges, isn't
> *equality for women* an urgent need everywhere? And what can the differ-
> ent religions... contribute in the postmodern paradigm on the basis of a
> feminist religious feeling to a change in global consciousness, to the
> realization of political and social human rights and so to the dimension
> of the *partnership* of man and woman?[48]

Peter Hodgson uses 'postmodernity' in a similar way. It is about

---

45. David Lyon, *Postmodernity* (Buckingham: Open University Press, 1994),
pp. 19, 21.

46. This position has recently been strongly urged by Kieran Flanagan, in his
The Enchantment of Sociology (London: Macmillan, 1996); see also the discussion
in John Orme Mills, OP (ed.), 'The Sociologist and God: Facing the Issues Raised
by Kieran Flanagan's *The Enchantment of Sociology*', *New Blackfriars* 78.113
(1997), pp. 102-52.

47. Hans Küng, *Christianity: The Religious Situation of Our Time* (London:
SCM Press, 1995), p. 773.

48. Küng, *Christianity*, p. 777 (author's emphasis).

the 'passage' of history—the passing of Western bourgeois culture, with its ideals of individuality, patriarchy, private rights, technical rationality, historical progress, capitalist economy, the absoluteness of Christianity, and so on.[49]

Almost all writers associate modernity with the triumph of science over other modes of knowledge, and a naïve belief in progress.[50] 'The post-modern', continues Hodgson, 'does not cancel the essential gains of modernity—rationality, freedom, human rights, subjectivity, dialogue, etc., but rather appropriates and reconfigures these modes of thought and action in new circumstances, often quite radically'.[51] Modernity has bequeathed to us a series of crises, cognitive, historical, political, socio-economic, ecological and religious. But two further crises of modernity are to do with sex and gender:

> The sexual revolution has exposed the repression deeply ingrained in Western culture and Christianity, but it has also led to a great deal of freedom of sexual practice beginning in adolescence, much of it destructive, and it has rendered problematic all of the established sexual institutions, including the nuclear family and marriage ... There is also a gender crisis—the beginning of the ending of patriarchy as a way of organizing male-female relations and distributing social power.

Marriage without doubt is one of the 'established sexual institutions' which are now rendered problematic by the crises of modernity.[52]

> The sexual crisis unmasks the linkage of religious belief with sexual repression and calls into question the authority of scripture on issues vital to human sexuality, while the gender crisis is disrupting long-established ways of imaging divine power and presence, namely in androcentric and patriarchal terms.[53]

49. Hodgson, *Winds of the Spirit*, p. 53. See William D. Lindsey, 'Crossing the Postmodern Divide: Some Implications for Academic Theology', *TheolSex* 7 (1997), pp. 53-69, and the sources cited there.

50. E.g., Diogenes Allen, *Christian Belief in a Postmodern World:The Full Wealth of Conviction* (Louisville, KY: Westminster/John Knox Press, 1989), pp. 4-5: J. Richard Middleton and Brian J. Walsh, *Truth is Stranger Than It Used To Be: Biblical Faith in a Postmodern Age* (London: SPCK, 1995), p. 20; Küng, *Christianity*, pp. 765-70. See also, Terrence W. Tilley, *Postmodern Theologies: The Challenge of Religious Diversity* (New York: Orbis Books, 1995).

51. Hodgson, *Winds of the Spirit*, p. 57.

52. See Jeffrey Weeks, *Invented Moralities: Sexual Values in an Age of Uncertainty* (Cambridge: Polity Press, 1995), pp. 25-26.

53. Hodgson, *Winds of the Spirit*, p. 62.

The 'postmodern condition' is 'marked by a plurality of voices vying for the right to reality'.[54] Hodgson thinks that the various crises brought about by modernity have led to an absence of God in postmodern consciousness.[55] That is certainly a shared assumption of the secular writers assessed later (below, 2.2). One of the objectives of this volume is to show how the partnership of marriage, conversely, is capable of mediating the divine presence.

b. *Marriage and Modernity*
The Christian understanding of marriage is set in the long 'premodern' period prior to the changes of modernity. It will be necessary to refer continuously to the diverse premodern traditions of marriage while reinterpreting what is found there in the light of the demands of the postmodern social and cultural situation. The Bible has no guidance for us about the right age for marriage, nor about any ceremony. There is clear tension in the New Testament between the concessionary view of marriage (1 Cor. 7.19) and the estimation of it as the great mystery symbolizing the union of Christ and the Church (Eph. 5.32). Marriage is discouraged in the light of the imminent return of Christ. In the next century it is discouraged because of negative attitudes to sexuality and because of the moral priority given to celibacy. A wedding ceremony was, until modern times, never a requirement, and the principal justification for the inferior way of marriage was that of having children. Only in the second millennium did marriage become a sacrament, and the meaning of 'sacrament' has changed completely since then. Betrothal was a common means of entry into marriage (below, 4.2), and vows could be made when the parties were as young as seven. The cultural discontinuities between premodern times and our own will render the premodern legacy strange to us; yet its very strangeness, its power to surprise and sometimes to amaze, will help to provide a critical resource for reviewing our own practice.

The social changes associated with modernity are crucial for this study, and discussion of them will be a prominent feature of Chapters 3 and 4. Modernity is associated with the rise of state bureaucracy, with 'the classificatory, controlling impulse seen in sphere after sphere'.[56] The Marriage Act which took effect in England and Wales in 1753

54. Middleton and Walsh, *Truth is Stranger*, p. 13.
55. Hodgson, *Winds of the Spirit*, p. 63.
56. Lyon, *Postmodernity*, p. 26.

represents the apex of modernity as it effects marriage, for prior to this date, ecclesiastical ceremonies and official registration were not legally required for a valid marriage to be enacted. The entry into marriage was less formal, and in some periods betrothal licensed sexual intercourse prior to the actual marriage ceremony. Courtship and attitudes to sexual intercourse prior to marriage were different prior to the Act and it will be necessary to 'lift the veil of modernity' (below, 4.2.a) in order to suggest that the informal entry into marriage via cohabitation, which our contemporaries have largely accomplished for themselves, is a partial return to premodern nuptial orthodoxy. In the eighteenth century the entry into marriage, at least in most of Britain, is effectively policed, and law becomes a principal means of enforcing social compliance. As we shall see these changes had more to do with the handing down of property than with the gospel, and we will need to be wary of them.

Marriage within modernity becomes increasingly associated with romantic love, the growth of individuality, the choosing of partners by each other, and (in Protestant countries) the ending of clerical celibacy. The most far-reaching change of all in the modern period is the mass production of reliable contraceptives, in particular the sheath in the nineteenth and 'the pill' in the second half of the twentieth century (below, 6.1).[57] The vigorous opposition to the use of contraceptives, even within marriage, by the Roman Catholic Church (below, 6.2) is a correct discernment that contraception changes sexual experience forever, since sexual intercourse need no longer be associated with the transmission of life.

c. *Marriage after Modernity*

In this book, postmodernity will be understood principally as a new opportunity for Christian thought and practice, coincidentally situated at the beginning of a new millenium. I agree with the analyses of Küng and Hodgson: the seizure of a new opportunity does not overlook that Christian theology is in some respects in a weaker position than it was even half a century ago; that it has lost many of the privileges it once had in the academy; that religious pluralism and moral relativism render it more difficult for Christian theology to obtain a hearing; and that indifference to anything that might be said in the name of Christ

57. See my 'Postmodernity and Chastity', in Jon Davies and Gerard Loughlin (eds.), *Sex These Days: Essays in Theology, Sexuality and Society* (Sheffield: Sheffield Academic Press, 1997), pp. 122-40 (127).

may be growing. Theology is still able to *earn* a hearing, insofar as it speaks positively and meaningfully to people's experience. My own use is best defined by grounding it in each of the six areas discussed in the previous section.

Loyalty to *Jesus Christ* transcends all periods of history and their accompanying changes. 'Jesus Christ is the same yesterday, today, and for ever' (Heb. 13.8). Jesus Christ provides the continuity throughout all ages, yet what counts as loyalty to Christ changes profoundly over time, and is differently configured in postmodernity. Postmodernity licenses new respect for differences, whether religious, social, cultural or ethnic. Loyalty to Christ must not, as in much liberal theology, collapse into altruistic humanism. Rather Christian identity will re-emerge in a postmodern context seeking new ways of expressing the reign of God.

Loyalty to *the Bible* is expressed by the insistence that its witness is to Christ, and that the 'symphonic imperative' provides a practical guide to its interpretation. Loyalty to *tradition* requires Christians to query the way of 'detraditionalization'. This is the series of processes whereby contemporary people lose contact with social traditions and value them less. But traditions are essential for maintaining identity. Loyalty to tradition requires a reclamation and rereading of it in the light of loyalty to Christ. And this is emphatically separable from hierarchical social forms and androcentric world-views.

Loyalty to *experience* requires giving priority to the testimony of contemporary men and women in the area of sexuality, and being willing to rethink the adequacy of premodern and modern institutions and assumptions which have regulated family and sexual life in the past. Loyalty to *culture* demands that the products of postmodern culture, especially the use of contraception, the widespread practice of cohabitation, the freedom associated with divorce, the weakening of conventional gender roles, and the high visibility of lesbian and gay people with legitimate demands for recognition, be assessed only after admitting the possibility that some of these products may be prompted by the Spirit of God. Such possibility is fully consistent with Christian teaching about the pervasiveness of sin, but it frees Christians from excessive attachment to the *status quo* and enables them to address the Bible and tradition with new questions. Loyalty to the *people of God* requires the process of making available to them the resources of the Bible and tradition as they might be understood by an encounter with postmodern experience and culture.

Chapter 2

CHRISTIAN MARRIAGE: THE TWO DIALOGUES

Marriage has become a focus of controversy within and between the churches. It raises questions about how the six theological loyalties discussed in Chapter 1 are to be expressed. In this context Christians will be engaging in two dialogues simultaneously. There is an internal dialogue among Christians about how the Bible and tradition are to be appropriated. The internal dialogue will attend to the incongruities, disagreements between churches, exegetical and hermeneutical problems which are encountered by Christians now. This dialogue must not be allowed to inhibit the more important external dialogue between Christians and their more secular neighbours who have concluded that Christians have nothing important to say to them. The Christian response to these contemporary challenges has to be made while recognizing internal difficulties within the churches' own teaching. This chapter is a contribution to both these conversations. The first part recognizes internal difficulties within the Christian understanding of marriage. Effort will be made to use these difficulties creatively as a source of insight, and as a series of markers for the theology of marriage. The second part examines marriage as it is treated in postmodern culture. The third part reinforces the conclusion that the postmodern understanding of marriage is in important respects deficient, and actually requires a Christian theology of marriage for its completion and coherence.

1. *The Internal Dialogue*

These two theological dialogues about the meaning and development of the doctrine of marriage share a single important function: they are essential in contributing to the living tradition of theology. Alasdair MacIntyre's definition of a tradition is central to our concerns here. 'A tradition', he writes, is an argument extended through time in which certain fundamental agreements are defined and redefined in terms of two kinds of conflict: those with critics and enemies external to the tradition who reject all or at least key parts of those fundamental agreements, and those internal, interpretative debates through which the meaning and rationale of the fundamental agreements come to be expressed and by whose progress a tradition is constituted.[1]

This definition is well suited to the task of charting a passage through the contemporary ferment which is marriage. Fundamental agreements between Christians are being defined and redefined in the light both of opponents' criticisms and through those painful 'internal, interpretative debates' many of which are prompted by the social changes which earlier theologians could never have anticipated. Attention to each type of disagreement is necessary both for the growth of the tradition in time, and for its health.

a. *A Concession to Lust?*
St Paul taught the church at Corinth that marriage is better avoided. It is a concession, a second best, an escape for those who cannot control their sexual feelings. 'To the unmarried and to widows I say this: it is a good thing if like me they stay as they are; but if they do not have self-control, they should marry. It is better to be married than burn with desire' (1 Cor. 7.8-9). Marriage is a source of 'anxious care', and husbands and wives are 'pulled in two directions' as they seek to 'please the Lord' as well as please each other (1 Cor. 7.32-4). This is a pessimistic view of marriage which turned it into a *remedium*, a remedy for the sickness of sexual desire. Peter Brown, historian of early Christian attitudes to sexuality, observes

> What was notably lacking, in Paul's letter, was the warm faith shown by contemporary pagans and Jews that the sexual urge, although disorderly, was capable of socialization and of ordered, even warm, expression within marriage. The dangers of *porneia*, of potential immorality brought about by sexual frustration, were allowed to hold the center of the stage. By this essentially negative, even alarmist, strategy, Paul left a fatal legacy to future ages.[2]

---

1.   Alasdair MacIntyre, *Whose Justice? Which Rationality?* (London: Gerald Duckworth, 1988), p. 12.

2.   Peter Brown, *The Body and Society: Men, Women and Sexual Renunciation in Early Christianity* (London: Faber & Faber, 1989), p. 55.

In contradistinction to this negative view of marriage, an extraordinarily positive view of marriage emerges elsewhere. Marriage is also thought to signify the great mystery of the relationship between Christ and his Church (Eph. 5.21-33). The love between married partners is a sharing in the sacrificial love of Christ for the Church. The International Theological Commission of the Roman Catholic Church says this text 'places Christian marriage within the framework of the paschal *mystèrion*'. The passages teaches 'the conjugal love of the Lord for his people… It is into this paschal *mystèrion*, under its conjugal dimension, that the conjugal love between a Christian man and a Christian woman is inserted'.[3] Not only is married love thought to be a sharing in the love of Christ for the Church, the love of Christ is itself identified as a *conjugal* love. By speaking of the insertion of one love into the other, an uncompromisingly positive, contemporary, official view of marriage is stated which leaves the pessimistic view behind. The term *mystèrion*, used in Eph. 5.32 of Christ's love for the Church, was translated in the Vulgate by *sacramentum*. It laid the foundation for the sacramentality of marriage in later ages.

The tension between the *remedium* with its sexual pessimism, and the *sacramentum* which, at least in contemporary accounts, inserts conjugal love into the conjugal love of Christ for the Church, has never been resolved. 'There is not a biblical theology of marriage as a unified set of ideas and concepts. Instead one has to view the richness and diversity of the various early traditions.'[4] But the assumption that uniformity in the biblical teaching about marriage is achievable, is deeply entrenched. A good example of this is Karl Barth's treatment of marriage. Paul told his male Corinthian readers they should not have sex with prostitutes. He offers them an argument based on two assumptions; that a Christian man is a member of the mystical body of Christ; and that sexual intercourse of a man with a woman involves becoming one flesh with her (1 Cor. 6.12-19). A Christian man who uses prostitutes is

3.   Mgr. Philippe Delhaye, 'Propositions on the Doctrine of Christian Marriage', in Mgr. Richard Malone and John R. Connery, SJ, *Contemporary Perspectives on Christian Marriage: Propositions and Papers from the International Theological Commission* (Chicago: Loyola University Press, 1984), pp. 17-18. See also *Gaudium et spes*, §49.

4.   Francis Schüssler Fiorenza, 'Marriage', in Francis Schüssler Fiorenza and John P. Galvin (eds.), *Systematic Theology: Roman Catholic Perspectives* (2 vols.; Minneapolis: Fortress Press, 1991), II, pp. 305-46 (316).

therefore said to put himself in the impossible position of being both spiritually united to Christ and physically united with a whore.

At this point Barth's endorsement of the remedial view of marriage emerges unmistakeably. He explains the impossibility just described as the predicament of a male Christian 'who is one spirit with the Lord, is joined in body with a harlot, and therefore at root frivolously, unfaithfully and in sheer lust'.[5] However in the very next sentences Barth continues,

> The choice of marriage is justified as a means of avoiding this impossibility. If a Christian finds that he must become one body with a woman, then in accordance with the fact that he is one in spirit with the Lord this must take place seriously and wholeheartedly, and not as in *porneia*.

But is this not both an endorsement and a restatement of the remedial view of marriage? It is obviously androcentric and assumes that women are available to help male Christians discharge their sexual urges legitimately. Yet a few pages later Barth confidently affirms marriage to be a 'vocation'.[6] Barth has endorsed the *remedium* theory of marriage in one place, the vocational theory of marriage in another, and failed to spot their incompatibility. There is an easy assumption among theologians that New Testament teaching about marriage can be conveniently harmonized. Yet the positive and negative views cannot be reconciled so easily.[7]

b. *Indissoluble and Inseparable?*
Central to the teaching of Jesus is that God joins married partners together and 'what God has joined together, man must not separate' (Mk 10.9). But is it to be understood that *every* couple formally joined together in the name of God is actually, ontologically, joined by God? God may be said to bless marriage *generically*, as an institution which is part of creation. That God created marriage along with creation itself was taught by Jesus (Mk 10.6). But does God join each and every individual couple? It seems that both Catholics and Protestants answer this question negatively.

5.   Karl Barth, *Church Dogmatics*. III. *Doctrine of Creation*, Part 4 (Edinburgh: T. & T. Clark, 1961), p. 145.

6.   Barth, *Church Dogmatics*, III, p. 183.

7.   Joel F. Harrington calls this the 'pronounced duality of Christian ideals'. See his *Reordering Marriage and Society in Reformation Germany* (Cambridge: Cambridge University Press, 1995), p. 48.

The Roman Catholic Church increasingly allows marriages to be annulled on the grounds of defective consent (below, 8.3). The practice of the annulment of marriage, together with an insistence that marriage is unable to be dissolved, is shaky, to say the least.[8] It relies on the ancient belief that the consent of the parties is what makes the marriage, and not the blessing of the priest during the wedding ceremony. If the consent is defective, the marriage is invalid. It follows, on this view, that couples who are pronounced wife and husband, need not be; and that the words 'Those whom God has joined together, let no-one separate' (or their many variations and equivalents), said to a marrying couple by a priest or minister at a wedding, confer no assurance at all that God has joined them together. It surely follows that couples can *never* know they have married in the sight of God.

Let us again take Karl Barth's teaching about marriage as an example, this time of Protestant teaching about marriage. Barth offers no assurance that people who are married in the name of God are joined together by God, or (what amounts to the same thing) receive the blessing of God upon their marriage. That is because there are two institutions of marriage—divine and human—providing literal credence to the adage that 'Marriages are made in heaven'[9]. The problem is that while God *might* join a particular woman and man in matrimony, the divine act of joining them together is not identified with any objective human act, whether consent, the exchange of promises, love-making, priestly blessing, or any other act. God's joining is said to rest instead on faith and the word of God.[10]

Protestant and Catholic then appear to agree on three unlikely propositions: First, a married Christian couple cannot know that a Christian marriage ceremony constitutes a marriage which is recognized or blessed by God. In the Catholic case the doubt is caused by the possibility, retrospectively established, that the consent exchanged at the

---

8. For the Anglican dislike of annulment, see *Marriage and the Church's Task*, pp. 80-81, §§221-24. William Basil Zion, an Eastern Orthodox Theologian, speaks of the 'hideous abuses' which 'the system of annulments' has brought about. Not only is the practice of annulment theologically flawed, Zion thinks it covers up 'the evils attendant upon marital breakdown and the acknowledgement of sin in such instances'. See his *Eros and Transformation: Sexuality and Marriage: An Eastern Orthodox Perspective* (Lanham, MD: University Press of America, 1992), p. 119.

9. Barth, *Church Dogmatics*, III, p. 215.

10. Barth, *Church Dogmatics*, III, p. 208.

ceremony was defective. In the Barthian case, while any marriage ceremony may be humanly valid because it would belong generically to
marriage as a human institution, a couple cannot know whether they
share in the divine institution.

Secondly, some marriages *are* dissoluble. Although valid marriages
are indissoluble, invalid marriages are emphatically dissolvable, in the
Protestant case by divorce, in the Catholic case by annulment. Barth
emphatically states that formally valid marriages 'which God may
never have joined together' *are* dissolvable,[11] and that 'man can, and
perhaps in certain situations must, dissolve' such marriages.[12]

It also appears to follow, thirdly, that just as married people may not
be married, so unmarried people may be married. The Barthian separation of the divine and human acts of joining together allows for a
position he does not consider, that is, the possibility that God's blessing
of a couple is independent of all acts which signify a human marriage.
In the Catholic case, the church allows that a non-Christian couple who
have exchanged consent and who have sexual intercourse, are legitimately married. This is because marriage belongs to creation *and*
redemption. Since it belongs to creation, it is God's gift to all women
and men irrespective of their status as baptized Christians. Such persons enjoy the blessing of Christ (whether they have heard of him or
not) on their marriages, which are covenants, but not sacraments:

> The strength and greatness of the grace of Christ are extended to all
> people, even those beyond the Church, because of God's desire to save
> all mankind. They shape all human marital love and strengthen created
> nature as well as matrimony 'as it was from the beginning'. Therefore,
> men and women who have not yet heard the gospel message are united
> by a human covenant. This legitimate marriage has its authentic good-
> ness and values, which assure its consistency. But one must realize that
> these goods, even though the spouses are not aware of it, come from
> God the creator and make them share—in an inchoate way—in the mari-
> tal love which unites Christ with his Church.[13]

This is a highly significant official statement. It offers the churches a
new strategy of evangelism to married couples—helping them to recognize that all the authentic goodness and values of their relationships is
already a gift of God and a sharing in Christ's own relationship with the

---

11. Barth, *Church Dogmatics*, III, p. 209.
12. Barth, *Church Dogmatics*, III, p. 211.
13. Delhaye, 'Propositions', p. 22.

Church. Evangelism would seek to help couples experience this sharing in a more explicit and advanced, instead of a merely inchoate, way. It also suggests the blessing of God rests on informal or 'common law' marriages (below, 4.2).

The solution to these problems which will be adopted later will be a refashioning of the teaching that a valid marriage is indissoluble (below, 8.3). Once the notion that indissolubility is something conferred on marriages at the beginning is replaced with the notion that it is something to be attained through the marriage,[14] through the deepening love of the spouses, a more dynamic understanding of marriage will have been reached. On this view the more Christian a marriage becomes, the more indissoluble it actually is.[15]

But we are not yet finished with unresolved problems generated by indissolubility. Suppose we were to take the words of Jesus '…what God has joined together, man must not separate' (Mk 10.9: Mt. 19.6) with a zealous literalism, it would still not follow from this injunction that *God* must not or cannot separate couples joined in marriage. This view was held in the mediaeval church.[16] The church allowed separation for partners who subsequently entered monasteries, appealing directly to the saying of Jesus, 'Truly I tell you: there is no one who has given up home, *or wife*, brothers, parents, or children, for the sake of the kingdom of God, who will not be repaid many times over in this age, and in the age to come have eternal life'[17] (Lk. 18.29-30). This practice of separation overtly relied on the assumption, stated by Jerome, that *God* can separate those whom God has joined.[18] However,

---

14. Both Cathy Molloy and Theodore Mackin trace the idea of indissolubility as *attainment* to Edward Schillebeeckx's late essay, 'Christian Marriage and the Human Reality of Complete Marital Disintegration' (1974). See Cathy Molloy, *Marriage: Theology and Reality* (Dublin: Columbia Press; Toronto: Novalis, 1996), p. 44; and Theodore Mackin SJ, *The Marital Sacrament* (Mahwah, NJ: Paulist Press, 1989), p. 622.

15. See Bernard Cooke, 'Indissolubility: Guiding Ideal or Existential Reality?', in William P. Roberts (ed.), *Commitment to Partnership: Explorations of the Theology of Marriage* (New York: Paulist Press, 1987), pp. 64-78 (71).

16. Philip Lyndon Reynolds, *Marriage in the Western Church: The Christianization of Marriage During the Patristic and Early Medieval Periods* (Leiden: E.J. Brill, 1994), Chapter 10, 'Separating to Serve God', pp. 227-38.

17. Reynolds, *Marriage in the Western Church*, pp. 230-31.

18. Reynolds, *Marriage in the Western Church*, p. 231.

once the principle is established that God can separate those whom God has joined, that same principle can hardly be confined to the case of entering the cloistered life. Is this really the only reason why God might separate married partners? The Orthodox Church has long assumed that 'as steward of the sacraments and by virtue of the authority to bind and loose conferred upon it by Christ himself' (Mt. 16.19; 18.18; Jn 20.23), it 'has the right to release the couple from the marriage bond and to permit a remarriage'.[19] So God can and does release married couples from their vows through the agency of the Orthodox church. I shall return to the meaning of indissolubility later, asking whether its use in forbidding divorce and remarriage has rightly interpreted the mind of Christ.

c. *Holy Matrimony or Unholy Misery?*
The tension between marriage as a remedy for sin and as a sacrament of salvation has already been noted. A further tension exists between the many prudential warnings against marriage in parts of the Christian tradition and the expectation in other parts that marriage is a source of divine grace. Gregory of Nyssa and John Chrysostom might serve as two examples from the many that might be given of the former, although hundreds of other saints and scholars might doubtless be cited. Gregory's treatise *On Virginity* contains a catalogue of negative personal consequences which inevitably attach to the married state and which intending husbands should ponder. Even in a happy marriage the inevitable death of one partner before the other brings pain which the unattached life avoids. Summarizing the tone of this warning against the oppressive dangers of marriage, Zion comments,

> St. Gregory comes up with a host of dark possibilities. Parents are blamed by their offspring, charges are made against the divine economy. Tragedy stands ever at hand. Even if there are children one lives a life of fear lest some harm come to them. Women suffer both from oppression by their husbands and from the loss of them. Widowhood is an unfortunate state, where a woman suffers grievously at the hands of relatives and enemies. If such evils attend the happy ones, the unhappy will have multiple woe... Marriage is fraught with miseries which the law courts

19. Kallistos Ware, 'The Sacrament of Love: the Orthodox Understanding of Marriage and its Breakdown', *Downside Review* 109 (1991), pp. 79-93 (87). See also John Meyendorff, *Marriage: An Orthodox Perspective* (St. Vladimir's Seminary Press, 1975), pp. 60-65.

reveal by their mass of marital cases. In fact, misery abounds for the married.[20]

If marriage is in any sense a sacramental state, it is hard to find evidence in these onslaughts against it.[21] According to Gregory 'everyone knows that the function of bodily union is the creation of mortal bodies, but life and incorruptibility are born instead of children, to those who are united in their participation in the Spirit'.[22] John Chrysostom also links virginity with life and marriage with death. In an early account, marriage is said to be 'bondage for both partners, but particularly for a woman'. It is a 'grim' picture, 'of a man tied to a woman who has a multitude of faults, who is wicked, talkative, wasteful, or of a woman tied to a man who is proud, impudent, or immoral... Indeed, for him marriage is precisely a bond, a tie, which enslaves and enchains the partners'.[23]

At present we are noting internal difficulties within Christian doctrine on marriage, and the one noted here is the difficulty that marriage is both commended as a good, given in creation, a symbol of Christ's love for the Church, a sacrament, and also warned off it as endangering our souls and imprisoning our bodies. Countless authors, at least in the first three quarters of the Christian era have spoken like this, and some still do. A contemporary theology of marriage which tries to remain loyal to Christian traditions is surely required to make sense of this contradiction. But there are different ways of making sense of it. A revisionist strategy of appropriating the text might be to off-load the many reservations which Christians have expressed about marriage onto the historical context, and then seek to show that the elements of

20. Zion, *Eros and Transformation*, p. 62.

21. Nonetheless, it is possible to read Gregory *ironically*, redirecting his criticism away from 'marriage *per se* and toward the desire for pleasure and misguided expectations of happiness which are the basis of most marriages'. See Mark D. Hart, 'Reconciliation of Body and Soul: Gregory of Nyssa's Deeper Theology of Marriage', *TS* 51.3 (1990), p. 451, discussed in Zion, *Eros and Transformation*, p. 67. While both writers seek to minimize Gregory's strictures against marriage, they fail to take account of the extent of the influence of the Platonic dualism which renders inevitable a negative estimation of the passions, desire and the body.

22. See Zion, *Eros and Transformation*, p. 65.

23. Zion, *Eros and Transformation*, pp. 76-77. Zion is anxious to indicate that Chrysostom's mature thought contains a more positive account of marriage. If his exegesis of Chrysostom's developing theology of marriage is sound, the outcome still faces other difficulties.

Christian thought which commend marriage are original, enduring and right. But this is a strategy which is too easy.

In the first place, the tradition that celibacy is better, is preserved in the Roman Catholic Church and other churches which do not permit any, or higher ranking, officials to marry. Clearly marriage is more than a disadvantage in such cases—it is a disability. But secondly, there is a remarkable convergence between ancient, theological criticisms of marriage made by celibate men and contemporary criticisms of marriage made by women, whether theological or non-theological, celibate or non-celibate. To such critics the reservations of the ancient celibates are seriously correct. The early theologians were right to point out that misery may abound for the married. The law courts are probably more full of marital cases today than they were in the ancient world of the fourth century: the argument has achieved the verification of centuries. Marriage, they would say (in ironic agreement with Gregory of Nyssa), has always been 'bondage for both partners, but particularly for a woman'. Contemporary critics of marriage, if they knew where to look, would find several of the 'Fathers' of the Church had already done much of the job for them. The confluence of these separate streams of marital criticism, is a remarkable feature of postmodernity: it is available to contemporary theology, waiting to contribute to the imaginative restatement of Christian marriage.

d. A Sacrament?

By the twelfth century, the mystery (*mystèrion*) which is marriage (Eph. 5.32) had become formally a *sacramentum* or sacrament. The Vulgate translation of this verse in the fourth century CE had used the term *sacramentum*, but the meaning of the term was a 'pledge of fidelity', well exemplified by the oath of allegiance sworn by a Roman soldier on enlistment. Article 25 of the Book of Common Prayer of the Church of England defines sacraments as 'certain sure witnesses, and effectual signs of grace, and God's good will towards us, by the which he doth work invisibly in us, and doth not only quicken, but also strengthen and confirm our Faith in him'. Marriage however, is expressly excluded along with others, from the list, leaving only baptism and 'the Supper of the Lord'. Protestants differ from Roman Catholics and Orthodox Christians about whether marriage is formally to be counted as a sacrament.[24]

---

24. Greater flexibility of definition and interpretation has eased this problem

There is however a more serious problem for the majority of Christians who hold that marriage *is* a sacrament. This is a different problem from the problem posed by the contrast between *remedium* and *sacramentum*, or the problem whether matrimony entails misery. The sacramental problem is about the conceptual intelligibility of what is proposed. There have been perpetual disagreements over what constitutes the sacrament of matrimony (consent? priestly blessing? sex?); who confers it (the priest or the marrying couple?); what exactly is conferred, and to whom sacramental grace is available. The traditional answer to the latter question is of course that for the baptized only is marriage a sacrament, but does not this answer needlessly restrict the generosity of God in the distribution of divine grace (below, 7.2.e)? Are baptized, lapsed, Christians deemed to be recipients of the sacrament, albeit unworthy ones, while unbaptized partners automatically exclude themselves from the experience of grace?[25]

A vigorous, positive account of marriage as a sacrament will be pursued later (below, 7.2), but this can only be done after repairing some of the suspect foundations of the doctrine. We know that those Christians who elevated marriage to the status of a sacrament thought the grace bestowed was a *medicinum*, medicine for the sickness of sexual desire and the inevitability of physical pollution through sexual intercourse. Theodore Mackin, that great historian and exegete of marriage in the Roman Catholic Church, remarks,

> Everyone knew what goes on in marriage: erotic love, bodily passion running out of control, sin-infected flesh satisfying itself sexually. There is grace given in the sacrament, so the explanation went, but it is not sanctifying; it is medicinal. It is a divine help for keeping passion not only inside one's marriage, but even within it confined to the innocent and therefore permissible motive for having intercourse, which is to conceive a child. It is grace fitted perfectly to enable spouses to deliver the good of their contract, and to keep their passion within the terms of the contract.[26]

Through the sacrament, it was hoped, at least the desire for one another

considerably. See Stuart and Thatcher, *People of Passion*, pp. 76-78.

25. See, e.g., Karl Lehmann, 'The Sacramentality of Christian Marriage: The Bond between Baptism and Marriage', in Malone and Connery (eds.), *Contemporary Perspectives*, pp. 91-116.

26. Theodore Mackin, SJ, *What is Marriage?* (New York: Paulist Press, 1982), p. 32.

could perhaps be converted into the desire for children and so not throw the married partners into mortal sin. There is both a negative and a positive aspect of this understanding of the sacrament. Negatively one is bound to ask how the Church ever developed such a theology. Positively one is bound to note that the theology of marriage has changed remarkably since the twelfth century. It had to. And the fact of the accomplishment of the change will hearten those Christians who presently argue for a further shift in marital doctrine.

e. *Whose Experience, Whose Gender?*

What difference does it make to speak of marriage as a sacrament, or as not a sacrament, when countless volumes about marriage (mostly written by unmarried men) have largely ignored the actual experience of marriage, and particularly the experience of women. They provide, in Rosemary Haughton's telling phrase, 'a theology of marriage shattered by experience'.[27] There are three associated problems here. First, the closed, heavily androcentric bias of historical Christian theological writing about marriage is frankly unreliable and inadequate for contemporary use. That is because marriage is fundamentally a partnership, and no account, theory, explanation or evaluation of a partnership is reliable if it does not give equal regard to each of the partners. The omission of women from theology is at its most damaging in the theology of marriage. In this book there are 295 works listed in the bibliography where the gender of the author is discernible, 225 written by men, 70 by women.

Secondly, when attention is given to the actual experience of women in marriage, evidence suggests many women find the institution, as currently practised, unjust and oppressive. In the United States, one person in four will avoid marriage completely.[28] Any theology of marriage, procedurally rooted in experience, will find unsettling the work of Jessie Bernard, who demonstrated that every marriage is best understood as two marriages or sets of experiences, his and hers, and hers is uniformly worse.[29] Bernard's 'simple assertion of a gendered difference in

27. Haughton, 'The Meaning of Marriage', p. 149.

28. There are 209.2 million people in the United States aged 15 and over. In March 1998 58.3 million of them had not experienced marriage. US Census Bureau, *Current Population Survey Reports*, March 1998.

29. Jessie Bernard, *The Future of Marriage* (New Haven: Yale University Press, 1973).

expectations, rewards, obligations and duties opened up new avenues of social inquiry into marriage'. It was found that 'men and women "explain" themselves in different ways, arising out of their contrasting biographies and socially constructed attributes'.[30] Women's 'marital deficit' covers work, physical and mental health, child care and safety. According to a recent study wives are likely to suffer a 'double burden' of dissipated energy and moral guilt as a result of social expectations about the value of men's work:

> Men frequently experience and see marriage as something that supports them in the world of work, providing the domestic back-up which makes their working lives easier, and may even enhance their job prospects. They will expect this process to begin when they get married, often with 'wife' taking over where 'mother' left off, and to go on uninterrupted ... By contrast, when women get married they are likely to experience immediate tensions between the demands of paid work outside, and those of their unpaid labours inside the home. These will not only be pressures of time and physical energy; housework and cooking are also 'moral' categories which 'say something' about a woman's feelings for her husband and their marriage and which communicate to significant others such as parents, siblings and friends.[31]

Married people enjoy better health than single people, but married men enjoy much better health than married women.[32] Husbands are reckoned to be psychologically dependent on their wives to an extent which is not reciprocally available to the wives themselves,[33] while

> levels of psycho-social illness are at their highest for young mothers at home with their children, especially when the women also lack a confidante or close relationship outside of the marriage, such as with a friend or mother. It is clear from this that the reverse side of the marriage relationship, which protects and bolsters the psycho-social well-being of men, is the one which impoverishes that of women. To that extent the marital world may become a psychic prison, rather than a haven; a place

30. David Clark and Douglas Haldane, *Wedlocked? Intervention and Research in Marriage* (Cambridge: Polity Press, 1990), p. 26.

31. Clark and Haldane, *Wedlocked?*, p. 27.

32. S. Macintyre, 'Marriage is good for your health; or is it?' (Lecture given to the Royal Philosophical Society of Glasgow, 11 December 1985), discussed in Clark and Haldane, *Wedlocked?*, p. 30.

33. Clark and Haldane, *Wedlocked?*, p. 30. They cite L. Eichenbaum and S. Orbach, *What Do Women Want?* (New York: Berkeley, 1984).

more likely to destroy than nurture. This is shown most graphically of all in studies of wife abuse.[34]

An investigation in Philadelphia, USA, into why women divorce published in 1995 showed women leave 'because of discontent with male control and traditional gender roles, violence, and their husbands' use of drugs and alcohol'.[35] Twenty-five per cent of all violent crime in Britain is wife assault.[36] Violence against women is common in Christian congregations. In the United States Pamela Cooper-White has written of her involvement in over one hundred cases of clergy abuse and confirms that power rather than sex lies at the root of them all.[37] A recent American church report on sexuality confirmed that almost 40% of rapes happen inside heterosexual marriages.[38]

Thirdly, the mismatch between doctrine and experience leads to a credibility gap.[39] Theological questions about whether marriage is thought to be a sacrament, whether grace is conferred, and so on, simply cannot be allowed to continue *in vacuo* as if the quality of the experience of marriage for wives and husbands was simply of no account. But the quality of that experience cannot be separated from pressing social influences, which include gender and role expectations, and the availability of employment and money. While Christianity is ever alert to the distorting and destructive power of sin, in marriage as elsewhere,

34. Clark and Haldane, *Wedlocked?*, p. 31, citing G. Brown and T. Harris, *The Social Origins of Depression* (London: Tavistock, 1978), and R.P. Dobash and R.E. Dobash, *Violence Against Wives* (Shepton Mallett: Open Books, 1980).

35. Demie Kurz, *For Richer, For Poorer: Mothers Confront Divorce* (London: Routledge, 1995), p. 74. See chapter 3, 'How Marriages End'. The study was based on a random sample of 129 divorced women with children in Philadephia. 19% of women gave violence as a principal reason for divorce; 19% their husbands' involvement with another woman; 19% personal dissatisfaction with their marriages; and 17% their husbands' 'hard-living' (26% 'other reasons'). See p. 45.

36. Elizabeth Stuart, *Just Good Friends: Towards a Lesbian and Gay Theology of Relationships* (London: Mowbray, 1995), p. 107.

37. Pamela Cooper-White, *The Cry of Tamar: Violence Against Women and the Church's Response* (Minneapolis: Fortress Press, 1995), p. 129.

38. General Assembly Special Committee on Human Sexuality, Presbyterian Church (USA), *Keeping Body and Soul Together: Sexuality, Spirituality and Social Justice* (1991), p. 53.

39. 'The purposes of marriage as set out in the ASB [Alternative Service Book of the Church of England] are not being fulfilled for a large number of people'. See Stuart, *Just Good Friends*, p. 108.

the very doctrine has come down to us, as if it were formulable irre-spective of its impact on those who enter into it. A fresh account of the grace of marriage is overdue.

f. *Inevitable Patriarchy?*

Perhaps most crucial of all that is considered in this chapter, the prob-lem of patriarchy[40] looms large. All traditions of marriage (except per-haps very early Christian ones) assume the domination of men and the subjugation of women. The history of marriage is one of patriarchy and inequality. Are there theological resources for re-visioning marriage as a sacrament of partnership and mutuality? The two issues to be charted briefly here are the sheer extent of patriarchal attitudes within marriage and the theology of marriage, and the extent to which the deconstruc-tion or transformation of patriarchy is possible. Rosemary Haughton rightly links the problem of male domination within marriage to male domination over everything else in an over-arching, patriarchal mind-set:

> Women's consciousness of themselves is inextricably linked to their awareness of the plight of the planet, even if not all make the connection explicit. That is why the theology of marriage touches the heart of the matter. What a society or a religious system thinks and does about mar-riage is bound to be the truest indication of its attitudes in every other sphere. The norms for relations between the sexes govern attitudes to education, to sex roles in work and home, and in so doing express the value judgment of a society on the characteristics supposed to belong to each. Whether intellect and power, analysis and control are valued, or whether wisdom and intuitive grasp, feeling, nurturance and imagination are highly regarded, shapes decision at every level of social and political life.[41]

A second problem for all students and practitioners of marriage is whether it is an institution which structurally and inevitably leads to an imbalance in the roles and duties of husbands and wives. John Gillis, an influential historian of marriage, believes so. He coins the term 'the conjugal myth' to describe the unavoidable conflict between the mod-ern emphasis on the equality of the partners and the equally modern

40. Thatcher, *Liberating Sex*, pp. 3-12: Rosemary Radford Ruether, *Gaia and God: An Ecofeminist Theology of Earth Healing* (London: SCM Press, 1993), Chapter 6; Stuart and Thatcher, *People of Passion*, pp. 10-13.
41. Haughton, 'The Meaning of Marriage', p. 149.

*de*emphasis of the unequal burdens born by wives. Gillis observes,

> The tension between love and marriage, between the myth of the con-
> jugal and the fact that the woman's marriage is still very different from
> the man's marriage, is by no means resolved. In the 16th and 17th cen-
> turies people took the incompatibility of love and marriage for granted
> and, through various ritual means, put aside intimacy and equality when
> they founded a household and family. The conjugal myth is so dominant
> today that many would deny there is anything fundamentally irreconcil-
> able between the egalitarian dimension of conjugal roles and the roles
> women and men assume when they set up homes and have children.
> Even the marriage law now pretends there is no difference between hus-
> bands and wives as far as their respective rights are concerned.[42]

If there is a change towards an equal sharing in domestic and parenting responsibilities it is slow in coming.

> Large-scale studies show men taking up more domestic work at a snail's
> pace … Meanwhile, here are still significant numbers of couples trapped
> in deeply unequal relationships in which intimacy is at best the forced
> intimacy of a coercive and controlling dominant figure.[43]

Christians look for visions, especially re-visions, not for illusions.
The hope remains that the practice of marriage can change. An adequate theology of marriage will nurture the hope that non-patriarchal
marriage is possible. If achieved it will be a reclamation of God's gift
in creation. It will recognize that marriage is both a public and a private
institution, both personal and social, and it will look for renewal at each
level. This book is a small contribution to the task. Good marriages are
bold experiments in mutual loving, caring, giving and living. Ruether
calls for 'a redefinition of the relationship between home and work
which would allow women to participate in the educational, cultural,
political, and job opportunities of the public world, while integrating
males into co-responsibility for parenting and homemaking'. She envis-
ages 'a new culture of men and women, both as co-parents and partners
in marriage and as co-workers in society, rather than a dichotomized

42. John Gillis, *For Better, For Worse: British Marriages, 1600 to the Present*
(Oxford: Oxford University Press, 1985), p. 310. In similar vein Clulow and Mattinson speak of 'the illusion of equality'. See Christopher Clulow and Janet Mattinson,
Marriage Inside Out: Understanding Problems of Intimacy (Harmondsworth: Penguin Books, 1989), pp. 16-19.

43. Lynn Jamieson, *Intimacy: Personal Relationships in Modern Societies*
(Cambridge: Polity Press, 1998), p. 169.

culture that places them on opposite sides of the home-work division.[44] The new culture she calls for has to be a social creation since Christians cannot by themselves bring it about. The quest for non-patriarchal marriage also forces the churches to think socially, to admit the impact on individual marriages of social forces, and to contribute to the broader rethinking of marriage which is a human, and not merely a Christian, priority.

2. *The External Dialogue*

We have looked at what MacIntyre called an 'internal, interpretative debate' within the Christian tradition of marriage. It is now time to examine the external dialogue between that tradition and those who reject all or part of it. Of course, postmodern writers on marriage are *not*, in general, in dialogue with Christian theologians. This is because (as it will turn out) they associate Christian faith either with an age that has passed away, or with oppressive sexual moralities which legitimize the subordination of women and the stigmatization of lesbian women and gay men. While there is a certain eerieness about this dialogue (who is talking to whom any more?), Christians are bound by a characteristic generosity of mind in assuming that God the Spirit has much to say to us through secular experience (above, 1.2.e) and writing, so patient, grateful listening is demanded. Without understanding there cannot be a basis even for disagreement. They are equally bound by the conviction that Christian faith provides the postmodern world with possibilities for thought and life of which it is almost wholly unaware. In a spirit of openness and conviction, then, it is necessary to listen carefully to voices of integrity far outside the churches. Four well known authors from three different countries have been chosen as participants for the external dialogue that is conducted in the next few pages.

a. *Plastic Sexuality and Pure Relationship*
'Heterosexual marriage', says the influential social theorist Anthony Giddens, 'has been largely undermined by the rise of the pure relationship and plastic sexuality'.[45] Whereas in Christian thought a 'pure

44. Rosemary Radford Ruether, 'Church and Family V: Church and Family in the 1980s', *New Blackfriars* 65 (1984), pp. 209-10.
45. Anthony Giddens, *The Transformation of Intimacy: Sexuality, Love and Eroticism in Modern Societies* (Cambridge: Polity Press, 1992), p. 154.

relationship' may conjure up thoughts of chastity, fidelity and continence, the term has a very different meaning outside Christian piety.

> A pure relationship has nothing to do with sexual purity ... It refers to a
> situation where a social relation is entered into for its own sake, for what
> can be derived by each person from a sustained association with another;
> and which is continued only in so far as it is thought by both parties to
> deliver enough satisfactions for each individual to stay within it.[46]

In late modern societies both sexes have a highly developed sense of
individuality—Giddens calls this 'the reflexive self'[47]—and they are
involved as never before in the creation of their identities. When
Giddens says 'Marriage ... has veered increasingly towards the form of
a pure relationship',[48] he means that married partners look to the relationship primarily in terms of what the relationship provides for them,
and this is something endlessly revisable and negotiable. Increasingly
marriage functions in late modernity less as a settled, permanent social
institution with settled roles for each partner, and more a convenient
social arrangement with an uncertain future in the on-going, negotiated
histories of married couples.

'Plastic sexuality', says Giddens, 'is crucial to the emancipation
implicit in the pure relationship, as well as to women's claim to sexual
pleasure. Plastic sexuality is decentred sexuality, freed from the needs
of reproduction, a *usurption* of it.'[49] Sexuality, then, is capable of being
shaped or formed as never before, through personal choice. But these
choices are made by individuals who have little or no contact with the
social and religious traditions which have led to their current freedoms.[50] Such individuals are importantly rootless, a social fact which
renders sexual intimacy yet more desirable. Maximum freedom is
available at the same time as minimum constraint. Since the pure
relationship assumes equality between the partners, intimate life has
become democratized. We are said to be witnessing 'the translation of
marriage into a signifier of commitment, rather than a determinant of
it'.[51] Commitment there may still be, but it is revisable and not fixed.

46. Giddens, *Transformation*, p. 58.
47. Giddens, *Transformation*, pp. 28-32.
48. Giddens, *Transformation*, p. 58.
49. Giddens, *Transformation*, p. 2.
50. This is what Giddens hints at by his term 'the sequestration of experience'
(Giddens, *Transformation*, pp. 175, 180).
51. Giddens, *Transformation*, p. 192.

'All relationships which approximate to the pure form maintain an implicit "rolling contract" to which appeal may be made by either partner when situations arise felt to be unfair or oppressive.' An ethical framework is provided for the pure relationship by 'confluent love', or 'opening oneself out to the other'.[52] Confluent love suggests the framework

> for the fostering of non-destructive emotion in the conduct of individual and communal life. It provides for the possibility of a revitalising of the erotic—not as a specialist skill of impure women, but as a generic quality of sexuality in social relations formed through mutuality rather than through unequal power.[53]

Giddens and the other authors studied in this section do not advocate the states of affairs they describe. They seek only to describe them, and to offer explanations for what is described. Sociologists are the allies of theologians in telling them how things are, while theologians will have their own accounts of how things might be. That said, the first and glaring difference between traditional Christian marriage and marriage as Giddens describes it, is that with the former marriage *is* the framework for sexual and erotic experience, whereas with the latter *the pure relationship provides the framework* and marriage is one of the possibilities within it. The pure relationship would seem to bring new problems in the wake of those it removes. Gone is the subordinate position of women, at least in their sexual relationships with men: the pure relationship is the deliberate undoing of patriarchy. Heterosexual people, as Giddens acknowledges, have much to learn from lesbian and gay relationships about how mutual, non-patriarchal relationships might be conducted.

But if the parties to the pure relationship are committed to it only relatively and as long as it delivers sufficient satisfactions for it to be mutually sustainable, is there not something intrinsically selfish and self-seeking about this?[54] Who is this modern subject, pursuing his or

---

52. Giddens, *Transformation*, p. 61.

53. Giddens, *Transformation*, p. 202.

54. Mellor and Shilling note that confluent love presupposes 'the essential *separateness* of sexual partners', 'the inherent *transience* of modern relationships', and their 'thoroughly *contractarian*' character. See Philip A. Mellor and Chris Shilling, 'Confluent Love and the Cult of the Dyad: The Pre-contractual Foundations of Contractarian Relationships', in Davies and Loughlin (eds.), *Sex These*

her reflexive life-project, episodically annexing others to himself or herself in the realization of ultimately selfish ends? The sheer individualization of the human being which the account of the pure relationship assumes is an issue for theology, and is taken up later. Undoubtedly there are unmarried people in partnerships with deep commitments, and married people in *de facto* pure relationships. Marriage by contrast offers the possibility of a relationship where the checklist of delivered satisfactions does not have to be endlessly reviewed, because the commitments are permanent ones.

The worth of Christian marriage may be demonstrated in societies where, as Giddens puts it, experience is 'sequestered'. Individuals living their lives in a continuous present forgetful of all past constraints, social expectations and religious beliefs may benefit from an encounter with an understanding of relationships which Christianity offers them. Christian faith remains a tradition, however much it may in its organizational aspects have become enfeebled, and at a time when traditions of all kinds are generally undervalued. Beyond doubt the Christian tradition provides continuity with a past that is all but lost. It is able to recognize that the confluent love and the endless negotiations of the pure relationship need a durable framework which expects, engenders and enhances commitment, and puts people in touch with divine grace in fulfilling their mutual love for each other.

There would seem to be other ways in which the relevance of the Christian story to the pure relationship can be suggested. Plastic sexuality makes bodies increasingly vulnerable even as it transforms reproductive capacity from necessity to choice. A sexual ethic which proclaims the advantages of chastity may be said to provide protection for people who live by it. The democratization of intimacy would seem also to require a durable framework for it to be effective. While there is a clear benefit, especially for women, in heterosexual relationships where negotiation replaces submission, democracy may be of little use when relationships come to a premature end. Termination requires only a single vote. Endings are generally painful. The thriving of intimacy may need a more satisfactory framework than the pure relationship can provide.

Days, pp. 51-78 (55-56) (authors' emphases). On Durkheimian grounds they argue that '"confluent love" rests on an egoistic and cognitive misconception of the thoroughly social and embodied nature of sexual relationships' (p. 51).

b. *Reinventing Humanism*

Jeffery Weeks has provided a valuable exposition of a sexual ethic for postmodern and post-Christian times. He simply assumes that Christianity has nothing to contribute to the shaping of an adequate ethic of relationships. He speaks of 'us post-Christians' who have 'escaped the ethical codes of the Christian era...'[55] Members of postmodern societies 'can no longer rely on pre-existing narratives to shape our hopes for the future'.[56] There is 'no longer a hegemonic master discourse telling us how we should behave',[57] and the reason given is that 'the narrative comforts of the Christian tradition have long suffered the corrosive effects of scepticism and critique, creating the space for fundamentalist revival alongside liberation from superstition'.[58] 'We have lost confidence in the cure of souls, so we have sought meaning in the cure of individual bodies.'[59] While Christianity is nowhere directly criticized in the book, a reader is likely to conclude that its confinement to irrelevance is more damaging than the corrosive critiques of an earlier Christian age. The 'contemporary challenge' for sexual ethics, thinks Weeks, 'is not to seek a new morality but to invent practices which eschew the models of domination and subordination, sin and confession, the natural and the perverse: practices which are "practices of freedom"'.[60]

One might wonder whether the invention of practices of freedom is an exclusive activity which Christians are disqualified from undertaking. Does it really have to be done shorn of all contact with the beliefs of billions of Christians who, in Weeks's estimation, are not yet aware that their deepest life-shaping beliefs have no place in postmodernity? How is this challenge to be met? Weeks agrees with Giddens that the starting place for the reinvention of sexual relationships is what Giddens describes as the democratization of intimacy.

> The democratization of sexuality and relationships that is now on the cultural agenda, only partially realized though it may yet be, creates the

55. Jeffery Weeks, *Invented Moralities: Sexual Values in an Age of Uncertainty* (Cambridge: Polity Press, 1995), pp. 55-56.
56. Weeks, *Invented Moralities*, p. 5.
57. Weeks, *Invented Moralities*, p. 27.
58. Weeks, *Invented Moralities*, p. 25.
59. Weeks, *Invented Moralities*, p. 165.
60. Weeks, *Invented Moralities*, p. 56.

space for rethinking the ethics and values of personal relationships, for exploring what we mean by terms like responsibility, care, concern and love.[61]

The 'regulative principle', of a democratic ethic, continues Weeks, 'must be one's sense that each individual's actions are given meaning through mutual involvement with others'.[62]

> Justice demands not only the avoidance of unnecessary pain to the other but the fostering of care and responsibility for the other. This is not the same as subsuming one's own needs abjectly to the needs of others, because similarly the other's self-determination depends on his or her recognition of responsibility for you. But though reciprocity is a good, responsibility and care for the self and the other cannot depend on one's expectation of return ...

> Care and responsibility ... imply, for example, that the commitment must be not to a paternalistic care but to a 'lightness of care' which recognizes the limits of others, and the necessity to limit your own actions. Care requires a drawing in of others to your interpretative frame, a willingness to hold open a space in which difference can unfold in all its peculiarity and specialness.[63]

There is much in Weeks's reinvention of personal morality for Christians to appreciate. What he says about care and reciprocity conveys what Christians mean by *agape*, and it does so without the hectoring assumptions that sometimes accompany the theological proclamation of that doctrine.[64] His determination to invent practices which avoid domination and subordination will be welcomed by everyone who opposes patriarchy. Nonetheless there are five areas where a robust theological response is appropriate. First it is necessary to ask whether a break with patriarchy is possible without a break from Christianity. The question is begged whether Christianity and patriarchy are too intertwined to be

61. Weeks, *Invented Moralities*, p. 42.

62. Weeks, *Invented Moralities*, p. 71. Weeks acknowledges his debt here to A. Heller and F. Fehér, *The Postmodern Political Condition* (Cambridge: Polity Press, 1988), p. 36.

63. Weeks, *Invented Moralities*, p. 72. The phrase 'lightness of care' is from S.K. White, *Political Theory and Postmodernism* (Cambridge: Cambridge University Press, 1991).

64. Weeks's treatment of the concept of care compares well with Jennifer L. Rike's excellent treatment of it in 'The Lion and the Unicorn: Feminist Perspectives on Christian Love as Care', in Thatcher and Stuart (eds.), *Christian Perspectives*, pp. 247-62.

distinguished. There is a world of difference between 'all' and 'some'. Some religious ethics are patriarchal, but all of them need not be. It will be suggested later that God the Spirit creates a mutuality among persons (the earliest church is an example of this) which is not patriarchal. Just as Marxists were generally surprised to find revolutionary forms of Christianity, so post-religious humanists may be surprised to find religious forms of humanism.

Secondly (as readers will be wondering), where is marriage in this invented, but not new, morality? The question expresses the concern: marriage is scarcely there at all. Surprise is expressed that heterosexual relationships remain largely 'wedlocked'.[65] It is acknowledged that people still get married in droves, but only (allegedly) because they are searching (honourably) for 'a satisfactory relationship entered into and sustained only for as long as it delivers emotional satisfaction'. We have already found Giddens saying this. This may well be a plausible explanation for an entrenched social habit. The possible truth of it provides a powerful argument both for a re-examination of the motives for entering into marriage and the search for a structure which actually supports the commitment which partners in pure relationships make, often with immense optimism and good will.

A third difficulty with the invented morality is that no consideration is given to children *at all*. The topic of children appears in the index of the book only in connection with their abuse by adults. But sexual moralities, at least for straight people, are not so easily separable from the having of children, and connections are easily made between pure relationships and their unintended consequences (abortions and babies). Children *happen*. Many people at some times in their lives want them. The more children are brought within the framework of a sexual ethic, the less adequate is plastic sexuality to deal with them.

Fourthly, most of the inadequacies of Giddens' view, also emerge here. Faith also offers continuity with the past as a rich resource for living, and need not be seen as a hegemonic master discourse mediating only oppression for those who live by it. Mutual relationships are not so neatly manageable as the democratizers of intimacy allow.

These difficulties lead to a further observation about the impossibility of abolishing sin. Christians may want to 'eschew' the model of 'sin and confession' as understood by Foucault and his followers, but the

---

65. Weeks, *Invented Moralities*, p. 35. The term 'wedlocked' is borrowed from the title of Clark and Haldane, *Wedlocked?*

collapse of confession as a practice and of sin as a meaningful concept make no difference to the root identification in Christian theology between selfishness and sin, and this identification appears to be confirmed by both of the analyses we have so far considered. There has to be a framework which nurtures commitments, including commitments to children, which is not questionable or ephemeral, just because the selfishness of individuals is likely to erupt destructively. Of course sin as selfishness is a gendered concept,[66] and selfishness a problematic one. Weeks's analysis recognizes the danger of selfishness when he insists that care must not be allowed to depend on any reciprocal response. Perhaps theology provides a more realistic moral narrative after all. If plastic sexuality is widespread, then the analysis of sin as a social and structural condition[67] would appear to receive additional confirmation.

c. A Pragmatic Sexual Ethic

Steven Seidman's *Embattled Eros* has many similarities with the two works we have just considered. The United States is regarded as a post-modern, post-Christian, pluralistic society where no single ethical code, still less a religious one, can be expected to regulate the sexual experience of its citizens. Seidman's book advocates a 'pragmatic sexual ethic'. He arrives at this by analysing the polyverse sexual styles and behaviours in the United States by means of two rival ideologies, libertarianism and romanticism, and then through criticism and appreciation going beyond both of them to his chosen pragmatic solution.

Seidman claims that in a libertarian sexual ideology,

> sex is viewed as a positive, beneficial, joyous phenomenon. Its expression is connected to personal health, happiness, self fulfillment, and social progress. Sex is said to have multiple meanings; it can be justified as an act of self expression or pleasure, a sign of affection, love or a procreative act. Sexual expression is said to be legitimate in virtually all adult consensual social exchanges, although most libertarians place sex in a romantic, loving bond at the top of their value hierarchy.

66. Anne Carr, *Transforming Grace: Christian Tradition and Women's Experience* (New York: Harper & Row, 1988), p. 58.

67. Rosemary Radford Ruether, 'Spirit and Matter, Public and Private: The Challenge of Feminism to Traditional Dualisms', in P. Cooey, S.A. Farmer and M.E. Ross (eds.), *Embodied Love: Sensuality and Relationship as Feminist Values* (San Francisco: Harper & Row, 1987), p. 66.

Opposed to this libertarian sexual construction is what I call sexual romanticism. Romanticists may very well affirm the sensually pleasurable and expressive aspects of sex while simultaneously emphasizing its dangers—from sexual objectification and dehumanization to promoting relational instabilities, unwanted pregnancy, violence, and exploitation. Whereas the libertarian wishes to release sexual expression from social constraints in order to activate its beneficient (*sic*) powers, the romanticist counsels controlling and sublimating eros to receive its self-enhancing benefit. The romanticist believes that to harness the beneficial aspects of sex, eros must be connected to and kept intertwined with emotional, social and spiritual intimacies. The romanticist holds that sex should always be a way to show affection and love. It should exhibit tender, caring, loving qualities, or qualities that are always respectful of the other as a integrated, whole person. Erotic pleasure should be limited and connected to social and spiritual feelings so as not to reduce the other to a mere body or vessel of pleasure.[68]

Much of *Embattled Eros* demonstrates how 'the feminist sexuality debates' and the 'gay sexuality debates'[69] draw on, modify, develop or oppose the two core sexual ideologies. After a long and careful analysis, this is Seidman's overall judgment of the benefits and weaknesses of each:

The strength of romanticism lie (*sic*) in its attentiveness to the qualitative aspects of sex, i.e., to issues of the emotional and social aspects of the social exchange as well as to considerations of power. This has allowed romanticists to spotlight the perceived dangers of sex. At the same time, this emphasis on judging sexual expression by its qualitative aspects has often led them to be unnecessarily restrictive and intolerant of sexual difference. In this regard, I have praised libertarians for their tolerance of the multiple forms of sexual and intimate expression. Libertarians are to be valued for their role in challenging sexual orthodoxies. But if romanticism is too restrictive, I fault libertarians for failing to provide sufficiently differentiated standards to guide sexual decision making and evaluate sexual practices.[70]

Seidman is aware that these judgments cannot be made from nowhere. This leads him to make explicit his own position and to commend it as a 'pragmatic sexual ethic'. This is where his problems multiply. His 'postmodern premises' lead him to repudiate 'all appeals to a

68. Steven Seidman, *Embattled Eros: Sexual Politics and Ethics in Contemporary America* (London: Routledge, 1992), pp. 5-6.

69. Seidman, *Embattled Eros*, Chapters 3 and 4.

70. Seidman, *Embattled Eros*, p. 190.

natural, divine, morally given order capable of grounding a particular sexual ethic or moral classification of sex practices and lifestyles'.[71] An adequate ethic 'would grant a minimal respect and legitimacy to the empirical differences in sexual concepts and practices we encounter across social space'. These differences 'proliferate as combinations of age, race, sexual orientation, gender, class, physical ableness, and ethnicity are seemingly infinite'.[72] Any judgment 'to the effect that an entire cultural pattern is narcissistic, anomic or immoral for whatever reason' is itself bound to be immoral, both because it is based on a restricted understanding of genuine diversity, and because there are no 'absolutist standpoints' or 'totalizing critiques' that are not 'authoritarian and dangerous'.[73] The two 'general norms' for the pragmatic sexual ethic are 'choice and consent' (a single norm) and 'responsibility'. Seidman is careful to strengthen the concept of consent to include various constraints, for example, 'women's economic position, the realities of violence and harassment, and cultural constructions that bind femininity to the roles of wife and mother'.[74] Similarly 'responsibility' is strengthened by taking into account 'the anticipated impact of an action on the welfare of others'.[75] This is a 'communitarian' notion of responsibility.[76] It presupposes

> viewing the individual as implicated in a social community to whom he or she bears obligations ... Sex should be viewed not simply as entailing a self-relation, but relations to others and to the community with whom we each share a common world.

With Seidman's work the trajectory of thought away from Christianity gathers momentum. One wonders whether the controlling bipolarity in the work between libertarianism and romanticism can quite bear the weight placed upon it. The churches have made a huge contribution to the understanding and practice of sex in North America,[77] but there is

71. Seidman, *Embattled Eros*, p. 191.
72. Seidman, *Embattled Eros*, p. 193.
73. Seidman, *Embattled Eros*, p. 194. So-called 'global judgments' suffer from the same rough treatment. See p. 195.
74. Seidman, *Embattled Eros*, p. 197.
75. Seidman, *Embattled Eros*, p. 199.
76. Seidman, *Embattled Eros*, p. 206.
77. According to Peter Gardella it was 'Christian influences, working through popular culture, [which] led Americans to seek ecstatic pleasure and to expect freedom from guilt in their sexual relations'. Even 'experts' on sex 'inherited their

not a hint of this in the book. Any view of sex which counsels restraint, or connects sexual activity with love or with religious or moral purposes is labelled 'romantic'. The view that there are no absolute standpoints is itself an absolute standpoint. The two norms for pragmatism, however important, are notoriously flimsy (as Seidman acknowledges). The end product is a liberalism which belongs to modernity, not a pragmatism of postmodernity as Seidman wants.

The more troubling aspect of the work is the lack of space afforded to marriage as an enabling framework for relationships of long-term commitment. Marriage seems to belong to premodernity and modernity. It appears to be significant chiefly for the problems it causes for the people who choose it. Once more there are almost no references to children. They appear to be written out of the texts of postmodernity rather as lesbian and gay people used to be written out of earlier ones. There is beginning to emerge a pattern in writings of this kind. Marriage is either a historical or a problematic relationship, one which few postmoderns will choose. Separation of sexuality from procreation is so far advanced ('sequestered', we might say) that having babies as a result of it is about as relevant as the institution of marriage itself.

d. *The Secular Religion of Love*

Several of the themes pursued in this chapter are confirmed by the final, and German, case-study, *The Normal Chaos of Love*.[78] The authors, Ulrich Beck and Elisabeth Beck-Gernsheim, argue for three theses. First, the 'prescribed gender roles' which are being subverted in the present century, 'are the *basis* of industrial society, and not some traditional relic which can easily be dispensed with'.[79] The second thesis is that

> the dynamics of change, making individuals out of members of social classes, do not stop short at the family's front door. With a mysterious force which they do not understand themselves, although they personify it, whatever strange form it takes, people are shaking off rigid gender roles, bourgeois maxims, set ways, or being shaken to the very depths of

faith in liberation through orgasm from Christians who had found freedom from sin in moments of religious ecstasy'. See Peter Gardella, *Innocent Ecstasy* (New York: Oxford University Press, 1985), pp. 3, 7.

78. Ulrich Beck and Elisabeth Beck-Gernsheim, *The Normal Chaos of Love* (trans. Mark Ritter and Jane Wiebel; Cambridge: Polity Press, 1995).

79. Beck and Beck-Gernsheim, *Chaos*, p. 23 (authors' emphasis).

their being. The belief that comes over them is *I am myself* and after that I am a woman. *I am myself*, and after that I am a man. 'I' and the *expected* woman, 'I' and the *expected* man are worlds apart.[80]

The third thesis is that 'the family is *only the setting, not the cause* of events'. The crisis afflicting marriage and the family is to be explained primarily as a social phenomenon, the product of social forces, and only secondarily as a personal and moral one, since the family is merely the internal site where the external tensions generated by the demands of employment in market economies, and the increasing access of women to opportunities once confined to men, are expressed.

These three theses help to explain what might be called the 'paradox of intimacy'. 'Individualization may drive men and women apart, but paradoxically it also pushes them back into one another's arms. *As traditions become diluted, the attractions of a close relationship grow.* Everything that one has lost is sought in the other'.[81] Now that God and the church are 'displaced', and no comparable substitutes are discoverable, romantic love replaces the lost belongingness to church, family and community.

> The direction in which modern developments are taking us is reflected in the way we idealize love. Glorifying it in the way we do acts as a counterbalance to the losses we feel in the way we live. If not God, or priests, or class, or neighbours, then at least there is still You. And the size of the 'You' is inversely proportional to the emotional void which otherwise seems to prevail.[82]

The prospects for marriage in the normal chaos of love are bleak. People look to intimacy to satisfy an increasing range of personal needs, and they may look to marriage as a means of enhancing and preserving it. But intimacy, whether or not formalized by marriage, is likely to be desired at least partly for selfish ends. Our partner is present to us as a means towards our own self-discovery:

> The fundamental theme behind marriage is not just the social structure of our lives; it is also increasingly a matter of identity. This is the aspect revealed particularly by psychological studies of marriage: in seeking an exchange on many levels with our partner we are also seeking ourselves. We are searching for the history of our life; we want to reconcile ourselves with hurts and disappointments, plan our goals and share our

80. Beck and Beck-Gernsheim, *Chaos*, p. 24 (authors' emphases).
81. Beck and Beck-Gernsheim, *Chaos*, p. 32 (authors' emphasis).
82. Beck and Beck-Gernsheim, *Chaos*, p. 33.

hopes. We mirror ourselves in the other, and our image of a You is also an idealized image of I.[83]

Under these circumstances the decision of couples to have children is said in many cases to be fraught with dangers for the children themselves. Children are thought to be simultaneously both obstacles and love-fetishes, the undeserving victims of the contradictions faced by their parents. 'On the one hand a child is regarded as an impediment to one's own progress.' On the other hand, 'the child becomes the last remaining, irrevocable, unique primary love object. Partners come and go, but the child stays. Everything one vainly hoped to find in the relationship with one's partner is sought in or directed at the child.'[84]

Alternatively, children may function as compensation for the transience of short-term relationships, as permanent companions in the multifluctuations of modern life. It is children who are surrogates now, not just mothers. They too are substitutionary figures, perhaps for absent or inadequate parenting partners. If parents 'feel rejected and unloved by their adult partner, surrounded by indifference and cold silence, people are glad to lavish their love on their child,[85] whatever the harmful consequences may be. Or perhaps a child is a sought-after compensation for the boredom and routine of working life. Children may help parents

> to rediscover some of their gifts and express some of their needs which they sorely miss in high-tech life: being patient or calm, solicitous and sensitive, affectionate, open and close. Motherhood seems to offer the women an alternative refuge from the working world... committing yourself to a child means contradicting the cognitive side of life, and finding a living counterweight to all that soul-destroying routine.[86]

The fate of children in post-traditional families will concern us later (below, 5.2.a). The authors' analysis of romantic love as itself a

83. Beck and Beck-Gernsheim, *Chaos*, p. 51. Increasingly couples now enter into marriage contracts which can specify the smallest detail of who does what within the marriage, whether there will be children and if so when and how many, and, of course, what is to happen if/when the marriage ends. The authors wryly comment: 'under voluntary contracts of this kind...one can presume that enduring such a marriage is easier, and this very fact encourages the participants to consider ending it earlier. Marriage turns into a tenancy for temporarily satisfying mutual needs' (p. 157).

84. Beck and Beck-Gernsheim, *Chaos*, p. 37.

85. Beck and Beck-Gernsheim, *Chaos*, p. 75.

86. Beck and Beck-Gernsheim, *Chaos*, p. 106.

surrogate, a substitute for religion, is important for the attempt to understand the contemporary context within which the presentation of Christian marriage is to be set in this book. The authors say they are 'immod-
estly and tentatively looking for the meaning of life in a post-Christian
modern society, and our discovery is, quite simply and unsociologi-
cally, love'.[87] They do not approve, however, of what they see. They
believe 'that the structure of industrial society which laid down gender,
family and occupational roles is crumbling away, and a modern form of
archaic anarchy is breaking out, with love on its banner, and a thousand
delights and obstacles in its path'.[88] 'Marrying for love has existed only
since the beginning of the industrial revolution and was its invention.'[89]
The shocking absoluteness of the commitment to romantic love can be
measured by the fact that 'Abandoning one's own children for someone
else is not a breach of love but a proof of it... This illustrates the
extraordinary power love already exerts over us'.[90] 'Our faith in love is
linked to its lack of tradition.' In its place love is 'a non-traditional,
post-traditional religion which we are hardly aware of because we ourselves are its temples and our wishes are its prayers'.[91] 'As religion
loses its hold, people seek solace in private sanctuaries.'[92] 'Faith in love
means you love your lover but not your neighbour, and your loving
feelings are always in danger of turning into hate.'[93] 'Love as an
encounter of egos, as a re-creation of reality in terms of you-me, as a
trivialized Romanticism without any prohibitions attached, is becoming
a mass phenomenon: a secular religion of love.'[94]

A major difference between *The Normal Chaos of Love* and the other
writings considered in this chapter is the welcome attention to the experience of children in post-religious, detraditionalized societies. Sometimes children are loved excessively; sometimes they are loved for the
wrong reasons; sometimes they are not loved at all. These grievous
descriptions of the unnecessary sufferings of children at the hands of

87. Beck and Beck-Gernsheim, *Chaos*, p. 169.
88. Beck and Beck-Gernsheim, *Chaos*, p. 170.
89. Beck and Beck-Gernsheim, *Chaos*, p. 172.
90. Beck and Beck-Gernsheim, *Chaos*, p. 174.
91. Beck and Beck-Gernsheim, *Chaos*, p. 177.
92. Beck and Beck-Gernsheim, *Chaos*, p. 179.
93. Beck and Beck-Gernsheim, *Chaos*, p. 180.
94. Beck and Beck-Gernsheim, *Chaos*, p. 184. The authors also consider some
'enormous differences' between romantic love and genuine religion. See p. 180.

their parents will contribute to the theology of liberation for children in Chapter 5. A second difference is the elevation of love to the status of a surrogate religion. Apart from these differences the work shares similarities with its British and American counterparts (without apparently being aware of them). We are post-Christians. We lack contact with our formative traditions. We are preoccupied with self-identity. We are ensnared by the attractions and limitations of intimacy.

3. *Christian Marriage: The Revised Agenda*

This chapter began with the claim that two separate but related theological dialogues were necessary in order to advance the Christian doctrine of marriage and extend the Church's marital tradition. Both of these dialogues have been reviewed. It is now time to examine how each might impinge creatively on the other, enabling new syntheses and insights to appear.

The internal dialogue within theology and the churches flagged up several theological problems. Could the recognition of the diversity of attitudes to marriage in the New Testament actually contribute constructively to contemporary accounts of marriage? Were assumptions about the indissolubility of marriage essential to Christian faith, or did they function instead to enforce the misery of marriages which had already failed? There were warnings against the oppressive nature of marriage which actually came from some of the Church's most famous theologians. What remarkable points of agreement might there be, as yet unexplored, between ancient theological and current feminist criticisms of marriage? Was marriage a sacrament? What other issues were at stake in probing the possible sacramentality of marriage? How far are all theologies of marriage invalidated by being premised on the experience of men? Is a non-patriarchal form of marriage as an institution a social possibility?

Some of these questions will receive detailed answers in the rest of the book. But the answers which are given will be honed by the whetstone of the secular, post-Christian agenda, since this is the generation with which the contemporary churches are responsible for sharing their Good News. Readers dismayed at the difficulties presented by the internal agenda are invited to channel their energies into making connections between living faith and the external, secular agenda. This is a practice which will in any case cause the internal difficulties to shrink in significance, and in some cases to disappear.

a. *Common Features of a Post-Christian Sexual Ethic*
The short survey of some postmodern writings on sexual ethics in this chapter reveals at least ten common features. Against each of them it is possible to juxtapose a clear Christian alternative. The features are:

1. *The marginalization of marriage* as a distinct framework, institution, or objective relationship within which people embark on life together. It is simply assumed that lifelong marriage is a forgotten, or discredited or unworkable option.
2. *The evacuation of the traditional meanings of marriage.* Marriage, inasmuch as it remains at all, is what partners make it. There are no longer discernible guidelines to be found among the 'pre-existing narratives' or 'hegemonic discourses' (Weeks's phrases) of premodernity and modernity. In postmodernity 'the pure relationship' prevails, even among the married.
3. *Missing children.* The place of children is deeply ambiguous in these accounts. They scarcely feature in them. Only one of the four books, *The Normal Chaos of Love*, dealt honestly with children (showing them generally to be victims of the normal chaos of love).[95]
4. *An individualistic view of the human person.* The terminology of the pure relationship, plastic sexuality and confluent love, presupposes a highly self-centred, reflexive, autonomous human subject. While there may be considerable support for this view of the subject in Western, especially Protestant societies, the reflexive self pursuing its own life-project may be a popular cultural myth.
5. *An idolatry of romantic love.* The overriding priority of falling and feeling in love may have become a surrogate religion.
6. *Personal identity as a lifelong project.* The question 'Who am I?' is endlessly worked out self-referentially, and only incidentally and ephemerally are significant others integrated into it.

95. Reviewing recent theological literature about sexuality Jon Davies observes 'It is, in all of these radicalisms, perhaps easy to miss what has been the greatest of all sexual transformations: the elimination of the child'. See Jon Davies, 'Neither Seen Nor Heard Nor Wanted: The Child as Problematic. Towards an Actuarial Theology of Generation', in Michael A. Hayes, Wendy Porter and David Tombs (eds.), *Religion and Sexuality* (Sheffield: Sheffield Academic Press, 1999), pp. 326-47 (326).

7.   *The superficiality of a secular, post-traditional ethic.* The question of how ethical wisdom is to be found in a post-religious age is far from settled. Weeks's honest 'invention' of a neo-humanism goes some way towards a Christian understanding of reciprocity, but his rejection of any and every meta-narrative is premature. Seidman's pragmatic ethic is superficial. And where is sacred order to be found in the 'normal chaos' which is love?

8.   *The tradition of late, secular humanism.* Despite the protestations that detraditionalization has taken place, that experience is sequestered, and individuals are no longer attached to their historic roots, the replacement tradition offered to us cannot of course come from nowhere. Neither is it new. It is late, secular humanism which sits well in an unbroken, European, Enlightenment and post-Enlightenment tradition of anti-religious thought, and which now has decided that religious influences have declined to the point at which they can be safely ignored. This is a very premature assumption. It is, however, disingenuous to offer post-traditional societies a very traditional (secular) ethic.

9.   *Ephemeral sexual relationships.* Relationships which exist only for the satisfactions which they provide seem pre-disposed to coming to an end. 'Relationships structured by such a mentality tend to break down more easily than those of a less egoistic character: the more people commit themselves to the notion of the pure relationship, the less viable their relationships are likely to be.'[96]

10.   *Post-patriarchal, post-religious ethos.* The ethos of secular ethics is post-patriarchal, and religion is seen as complicit in patriarchy's long reign.

b. *Christian Alternatives to the Post-Christian Sexual Ethic*
Christian faith posits clear alternatives to these features of postmodern sexual ethics. With regard to marriage the following table indicates some of the differences.

96. Mellor and Shilling, 'Confluent Love', p. 73. They follow empirical work reported by D.R. Hall, 'Marriage as a Pure Relationship: Exploring the Link between Premarital Cohabitation and Divorce in Canada', *Journal of Comparative Family Studies* 27.1 (1996), pp. 1-12.

Postmodern approaches to marriage	Christian approaches to marriage
1. the marginalization of marriage	1. centrality of marriage as an ethic of mutual self-giving
2. the evacuation of the traditional meanings of marriage	2. recovery of the traditional meanings of marriage, children, fidelity, sacramentality
3. missing children	3. children as the blessing of God on the marriage
4. an individualistic view of the human person	4. a social view of the human person as a person-in-relation
5. an idolatry of romantic love	5. a divine-human love rooted in the divine Trinity
6. personal identity as a lifelong project	6. Christian identity conferred by being with others in relationship
7. superficiality of a secular, post-traditional ethic	7. depth of the Christian 'passionate ethic': the communal character of morality
8. the tradition of late, secular humanism	8. the recovery of the historical, developing, Christian tradition
9. ephemeral sexual relationships	9. lifelong covenant with one person
10. post-patriarchal, post-religious ethos	10. post-patriarchal, authentically religious ethos

Most of the items in the right hand column receive a detailed (and revised) treatment later in the book. In Christian thought vowed, covenanted commitment to one person for life is intended as a liberating structure precisely because it forecloses the prospect of termination when the endless negotiations founder or the supply of satisfied needs is temporarily interrupted. Marriage offers the prospect of mutual self-giving irrespective of the extent of care which each partner actually requires. In its Christian form marriage carries with it certain meanings about becoming one flesh with a partner for life, about a covenant which reflects God's loving commitment towards God's people, about having and caring for children, and about 'the mutual society, help, and comfort, that the one ought to have of the other, both in prosperity and adversity'.[97] The bringing of children into the world and the bringing up of children in the world is one of the great purposes and delights of marriage.

The full resources of traditional faith are available to Christians who wish to counter the individualistic anthropologies and self-centred motivations of secular postmodern ethics. Biblical faith has a communitarian view of individuals which locates them in the community of the whole people of God and defines them as members of the one, inclusive body of Christ. Theology has an understanding of the human person as a person-in-relation which is ultimately derived from belief in the nature of God as a communion of coequal Persons-in-relation. The divine love which enables and sanctifies marital commitments mingles with human love as the partnership of marriage is also a partnership of faith.

Christians ultimately derive their personal identity from their baptism in the name of the triune God. Identity is conferred, not discovered. Whatever else they are or become, they are first of all Christians, belonging to God through incorporation in the gift of Christ. This identity is prior to all others and relativizes lesser identities of birth, class or status. Instead of a naturalistic ethic, the depth of the Christian 'passionate ethic',[98] rooted in the co-solidarities with Christ and with the vulnerable, suffering neighbour, becomes constitutive for the practice of faith. The communal character of morality which is expressed in the Christian virtues of faith, hope and love is counterposed to post-traditional ethics, and the recovery of the historical, developing, Christian tradition is offered in place of detraditionalization. The prospect of a lifelong covenant with one person in matrimony belongs to the virtue of hope, and the abolition of male dominance, in marriage, Church and society, while still far away, is, so it will be argued, the fruit of authentic faith.

Such contrasts are admittedly dangerous. They are made only to draw attention to genuine differences in outlook, not to polarize fixed positions. The line between them is blurred. The claims just made for Christian marriage will seem to some readers just plain wrong, and unsupported. In what follows, these claims will be made good. In the

97. This is the third of the three purposes of marriage in the Book of Common Prayer.
98. See Stuart and Thatcher, *People of Passion*, Chapter 2, pp. 25-57.

process of rediscovering a theology of marriage in the postmodern context, many of the conundrums identified in the internal and largely premodern agenda will also come to be seen in a fresh light.

Chapter 3

THE BIBLICAL MODELS OF MARRIAGE

In this chapter the biblical roots of Christian marriage will be briefly described. The term 'biblical roots' suggests deep, established historical sources which have brought forth fruitful, luxurious growth. This is a useful metaphor, provided that a little root-pruning is also allowed. However, the term 'model' is preferred, because it registers the gap between a model and what is modelled. Good models provide partial representations of what they model, and at the same time nudge their viewers and readers to engage imaginatively with what is beyond adequate representation. When this happens, insight may occur and the models may begin to be appropriated in new ways.

There are two major and three minor models of marriage in the Bible. While the major models are familiar, the minor models are less so. But the intention here is to examine biblical teaching as a whole and not to ignore those minor but significant passages which can only with difficulty be integrated into an *apologia* for Christian marriage. Considerable work will be done on the two major models, and the conclusions taken forward to Chapter 7 where a contemporary picture of the meaning of marriage is sketched. Heeding the warning (above, 2.1.a) that there is a bewildering diversity of views about the meaning of marriage in the Bible which may not be readily harmonized, let us identify the two main models of marriage in the Bible, as those of *covenant* (3.1.a) and *union* (3.1.b). But the Bible also speaks of marriage as a 'dubious necessity' (3.1.c), a 'worldly concession' (3.1.d), and as passionate mutual *love* (3.1.e). These are the minor models. Each of the models will be revisited in 3.2 to assess their significance for a contemporary re-visioning of Christian marriage and to contribute to the doctrinal reconstruction of later chapters.

1. *The Biblical Models of Marriage*

a. *A Covenant*

From at least the eighth century BCE marriage was regarded as a covenant, modelled on the divine-human covenant between Yahweh and the Jewish people. The Hebrew term for covenant (*berit*) 'seems to have the root meaning of "bond, fetter", indicating a binding relationship'. It

> signifies a relationship based on commitment, which includes both promises and obligations, and which has the quality of reliability and durability. The relationship is usually sealed by a rite—for example, an oath, sacred meal, blood sacrifice, invocation of blessings and curses—which makes it binding.[1]

A preliminary move towards emphasizing marriage as a covenant is to make the contrast between a covenant and a contract as this was understood in the ancient world:

> The binding and inviolable character of covenants derived from the divine sanctions attached to the covenant agreement. Contracts have people as witness, and human or civil society as guarantor. Covenants have God or the gods as witness, but not in the sense that the gods or God simply vouch for the correctness of the agreement; they act as guarantors that the terms of the treaty, alliance, or covenant will be carried out.[2]

There is a strong covenantal implication in the foundational text of Gen. 2.24: 'That is why a man leaves his father and mother and attaches himself to his wife, and the two become one.' The man who 'leaves' (Heb. *asav*) his father and mother is said to *sever a covenant* with them. When he 'attaches himself (Heb. *davaq*) to his wife' he creates a covenant with her.[3] Gordon Hugenberger has argued at length the likelihood 'that sexual union was understood as a complementary covenant-ratifying oath-sign, at least by some biblical writers', and that in contradiction to the rival theory of marriage by purchase, sexual union was 'the indispensable means for the consummation of marriage both in the

---

1. Bernhard W. Anderson, 'Covenant', in Bruce M. Metzger and Michael D. Coogan (eds.), *The Oxford Companion to the Bible* (Oxford: Oxford University Press, 1993), p. 138.

2. Paul F. Palmer SJ, 'Christian Marriage: Contract or Covenant?', *TS* 33 (1972), pp. 617-65 (618).

3. Mackin SJ, *The Marital Sacrament*, p. 28.

Old Testament and elsewhere in the ancient Near East'.[4] The relationship between God and God's people is a covenant-relationship. The relationship between covenanters in the ancient world was originally that between kings and their subjects, between lords and their vassals.[5] Later, the prophets come to speak of the covenant in terms of divine love and fidelity. This leads them to utilize the human marriage covenant as a way of expressing the divine-human covenant between God and the people of God. While this is in part a deepening of the understanding of the covenant-relationship, it is also regressive, because the metaphorical meanings required to establish the cognitive transfer from the divine-human covenant-relationship between God and the people of God to the human covenant-relationship of marriage have unacceptable consequences. Women are stereotyped as inferior and unfaithful partners, a caricature upheld and reaffirmed many times over in Christianity. So it is necessary to inquire further into the development of the understanding of marriage as a covenant, and to ask the question whether the covenant idea has a part to play in any contemporary Christian vision for marriage.

Hosea. Hosea's actual or fictitious marriage to Gomer, his adulterous wife, and the symbolic power of the marriage to stand as a model of the broken covenant between God and God's people is well known. Gomer is not to be divorced or killed (as Deut. 22.22 sanctioned) for her crimes: rather her anguished husband shows his love for his faithless wife by forgiving her and taking her back. Their reconciliation will be the precursor of a new covenant between God and Israel which includes 'the wild beasts, the birds of the air, and the creatures that creep on the ground' (Hos. 2.18). The means of waging war are swept from the earth, and then, says God, 'I shall betroth you to myself for ever, bestowing righteousness and justice, loyalty and love; I shall betroth you to myself, making you faithful, and you will know the Lord'[6] (Hos. 2.19-20)[6].

4.   Gordon Paul Hugenberger, *Marriage as a Covenant: A Study of Biblical Law and Ethics Governing Marriage Developed from the Perspective of Malachi* (VTSup, 52; Leiden: E.J. Brill, 1994), p. 343.

5.   Palmer, 'Christian Marriage', p. 619.

6.   According to Hugenberger, there is a deliberate *double entendre* here, combining covenantal and sexual meanings of 'know'. 'In an extended marriage

So the covenant is re-established and the language of betrothal and marriage again deployed to express it. There is no doubt that the book of Hosea represents a great step forward in the theology of covenant. The covenant rests not simply on legal, but moral foundations: it is based on love, not simply on law. Forgiveness overrides forensic justice. The problem arises at the point at which the analogy between the human covenant and the divine-human covenant breaks down. Since analogies rest on known similarities and dissimilarities between what is compared, it is also important to state what is dissimilar when comparisons are being made, and this is where two lots of trouble arise. A covenant is not a relationship between equal parties, especially if one party is a king, a lord or a god. Insofar as marriage is a covenant, there is little evidence in the Old Testament that it carried with it a sense of equality between the partners. A divine-human covenant is clearly an asymmetrical relationship. The divine party calls all the shots. If or when this detail of the analogy is reflected back into the gender relations of the human parties, it has a shattering effect, as in Hosea 1–3. The man represents God. The woman represents God's faithless people. Gender stereotypes are reinforced. And that is exactly what happens in Hosea.

A second and more pressing problem is the extent of sexual violence which Hosea is prepared to contemplate in order to compel the return of his wife, prompting the shocked realization that it is the exercise of male power rather than forgiveness which the prophet will use to achieve his ends. Gomer's estranged partner is prepared to 'strip her bare and parade her naked' (2.3) presumably to teach her the lesson that her lovers, unlike her husband, are unable to defend her. Then he considers restraining her (2.6), so that her loss of freedom of movement will compel her to return to her husband because she will realize that her freedom is his gift. Finally seduction in a deserted place will be tried. 'I shall woo her, lead her into the wilderness, and speak words of encouragement to her' (2.3). As Renita Weems asks, 'how are we as biblical theologians to come to grips with the prophet's association of God with sexual violence?', and observes 'For women who have been

metaphor Hos. 2.22 uses "know", to describe the point at which Israel will "acknowledge" Yahweh as her covenant partner. This fact appears to confirm our hypothesis that sexual union, as a marriage covenant-ratifying act, is the decisive means by which an individual "acknowledges" his or her spouse as covenant partner'. See Hugenberger, *Marriage as a Covenant*, p. 343.

the victims of domestic and sexual violence, the image of God as rav-
aging husband may be intolerable'.[7] Whatever literary or symbolic
power Hosea's failing marriage may have had, there is little mutuality
either in the marriage itself or in its use for how things stand between
Yahweh and the chosen people.[8]

Jeremiah and Ezekiel. Jeremiah and Ezekiel also deploy the language
of broken marriage to expose the broken relationship between the Lord
and the Lord's people. The Lord is the wronged husband whose marriage with the people of Israel has been sabotaged by his bride's
unfaithfulness. 'I remember in your favour the loyalty of your youth,
your love during your bridal days, when you followed me through the
wilderness, through a land unsown' (Jer. 2.2). But the long-suffering
Lord is not always the forgiving husband: *he is also the initiator of
divorce.* The collapsed northern kingdom (Samaria) is depicted to the
tottering southern kingdom (Judah) as a sister divorced by her divine
husband: Judah is about to share a similar fate.

> Even after she [Samaria] had done all this I thought she would come
> back to me, but she did not. That faithless woman, her sister Judah, saw
> it; she saw too that I had put apostate Israel away and given her a cer-
> tificate of divorce because she had committed adultery. Yet that faithless
> woman, her sister Judah, was not afraid; she too went and committed
> adultery (Jer. 3.7-8; and see Ezek. 23).

In a series of disturbing images, Ezekiel depicts the southern kingdom as a foundling baby girl who 'was thrown out on the bare ground
in your own filth on the day you were born' (16.5). The Lord rescued
and tended the girl but decreed she should continue to live, unwashed,
in the blood in which she lay at birth. Later Ezekiel has the Lord say

> You came to full womanhood; your breasts became firm and your hair
> grew, but you were still quite naked and exposed. I came by again and
> saw that you were ripe for love. I spread the skirt of my robe over you

7. Renita J. Weems, 'Gomer: Victim of Violence or Victim of Metaphor?',
Semeia 47 (1989), pp. 100-101. Weems argues sexual violence is expressed in three
ways in Hosea 1–3. It shows the permitted length a husband may go to preserve a
marriage. It functions 'to underscore the point that punishment precedes reconciliation'. Thirdly, it functions 'as a poetic device to relate the punishment to the crime',
that is, because the wife dresses provocatively she *deserves* the humiliation of public nakedness. See pp. 97-98; and *idem, Battered Love.*

8. See Stuart, *Just Good Friends*, p. 122.

and covered your naked body. I plighted my troth and entered into a covenant with you, says the Lord God, and you became mine. Then I bathed you with water to wash off the blood: I anointed you with oil (16.7-8).

The young woman is next prepared by her divine husband to be his bride (16.10-13). No sooner has she become a beautiful queen (13-14) than she is accused of a catalogue of crimes of sex and violence which include prostitution, the killing of her own children (16.20-21), and 'countless acts of harlotry' (16.25). She is so eager to get laid she waives her prostitute's fee (16.31), and even pays some of her punters to screw her (16.34). As a punishment she too is stripped naked before her lovers, humiliated, then stoned and hacked to pieces by a mob (16.37-40).[9] Her crime? Like her sister (the northern kingdom) 'You are a true daughter of a mother who rejected her husband and children. You are a true sister of your sisters who rejected their husbands and children' (16.45). Yet even after this shocking oracle comes another which is more hopeful. While Judah is punished for breaking the former covenant (16.59), the new covenant will last forever. 'I shall establish my covenant with you, and you will know that I am the Lord. You will remember, and will be so ashamed and humiliated that you will never open your mouth again, once I have pardoned you for all you have done' (16.62-63).

A contemporary reader will find little to cheer her here. The images Ezekiel chooses cannot be understood without further inferences being made which render the 'symphonic imperative' (above, 1.2.b) difficult to achieve. The child has a deprived, restricted childhood and is entirely at the mercy of her condescending patron. There is a suggestion he is a voyeur, aroused by her adolescent but still naked body, so he marries her. She is powerless with respect to his will. The first exercise of freedom permitted to the young bride is to become a whore. Several stereotypes operate: women can't be trusted; women are naturally randy and unfaithful; prostitutes like sex; women's beauty is a source of sin; women deserve violence and humiliation as legitimate punishment. Even the depiction of the fresh start, the new covenant, will

9.   One plausible commentator thinks Ezekiel was 'a man possessed by fear and loathing of women and their sexuality, and by rage and envy that other men might partake of their sexuality'. See David J. Halperin, *Seeking Ezekiel* (Pennsylvania: Pennsylvania State University Press, 1993), p. 141. For the full horror of the pornographic detail of ch. 16, see p. 146.

induce a state of disabling female guilt, the weight of which renders women dumb and makes mutual participation in the covenant impossible. If the covenant idea can function as a foundation for Christian marriage, it clearly cannot be used as it is found here.

Deutero-Isaiah. Jeremiah and Ezekiel depicted Yahweh as alternately a wronged and angry husband, and a forgiving compassionate one. However a generation later the author of Isaiah 40–55 ('Deutero-Isaiah') moved towards a view of covenant-love as unshakeable and unaffected by human faithlessness. This prophet had suffered the pain of exile in Babylon and as a result of that experience he had come to believe that God would never again allow such affliction to befall the covenant-people. His hope for a renewed covenant is poignantly expressed by means of a prolonged marital metaphor. Israel the once barren, deserted wife will now have an abundance of children. (Isa. 54.1) Whereas under the previous covenant the Lord had divorced his young bride for her infidelity, under the new covenant, the prophet announces, the Lord will never again forsake his people. ' ... your husband is your Maker; his name is the Lord of Hosts. He who is called God of all the earth, the Holy One of Israel, is your redeemer' (54.5). The Jews' status as wife of the Lord is to be reconfirmed: 'The Lord has acknowledged you a wife again, once deserted and heart-broken; your God regards you as a wife still young, though you were once cast off' (54.6). The just punishment meted out by the angry husband is itself explained as a momentary lapse on the Lord's part, something he will not permit to recur. 'For a passing moment I forsook you, but with tender affection I shall bring you home again. In an upsurge of anger I hid my face from you for a moment; but now have I pitied you with never-failing love, says the Lord, your Redeemer' (54.7-8). The divine husband's new covenant with his wife is compared with his covenant with the peoples of the world after the time of Noah not to destroy them by flooding the earth (54.9).

> As I swore that the waters of Noah's flood should never again pour over the earth, so now I swear to you never again to be angry with you or rebuke you. Though the mountains may move and the hills shake, my love will be immovable and never fail, and my covenant promising peace will not be shaken, says the Lord in his pity for you (54.9-10).

Only in the last book of the Old Testament does the Bible expressly refer to individual Jewish marriages as covenants. The prophet Malachi, writing about 445 BCE, became outraged by the practice of Jewish husbands in abandoning their wives and marrying pagan wives in their place.[10] His argument against the practice relied on several distinct premises, which in order to appreciate the prophet's profound view of marriage as a covenant must now be made explicit.

First, all Jewish men and women share a common identity under God as Creator and Parent. Divorce is a breach of the covenant-solidarity which embraces male and female. 'Have we not all one father? Did not one God create us? Why then are we faithless to one another by violating the covenant of our forefathers?'(Mal. 2.10; also 2.15) Secondly, Malachi identifies individual breaches of the marital covenant with breaches of the divine-human covenant. Although one presumes a minority of husbands were divorcing their wives to marry pagan women, the whole nation is contaminated by the practice. 'Judah is faithless, and abominable things are done in Israel and in Jerusalem: in marrying the daughter of a foreign God, Judah has violated the sacred place loved by the Lord' (2.11). Thirdly, the remarriage of divorced Jewish men to pagan women invalidates all ceremonial worship and cultic sacrifice. Despite offerings and earnest tears, the Lord is said still to refuse

> to look at the offering or receive favourably a gift from you. You ask why. It is because the Lord has born witness against you on behalf of the wife of your youth. You have broken faith with her, though she is your partner, your wife by solemn covenant (2.13-14).

Liturgical acts do not compensate for immoral ones. The Lord gives evidence on behalf of divorced wives in the prosecution of selfish husbands. Fourthly, since marriage is itself an unbreakable covenant, divorce breaks its terms absolutely. 'Godly children' should follow marriage, not divorce (2.15). Finally, divorce is wrong because it is selfish, and because it involves the exercise of unequal power of men over women, it is also cruel.

> Keep watch on your spirit, and let none of you be unfaithful to the wife of your youth. If a man divorces or puts away his wife, says the Lord God of Israel, he overwhelms her with cruelty, says the Lord of Hosts. Keep watch on your spirit, and do not be unfaithful (2.15-16).

10. Mackin, *The Marital Sacrament*, p. 39. Despite Malachi's strictures, Bruce J. Malina notes his silence about divorce between Jew and Gentile. See Bruce J. Malina, *The New Testament World: Insights from Cultural Anthropology* (Atlanta: John Knox Press, 1981), p. 10.

Malachi contributes much to the biblical understanding of marriage and so of divorce. He anticipates the teaching of Jesus. In his support for the rights of women he is unsurpassed in the Hebrew Scriptures.

Ephesians 5. Neither Jesus nor Paul uses the term 'covenant' in relation to marriage. However, since 'covenant' comes to be increasingly qualified by 'steadfast love', it is appropriate to include in the present section part of the well known analogy from Ephesians 5 between husbands and wives and Christ and the Church. The text has been used in the past to legitimize a range of practices which today are rightly questioned, including the divine legitimation of the submission of wives to husbands, and the alleged *metaphysical* indissolubility of marriages. The text incorporates a 'household code' or *Haustafeln*[11] but in this case the conventional relationship between husbands and wives has been partly transformed by profound theological reflection.

Members of the Christian community are to 'be subject to one another out of reverence for Christ' (5.22). But the exercise of mutual subjection throughout the community as a whole should not tempt us to suppose that the power which some members have over others because of class, status or gender, is being substantially redistributed. Wives are to 'be subject to your husbands as though to the Lord' (5.22). The conventional wisdom of subjection to husbands is now given a theological rationale by means of two tightly related analogies. Subjection of wives to husbands is required 'for the man is the head of the woman, just as Christ is the head of the church. Christ is, indeed, the saviour of that body; but just as the church is subject to Christ, so must women be subject to their husbands in everything' (5.22-23).

All three household codes in the New Testament teach the subjection of wives to husbands.[12] Mackin translates the participal *hypotassomenoi*

11. There are three 'household codes' in the New Testament, Eph. 5.21–6.9: Col. 3.18–4.1; and 1 Pet. 2.18–3.7. Similar material is found in 1 Tim. 2.18–3.7, 6.1-2; Tit. 2.1-10. A household in the ancient world would be hierarchically ordered, from the male householder, down through to his wife, children, slaves and other property. For a thorough investigation in the light of contemporary questions, see Dunn, 'Household Rules', pp. 43-63.

12. Dunn agrees with feminist criticisms of subordinationism, but warns 'The fact that our moral sensibilities have been sharpened over a span of two millenia should not give us licence to find fault with those who, two millenia earlier, did not share our enlightenment' ('Household Rules', p. 60). The 'norm' provided by New Testament Christianity 'is not necessarily the specific command or injunction, but

(lit., 'being subject to') as 'defer to'.[13] Since the example to be followed in subjection to husbands is the subjection owed to Jesus Christ
himself, the inferior position of the wife in the marriage appears to be
divinely sanctioned. As it is between man and woman, so it is between
Christ and the Church. The writer introduces into New Testament
theology an entirely new insight. The individual relationship between
husband and wife *within* the Christian community is to be understood
alongside the transcendental relationship of Christ *to* the Christian
community. This is then unpacked by means of the familiar metaphor
of the Church as the 'body' of Christ.

The first use of the analogy is the simpler one. 'The man is head of
the woman, just as Christ is the head of the church.' 'Head' appears to
mean leadership of the marital community of two, just as head of the
Church means leadership of the ecclesial community of many.[14] But the
author does not lose sight of the analogical character of the argument.
The remark that 'Christ is, indeed, the saviour of that body' might
equally well have been used analogically to suggest that the husband is
the saviour of the wife. While he does not say this, deference to
husbands in everything along the lines of the Church's deference to
Christ nonetheless reinforces the wife's subordinate role in the marriage.

An important question to be raised is whether the redefinition of the
role of husbands in the subsequent verses is sufficiently far-reaching
and radical to counterbalance the asymmetrical deference of wives.
Everyone in the household must act 'out of reverence for Christ' (5.21):
for husbands this means loving their wives, 'as Christ loved the church
and gave himself up for it' (5.25). While the love of a wife would not
have been a surprising thought in the ancient world, the love that is
enjoined on Christian husbands here is novel and distinctively and
authentically Christian. The author takes for granted that the death of
Christ is to be understood as a sacrifice and that the sacrifice is a self-

the sensitivity to what was appropriate and practical and right and witness-bearing
within the social constraints of the time—their "healthy worldliness"' ('Household
Rules', p. 63).

13. Mackin thinks 'be subject to' may be too strong (*Martal Sacrament*, p. 71).
But the same verb is used in Col. 3.18 and 1 Pet. 3.1, where obedience seems
included among the appropriate attitudes the wife must show to her earthly
dominus.

14. Paul takes for granted that the man is head of the woman. See 1 Cor. 11.3.

giving. The verb *paredòken* 'signifies a relinquishing of oneself, a giving over of oneself for another'.[15] Husbands are to give themselves to their wives with all the devotion and totality with which Christ gave himself for the Church.

Christ's sacrifice for the Church is next qualified by images taken from bathing—the washing of baptism and the washing of the bridal bath. Consecration and cleansing by water and word (5.26) represent the process of union between the believer and Christ brought about symbolically by baptism. The presentation of the Church to himself as glorious and perfected 'puts Christ in a double role in the imagined wedding ceremony. He is the *prónubus*, the person who presents the bride to the groom. He is also the groom'.[16] Jewish readers would be mindful of the Lord's marriage to the foundling girl Israel who is first betrothed and then washed with water by the bridegroom, who then prepares her for the wedding ceremony (Ezek. 16.8-14). The Lord God's verdict on his bride was: 'Your beauty was famed throughout the world; it was perfect because of the splendour I bestowed on you' (Eph. 5.14).

The breadth of the basic analogy between husbands and wives, and Christ and the Church, is expanded by these images to include the new covenant inaugurated by the death of Christ. The new people of God are personified in the single image of the Church. In each case the people of God are depicted as God's bride. Because they are *God's* bride, they must be made perfect. The bride of the old covenant had splendour bestowed on her by the bridegroom (Ezek. 16.14). The bride of the new covenant was endowed with splendour by Christ's sacrifice. Nothing more is needed to make her an acceptable bride: the death of Christ has united the Church to himself irreversibly by his self-sacrifice. And the consequence for the Christian life is that husbands are required to love their wives in similar fashion.

b. *A 'One-Flesh' Union*
It is well known that the first account of the creation of the world in Genesis comes to its climax with the making of humankind on the sixth day. 'God created human beings in his own image; in the image of God he created them; male and female he created them' (Gen. 1.27). The second account of the creation of the world (Gen. 2.4b-25) has the Lord

15. Mackin, *Marital Sacrament*, p. 73.
16. Mackin, *Marital Sacrament*, p. 73.

God making a man. The Lord subsequently decides that the man needs a partner (2.8). All the animals and birds which God made are brought to the man, who names them, but finds no suitable partner among them. God then puts the man to sleep, takes one of his ribs, and builds it up into a woman. When the woman is brought to the man he exclaims 'This one at last is bone from my bones, flesh from my flesh! She shall be called woman, for from man was she taken' (2.23). There then follows an editorial comment on this saying. 'That is why a man leaves his father and mother and attaches himself to his wife, and the two become one' (2.24). A more familiar version of this comment is found in the RSV: 'Therefore a man leaves his father and his mother and cleaves to his wife, and they become one flesh.' The idea of oneness in flesh is thought to have its root metaphorical meanings in the man's recognition of the woman's flesh as coming from his own, and in the oneness of sexual intercourse. It came to be seen as 'a union of the entire man and the entire woman. In it they become a new and distinct unity, wholly different from and set over against other human relational unities, such as the family or the race'.[17]

Jesus. The term 'one flesh' was not influential in the formation of the Jewish doctrine of marriage (and divorce). It was not used against the legitimate practice of polygamy (Deut. 21.15-16). It does not occur again in the Hebrew Scriptures. The rabbis were more interested in whether the reference to the departure of the man from the family home to live with his wife, not a state of affairs to which they were accustomed, 'implies a matriarchal kind of society or whether it casts into question the patriarchal pattern with which the rabbis were so familiar in Israel'.[18] Since the text asserts the priority of the relationship of a man with his wife over his relationship with his parents, we may perhaps assume that, 1000 years BCE, the issue of a man's clash of loyalties between parents and wife was a troublesome one which the author was attempting to resolve. The text appears four times in the New Testament, twice in the Gospels, so it is a constitutive idea in the formation of Christian marriage. It is also well known that the teaching of Jesus about marriage in the Gospels arises contingently out of contem-

17. Derrick Sherwin Bailey, *The Mystery of Love and Marriage* (London: Camelot Press, 1952), p. 44.
18. Bruce Kaye, '"One Flesh" and Marriage', *Colloqium* 22 (1990), pp. 46-57 (49).

porary disputes about divorce.[19] In taking issue with the practice of divorce in Jewish society, Jesus appeals to a higher authority than the Mosaic law which provided for it (Deut. 24.1). The authority is the two texts from Genesis just cited. Mark has Jesus quote Gen. 1.27 and 2.24: 'In the beginning, at the creation, "God made them male and female". "That is why a man leaves his father and mother, and is united to his wife, and the two become one flesh"' (Mk 10.6-8; see Mt. 19.4-5). The decisively new element in the understanding of the term 'one flesh' is provided by the comment on it of Jesus himself. He says 'It follows that they are no longer two individuals: they are one flesh. Therefore what God has joined together, man must not separate' (Mk 10.8b-9; Mt. 19.5-6).

By this single comment Jesus adds to the then prevailing understanding of the term several new meanings. It indicates, first, that the 'attaching' or 'cleaving' of the man to his wife is a deep personal union which actually creates a new identity for each of them. The couple 'are no longer two individuals'. Each is who he or she is in relation to his or her partner. Secondly, the union is a permanent one. That this is so is made clear by the reaction of the disciples to Jesus' words. They think if a man cannot divorce a wife it would be better not to marry in the first place (Mt. 19.10; and see Mk 10.10). Thirdly, the union achieved by the man and the woman is achieved by the action of God. There is a holiness about the union which is marriage unhinted at in Genesis 2. God does not merely witness marriage vows: God ratifies them.[20] Fourthly, divorce is excluded from the reign of God (although Matthew allows the famous exception of *porneia*—19.9; 5.32; below 8.2.c). This follows not only from the permanence of the union but because of the uniting of the couple by God. And fifthly, polygamy too appears completely excluded. While neither Jesus nor Genesis 2 says anything directly about polygamy, the personal union envisaged by Jesus cannot accommodate it.

Paul. But there are two further New Testament references to Gen. 2.24,

19. Divorce is considered in Chapter 8, below. The task at present is to discern the teaching of Jesus about marriage from what he said about divorce. It will be argued there is a latitude to the teaching of Jesus about divorce which cannot be anticipated here.

20. We have already had good reason to query what is meant by saying God joins couples together (above, 2.1.b).

the earlier of which does not appear to support the interpretation put on 'one flesh'. To the male Christians who thought their freedom from moral law brought about on their behalf by Jesus extended to visiting prostitutes (above, 2.1.a) Paul admonishes 'You surely know that anyone who joins himself to a prostitute becomes physically one with her, for Scripture says, "The two shall become one flesh"' (1 Cor. 6.16). The fleshly union between a prostitute and her Christian client is clearly not a union of the moral kind envisaged by Jesus, brought about by God, and permanent. Does this therefore mean that Paul (who knew the teaching of Jesus about divorce—1 Cor. 7.10-11) drew a different conclusion about the meaning of becoming 'one flesh'?

No. In an answer to a different question (below, 3.1.d) Paul rules 'The wife cannot claim her body as her own; it is her husband's. Equally, the husband cannot claim his body as his own; it is his wife's' (1 Cor. 7.4). It is a mistake to read this passage as a statement about ownership. 'Belonging' is a better term, and the mutual belonging of the partners to each other is a striking element of the argument. It is best understood as a clear inference from the Genesis passage which Paul has just used. Since a husband and wife are 'no longer two individuals' but are one flesh, each is in a real sense part of the other. The unity which they make as a couple vetoes any sexual independence which they may once have had as single people.

The Author of Ephesians. The covenant analogy in Ephesians 5 leads, as we have seen, to an appeal to the Genesis 'one flesh' text. In illustrating the union which the writer believes to exist between Christ and the Church, he deploys the same insight just encountered in 1 Cor. 7.4, that the bodies of a married couple do not simply belong to each other—they importantly *are* each other. The Ephesian analogy continues: 'In loving his wife a man loves himself. For no one ever hated his own body; on the contrary, he keeps it nourished and warm, and that is how Christ treats the church...' (5.28b, 29). In part the observation is based on self-love. People care for their own bodies. But self-love comes to mean something quite different in Christian marriage. 'Self' can only be articulated *at all* through reference (*de*ference would be more accurate) to one's partner.

The insight that a married person receives a new identity from his or her partner is drawn from Gen. 2.24. This can be affirmed with some confidence because a further word of explanation quotes it in full.

'"This is why" (in the words of Scripture) "a man shall leave his father and mother and be united to his wife, and the two shall become one flesh" '(Eph. 5.31). But this use of the Genesis text is given a final tentative twist which seems to have provoked comment in every period of church history and is immensely important. Commenting directly on his own use of the Genesis text, the author says 'There is hidden here a great truth, which I take to refer to Christ and to the church. But it applies also to each one of you: the husband must love his wife as his very self, and the wife must show reverence for her husband' (Eph. 5.32-33).

The 'great truth' (*mystèrion mega)* is more usually translated 'great mystery'. Tertullian, Jerome and the Latin Vulgate render *mystèrion* as 'sacrament' (below 7.2). The writer thinks that the sacrificial love of Christ for the Church now enables the one flesh union of Gen. 2.24 to be Christianly understood in a way which, prior to the sacrifice of Christ, had not been possible. Christ's love is thought to exemplify the love which the writer believes is to be found in the one-flesh union of Genesis. But he is *tentative* about his own interpretation ('I take to refer to'). There is a confluence here between the author's use of Scripture and the contemporary method for reading the Bible advocated earlier (1.2.b, the 'symphonic imperative'). The author is writing about a real, existential, current concern, and searching the Scriptures in the light of the questions being faced by his community. The Genesis text is clearly fundamental to the issue. But as a Christian writer he will wish to interpret whatever he finds in the Hebrew Scriptures as referring in some way to Christ (*eis Christon*). Contemporary Christians pondering over what has become of marriage have similar, but also dissimilar questions to ask, and these will be determinative when we search the Scriptures for ourselves. We will arrive at different answers, but in common with every generation of Christians they too must be transparently *eis Christon*.

c. *A Dubious Necessity*
The Wisdom literature of the Hebrew scriptures contains a different model of marriage which alternates appreciation with suspicion. The attitude to marriage in this literature is entirely androcentric. In this literature women are alike

> the objects of passion, of admiration, of care, of gratitude, of caution, of suspicion, of contempt. Not even fictionally is any saying ever addressed

to a woman. Husbands are warned repeatedly against the other woman's allure. No wife is ever warned about a husband's fragile fidelity.[21]

It is hardly surprising that these sentiments were to be worked over by different generations of men keen to praise wifely domesticity or to justify celibacy. To a generation which has learned to appreciate feminist criticisms of gender bias (and where better to start?) there may be little to carry forward into a positive appreciation of Christian marriage.

A good wife is a blessing from God and immensely useful to a man. 'He who finds a wife finds a good thing; he was won favour from the Lord' (Prov. 18.22). The good wife is praised by her husband for her many virtues (Prov. 31.10-31). The measure of the 'good wife' is 'her net worth' (*mikrah*). A husband can expect to gain 'windfall profits' (*salal*, lit. 'spoil, plunder') if he puts his trust in such a wife. 'She works to bring him good, not evil, all the days of her life' (Prov. 31.12). 'A good wife makes a happy husband; she doubles the length of his life' (Ecclus 26.1; see also 26.2-4, 13-15; 7.19; 40.19-20). 'As beautiful as the sunrise in the Lord's heavens is a good wife in a well-ordered home' (Ecclus 26.16). He who acquires a wife has the beginnings of a fortune, a helper to match his needs and a pillar to give him support. Where there is no hedge, a vineyard is plundered; where there is no wife, a man wanders about in misery' (Ecclus 26.24-25).

A wife is therefore a necessity if a man is to be rich, successful, happy, long-lived, looked after and pampered. One of three sights that warms this author's heart is that of 'a man and wife who are inseparable' (Ecclus 25.1). But if marriage is a source of blessing for the husband, it is also a source of grief for him. While a wife is a necessity, she is a dubious one. In the following verses a wife who refuses to submit uncomplainingly to her husband's demands is worse than a snake; her beauty is a source of deceit; dependence on her enslaves him; her sex was responsible for sin entering the world; and she should be divorced:

> I would sooner live with a lion or a serpent
> than share a house with a malicious wife.
> Her spite changes her expression,
> making her look as surly as a bear.
> Her husband goes to a neighbour for his meals
> and cannot repress a bitter sigh.
> There is nothing so bad as a bad wife;

21. Mackin, *Marital Sacrament*, p. 50.

may the fate of the wicked overtake her!
It is as easy for an old man to climb a sand-dune
as for a quiet husband to live with a garrulous wife.
Do not be enticed by a woman's beauty
or set your heart on possessing one who has wealth.
If a man is supported by his wife,
he must expect tantrums, effrontery, and much humiliation.
Depression, downcast looks, and a broken heart;
these are caused by a worthless wife.
Feeble of hand and weak at the knees
is the man whose wife fails to bring him happiness.
Sin began with a woman,
and because of her we all die.
Do not leave a leaky cistern to drip
or allow a worthless wife to say whatever she likes.
If she does not accept your control,
bring the marriage to an end (Ecclus 25.16-26).

In the interests of comprehensiveness and truth this biblical[22] model of marriage, like the 'anxious care' model which follows, cannot be overlooked. The place of its sentiments in Christian marriage is discussed below (3.2.c).

d. *A Worldly Concession*

Paul gave advice to the church at Corinth about how to handle an ascetic faction that believed that all sexual experience was wrong. The apostle allows marriage, but as a means of avoiding immorality. 'In the face of so much immorality, let each man have his own wife and each woman her own husband' (1 Cor. 7.2). It is hard to find a positive evaluation of marriage in this chapter. Its justification lies in avoiding extra-marital sex. It is a concession (7.6). Singleness is preferable (7.7-8, 26). Marriage is for people who lack self-control (7.9). It is second best. 'Those who marry will have 'hardships to endure' (7.28) and 'anxious care' (7.32). Since the Lord's return is imminent marriage is a distraction from doing the Lord's work (7.29-31). Unmarried men and women are 'concerned with the Lord's business' (7.32-34). Married men and women are 'concerned with worldly affairs' (7.33-34). A

---

22. The book Ecclesiasticus, or The Wisdom of Jesus Son of Sirach, has always been part of the canon of the Roman Catholic Church. For Anglicans, it is one of 'the other Books … the Church doth read for example of life and instruction of manners … ' Book of Common Prayer, article 6).

betrothed man who lacks restraint is nonetheless permitted to marry his intended bride (7.36-37). If he marries her he 'does well', but if he can manage not to, he 'does better' (7.38).

Marriage in this letter is permissible but not commendable. This was to be the position taken by the Western church for more than a thousand years. But while marriage is second best when compared with singleness, a feature of Paul's account of marriage, often overlooked, is the substantial equality of partners within it. He acknowledges that the desire to marry to satisfy sexual desire moves women as well as men (1 Cor. 7.2). Once married they are under a mutual obligation to meet each other's sexual needs. 'The husband must give his wife what is due to her, and equally the wife must give the husband his due' (7.3). The reason for this is one met in the discussion of the implications of the 'one-flesh' model of marriage (above 3.1.b): 'The wife cannot claim her body as her own; it is her husband's. Equally, the husband cannot claim his body as his own; it is his wife's' (7.4). Neither is the 'anxious care' involved in marriage a one-way flow from wife to husband. Paul takes for granted that the 'aim' of a married man is 'to please his wife' (7.33) and the aim of a married woman is 'to please her husband' (7.34).

If marriage is a concession in Paul, it is to be avoided altogether in Luke. Matthew and Luke (Mt. 22.23-34; Lk. 20.27-38) both record an incident in the temple when some Sadducees ask Jesus a trick question. A woman has seven husbands, one after the other, with no children by any of them. Whose wife is she 'at the resurrection'? Matthew has Jesus answer with a comment about how life will be after death: 'In the resurrection men and women do not marry; they are like angels in heaven' (Mt. 21.30). But Luke has Jesus use the Sadducees' question to say that married people place themselves beyond the resurrection altogether:

> The men and women of this world marry; but those who have been judged worthy of a place in the other world, and of the resurrection from the dead, do not marry, for they are no longer subject to death. They are like angels; they are children of God, because they share in the resurrection (Lk. 20.34-36).

Here is an asceticism more severe than that of Paul.[23] People who marry are citizens of this world, not of the world to come, and their

---

23. For the context, see Brown, *Body and Society*, pp. 41-44.

married status actually endangers their partaking in the resurrection. These verses are almost entirely overlooked in attempts to arrive at an overall and consistent account of the biblical teaching on marriage. Leaving aside the problem of what was at stake in speaking, against the Sadducees, of resurrection, the verses provide clear evidence for the view not merely that celibacy is better than marriage, but those unwise enough to marry jeopardize their eternal salvation. And, moreover, this view is attributed to Jesus. It seems that even 'concession' is too weak a word. Only 'avoidance' is strong enough.

e. *Passionate Mutual Love*

The Song of Songs provides our final biblical model of marriage. Its delightful, overt, playful, erotic imagery has led to its being either ignored or, under the influence of Ephesians 5, converted into an allegory of the spiritual love of Christ for the Church. The book is a cycle of love songs, accompanied by music and dancing, sung at wedding feasts and other joyful occasions. Christian commentators today generally think of the Song as the 'joyous, tentative explorations of love of the betrothed couple, culminating in their marriage and full sexual union in 5.1'.[24] This judgment probably reflects the desire to impose on the text an anxiety about the marital status of the lovers, about which the text itself is shockingly indifferent.

It is significant that, as the recitative opens, the young woman is the first to speak:

> May he smother me with kisses.
> Your love is more fragrant than wine,
> fragrant is the scent of your anointing oils,
> and your name is like those oils poured out;
> that is why maidens love you.
> Take me with you, let us make haste;
> bring me into your chamber, O king (1.2-4).

The woman is the one who first 'voices her yearnings, her anxieties, her fears and her delights in a much more colourfully expressive way, and

---

24. Thus Tom Gledhill, *The Message of the Song of Songs* (Leicester: Inter-Varsity Press, 1994), p. 28. Roland E. Murphy argues 'There is no solid basis for identifying marriage as either the *primary* setting of the entire work or the purpose for which most of the individual poetic units were composed'. See Roland E. Murphy, *A Commentary on the Book of Canticles or Song of Songs* (Minneapolis: Fortress Press, 1990), p. 60.

more frequently than her lover does. She is the one who invites him to intimacy, she is the one who so often takes the initiative'.[25] In contrast to the asymmetry which is a feature of the covenant language of the Hebrew Scriptures, 'the Song subtly undermines the common type-casting of the male/female roles as dominant/submissive, active/passive, leader/follower, protector/protected, and so on. In the Song we have complete mutuality of desire, boy toward girl, girl toward boy'.[26]

The intense delight which the lovers take in each other is clearly an end in itself which is not justified by further reference to having children, pleasing God, or anything else.[27] 'Fertility and reproduction of the species are themes which barely surface in the Song.'[28] The sacrifice of Christ the bridegroom for his bride the Church was described in Ephesians 5 as a divine self-giving. In the Song there is a *human* self-giving, as the lovers give themselves to each other in consuming devotion. The young man speaks of his deep satisfaction in loving the young woman when he says,

> I have come to my garden, my sister and bride;
> I have gathered my myrrh and my spices;
> I have eaten my honeycomb and my honey,
> and drunk my wine and my milk (5.1).

Likewise the young woman, who having given herself to her lover, takes delight in the delight he has received from her:

> My beloved has gone down to his garden,
> to the beds where balsam grows,
> to delight in the gardens, and to pick the lilies.
> I am my beloved's, and my beloved is mine;
> he grazes his flock among the lilies' (6.2-3).

A further contrast invites attention: that between the natural beauty which the man finds in the woman, and the beauty conferred on the bride by the divine bridegroom of Ezekiel 16. In Ezekiel, he bathes,

25. Gledhill, *Message*, p. 93.

26. Gledhill, *Message*, p. 94. See also p. 140: 'This reciprocity, this mutuality is something that shines out from the Song, something of a protest against the male dominance and macho-masculinity which sin brought into the world.'

27. The case of the pious Tobit is very different. On his wedding night he prays to the Lord '"I now take this my beloved to wife, not out of lust but in true marriage. Grant that she and I may find mercy and grow old together". They both said "Amen, Amen", and they slept through the night' (Tob. 8.7).

28. Gledhill, *Message*, p. 134.

dresses and adorns her. Her beauty is perfect because of the splendour the bridegroom bestows on her (Ezek. 16.14). The bride here is praised by her bridegroom as she is. After marvelling at her eyes, hair, teeth, lips, neck and breasts, he cries,

> You are beautiful, my dearest,
> beautiful without a flaw (3.1-7).

2. *Reclaiming the Biblical Models*

The biblical models for marriage have now been briefly described. In this section of the chapter an attempt will be made to retrieve their significance for contemporary theology.

a. *A Covenant*

If the biblical model of covenant is to play a central role in a post-modern celebration of Christian marriage, clearly there are elements of it which are simply unserviceable. The survey of the covenant model of marriage quickly uncovered simmering issues of gender and power in the texts themselves. Where the marriage covenant is illuminated by the divine-human covenant, there must be no more transfer of divine power to the man, and of human fickleness and infidelity to the woman. There must be no more stereotyping of women as covenant-breakers. Any suggestion of sexual violence must be absolutely filtered out. The theological conviction that in relation to God, God alone takes the initiative, must not transmit to the human marriage relation that husbands alone take the initiative. Even in Ephesians 5 the bridegroom is the active partner who initiates the marriage and even prepares the bride for his wedding: the bride is the passive recipient of his ministrations, subject to him in all things. Her perfection and her passivity coincide. Any refashioning of the covenantal idea must first deal with these fundamental difficulties.[29]

Despite these difficulties I remain convinced that 'covenant' can and should remain central to the Christian doctrine of marriage, and that it is possible (indeed essential) to state how marriage as a covenant may be commended in ways that are free from sexism and gender

---

29. For a moderate view which nonetheless boycotts the text on the grounds of its historical harm to women, see Schüssler Fiorenza, 'Marriage', p. 330.

imbalance.[30] This will be attempted next by making and qualifying five claims about covenants, each of which builds on the previous one in a cumulative way.

(i). *Marriage is a covenant in the straightforward sense that it is an agreement between two people.*[31] Beginning with the deep-rooted meaning of covenant as a 'binding relationship', which includes commitment, promises, obligations, durability and concluding or sealing by

30. According to Karl Barth and many contemporary evangelicals, the subordination of women to men is ordered by God at creation and cannot be changed. See his *Church Dogmatics*, III. 'The essential point is that woman must always and in all circumstances be woman; that the command of the Lord, which is for all eternity, directs both man and woman to their own proper sacred place and forbids all attempts to violate this order' (p. 156). 'Man and woman are not an A and a second A...[They] are an A and a B, and cannot, therefore, be equated' (p. 169). Divine order is said to require 'the strong man' and the 'obedient woman' (pp. 176, 177). Woman is to be 'subordinate' but not 'submissive' (p. 179). 'She will endorse the strength of the strong' (p. 180). Her 'whole existence' is 'an appeal to the kindness of man' (p. 181). Not only is it difficult to see how this is good news for women, it endangers them. An influential group of evangelicals opposed to any vestige of 'feminism', defines biblical 'mature femininity' as 'A Freeing Disposition to Affirm, Receive and Nurture Strength and Leadership from Worthy Men in Ways Appropriate to a Woman's Differing Relationships [sic]'. See John Piper and Wayne Grudem, *Recovering Biblical Manhood and Womanhood: A Response to Evangelical Feminism* (Illinois: Wheaton, 1991), p. 36. Twenty-six chapters endorse Piper's doctrine of the submission of wives: 'the Biblical reality of a wife's submission would take different forms depending on the quality of a husband's leadership. This can be seen best if we define submission not in terms of specific behaviors, but as a *disposition* to yield to the husband's authority and an *inclination* to follow his leadership. This is important to do because no submission of one human being to another is absolute. The husband does not replace Christ as the woman's supreme authority. She must never follow her husband's leadership into sin. She will not steal with him or get drunk with him or savor pornography with him or develop deceptive schemes with him.

'But even where a Christian wife may have to stand with Christ against the sinful will of her husband, she can still have a spirit of submission—a disposition to yield. She can show by her attitude and behavior that she does not like resisting his will and that she longs for him to forsake sin and lead in righteousness so that her disposition to honor him as head can again produce harmony' (p. 47). Against such distortions, the attempt to redress the gender imbalance of the biblical texts underlying them acquires a new urgency.

31. It has not been forgotten that throughout the Bible and much of Christian history, marriage is an agreement between two *families*, not between two people. 'Covenant' is being rooted here in contemporary experience.

a rite, marriage fits the description of covenant very well. A covenant in the ancient world is likely to have a god or gods to witness it, thereby acting as guarantors of the agreement and underlining the seriousness of the pledges being made. Almost all Christian marriage services have the opening words which acknowledge God as witness.[32] No partner need promise anything that the other partner does not.[33] So there need be nothing detrimental to the mutuality of a marriage by its being a covenant in this sense.

(ii). *Marriage is better understood as a covenant, not as a contract.* Let us take Palmer's contrast between the two types of agreement. While he has probably exaggerated and polarized the differences between them, the general contrast is still useful. He writes,

> Contracts deal with things, covenants with people. Contracts engage the services of people; covenants engage persons. Contracts are made for a stipulated period of time; covenants are forever. Contracts can be broken, with material loss to the contracting parties; covenants cannot be broken, but if violated, they result in personal loss and broken hearts. Contracts are secular affairs and belong to the market place; covenants are sacral affairs and belong to the hearth, the temple, or the Church. Contracts are best understood by lawyers, civil and ecclesiastical; covenants are appreciated better by poets and theologians. Contracts are witnessed by people with the state as guarantor; covenants are witnessed by God with God as guarantor. Contracts can be made by children who know the value of a penny: covenants can be made only by adults who are mentally, emotionally, and spiritually mature.[34]

There is little doubt that the notion of contract has been more influential than that of covenant in the Christian tradition. It was John Calvin (*d.* 1654) who initiated a covenant theology of marriage.[35] The

32. For example, The Book of Common Prayer: 'Dearly beloved, we are gathered together here in the sight of God, and in the face of this congregation...'

33. That is, *unlike* The Book of Common Prayer, where the man must 'love her, comfort her, honour, and keep her in sickness and in health', and the woman must 'obey him, and serve him, love, honour and keep him in sickness and in health'. The thirteenth-century rite of Sarum requires the woman to say she obeys her husband.

34. Palmer, 'Christian Marriage', p. 639. Even in a health care context the term 'covenant' is useful. See James F. Childress, *Who Should Decide: Paternalism in Health Care* (New York: Oxford University Press, 1982), p. 42.

35. See John Witte, Jr, *From Sacrament to Contract: Marriage, Religion, and Laws in the Western Tradition* (Louisville, KY: Westminster/John Knox Press, 1997), Chapter 3, 'Marriage as Covenant in the Calvinist Tradition', pp. 74-129.

notion of marriage as a covenant has become more accepted in Catholicism since Vatican II,[36] but only in 1983 did Canon Law refer to marriage as 'the matrimonial covenant'.[37] The dominant secular understanding of marriage is that it is a contract[38] and it is ironic that while late modern societies return to a contractual understanding which was once the dominant Christian understanding, Christians are rightly discovering the fruitfulness of a covenantal understanding of the essence of marriage.

(iii). *Christian marriage is a covenant between husband and wife ratified by Jesus Christ.* The warrant for this assertion is given by an interpretation of Ephesians 5, which seeks to resolve the problems of power and gender discussed in 3.1.b. This is how such an interpretation might go.

First, the method of the author is to relate everything that is to what God has done in Jesus Christ. He has been 'granted the privilege of proclaiming to the Gentiles the good news of the unfathomable riches of Christ' (3.8). It is inevitable that the relationships governed by household codes will get the full 'christological treatment', for literally everything—including time and history, the earthly and heavenly realms and everything in them—is understood in the light of God's purpose in Christ. When marriage too receives this treatment, the daring analogy comparing husband and wife with Christ and the Church is introduced. It is clearly possible (and of course desirable) to retain the firmly Christocentric approach to marriage, while at the same time developing this approach in ways more sensitive to gender implications than the author believed necessary in first-century Ephesus.

Secondly, the Ephesian household code, determined by the revelation of the divine love in Jesus Christ, is prefaced by the injunction to the

---

36. John Paul II, *Familiaris consortio*, section 12, 'Marriage and Communion Between God and People': Pope John Paul II, *Letter to Families* (Vatican City: Vatican Press, 1994), section 7, 'The Marital Covenant': Michael G. Lawler, 'Faith, Contract, and Sacrament in Christian Marriage: A Theological Approach', *TS*, 52 (1991), p. 722; *idem*, 'The Mutual Love and Personal Faith of the Spouses as the Matrix of the Sacrament of Marriage', *Worship* 65 (1991), pp. 340-47; *idem*, *Marriage and Sacrament: A Theology of Christian Marriage* (Collegeville, MN: Liturgical Press, 1993), p. 70: Peter J. Elliott, *What God Has Joined: The Sacramentality of Marriage* (New York: Alba House, 1989), pp. 176-80.

37. *Codex Iuris Canonici* (1983), p. 359, §1604.

38. Witte, *From Sacrament to Contract*, p. 195.

whole church to 'Be subject to one another out of reverence for Christ' (5.21). Mutual subjection within the household is to be understood in the broader context of the theme of subjection in the whole letter, where 'all government and authority, all power and dominion' is made subject to Christ, for God 'put all things in subjection beneath his feet, and gave him as head over all things to the church which is his body' (1.21-2). Subjection to Christ in the community now anticipates the new age when all things will be subject to him. The vexed problem of 'headship' is also best dealt with by this author's wider conviction that Christ is head not simply of the Church but 'over all things'. The Christian community, which through the Spirit (2.13-4) anticipates the time when God's purposes in Christ are complete, lives that subjection now. Subjection, or if Mackin's term is preferred, 'deference', is for the entire community to express in the quality of its living together in Christ.

Thirdly, the sharing of the vision of how things might look when everything and everyone is subject to the love of Christ might start with the actual experience of contemporary families and households, where there is much evidence of things *not* being subject to Christ, where instead there may be sexual violence, the misuse of male power, the pursuit of selfish individualism, the exploitation of sexuality and the body, and the horrendous neglect and ill treatment of children. Thus relocated, the vision of mutual subjection 'out of reverence for Christ' is delivered from the archaic and historically contingent set of hierarchical relationships which were an inescapable fact of life in the ancient world, and which included slaves (6.5-9). It is able to focus instead on the real transformative work required for women and men to love each other as Christ loves them both, and for this love to encompass children and engage prophetically with the new slavery (i.e., the unjust burden of work which state and capitalist organizations alike impose upon their employees). Once subjection is disengaged from gender politics and reintegrated into the cosmic vision of the ultimate reign of Christ, marriage can prefigure the victory of love over violence that is the hope of Christians everywhere.

(iv). *Christian marriage is a covenant between equals, that is, between men and women who without distinction are equal recipients of the love of Christ.* This is a deliberate but simple amendment of the analogies in Eph. 5.22-28 in accordance with what has just been said about the christological method of the letter, about the headship of

Christ being over everything, and about 'subjection' referring prophetically to God's future when the reign of Christ over everything is
achieved. Paraphrased, the first analogy, addressed to wives only, says:

wives must be subject to husbands
as
the woman is subject to the man, and
as
the church is subject to Christ.

The second analogy, addressed to husbands only, also implies the subordination of wives. It says:

as Christ loved the church
so
husbands must love their wives.

The amendment, which would remove the subordinationist tenor of
both analogies, makes husbands and wives subject equally, both to each
other and to the Lord as head of the Church. The first analogy would
then read:

wives must be subject to husbands,
and
husbands must be subject to wives
as
the church is subject to Christ.

The second analogy, now addressed to husbands *and* wives, would
read

as Christ loved the church
so
husbands must love their wives,
and
wives must love their husbands.

The amended analogy removes the offensive gender identification of
the male marriage partner with the male Christ, and male initiative with
divine initiative. It does not remove the gendered requirement that
husbands must love their wives as Christ loved the Church. It *adds* the
gendered requirement that wives must love their husbands as Christ
loved the Church, and thereby removes the further offensive inference
that while men are capable of exemplifying Christ's love for their partners, women, who are not leaders and initiative takers, are capable only

of subjection.[39] It shares the insight earlier in the letter that Christ-like love is the responsibility of all members of the Christian community, since all of them have received the benefits of his sacrifice: 'In a word, as God's dear children, you must be like him. Live in love as Christ loved you and gave himself up on your behalf, an offering and sacrifice whose fragrance is pleasing to God' (5.1-2).

(v). *The human covenant of marriage is a participation in the divine-human covenant between Christ and the Church.* The analogies of Ephesians 5 and their amendments require a further inference to be made more explicit. The Christian life is not only or even principally an *imitation* of Christ, but also a *participation* in the risen life of Christ, and that means the life of all-embracing love which reconciles everything to God. The interweaving of the human with the divine-human covenant, is rooted in the steadfast love which is a mutually affirming partnership (below, 7.1). The mutual love in the Christian vision for marriage does not come from nowhere: in its formation, realization, growth and perpetuity, it is an *icon*[40] of the covenant love of Christ for the Church.

Can the covenant between Christ and the Church be understood without a restoration of the very inequality between partners which has plagued covenant models in both the Bible and tradition? And is there not a credibility gap between the Church understood as the bridegroom of Christ and the Church in its empirical manifestation as divided, hierarchical and uncomprehending? Karl Rahner has addressed these problems, and his solution is commendable. He acknowledges that both institutions, marriage and the Church, continually fall short of what they are intended by God to be. This falling short requires a distinction to be made in each case between the institution as a sign and what the institution is a sign *of*, that is, the signified. 'What the Church points to', observes Rahner,

39. I am influenced here by Margaret A. Farley's brilliant insights into covenant language. See Margaret A. Farley, *Personal Commitments* (San Francisco: Harper & Row, 1990), Chapter 8, 'Commitment, Covenant and Faith'. Of God's covenant-love she says, 'God's love serves as a model for the love between human persons. But what serves as a *model* here is precisely God's love for human persons, not human persons' love for God. That is, the way in which we are to love one another is the *way in which God loves us*, not the way in which we are called to love God' (p. 130, author's emphases).

40. See Stuart and Thatcher, *People of Passion*, pp. 37-39, and Guroian, *Ethics After Christendom*, Chapter 3.

is not herself. Rather as sign, i.e., as a socially organised community constituted by a common creed, a common cult and common works of charity, she is precisely the sign of that humanity, consecrated and united by grace ... the grace-given unity which extends far beyond the social organism of the church.[41]

In marriage too there is a gap between sign and signified. 'A particular marriage can sinfully be degraded into a lie when that which it is intended to manifest and to render present is not present in itself, namely the love that is grace-given and unifying.' But despite the failure of both marriage and Church adequately to signify that divine love which inspires and animates them, 'the basic parallelism between marriage and the Church continues to exist'. Both are signs,

> at the palpable level of historical and social human life, of the fact that *that* love is being made effective and victorious throughout the whole of humanity which is the love of God for us and of us for God, the love which comprehends and unifies all so long as no-one sinfully denies it.[42]

Rahner places Jesus Christ at the centre of his theology of marriage, but not as one whose male gender signifies power over his bride. Rather, the unsurpassed depth of the love of Christ (Eph. 3.18-19) is the guarantee of the ultimate victory over the sin in both marriage and Church which makes those institutions damaged signifiers of the love each is supposed to embody.

If these arguments are sound, Christians can continue to have confidence in covenant language. That being so, the distinction between a covenant and a contract helps to express the difference between the Christian and secular alternative accounts of marriage which were reviewed at 2.3.b above.[43] All ten features of 'the secular approaches to marriage' listed there are addressed by it. 'Covenant' grasps well what is lacking in the contractarian mentality. The act of faith and acceptance of risk involved in marriage is well preserved by the phrase 'plighting of troth'. To 'plight' meant 'to promise or bind by a solemn pledge', or 'to give one's solemn oath'.[44] 'Troth' meant one's good faith or

---

41. Karl Rahner, 'Marriage as a Sacrament', *Theological Investigations* (23 vols.; London: Darton, Longman & Todd, 1967), X, pp. 210-11.

42. Rahner, 'Marriage as a Sacrament', p. 211.

43. Neither should it be forgotten that, e.g., Albert the Great, Thomas Aquinas, Duns Scotus and countless other theologians have spoken of marriage as a contract.

44. The term came from the middle English *plighten*, which came from the Old English *plihtan*, 'to endanger', 'to put at risk', from *pliht*, meaning 'danger', 'risk'.

fidelity, coming from the Old English *trêowth*, 'truth'. The contractarian mentality preserves self-interest; the covenantal mentality commits itself to the betrothed. The contractarian mentality protects itself against risk; the covenantal mentality accepts risk and seeks to integrate it into the growth of the relationship. The contractarian mentality anticipates an end to the contract; the covenantal mentality anticipates togetherness without end.[45] The covenant mentality replenishes romantic love with unconditional love. It replaces the endless self-referentiality of modern intimacy, not with an 'other-referentiality' which robs the self of individuality, but in a covenant in which each resolves before God to cherish the other in mutual self-affirmation and self-giving.

b. A 'One-Flesh' Union

The notion of marriage as 'one flesh' in a patriarchal society has undoubtedly been used to incorporate the woman into the identity of the man, and so to transfer her and her property into his guardianship. Marriage then is too easily a loss. The new one flesh created by marriage has too often been *his*. Without a mutual contribution to the married relationship an entire 'gender-sex system'[46] is encouraged in which wives exist through their husbands and subordinate their interests to those of men. Such relationships are clearly unjust. Socially, the wife has been in danger of becoming the man's adjunct, someone attached to him in a permanently dependent and subordinate position, his representative in domestic matters, in particular, bearing and rearing *his* children and keeping his house clean. Her dependence on him in such circumstances is complete. There is not even any psychological space to think her own thoughts. What fragile sense of selfhood remains to her, if she exists only through him and for him?

The Sarum rite has bride and groom say 'ther to I plycht the my trouth(e)'.

45. It sounds trite to observe that for a covenant to have no end, the 'covenanters' must both seek to stay together. What happens when one or both do not so seek, cannot be discussed until Chapter 8.

46. I endorse Seyla Benhabib's definition: 'The gender-sex system is the grid through which the self develops an *embodied* identity, a certain mode of being in one's body and of living the body. The self becomes an I in that it appropriates from the human community a mode of psychically, socially and symbolically experiencing its bodily identity. The gender-sex system is the grid through which societies and cultures reproduce embodied individuals.' Seyla Benhabib, *Situating the Self: Gender, Community and Postmodernism in Contemporary Ethics* (Cambridge: Polity Press, 1992), p. 152.

The question to be faced is whether the one-flesh model of marriage operates to encourage gender imbalance, or whether the use of it by patriarchal churches, theologians and societies is responsible for this model reinforcing women's subordination. The Christian understanding of marriage is largely based on Jesus' own use of it. If it were to be abandoned by Christian theologians because it was deemed defective, serious questions would have to be asked about whether what remained was Christian marriage. Need that predicament be faced? Yes and no.

First, the all-important Genesis text from which Jesus quotes *does* assume that her flesh is his. The man was made first. The woman is made only after the failed search for a suitable companion for the man. The woman is made from the man's flesh, and when she is brought to him by the Lord God, it is *his* flesh that he recognizes. Moreover Paul (following the normal rabbinic exegesis of the time) reads the text in this way. On the one hand, the temporal priority of the first man over the woman is elevated by Paul to an ontological priority of men over women essentially, generically, functionally and timelessly.

> Man is the image of God, and the mirror of his glory, whereas a woman reflects the glory of man. For man did not originally spring from woman, but woman was made out of man; and man was not created for woman's sake, but woman for the sake of man (1 Cor. 11.7b-9).

On the other hand we have seen (above, 3.1.d) that Paul insists that the bodies of partners in marriage are equally shared, for neither's body is individually his or her own (1 Cor. 7.4).

Whether *Jesus* understood 'one flesh' as subordinating hers to his is much more doubtful. We have already noted how the disciples' reaction to Jesus' teaching on divorce indicated his far-reaching disagreement with conventional interpretations of both. Jesus' subsequent criticisms of one-sided divorce practice which permitted husbands to divorce their wives for trivial reasons (below 8.2) and did not permit wives to divorce their husbands for any reason (Mk 10.10-12) should lead us to think that Jesus was firmly addressing and correcting the androcentric bias of the Jewish establishment. The suggestion made here is that the one-flesh model is *not* of itself androcentric and offers a fine model of what Christian marriage might be. A difficulty with this suggestion is that to establish it beyond doubt would involve extracting a concept from the broader conceptual milieu of the time, and that milieu is androcentric beyond dispute. So any commendation of the one-flesh model must adopt the approach taken with the covenant-model earlier, that is, it will be legitimately put forward as a non-sexist model of marriage and contrasted with secular accounts of marriage and of the person.

When the idea of marriage as a union of a man and a woman becoming one flesh is added to the cocktail of individualistic notions of the human person characteristic of late modernity, it positively effervesces. The special case of human union which is marriage as envisaged by Jesus provides a convincing alternative to the secular ethic of 2.3.b above. Like 'covenant' it is a corrective to all ten features of the ethic described there. In particular it engages with features 1, 4, 5 and 6, the marginalization of marriage, the individualistic view of the human person, the idolatry of romantic love and the problem of personal identity.

While secular society allows many of the meanings of Christian marriage to drain away, the traditional one-flesh model retains and preserves a vision of lifelong partnership commended by Christ himself. Borrowing (and slightly extending) the momentous insights of the Church's first theologian of marriage (the author of Ephesians), we may say the Genesis one-flesh text *means* a lifelong union where each partner loves the other as that partner loves himself or herself. In starting out in faith to love the 'other' as one loves oneself, one engages in an adventure which embodies the love of God revealed in Christ, finds the face of Christ in the face of one's partner, and shares with him or her that love which Christ shared with the Church.

In contrast with the individualistic view of the human person, the partnership of marriage confirms the *relational* view of the person. Jesus' abbreviated use of the Genesis text which affirms male and female alike are made in the image of God ('God made them male and female': Mk 10.6, Mt. 19.4, citing Gen. 1.27) confirms that the image of God is to be understood *relationally*. Alistair McFadyen says 'If the image [of God] is construed in relational terms, then the structure of human and personal being may be seen to be ex-centric. By this I mean that persons are orientated upon themselves (centred) by moving towards the reality of others.[47] Marriage draws on the divinely created structure of human relations. 'The form which one's relations takes determines the form which one's personal centring and hence personal

---

47. Alistair I. McFadyen, *The Call to Personhood: A Christian Theory of the Individual in Relationships* (Cambridge: Cambridge University Press, 1990), p. 40.

identity takes. This can be expressed simply through the dictum that persons are what they are for others or, rather, the way in which they are for others'.[48] Marriage too, understood as a 'one-flesh union', appropriately qualified, is a 'form' of relationship, potentially the paradigmatic form for beings who are persons-in-relation.

In contradistinction to the idolatry of romantic love is contrasted the passionate love of God which bursts out in Christ's sacrifice of himself on behalf of the Church. This is a self-giving which is total, and so physical. The notion of 'flesh' of course suggests this. In contrast to the self-referential project of personal identity is the adventure whereby each partner in reaching out to the other receives him or her back again countless times over, and so allows his or her identity to be determined in part by the partner's. The union of partners in marriage as held by the author of Ephesians is meant to anticipate the union of all things in Christ. Christ's work brings together 'everything in heaven and on earth' (Eph. 1.10; 2.6). Christ's reconciling work brings into one body Gentiles and Jews 'so as to create out of the two a single new humanity in himself, thereby making peace' (2.16; 3.6). The author prays that his readers may 'be strong to grasp what is the breadth and length and height and depth of Christ's love, and to know it, though it is beyond knowledge' (3.17-19). The potential microcosm for this love, the most concrete instantiation of it, is the sacrament of Christian marriage.

c. A Dubious Necessity
How is the witness to marriage in the Wisdom literature to be handled now? Are Christians today able to treat marriage as it is depicted in the Wisdom literature as a musical score (above, 1.2.b) and play it as music which wives too can compose, play and enjoy? Assuming that the pessimism and androcentrism of this view of marriage cannot merely be ignored and lost among the obscurer parts of the Old Testament (or Apocrypha), or relativized to the point of irrelevance, how might Christian heterosexual women, perhaps unmarried now but intending marriage soon, or perhaps divorced, appropriate the 'dubious necessity' model as God's word?

One response might be to maximize the dubiety, and minimize the necessity. It is surely consistent with devotion to Jesus Christ that one should conclude that marriage is an unattractive prospect. The Church has long been suspicious of it. Men are scarcely able to complain if the

48. McFadyen, *The Call*, p. 40.

doubts they have historically expressed about women have caused or been replaced by women's doubts about men. Women are absent as subjects in the Wisdom literature. Their very absence opens the possibility of identification now with this silent perspective, a poignant reminder that marriage as it was actually experienced by women was, and in important ways still is, a patriarchal institution.

If this model provides a salutary warning against marriage, or serves as a reminder that marriage is in permanent need of the transformation which may be brought about by Jesus Christ, then it is yet able to express gospel truth. To adopt a perspective on marriage as dubious and unnecessary is to recognize the diversity of ways of pleasing God and living one's life. It may be difficult to square this perspective with the wholly positive commendations of the covenant and union models of marriage. But it may not be. If Christian marriage at its best is a microcosm of the unifying love of God, it still would not follow that marriage was for everyone. There are other ways by which the divine love may in faith course through our lives. Christian people share in God's covenant with them whether or not they share in God's covenant of marriage. Some men and women find the prospect of lifelong union with one person a truly suffocating prospect. They need not think they are missing out. A greater, or at least a different, range of possibilities for selfless loving remains open to them.

d. A Worldly Concession

The 'worldly concession' model of marriage in 1 Corinthians is more important for its advocacy of celibacy than for a commendation of marriage now. In particular the advice to marry in order to deal with one's own libidinous desires seems an inadequate defence for marriage. Marriage would then appear to function merely as a licence for having sex: that it might be a covenant involving sacrificial love, as in Ephesians, is not considered. The inconsistency in the theology of marriage is itself a powerful argument for the different authorship of each letter. We may also note that the reasoning behind the requirement that married partners must satisfy each other's desires overplays the one-flesh understanding of marriage. While the body of each partner is said also to belong to the other, what looks like equality of access to each other's bodies can only be acceptable if the power of husbands over wives is given up and replaced by power-sharing between them. Without such sharing, the statement that 'The wife cannot claim her body as her own:

it is her husband's' (7.4) has put countless wives in extreme danger.

These reservations aside, the temptation to relativize the text as unduly influenced by the belief in the imminent return of Christ must not be allowed to drown out the possibility that, with regard to the preference for singleness over marriage, Paul is actually right. One way of interpreting Paul's characterization of marriage as 'anxious care' is to believe him. While Paul may be optimistic in thinking that unmarried men and women are free from anxious cares,[49] a similar argument that the care of children and the pleasing of one's partner make particular demands which single people do not have seems obviously valid. Perhaps because Western Christians have lived through an era of 'mandatory marriage' (below, 4.2.d) it is still difficult for many people to realize that the destiny of marriage is far from inevitable. Once marriage is categorized as a 'vocation', the inference can be rightly drawn that significant numbers of people are *not* called to it. Paul uses the term *charisma* or gift in relation to singleness, marriage and temporary abstinence from sex (1 Cor. 7.7). People who honestly believe they cannot fulfil the obligations of marriage must actively resist any pressure on them to marry. Neither should they think unfitness for marriage is any kind of character deficiency! 'Each person has the gift God has granted him, one this gift and another that' (1 Cor. 7.7).

The hard saying of Jesus that marriage endangers a person's salvation is very difficult to integrate into a positive theology of marriage. It may be possible to regard this saying as one which helped 'to meet the needs and to validate the activities of a group of wandering preachers' in the aftermath of the sack of Jerusalem and the abandonment of the 'eccentric settlements' by the Dead Sea. These words of Jesus may have been appropriated by this 'particular small group'.[50] Equally, Christians with a strong commitment to marriage may be too eager to adopt disposal strategies of inconvenient texts. Perhaps one might find in this saying a warning against that kind of absorption in home and family which really is 'subject to death'. A perspective outside marriage, such as this text provides, enables elements of family life to be

---

49. Adrian Thatcher, 'Singles and Families', *TheolSex* 4 (1996), pp. 11-27 (13-14). The argument of Rodney Clapp that singleness is better than marriage, is also examined here, see pp. 12-17. Rodney Clapp, *Families at the Crossroads: Beyond Traditional and Modern Options* (Leicester: Inter-Varsity Press, 1993), Chapter 5 'The Superiority of Singleness', pp. 89-113.

50. Brown, *The Body*, pp. 41-42.

properly criticized as life-threatening, as real obstructions to the gift of salvation. Among these elements may be found an oblivious disregard of the wider world beyond the family, a lack of awareness of the damage which the continual closeness of married life is able to inflict on partners, a lack of awareness of the imbalance of power which remains a problem in many marriages, a spirit of selfishness and possessiveness which the maintenance of an affluent home encourages, and all those other features of marriage which led (above, 2.1.c) to the title 'unholy misery'.

e. *Passionate Mutual Love*
If the third and fourth models of marriage counsel caution or even avoidance, there is no such caution about the joys of human love in the Song of Songs. We have had good reason already to note that the love of God is found in the deep, playful, mutual and erotic love the young man and woman have for each other. In this milieu the woman takes the initiative in making love and expressing her feelings at least as often as the man. In contrast with the 'dubious necessity model' where women do not have a perspective at all, either on men or even on themselves, the woman of the Song is equal to the man in everything. Her *persona* as an overtly desiring (and black) woman is perceived neither as sinful, nor as threatening. There is no extrinsic justification for their love. The garden of their love may be a deliberate reversal of the fall of humanity in the garden of Eden. 'There is no expulsion here; no constraint or curse in the Song; no taint or shame'.[51] The unity of this couple subverts the gendered humanity of the fall, of Ezekiel and the household codes.

This model is particularly appropriate for a generation of men and women still influenced by awkwardness and embarrassment in relation to their bodies and the bodies of others. While there is strong evidence that many contemporary people have more than overcome their parents' and grandparents' reticence to discuss or to admit to enjoying sexual experience, most Christians are still not encouraged to link sexual intimacy with the intimacy of faith. Connections are still not being made between sexuality and spirituality.[52] Consequently, as the delights of mutual love are sampled and explored, these stirrings and

51. Heather Walton, 'Theology of Desire', *TheolSex* 1 (1994), pp. 31-41 (33).
52. See Stuart and Thatcher, *People of Passion*, Chapter 9, 'Spirituality', pp. 222-44.

intimations of human love are experienced without reference to the source of all love, poured out in the love of God for all things in Christ. Since divine love always surfaces in human love, the ongoing divorce between sexuality and spirituality means the most potentially fruitful experience for a person to discover, and grow, in faith, is repeatedly missed.

The attempt to reclaim the biblical models of marriage can be said to have had only limited success. The five models described are not all equally serviceable; indeed one of them is almost useless; one of them provides a positive disincentive to marry; and a third, while a celebration of passionate, mutual love, is linked to marriage largely by assumption. Both the remaining models require extensive theological work to be done on them before they can bear the required weight of supporting a contemporary theology of marriage. This is a disappointing conclusion, not one that a passionate supporter of Christian marriage, having searched the Scriptures, might expect to arrive at.

At least an attempt has been made to take seriously inconvenient sources. The confidence placed in the covenant and one-flesh models will begin to be justified only in Chapter 7 when a developed theology of marriage as a 'communal partnership (7.1) and as a 'mutually administered sacrament' (7.2) is attempted. A major justification for marriage is not found in any of the models discussed in this chapter. It is found in the need that children have to be loved by two parents. That discussion must be postponed to Chapter 5.

Chapter 4

COHABITATION, BETROTHAL AND THE ENTRY INTO MARRIAGE

What are the churches to say and do about the widespread practice of cohabitation prior to marriage, inside and outside the membership of the churches? These questions are tackled directly in this chapter by examining, historically and theologically, how the entry into marriage is achieved. The cautious acceptance of some forms of cohabitation advocated by the Church of England report, *Something to Celebrate*, is described and commended. However, this report does not discuss those historical forms of entry into marriage which would give its recommendations greater weight. Basic theological considerations about what makes a marriage are also excluded from the report. While the scope of this chapter is considerably broader than the problem of cohabitation and the regressive and reactionary response to that report in England, this chapter will, on its way, repair these two *lacunae* and provide historical and theological grounds for endorsing the report's conclusion about cohabitation. The conclusion is then further refined and extended. The deeper question, what marriage *is*, and how its meanings might be reappropriated in postmodern times, is postponed to the following chapters.

1. *Cohabitation and* Something to Celebrate

The practice of cohabitation before marriage has been rising steadily since the 1960s. *Something to Celebrate* records that in the late 1960s, a mere 6 per cent of women marrying in the United Kingdom had cohabited. In the late 1970s the figure was 33 per cent, and in the late 1980s 58 per cent.[1] In the 1990s it has risen further. This trend is

1. General Synod Board for Social Responsibility, *Something to Celebrate: Valuing Families in Church and Society* (London: Church House Publishing, 1995), p. 34.

replicated in many other industrialized countries. In the United States there are nearly six million 'households with two unrelated adults', and in 2.7 million of these there are no children in the household.[2] Cohabitation is common both before marriage and after it. 'The period of cohabitation tends to be short-lived. One-third of couples cohabit for less than a year and only 16 per cent live with their partner for more than five years. A cohabiting relationship lasts two years on average and then the couple either separate or marry.'[3] About half of all cohabiting heterosexual couples are young, unmarried or not yet married, and childless.

Reasons given for cohabitation before marriage include 'reaction to the clear failure of traditional patterns of partner selection, courting, marriage and setting up home';[4] the ability to avoid or delay conception through reliable contraception; the wish to avoid promiscuity; the wish to avoid the possible consequences of being married, like the cost of a legal divorce or of a big wedding. Other reasons include peer pressure; a saving on the rent; or waiting to conclude higher education. The distinction made in 1981 between three types of cohabitation remains useful.[5] The first type is 'temporary or *casual* cohabitation', entered into with little thought or commitment; the second type is conscious *preparation for marriage* or 'trial marriage'; the third type functions as a *substitute for marriage* either because the couple is opposed to marriage as an institution, or because they live in a society where cohabitation is an institution already.

Cohabitation has become the theological problem for the 1990s that 'sex before marriage' was for the 1960s. In a major survey of sexual behaviour in Britain in 1994 it was discovered that 'fewer than 1 per cent of men and women aged 16 to 24 were married at the time of their first sexual intercourse'.[6] While the near unanimity of practice does not make the practice morally right, it indicates the extent of the rejection

2.   US Census Bureau, Current Population Survey Reports (March 1998).
3.   *Something to Celebrate*, p. 34.
4.   *Something to Celebrate*, p. 111.
5.   Gary Jenkins, *Cohabitation: A Biblical Perspective* (Nottingham: Grove Books, 1992), pp. 4-5, and nn. 3, 5 and 6. For a more sophisticated typology see C. Barton, *Cohabitation Contracts* (Gower: Aldershot, 1985), p. 10.
6.   Kaye Wellings, Julia Field, Anne M. Johnson and Jane Wadsworth, *Sexual Behaviour in Britain: The National Survey of Sexual Attitudes and Lifestyles* (Harmondsworth: Penguin Books, 1994), p. 72.

of the churches' traditional teaching and prompts hard questions about the balance of reasons for it, which vary from the inability of the churches to connect with people's real experience, to the alleged extent of neopaganism or sinful unbelief which may be sweeping the West. What are the responses of the churches to this practice? Is it an obvious sign that in sexual relations we have now entered the 'post-Christian' era?

The Roman Catholic Church treats cohabitation under the rubric of 'free unions', and condemns those, along with adultery, divorce, polygamy and incest as 'grave offences against the dignity of marriage'.[7] Orthodox churches are authoritatively said to be unprepared even to raise 'the question of sexual activity outside of marriage',[8] and the same response is generally made by evangelical churches and their members.[9] However, the authors of *Something to Celebrate*, while acknowledging some 'concerns' among Christians over cohabitation, argue differently. They say,

> The wisest and most practical way forward therefore may be for Christians both to hold fast to the centrality of marriage and at the same time to accept that cohabitation is, for many people, a step along the way towards that fuller and more complete commitment. Such an approach has much to be said in its favour.[10]

A similar position was taken in 1991 by the report, *Keeping Body*

---

7.   Most recently in the *Catechism of the Catholic Church*, paras. 2380-2391, 2400. The Vatican position has scarcely changed since the Encyclical Letter of Pope Pius XI, *Casti Connubii*, warned 'There is danger that those who before marriage sought in all things what is theirs, who indulged even their impure desires, will be in the married state what they were before, that they will reap that which they have sown; indeed, within the home there will be sadness, lamentation, mutual contempt, strifes, estrangements, weariness of the common life, and, worst of all, such parties will find themselves left alone with their own unconquered passions' (*Casti Connubii* [Vatican City: Vatican Press, 1930], p. 34). See also Congregation for the Doctrine of the Faith, *Declaration On Certain Questions Concerning Sexual Ethics* (Vatican City: Vatican Press, 1975), section 7.

8.   Zion, *Eros and Transformation*, p. 119.

9.   An exception is Greg Forster who affirms there *are* 'circumstances in which a cohabiting couple ought to be regarded morally and socially as married'. See his *Marriage Before Marriage?: The Moral Validity of 'Common Law' Marriage* (Bramcote: Grove Books, 1988), p. 23; and in greater detail, *idem, Cohabitation and Marriage: A Pastoral Response* (London: Marshall Pickering, 1994).

10.   *Something to Celebrate*, p. 115.

and Soul Together of the Presbyterian Church of the USA. The authors raise the question

> By what strategy will sessions/congregations be encouraged to gladly receive cohabiting couples into the church family? Are we to ignore them with the expectation that they will one day 'see the light?'[11]

Since the stance taken by *Something to Celebrate* is important for this study, it is necessary to explore the authors' concerns and the reasons they give for their 'way forward'.

First, many Christians think 'the traditional Christian understanding situates sexual intercourse firmly within the context of the bond of marriage and therefore means that any non-married relationship involving sexual intercourse is wrong'. On this view, 'The rise of cohabitation is seen as a sign of lack of discipline, a giving in to the spirit of the age'.[12] Secondly, some Christians think 'that cohabitation poses a threat to the institution of marriage and the family as Christians understand them'. In particular marriage is a 'community event' with an unlimited commitment, while cohabitation 'tends to be an informal arrangement of a more private kind, involving consent but lacking the unlimited commitment of the vows of marriage'. And thirdly, 'cohabiting relationships appear to create less stable relationships when converted into marriage'.[13]

These concerns are outweighed by the counter-arguments. In an analysis of cohabitees in the early 1980s who subsequently became married, John Haskey pointed out that they were 50 per cent more likely to become divorced after five years than those couples who were not living together before their wedding. But if the length of the times of the living together of the two groups is compared, the figure is reduced. It is reduced in fact to 20 per cent after 15 years of living together.[14] As the authors of *Something to Celebrate* point out, 'the evidence does not

11. *Keeping Body and Soul Together*, p. 50. It should not be forgotten that the General Assembly of the Presbyterian Church, under the glare of intense media scrutiny at Baltimore in June 1991, threw the report out. For a distressing account see John J. Carey (ed.), *The Sexuality Debate in North American Churches 1988–1995* (Lewiston: Edwin Mellen Press, 1995), pp. 38-49.

12. *Something to Celebrate*, p. 113.

13. *Something to Celebrate*, p. 114.

14. John Haskey, 'Pre-marital Cohabitation and the Probability of Subsequent Divorce: Analyses Using New Data from the General Household Survey' (Population Trends, 68; London: HMSO, 1992), pp. 10-19 (10-11).

necessarily mean that cohabitation before marriage *causes* break-down'.[15] Such couples may have a lesser commitment to marriage in the first place or may inadvisedly proceed to marriage as an attempted solution to relationship difficulties.[16] The report also acknowledges the peculiar difficulty of cohabiting couples in rendering their relationship as normative and acceptable to the wider (and older) society. 'While cohabitation has become more socially acceptable, we have yet to establish a language and mode of behaviour with respect to the new form. Thus the couples themselves may find it difficult to present their relationship to the outside world.'

While there is an obvious difference between accepting that many people have a particular view and accepting that that view is or could be consistent with Christian teaching, the authors clearly argue for the latter position, and they do so on what might be deemed evangelistic, theological and pastoral grounds. It is evangelistic because 'it is a way of responding sympathetically and realistically to the increasing number of people who are seeking a different form of partnership from that traditionally accepted'. Secondly, 'in terms of the theology of marriage, cohabitation which involves a mutual, life-long, exclusive commitment may be a legitimate form of marriage, what might be called "pre-cere-monial" or "without ceremonial" marriage'.[17] The pastoral grounds for adopting a positive approach are based on 'changes and developments in modern life'. These include recognition of the value people place on 'intimate relations and sexual experiences', the optional link between intercourse and procreation, the 'shift in gender-role stereotypes', and the impact of the women's movement.

Something to Celebrate represents a promising and courageous attempt by the Anglican Church to understand the reasons for the increasing popularity of cohabitation and to begin to equip its pastors in dealing with it. But the report lays itself open to the charge of failure to provide sufficiently detailed historical and theological foundations for its recommendations. Sadly there was substantial opposition even to a motion in General Synod to 'take note' of it,[18] and much dislike of it by

15. *Something to Celebrate*, p. 114 (authors' emphasis).

16. See Greg Forster, *Healing Love's Wounds: A Pastoral Approach to Divorce and Remarriage* (London: Marshall Pickering, 1995), p. 13.

17. *Something to Celebrate*, p. 116.

18. For an account of this unhappy meeting of the Synod, see *The Church Times*, 8 December 1995.

conservative Christians.[19] The rest of this chapter provides further historical and theological reflection on the entry into marriage, which, if successful, will locate *Something to Celebrate* much more centrally within Christian tradition, while remaining importantly at the frontier of it.

2. Revisiting the Tradition

a. *Lifting 'the Veil of Modernity'*
Changes to marriage practice in England and Wales since the Hard-wicke Marriage Act of 1753 have become so entrenched that it has become difficult even to imagine that strange and informal world of conjugality that lies behind the veil of modernity. Moreover the impact of that Act was felt all around the British Empire which at that time included 13 colonies on the eastern seaboard of North America. The possibility to be opened up here is that alongside the near-universal assumption that marriage begins with a wedding, is another, equally traditional view that the entry into marriage is a process involving stages, with the wedding marking both the 'solemnization' of life commitments already entered into, and the recognition and reception of the changed status of the couple by the community or communities to which each belongs. If this possibility is sound, one of the consequences that will undoubtedly follow is that at least some cases of 'sex before marriage' which used to be frenetically discussed among Christians were misdescribed. The alternative view, that marriage is entered into in stages renders superfluous those easy temporal distinctions between 'before' and 'after', provided by the identification between the beginning of a marriage with a wedding.

It is necessary to begin as far back as the twelfth century for the alternative view to emerge, although its roots are earlier. The twelfth century Western church developed two rival theories of what made a marriage. Gratian and the Italians held to a two-stage theory of initiation and completion. The exchange of consent was the first phase; first

19. See Alan Storkey, *Marriage and its Modern Crisis: Repairing Married Life* (London: Hodder & Stoughton, 1996), pp. 218-19. Storkey, a member of the working party that produced *Something to Celebrate*, resigned from it prior to the report's publication.

intercourse was the consummation.[20] This view combined the emphasis in Roman law on marriage being defined by mutual consent, together with the biblical emphasis on marriage as a 'one-flesh' union of partners. Lombard and the Parisians held consent alone made the marriage. A principal reason was the strong belief, unquestioned at the time, that the marriage of Mary the mother of Jesus, and *virgo perpetua*, to Joseph was never physically consummated. This was one of the reasons why it was believed to be a perfect marriage. Consent could be made in either the present or the future tense: *de praesenti* or *de futuro*. Consent in the present tense was marriage. Consent in the future tense was not marriage, but betrothal (*sponsalia*). Betrothal 'was dissoluble by mutual agreement or unilaterally for good cause'.[21] Luther called the two different kinds of consent a 'fool's game'[22] and saw them as an excuse for much promiscuity.

Catholic teaching about what constitutes a marriage, to this day, is based on a compromise between these two rival mediaeval views. Consent is what makes a marriage, is what makes it valid (*ratum*). However, consummation through sexual intercourse (*consummatum*) is what renders it indissoluble, thereby making non-consummation or male impotence grounds for annulment. A person could be betrothed at seven years old. A girl could be married at 12, a boy at 14. The first known instance in the West of a blessing by a priest during a wedding ceremony is the 950 CE ritual of Durham, England.[23] Although the fourth Lateran Council of 1215 required the blessing of a priest, it was unnecessary for the validity of the marriage. Only after the Council of Trent in 1563 was a ceremony compulsory for Roman Catholics. Only in 1754, after the Hardwicke Marriage Act had been passed, was a ceremony a legal requirement in England and Wales.

---

20. For the background see James A. Brundage, *Sex, Law and Marriage in the Middle Ages* (Aldershot: Variorum, Ashgate Publishing, 1993), pp. 407-11; Christopher Brooke, *The Medieval Idea of Marriage* (Oxford: Clarendon Press, 1989), pp. 126-39.

21. Brundage, *Sex, Law and Marriage*, p. 409. See also, Eric Josef Carlson, *Marriage and the English Reformation* (Oxford: Basil Blackwell, 1994), p. 20.

22. See Harrington, *Reordering Marriage*, p. 30.

23. Jean-Baptiste Molin and Protais Mutembe, *Le rituel du mariage en France du XIIème au XVIème siècle* (Paris, 1974), pp. 29-30.

b. *'Spousals' and 'Nuptials'*

The importance of the distinction between betrothal and marriage, and the transition from one to the other cannot be overestimated. The distinction continued until well after the Reformation.[24] Up to the sixteenth century, the spousal or spousals were undoubtedly more important than the nuptials. Children born to couples who conceived during betrothal would be regarded as legitimate, provided the couple married. According to Macfarlane

> it was really only in the middle of the 16th century that the betrothal, which constituted the 'real' marriage, was joined to the nuptials or celebration of that marriage. Consequently, during the Middle Ages and up to the 18th century it was widely held that sexual cohabitation was permitted after the betrothal.[25]

In France sexual relations regularly began with betrothal, at least until the sixteenth century when the post-Tridentine church moved against it.[26] In Britain, 'Until far down into the sixteenth century the engaged lovers before the nuptials were held to be legally husband and wife. It was common for them to begin living together immediately after the betrothal ceremony'.[27] According to the social historian John Gillis,

24. Alan Macfarlane, *Marriage and Love in England: Modes of Reproduction 1300–1840* (Oxford: Basil Blackwell, 1987), p. 291.

25. Brundage, *Sex Law and Marriage*, p. 305.

26. See Jean Rémy, 'The Family: Contemporary Models and Historical Perspective', in Andrew Greeley (ed.), *The Family in Crisis or Transition*, *Concilium* 121 (1/1979), p. 9: '[in France] in the 16th century the churches began to lead a campaign against premarital sex. Previously the engagement or betrothal carried great weight. If the Church frowned on the unblessed marriage she did not forbid it. Very often, above all in the country, the church marriage took place when the woman was pregnant, sometimes towards the end of her pregnancy. What is more, in many places intercourse took place as a kind of test of fertility. One only married the girl when she was pregnant. All this implies a society in which fertility was central to the meaning of marriage. The Church, which played no part at the time of the betrothal, emphasised the sole validity of marriage and was increasingly direct in her opposition to premarital relations. This was an historic struggle which possibly still colours the Church's reactions today.'

27. Macfarlane, *Marriage and Love*, p. 291, citing Howard, *Matrimonial Institutions*, i, 374. See also the judgment of Lawrence Stone: 'Before the tightening up of religious controls over society after the Reformation and the Counter-Reformation in the mid-16th century, the formal betrothal ceremony seems to have been at least as important, if not more so, than the wedding. To many, the couple were from that moment "man and wife before God", and the temptation to sexual

'Although the church officially frowned on couples taking themselves as "man and wife" before it had ratified their vows, it had to acknowledge that vows "done rite" were the equivalent of a church wedding'.[28]

The term 'processual marriage' is sometimes used to describe these arrangements, that is, 'where the formation of marriage was regarded as a *process* rather than a clearly defined rite of passage'.[29] This was clearly the arrangement practised in Somerset, England, among farm workers. 'In effect for the peasant community there was very little premarital sex. Most of the acts seen as such by Church and State were interpreted by the village as activities within marriage—a marriage begun with the promise and irreversibly confirmed by pregnancy.'[30] The promise 'was often *presumed* by local opinion so as to avoid illegitimacy and any consequent charge on the rates'.[31] Far from this practice being seen as promiscuous or immoral, it should be seen instead as a practice which was approved and enforced by the community.[32] Such practice was very common in the seventeenth and eighteenth centuries.

It is no longer generally known that the Anglican marriage service was an attempt to combine elements of two separate occasions into a single liturgical event. Alan Macfarlane develops the point in detail:

> Behind the English wedding as it developed over the centuries there lay separate acts, one essential and one voluntary. In Anglo-Saxon England the 'wedding' was the occasion when the betrothal or pleding of the couple to each other in words of the present tense took place. This was in effect the legally binding act; it was, combined with consummation,

intercourse before the marriage ceremony in the church was very great. The Church itself recognized this situation, and as late as 1619 in the Deanery of Doncaster a betrothal was successful as defence against an accusation in the courts of pre-nuptial fornication' (Lawrence Stone, *The Family, Sex and Marriage in England 1500–1800* [London, Weidenfeld & Nicolson, 1979], p. 628).

28. Gillis, *For Better, For Worse*, p. 20.

29. Stephen Parker, *Informal Marriage, Cohabitation and the Law, 1750–1989* (New York: St Martin's Press, 1990), p. 19.

30. G.R. Quaife, *Wanton Wives and Wayward Wenches: Peasants and Illicit Sex in Early Seventeenth Century England* (London: Croom Helm, 1979), p. 61, cited by Parker, *Informal Marriage*, p. 19.

31. Parker, *Informal Marriage*, p. 19 (emphasis added).

32. It was 'located in a general belief in the ability of public opinion to command obedience to community values'. Parker, *Informal Marriage*, p. 19, citing J.M. Golby and A.W. Purdue, *The Civilization of the Crowd: Popular Culture in England 1750–1900* (London: Batsford, 1984), p. 3, and G. Alderman, *Modern Britain 1700–1983* (London: Croom Helm, 1986), p. 3.

the marriage. Later, a public celebration and anouncement of the wedding might take place—the 'gift', the 'bridal', or 'nuptials', as it became
known. This was the occasion when friends and relatives assembled to
feast and to hear the financial details. These two stages remained separate in essence until they were united into one occasion after the Reformation. Thus the modern Anglican wedding service includes both
spousals and nuptials. An important feature of the first act was that it
originally involved no religious or ritual element. It was a purely personal, private, civil contract, only to be entered into by the couple. There
was no necessity for a clergyman to be present, or for any religious
ceremony.[33]

This premodern distinction between *spousals* and *nuptials* has been
largely forgotten; indeed, its very recollection is likely to be resisted
because it shows a cherished assumption about the entry into marriage,
that it necessarily begins with a wedding, to be historically dubious.
'Betrothal', says Gillis, 'constituted the recognized rite of transition
from friends to lovers, conferring on the couple the right to sexual as
well as social intimacy'.[34] Betrothal 'granted them freedom to explore
any personal faults or incompatibilities that had remained hidden during the earlier, more inhibited phases of courtship and could be disastrous if carried into the indissoluble status of marriage'.[35]

It has also been forgotten that about half of all brides in Britain and
North America were pregnant at their weddings in the eighteenth century.[36] According to Stone, 'this tells us more about sexual customs
than about passionate attachments: sex began at the moment of engagement, and marriage in church came later, often triggered by the pregnancy.[37] He concludes that 'among the English and American plebs in
the last half of the 18th century, almost all brides below the social élite
had experienced sexual intercourse with their future husbands before
marriage'.[38] This remarkable statistic is made yet more extraordinary

33. Macfarlane, *Marriage and Love*, pp. 309-10, citing also Whitelock, *English
Society*, p. 152, and Howard, *Matrimonial Institutions*, p. 381.

34. Gillis, *For Better, For Worse*, p. 47.

35. Gillis, *For Better, For Worse*, p. 47.

36. Lawrence Stone, 'Passionate Attachments in the West in Historical Perspective', in Scott and Warren (eds.), *Perspectives on Marriage*, p. 176. The figure cited
here is 'at least half of all brides'. Elsewhere Stone says the figure is 'over 40%'
(*The Family*, p. 609).

37. Stone, 'Passionate Attachments', p. 176.

38. Stone, *The Family*, p. 609.

by the fact that early conception was discouraged, and that, as Jarrett says, 'For the great majority of people in eighteenth century England, the most urgent problem in life was how to prevent it'.[39] For we post-moderns, socialized into the belief that widespread premarital sex is a new phenomenon, disbelief is easy to comprehend. While the Reformation had succeeded in greatly reducing prenuptial pregnancies, largely through the surveillance system of the church courts, this development was a temporary one. Stone's explanation of this 'gigantic rise of pre-nuptial conceptions' is not 'a massive violation of accepted standards in sexual behaviour', but rather 'a change in those standards'. His judgment is that:

> In the eighteenth century it looks as if the spousals again became the generally accepted moment at which sexual relations could begin, the marriage ceremony occurring later, often when the bride was quite far advanced in pregnancy. The man's honour was not damaged in the public consciousness, provided that he lived up to his promise to marry despite any possible second thoughts he might subsequently have had; and the woman's honour was not damaged in the public consciousness merely for having commenced sexual relations after the spousals but before the marriage.[40]

Emmanuel Ntakarutimana reminds Western readers that in many African countries today a marriage is not deemed to be consummated until the birth of the betrothed couple's child. He writes

> Where Western tradition presents marriage as a point in time at which consent is exchanged between the couple in front of witnesses approved of by law, followed by 'consummation', the tradition here recognizes the consummation of a marriage with the birth of the first child. To that point the marriage was only being progressively realized.[41]

---

39. D. Jarrett, *England in the Age of Hogarth* (St Albans: Paladin, 1976), p. 58, cited by Parker, *Informal Marriage*, p. 22. A well known and influential study in 1965 delicately pointed out the 'striking difference' between the informal marriage customs of the sixteenth, seventeenth and eighteenth centuries and 'those which are now universally regarded as standard and required practice amongst Christians'. See, Peter Laslett, *The World We Have Lost* (London: Methuen, 1965), p. 141.

40. Stone, *The Family*, p. 629.

41. Emmanuel Ntakarutimana, 'Being a Child in Central Africa Today', in Junker-Kenny and Mette (eds.), *Little Children Suffer*, p. 15. Ntakarutimana speaks of the 'Africa of the Great Lakes' and reminds us that marriage is a joining of two wider families, not merely of two individuals.

There are close similarities between pre-modern entry into marriage in Europe and the entry into marriage still practised in parts of Africa. Both will help in the reclamation of betrothal (below, 4.3).

c. Clandestine Marriages

Since a church ceremony was not a legal requirement for a valid marriage, and the church recognized the vows made by marrying couples whether in church or not, many marriages were conducted in secret, that is, they were clandestine. 'A paradox at the heart of the Church's teaching on marriage was that while it condemned clandestine marriages it continued to recognize their validity.'[42] The term 'clandestine marriage' also covered any marriage that 'failed to conform to the requirements of the canon law as to place, time and procedure'.[43] The practice led to widespread irregularities and frequent abuse. Since a private or informal marriage was often difficult subsequently to verify, the practice was conducive to bigamy and also clandestine divorce.

The Hardwicke Marriage Act of 1753 required registration of all marriages in England and Wales, and set up a bureaucratic apparatus for doing so. Verbal contracts or pledges were no longer regarded as binding. Couples were offered the choice of having banns called in the parish of one of them, or of obtaining a licence to dispense with the banns: marriages at first took place in parish churches; priests seeking to conduct informal marriages were liable to transportation to America.[44] The creeping extension of the bureaucratic state to encompass the entry into marriage is characteristic of the apparatus of modernity. Uniformity was imposed and policed. Betrothal no longer had any legal force. While the working classes continued to practice alternatives to legal marriage, for example, besom weddings, living tally,[45]

---

42. Art Cosgrove, 'Consent, Consummation and Indissolubility: some evidence from medieval ecclesiastical courts', *Downside Review* 109 (1991), pp. 94-104 (97).

43. See R.B. Outhwaite, *Clandestine Marriage in England, 1500–1800* (London: Hambledon Press, 1995), p. xiv, and throughout.

44. Outhwaite, *Clandestine Marriage*, pp. 84-85.

45. See Gillis, *For Better, For Worse*, pp. 198-200, 206. At a besom wedding, 'couples lept over a birch besom in the open doorway of a house, in presence of witnesses', p. 198: and see Parker, *Informal Marriage*, p. 18. Gillis says 60% of baptisms in the Ceiriog Valley of North Wales (1769–99) showed 'some kind of irregular marriage had been practiced…which…while not yet formally solemnized in church, were nevertheless sufficiently stable to be recorded as separate from those births in which no father was declared'. '…in almost every part of Britain the

handfasting,[46] and so on, the stigma of illegitimacy now attached itself to children whose parents had not been through a wedding ceremony. Gone was the transitional phase from singleness to marriage.

My concern in this chapter is the entry into marriage. However, tumultuous changes in the understanding of marriage occurred between the sixteenth and nineteenth centuries. These included the Protestant disregard for priestly celibacy and the denial that marriage was a sacrament. In the wake of the Reformation and ecclesiastical disruption, the institution of the family assumed greater importance as an influence for social stability. In Reformation Germany 'the well-known head of the household, or *Hausvater*, was joined in sixteenth-century rhetoric by two other paternal authority figures—the *Landesvater* (political ruler) and the *Gottesvater* (God the Father)'. Luther called these 'the three orders of Christian Society'. Harrington comments, 'Like the kings and patriarchs of ancient Israel, the *Hausvater* possessed an authority that was both divinely ordained and inviolable; those who would undermine it risked the wrath of the *Gottesvater* himself'.[47] In the sixteenth and previous centuries marriage was generally arranged by parents, who had their own economic and social objectives for their offspring to achieve.[48] The rise and rise of individualism in social and economic life profoundly affected marriage. By the eighteenth and nineteenth centuries, says Lawrence Stone, 'individualism had so far taken precedence over the group interests of the kin that the couple were left more

term "living tally" established itself…The origin of the term *tally* is obscure. It may have come from the Welsh word for love token, *tali*, or it may refer to the tally stick that miners used to mark the amount of coal dug. But, whatever the origins, the term itself first became widespread in the nineteenth century, indicating the growth of a practice that was clearly distinct from both casual cohabitation and formal marriage. It conveyed a notion of definite, if conditional, contract or "bargain", based on the consent of both parties and protecting the woman in case of motherhood. Furthermore, it suggested a partnership based on some degree of affection' (Gillis, *For Better, For Worse*, p. 206).

46. Handfasting 'involved the exchange of promises before witnesses with the man and woman joining hands. The couple lived together for a year and a day and, if pleased with the arrangement, could extend it for life. The conception of a child within the time limit made the union binding…' See Parker, *Informal Marriage*, p. 18, also citing J.H. Baker, *An Introduction to English Legal History* (London: Butterworth, 1979), p. 32.

47. Harrington, *Reordering Marriage*, pp. 39-40.

48. Stone, 'Passionate Attachments', p. 173.

or less free to make their own decision, except in the highest aristocratic and royal circles'.[49] Embedded in these changes is the astonishing rise of something called romantic love, and with it, *companionate marriage* which soon became the dominant understanding of marriage in Protestant Christianity.[50] I shall return to these trends when discussing the relationship between marriage and human love (7.1).

d. *The Triumph of the Upper Classes*

A final piece of evidence in the inquiry into the beginnings of marriage is the social enforcement of the new marriage ideal enshrined in the Hardwicke Act. The achievement of the widespread belief that a marriage begins with a wedding was not so much a *religious* or theological, but a *class*, matter. The upper and middle classes had the political clout to enforce the social respectability of the new marriage laws, and they used it. As John Gillis writes,

> In the course of the previous hundred years [prior to 1850] both betrothal and wedding had become the subject of passionate controversy, *an issue not so much of religion but of class*. People in different parts of Britain now married in quite different ways; the distance between the mores of ordinary people and those of the educated élites had never been greater. The ideal of the nuclear family and companionate marriage, something that divided the middle class from the aristocracy in the seventeenth century, now united them in common opposition to the less strictly monogamous behavior of their social inferiors. From the mid eighteenth century onwards *sexual politics became increasingly bitter as the propertied classes attempted to impose their standards on the rest of society.*[51]

New social institutions, like ballrooms and balls where the sons of gentlemen could initiate romantic attachments, ostentatiously expensive white weddings, and 'honeymoons' which separated the couple from their kin as soon as the ceremony had taken place, were all introduced in this period and quickly announced themselves as normative.[52] Gillis explains that,

---

49. Stone, 'Passionate Attachments', p. 175.

50. The idea that one might marry because one was in the romantic state of being 'in love' was originally regarded as 'imprudent folly and even madness'. See Stone, 'Passionate Attachments', p. 181.

51. Gillis, *For Better, For Worse*, p. 135 (emphases added).

52. Gillis, *For Better, For Worse*, pp. 135, 138, 164.

until the rise of the joint stock company the family was a crucial means of capital accumulation and economic enterprise. Marriage played a central role in mobilizing wealth and power, and the control of courtship, particularly that of heirs and heiresses, remained essential. While young people were told they must marry for love and were given a certain latitude in the choice of mates, the courtship process was carefully constructed to prevent misalliances.[53]

The upper and middle classes borrowed the earlier Puritan conception of marriage and used it to distinguish their own practice from the less formal, more traditional alternatives. By the mid-eighteenth century they were able 'to impose their will on the established church'.

> They were now convinced that the legality of betrothal together with the church's toleration of clandestine marriage were, as Daniel Defoe was so fond of pointing out, crimes against both property and patriarchy: 'a Gentleman might have the satisfaction of hanging a Thief that stole an old Horse from him, but could have no Justice against a rogue for stealing his Daughter'.[54]

In contrast to plebeian practice where betrothal continued long after it had any legal force,[55] in the upper class new courtship procedures required preceremonial virginity of brides, for social rather than moral reasons.

> For all women of this group virginity was obligatory. Their class had broken with the older tradition of betrothal that had offered the couple some measure of premarital conjugality and had substituted for it a highly ritualized courtship that for women began with the 'coming out' party and ended with the elaborate white wedding, symbolizing their purity and status. Couples did not really come to know one another until marriage, a condition that was compensated for by the honeymoon, another of the innovations peculiar to the Victorian upper middle class.[56]

53. Gillis, *For Better, For Worse*, pp. 135-36. A similar process may have occurred in France. When the church 'set impossibly high standards of family and sexual morality' in the first half of the eighteenth century, 'one can point to the bourgeoisie as pioneers of this new morality'. See Antony Copley, *Sexual Moralities in France, 1780–1980* (London: Routledge, 1989), p. 11. Copley cites J.L. Flandrin, *Families in Former Times* (Cambridge, 1976), p. 240.

54. Gillis, *For Better, For Worse*, p. 140.

55. Gillis, *For Better, For Worse*, pp. 179-81.

56. Gillis, *For Better, For Worse*, p. 164. Stone concurs: 'The value attached to chastity is directly related to the degree of social hierarchy and the degree of property ownership. Pre-marital chastity is a bargaining chip in the marriage game,

Many other changes to marriage occurred in this period that cannot be described now. Welfare legislation was frequently revised in order to discriminate against those who were not legally married. The period 1850–1960 has been called 'The Era of Mandatory Marriage'.[57] People married earlier. Secular engagement[58] replaced betrothal, and gender roles—the man the principal breadwinner, the woman the dependent wife and mother—seemed firmly established.

e. *Learning from Premodern Marriage*

I hope it is by now apparent that the widespread entry into marriage in the 1990s through cohabitation represents remarkable parallels with at least some practice in premodern England. The rise in the age of first marriage in the last quarter of the present century, to 28 for men, and 26 for women, is a precise return to what it was (for both sexes) during the reign of Elizabeth I. The figure for both sexes is identical in the United States.[59] The destigmatization of pregnancy prior to a wedding is a return to premodern ways. The recent licensing of hotels, casinos and football stadia as places where marriages may be conducted replicates earlier freedoms where wedding vows could be exchanged anywhere.[60] Gillis's verdict, written in 1985, is that

> Together law and society appear to have reinstated a situation very much like that which existed before 1753, when betrothal licensed pre-marital conjugality. It is also like the situation that existed in the late eighteenth and early nineteenth centuries when so many people made their own

to be set off against male property and status rights. Pre-marital female sexual repression is thus built into the social system, since male and female are bargaining on the marriage market with different goods, the one social and economic, the other sexual' (*The Family*, p. 636).

57. Gillis, *For Better, For Worse*, p. 229. The phrase is the title of Part 3 of the book.

58. Is it not strange that conservative documents emphasizing tradition should ignore betrothal in favour of 'engagement'? See, e.g., Pontifical Council For The Family, *Preparation For The Sacrament Of Marriage* (Vatican City: Vatican Press, 1996), §§16-17.

59. I.e., in 1990 it was 28.7 years for men, and 26.7 for women. US Census Bureau, *Monthly Vital Statistics Report* 43.12 (supp.) (1995).

60. Walter Kasper forthrightly reminds us that the church long recognized civil marriages without ecclesiastical ceremony, because their validity rested on consent, and nothing else. See Walter Kasper, *Theology of Christian Marriage* (London: Burns and Oates, 1980), pp. 74-76.

private 'little weddings', postponing the public, official event until such time as they could gather the resources necessary to a proper household.[61]

This conclusion, that there are remarkable parallels, between pre-modern times and our own, is deeply significant. It should not, however, be accepted without due caution. The 'pre-marital conjugality' of the earlier period occurred within a theological and social framework which was nonetheless strict with regard to promiscuity,[62] which insisted on marriage as the precondition of raising children, and was fiercely insistent on fathers assuming responsibility for the welfare of the children they conceived. Pre-industrial communities were largely self-regulating, and the full sexual experience practised by betrothed couples was, unlike much of the same practised by cohabiting couples today, *emphatically premised by the intention to marry*. Once a marriage had been contracted it was indissoluble, and divorce, aside from special Acts of Parliament, was unavailable. However, despite these dissimilarities, there are some tentative conclusions that may be drawn from a consideration of the entry into marriage during earlier periods.

First, there is no longer any formal provision for the staged entry into marriage. In the absence of this, it is possible to read the practice of cohabiting but not-yet married couples as a return to earlier informalities, and as a rejection, not so much of Christian marriage, but of the bourgeois form of it that became established at the end of the eighteenth century and was then consolidated in the Victorian era. Secondly, Christian marriage in the modern period has accommodated enormous changes (which have largely been forgotten) and must be expected to accommodate further changes in the next century which is upon us. The Protestant denial of sacramentality, the social permission afforded to marrying parties to choose their partners, the incorporation of romantic love into the meanings of marriage, and the abolition of betrothal and informal marriage all indicate, once more against social expectation, that Christian marriage is a remarkably flexible institution. There may be a deep irony here. Those conservative Christians who are

---

61. Gillis, *For Better, For Worse*, p. 310.

62. Stone has used the term 'social eversion' to describe how 'both sexual repression and sexual permissiveness eventually generate extremist features, which in turn set in motion counterforces', or 'long-term see-saw oscillations'. He estimates 'the duration of each of these swings of religio-ethical attitudes towards sexuality seems to have been about one hundred years' (*The Family*, p. 545).

generally opposed to changes to marriage on historical grounds do not always appear to be familiar with the changes in the history of marriage which can plausibly be construed to support a different conclusion.

Thirdly, Christian morality should not equate premarital chastity with the expectation that marrying couples should not make love before their wedding. It would be dishonest to assert or assume that the tradition is unanimous about the matter or that no other way of entry into marriage had ever been tried, or that no theological grounds were available for thinking differently. Yet this is what much official Christian literature does. There are grounds for thinking this is a new orthodoxy, not an old one. Fourthly, the possibility exists that the old mediaeval theories of marriage which were responsible for the practice of betrothal may be serviceable in the construction of a postmodern theology of entry into marriage which would have considerable practical value at the present time.

3. Betrothal: Reclamation and Reinstatement

a. *The Extension of 'Consent' and 'Consummation'*
In 1977 a strong case for reinstating betrothal was made by the Roman Catholic André Guindon.[63] Beginning with the mediaeval theories just discussed (above, 3.2.a) he observes that a marriage in the Roman Catholic tradition is legally valid and sacramental (*ratum*) when the free consent of both parties is exchanged.[64] However, at first intercourse, the marriage is consummated (*consummatum*), and once consummated it is indissoluble by any human power. Therefore, reasons Guindon, 'according to the canonical view, coition strengthens the bond of indissolubility'.[65] The tradition then, is said to acknowledge the insight that intercourse strengthens the marriage. This insight is next brought forward as a principal reason why the chronological order of *ratum* and *consummatum* is able to be reversed.

---

63. André Guindon, 'Case for a "Consummated" Sexual Bond before a "Ratified" Marriage', *Eglise et Théologie* 8 (1977), pp. 137-81. The whole edition of this journal was about 'Christian pre-ceremonial couples'. The views expressed were condemned by the Commission Théologique Internationale, *Problèmes doctrinaux du mariage chrétien* (Louvain-La-Neuve: Centre Cerfaux-Lefort, 1979). Twenty years on, it is time for his arguments to be revisited.
    64. *Code of Canon Law*, c. 1081, §1.
    65. Guindon, 'Sexual Bond', p. 141.

The notion that marriage rests on the irrevocable consent of the parties alone is said to rest 'on an extremely weak foundation'.[66] Its acceptance in the church was due to the negative view of sexual intercourse in the mediaeval period and the idealization of the allegedly perfect, virginal marriage of Mary and Joseph. And it fails to do justice to the biblical view that marriage is a union of two people in 'one flesh'. The marriage of Mary and Joseph was emphatically not 'prototypic'. The 'astonishing fact' that the Roman church, after the Council of Trent 1563, continued to acknowledge the dissolubility of unconsummated marriages is taken as admission of the weakness of the consent theory. Guindon wants to reinstate the joint basis for marriage in consent and consummation, and to enlarge the church's understanding of both so that each is able to encompass the experience of today's young persons beginning marriage.

The idea of consummation is broadened by pointing out that its equation in the tradition with the first act of sexual intercourse is extremely limiting and inadequate. 'Consummation is a far richer experience than anything which is expressed in the first coitus after the marriage ceremony.'[67] What counts as consummation cannot in any case be worked out 'in a non-cultural fashion'.[68] It is 'an interpersonal process'. The first single act of intercourse, assuming *per impossibile*, that it happens after a wedding ceremony, cannot bear the meaning of consummation. We have already noted that, in an African context, such a meaning would be regarded as curiously Western. The 'consummation element' of marriage, Guindon reminds us, is thought in the tradition to express the symbolic union between Christ and the Church (Eph. 5.32). Yet 'a single act of copulation'[69] clearly cannot symbolically represent the union between Christ and the Church without distorting it. Finally, consummation in a single act is called 'sexual and sacramental automatism',[70] a transaction which has more in common with 'the sympathy magic found in the fertility cults' than with the growth in grace more characteristic of Christian marriage. In the 'totally new sociological framework' (Canada in the 1970s),

66. Guindon, 'Sexual Bond', p. 150.
67. Guindon, 'Sexual Bond', p. 153.
68. Guindon, 'Sexual Bond', p. 155.
69. Guindon, 'Sexual Bond', p. 156.
70. Guindon, 'Sexual Bond', p. 157.

not only will *love* be the decisive element in both the decision to marry
and the survival of this marriage, but this love must be built on a very
thorough and lucid knowledge of self and of other, both as individuals
and as parts of a conjugal unit. How will this ever be achieved for *many*
people today, without a real experience of conjugal living?[71]

Consent, like consummation, is broadened in this theology of marriage. Its meaning is extended from that expressed by a single act (the
vows) to 'the lived reality of a conjugal commitment'. But Guindon
alleges this always was the mediaeval meaning of marital consent and
consummation, that is, joint consents which form a *societas* of the
couple and which, since they were not required to be expressed in any
ecclesiastical ceremony, were expected to be expressed instead in the
maritalis affectio, that is, in treating the spouse as a loved partner.[72] On
this view consent is expressed not merely by the ceremony but by the
quality of mutual affection found in the lives of the consenting persons.[73] That consummation is something much more profound than first

71. Guindon, 'Sexual Bond', p. 160.

72. Guindon, 'Sexual Bond', pp. 172-73. This insight leads to another argument
which cannot detain us here. Speaking of his church's willingness to annul marriages on the grounds of 'defective consent', Guindon argues that the real ground in
such cases is defective *consummation*.

73. *maritalis affectio* was also the ground for recognition of a relationship of
concubinage. The acceptance of concubinage by the church for long periods
provides further disconfirmation of the widely accepted view that the church has
always taught that sex before, or outside marriage, is wrong. In the Roman Empire
concubinage but not marriage was permitted between persons of different classes.
Following, but deliberately revising, Roman law, Pope Callistus I (217–22) allowed
that while such unions were unrecognized as marriages by the state, they might be
recognized by God. Until at least the fifth century, 'if fidelity and monogamy were
observed', Christian men and their concubines 'were usually not precluded from
baptism and eucharist'. (Reynolds, *Marriage in the Western Church*, p. 167, and
see pp. 156-57.) But Gratian's *Decretum* (c. 1140) explicitly *ascribed to the concubinage relationship* the quality of marital affection which the Roman jurists had
reserved for marriage unions. He 'conceived of concubinage as an imperfect, informal marriage, a marriage which lacked legal formalities and full legal consequences, but which was nonetheless a true and valid marriage. This meaning of
concubinage became the reigning sense of the term among the canonists of the high
middle ages' (Brundage, *Sex, Law and Marriage*, pp. 3-4, and see also p. 827).
While concubinage was a less equal power-relation for women even than marriage, a reassessment of it is long overdue. What *Something to Celebrate* rightly
acknowledges as loving relationships which are not formal marriages yet which

intercourse is increasingly emphasised in Catholic mainstream (but unofficial) thought.[74] The refusal of the church to recognize preceremonial couples 'contradicts the ancient and long-standing ecclesial practice of sacramentalizing the *existing* marriage, and not some marriage imported from the Platonician sky of subsistent ideas'.[75] Couples, then, are fully justified in living together and thereby 'initiating a real marriage project', while simultaneously wishing 'to avoid the incongruity of saying their total love commitment publicly to the community before having brought it to fullness and said it with truth and realism to one another.[76]

When would it be appropriate, on Guindon's view, for a couple to go public on their marriage? When would the consummation of it be sufficiently advanced for the couple to ask the church to ratify their marriage as the sacramental reality it already is? The answer is:

> When they *experience* the sort of sexual fecundity which calls forth its most privileged fruit, a child of love, they may discern that they have become a socially responsible unit. The conjugal bond has probably reached a point of consummation where legal ratifications make sense.[77]

However in the book which followed nine years after the article, Guindon moves from the position that a marriage ought to be consummated when the couple wish to have children, to the position that marriage should be *confined to those who have children*. He writes,

> I have come to believe that the profound mind of the Christian Tradition concerning the institution of marriage is that it is to be entered into by

approximate to them, a much earlier generation of Christians would probably have described by means of the term *maritalis affectio*.

74. Michael Lawler thinks the identification between first intercourse and consummation 'overly romantic and unrealistic'. See Lawler, 'Mutual Love', p. 360. He follows the weighty judgment of Theodore Mackin that consummation means 'to bring the marital relationship to its fullness'. See Mackin, *The Marital Sacrament*, p. 674.

75. Guindon, 'Sexual Bond', p. 177.

76. Guindon, 'Sexual Bond', p. 178.

77. Guindon, 'Sexual Bond', p. 166 (author's emphasis), and see also pp. 175, 181. William Countryman has argued that 'At the present time, the church would perhaps be better advised not to solemnize marriages at the inception of the relationship itself, but to wait a period of some years before adding its blessing' (*Dirt, Greed and Sex: Sexual Ethics in the New Testament and their Implications for Today* [London: SCM Press, 1989], p. 263).

those who *wish* and *can* effectively establish a family, that is to say a
social cell in which descendants secure the historical lineage.[78]

It would be more coherent with the sense of the Tradition, I would
claim, to clearly distinguish, both theologically and ritually, between two
realities. Those unions between a man and a woman which have fructi-
fied into family and are lived as a faith event would be seen as sacramental marriages and celebrated liturgically as such. A man and a
woman who wish to be united to one another with the publicly manifested intention to share their existence, support each other (but not
children), and grow together in the capacity for caring through their
mutual life-time, are undertaking a morally, civilly and religiously worth-
while enterprise. *This enterprise is distinct, nevertheless, from what has
been traditionally called 'marriage'.* We could imagine that both a
specific legal status and special ecclesiastical blessings could be conferred upon such a conjugal union.[79]

b. *Problems over 'Trial Marriages'*

Guindon's work on consent and consummation in this theology of
marriage is most valuable, although I shall not adopt his more recent
position on two types of unions, the childless but conjugal union, and
the sacramental, child-creating matrimonial union. For reasons yet to be
given (below, 5.1.b) it will be urged that having children is an indis-
pensible purpose of marriage. Nonetheless marriage can hardly be
confined to those who intend to have children and can verify that they
can have them or be denied to those couples who do want children and
cannot have them. One further proposal regarding betrothal will be very
briefly considered before the overall case for betrothal is assessed.
Bishop John Spong has defined betrothal as 'a relationship that is
faithful, committed, and public but not legal or necessarily for a life-
time'.[80] For some a betrothal will be 'a stage of life preliminary to
marriage, or it may be for others a relationship complete in and of itself
and that has meaning for both partners in a particular context in which a
lifetime vow is neither expected nor required'. There should be a liturgical form for betrothal which would 'include a declaration that the

---

78. André Guindon, *The Sexual Creators: An Ethical Proposal for Concerned
Christians* (Lanham, MD: University Press of America, 1986), p. 88.

79. Guindon, *The Sexual Creators*, p. 89 (emphasis added).

80. John Shelby Spong, *Living in Sin? A Bishop Rethinks Human Sexuality* (San
Francisco: Harper & Row, 1988), Chapter 12, 'Betrothal: An Idea Whose Time Has
Come', p. 177.

couple intends to live together in love and faithfulness for a period of time in a bonding relationship'. 'The conception and birth of children would not be appropriate to this relationship of betrothal.' The reason for the exclusion of children from betrothal is that 'A child born of both intention and love deserves to have the nurture available in and the security provided by a legal bond of marriage, with permanence of commitment being the expectation of both the father and the mother'.[81]

Spong's argument for betrothal is based on social and pastoral considerations. Children reach puberty earlier and marry later. Adolescents cannot be expected to 'suppress their sexual drives'. The damaging guilt induced largely by redundant religious (and especially Roman Catholic) attitudes to sex is being thrown off in the wider society. Reliable contraception has removed the fear of pregnancy, the main historical inhibitor of premarital and extra-marital sex. Opportunities for privacy have increased, chaperoning has been abandoned, and people are mobile. More surprising than promiscuity is that so many young people have maintained high, but different, moral standards, with no help from their elders. Spong thinks that when a couple's relationship has

> reached a certain intensity, when it is committed and exclusive, when their peers begin to relate to them as a couple, *and when they want to begin a trial period of living together*, then such a relationship might be blessed by their church because that relationship carries with it the possibility of life-giving holiness.[82]

The argument that such betrothed couples break too easily is dismissed. Broken betrothals heal more easily then broken marriages.[83] Betrothal 'would honor the power of sex by taking it seriously', and would 'send shock waves through a generation that is quite sure that religion in general and the church in particular has nothing of substance to offer their lives'.[84]

A clear difference between *Something to Celebrate*'s acceptance of cohabitation and Spong's advocacy of betrothal is that Spong's proposal allows for betrothal to be an end in itself, and not, as in

81. Spong, *Living in Sin?*, p. 178.
82. Spong, *Living in Sin?*, p. 184 (emphasis added).
83. Cf. Storkey (*Marriage and its Modern Crisis*, pp. 99-100) for the argument that a failed 'trial-marriage' is not worth the hurt that it will inevitably cause. That such arrangements might *prevent* failed real marriages is not considered.
84. Spong, *Living in Sin?*, pp. 186-87.

Something to Celebrate, 'a step along the way' to the more complete commitment of marriage. It might be 'a stage of life preliminary to marriage', but it might not be. It might be 'a relationship complete in and of itself'. It is difficult to see how these provisions are reconcilable with the recovered Christian tradition of betrothal, although they might be offered as a plausible development of it. Betrothal *always was a promise to marry*, even though the promise could be hedged with conditions. Spong's proposed betrothal would render optional the connection between one and the other. This deficiency is further complicated by the expectation that a betrothed relationship which excluded marriage and children could, logically and psychologically, *ever* be 'complete in and of itself', since the dynamics of relationships are unpredictible, and a relationship which precluded growth would be destructive, even if it were possible. It is hard to see how even a happy, long-established marriage might be deemed 'complete', and so much harder to figure out how completeness could be a characteristic of a relationship which is in its infancy.

Spong's proposal runs into other difficulties. While the betrothed couple are sexually exclusive and committed to each other while the betrothal lasts, serial betrothal clearly cannot be ruled out if this is all betrothal is. One might just have lots of partners and be faithful to each of them while they happen to be, so to speak, 'in the frame'. However this argument is also effective against divorce, for divorce makes serial monogamy possible. A stronger argument might begin by asking just what is involved in being sufficiently committed to a partner to want to become betrothed to him or her. While these commitments will involve economic and domestic commitments, what personal commitments are entailed by the semi-formal status of the new betrothal? They will live together 'for a period of time'. Five weeks and fifty years are periods of time. There appears to be a deliberate vagueness about key aspects of the proposal. Perhaps a studied indefiniteness is a necessary element in any definition of betrothal, but there needs to be more clarity about what expectations are being shared both by the couple and by any Christian community which might recognize their union liturgically.

While Spong dislikes the term 'trial marriage' he allows himself to speak of a 'trial period of living together', and he uses 'trial marriage' and 'relationship of betrothal' interchangeably. The problem here is largely one of terminology. Partners presumably are not to be treated as goods which can be bought for a trial period by a consumer and then returned to the vendor if the purchaser is not completely satisfied. A trial period of living together if the couple were considering marriage as a future possibility could make good moral sense.[85] It is often urged that trial marriages can never replicate real marriages because the former can be terminated while the latter, at least in traditional Christian thought, cannot. This objection simply neglects two factors. It does not acknowledge that decisions require experience and information, and that in the case of the decision to marry or refrain from marriage, perhaps the most momentous decision one ever makes, as much information as possible about one's partner and one's own dispositions towards him or her, is desirable. The objection also overlooks the kind of difference which might be exemplified by the difference between a rehearsal and a performance of a play or piece of music. While performance cannot be *replicated*, it can be, and ought to be, *anticipated*, as far as possible. Why not the same for marriage?

c. *No Betrothal without the Prospect of Marriage*
These arguments, however valid, must not be allowed to sideline the central point. Traditional betrothal was allowed to couples who, hedged about with qualifications, intended marriage. A betrothal which is an end in itself is a misdescription—a rehearsal (to extend the analogy) for a performance that never happens. This negative conclusion about part of Spong's proposal need not veto his pastoral desire to afford liturgical recognition to couples who are living together in the circumstances he describes. There is surely scope for the greater involvement, including liturgical involvement, of the churches in the prolonged adolescence of their members' lives. Much of this will doubtless be semi-official. If this involvement includes a service of betrothal, to whom should it be offered? It might be desirable to follow ancient practice and to stipulate that betrothal be open only to those couples who express an intention to marry. I think this would make the defining condition too strong.[86] There are at least three reasons for this.

First, the connection between intention and action is complex even in the case of single intentions like intending to go home for lunch and

---

85. The large assumption, to be examined in Chapter 6, is that the use of contraception in these circumstances is morally legitimate.

86. It would also take us into a philosophical minefield. For some of the logical problems, see William Lyons, *Approaches to Intentionality* (Oxford: Oxford University Press, 1997).

doing it. The intention to marry is a vastly *multiple* intention, for it entails that *all* one's life and *all* one's personal relationships with others will be changed forever. It cannot therefore be treated as a single intention at all. Secondly, there is likely to be a lapse of time between intention and action however small.[87] Yet in the case of getting married, the intervening period may be several years. In several years, several things can change, so the intention to marry must be *revisable*, at least up to the point of marriage. Thirdly, unlike most intentions, one cannot carry out the intention to marry unless one's partner simultaneously carries out his or her intention to marry. But one's partner's intention to marry may become less strong or more doubtable, and so might one's own. My concern here is to *preserve the ancient link between betrothal and marriage* while acknowledging that betrothal is not yet marriage and so does not yet preclude the possibility of revoking the complex set of multiple intentions which end in marriage. This may be possible by saying that a defining condition of betrothal is *openness to the probability of future marriage*. Spong's temporary and self-sufficient relationships would thereby fall outside the definition. So would casual cohabitation and deliberate marriage substitution (above 3.1). This defining condition is admittedly vague. It will be strengthened after the treatment of our responsibilities to children and of the place of contraception in beginning marriage in the next two chapters.

Guindon's *apologia* for the recognition of preceremonial marriage is more convincing. But this term is misleading since it suggests marriage before marriage (another term which he accepts). While his arguments are directed to Roman Catholic theologians and administrators, the theological case for retaining and expanding the traditional criteria of consummation and consent, and utilizing both of them as an index of readiness for marrying couples to seek the blessing of the church, has much to commend it. He acknowledges the sociological contexts within which the process of marrying is inevitably rooted, and accepts the psychological reality that as partners in a relationship grow towards each other, their love will receive sexual, though not necessarily genital expression.[88] When that point is reached the relationship takes on a new

---

87. It has not been overlooked that intentions may be a class of explanations of actions open to us to deploy *after* actions have been carried out.

88. Guindon's earlier book (*The Sexual Language: An Essay in Moral Theology* [Ottawa: University of Ottawa Press, 1976], pp. 90-95), condones sexual experience which excludes sexual intercourse for pre-married couples. I take up this case

dimension and if the couple is not ready for the joint responsibility of parenthood, the joint responsibility for contraception must be exercised.[89] The social and historical case, based on the considerations in 3.2 above, makes his position even stronger.

d. *Celebrating* Something to Celebrate

We are now in a better position to contribute to the case made by *Something to Celebrate* for recognizing cohabitation. At least two of the 'concerns' reported in 3.1 above are mitigated by this study. Christians who think *all* preceremonial sex is wrong have wrongly assumed that the ceremonial requirement of a wedding, in fact a requirement of modernity, has always been normative. It has not. Indeed a ceremony until relatively recently, has not been a requirement. The objection that cohabitation presents 'a threat to the institution of marriage and the family' assumes there are fixed, not changing institutions, of marriage and family, and so 'defending' marriage entails defending a peculiar inherited version of it. The re-establishment of betrothal as a way of entry into marriage is, in part, the advocacy of a premodern institution. Since it is a part of the Christian tradition *already*, conservative orthodoxies can hardly continue to ignore it.

So there are considerably stronger grounds for accepting that type of cohabitation 'which involves a mutual, life-long, exclusive commitment' than the authors of *Something to Celebrate* put forward. First, the report avoids the use of the idea of betrothal. This is understandable,

---

myself in 'Safe Sex, Unsafe Arguments', *Studies in Christian Ethics* 9.2 (1996), pp. 66-77; and in 'Postmodernity and Chastity', pp. 122-40.

89. Evelyn Eaton Whitehead and James D. Whitehead helpfully suggest Christians anxious about engaged couples having sex might be more profitably concerned with whether their intimacy is *confined* to having sex. 'The notion of marriage as a passage with stages of deepening intimacy and commitment threatens the conventional Christian understanding that all genital expression is forbidden before marriage. In the past, Christians have been concerned that the growing intimacy between the engaged couple not reach genital expression. A more contemporary concern of Christians might be that this intimacy *not be limited to genital expression*. Many young adults today find sexual sharing easier than psychological and religious self-disclosure. Christians hope for a growing intimacy which is more than improved sexual compatibility: an increase in intimacy which includes a greater openness not only to each other's bodies but also to each other's dreams and faith.' See Whitehead and Whitehead, 'The Passage into Marriage', in Scott and Warren, *Perspectives on Marriage*, pp. 136-45 (138).

given its intended readership and that the term has lost the currency it once had. Yet it is hard to avoid the conclusion that the recovery of the theology and practice of betrothal would provide a stronger theological argument than any given in the report in support of cohabitation. Secondly, its acceptance of cohabitation on the ground simply that couples do it or that they 'are seeking a different form of partnership from that traditionally accepted' is certain to invite charges of capitulation to 'the spirit of the age' of which the authors are aware.[90] People often do things they should not do. People sometimes do things in great numbers that collectively they should not do. The Christian doctrine of sin gives a good reason why this is so. If people are looking for different and non-traditional forms of partnership, they may be doing so *sinfully*. They may have poor reasons for looking for these things. If mere difference from traditional forms of partnership is sought, threesomes and foursomes, provided they were accompanied by suitable vows, would suit the specification admirably.

Thirdly, there is a similar ambivalence about accepting 'that cohabitation is, for many people, a step along the way' to marriage and accepting that cohabitation is permissible moral behaviour for Christians, in line with the will of God. Accepting that many people believe their horoscopes does not require that we believe their horoscopes. We may believe that people who believe their horoscopes are daft. The point is that there are stronger reasons for accepting betrothal than the subjective states of cohabitees and the behaviour which follows from these. They are historical and theological. Christians have done these things before and it is the present arrangements which begin marriages with weddings that are new.

Fourthly, there remains a question about what is meant by saying that lifelong cohabitation 'may be a legitimate form of marriage, what might be called "preceremonial" or "without ceremonial" marriage'. Is it or isn't it? For Roman Catholics prior to 1564, when the papal bull requiring compliance to the decision of the Council of Trent, and for citizens of England and Wales prior to 1754, a *valid* marriage needed no ceremony. Provided the conditions of consent and consummation were met, the marriage would be recognized as valid. Common law marriages are still recognized in Scotland. However since these informalities are no longer generally recognized by church and state, it is misleading to say lifelong cohabitation may be a legitimate form of

90. E.g. Storkey, *Marriage and its Modern Crisis*, p. 218.

marriage. It is not. Could it mean that in the absence of recognition by church and state, some marriages are recognized by God as marriages because of certain qualities which they possess? Some Christians would be prepared to run with this argument. It is the 'marriages-are-made-in-heaven' argument but it is not advanced explicitly in the report. Lifelong cohabitation is made equivalent to 'preceremonial' marriage, but as these cohabitations are, at least in principle lifelong, they are not 'pre-' anything.

If the entry into marriage were accepted as a process which involved, as steps within it, betrothal and ceremony, the anomalies presented to the church by cohabitees could be more easily handled. Furthermore, the actual availability of a betrothal liturgy or liturgies would help considerably in providing the missing language which renders cohabitation socially problematic (above, 3.1). It would also meet the concern that, while marriages are public, cohabitation is largely a private matter.[91] A betrothal ceremony would provide precisely the public language and community dimension which are currently properties of weddings.

Despite these reservations, *Something to Celebrate* makes an impressive contribution to the churches' teaching about the entry into marriage because it acknowledges that some types of cohabitation are consistent with the practice of the faith. This is itself an impressive achievement. Our earlier findings (above, 3.2.e) that present cohabitation trends may in part be a product of the eclipse of betrothal; that the eclipse of betrothal had more to do with the transmission of wealth than with the transmission of tradition or faith; and that the recovery of betrothal is essential to the recovery of marriage as a life-process, all add weight to this conclusion. The increasing popularity of cohabitation was said to be 'an opportunity and a challenge to the Church to articulate its doctrine of marriage in ways so compelling, and to engage in a practice of marriage so life-enhancing, that the institution of marriage regains centrality'.[92] The report provides an opportunity to reconsider betrothal and to thank God for the hundreds of thousands of couples who, in defiance of the churches' official teaching, are reminding us in the churches that they are sharing part of the Christian tradition after all.

---

91 Forcibly stated by Jo McGowan, 'Marriage versus Living Together', in Scott and Warren, *Perspectives in Marriage*, pp. 125-29 (127).

92. *Something to Celebrate*, p. 118.

Chapter 5

A THEOLOGY OF LIBERATION FOR CHILDREN

The argument of this chapter will establish a renewed emphasis on the importance of children to the institution of marriage, and so to its contemporary meaning. Children quickly became the chief justification for marriage in the early church. The internal dialogue (above, 2.1) within the early church about the purpose of marriage will be examined, and some of the conclusions reached there about the place of children will be retained. But the exigencies of the external dialogue (above, 2.2) provide the principal reasons for emphasizing the centrality of children in marriage. Many children deprived of the long-term care of both parents *suffer*. They experience childhood as a *form of oppression*. A theology of liberation for children is required which represents children's interests, and incorporates them into a postmodern theology of Christian marriage. Such a theology ironically shares considerable common ground with ancient theologies of marriage, proving once more that very different arguments are capable of yielding very similar conclusions. Now that the old procreationism has fallen away (except for official Roman Catholicism), a newer, wiser, child-sensitive, heterosexual, Christian, sexual ethic appears set to announce itself. The Christian faith *is* the gift and practice of liberation. Liberation is the experience of deliverance from all kinds of sin, whether individual and personal, or social and structural, through the victory over sin secured for all of us by Jesus Christ. How might Christian liberation impinge upon children and their parents?

1. Beginning with Children

It must first be admitted that children do not occur in *any* of the biblical models for marriage examined and represented in Chapter 3. Perhaps the connection between marriage and children was simply taken for granted. The children of Hosea and Gomer add to the pain of Judah's infidelity to the covenant. Their names derive from the estrangement between their parents,[1] and they call their mother to account for her neglect. This detail might support the common-sense view that children are adversely influenced by the perpetual lack of parental care, but it does not support the view that the marriage covenant is primarily for children. There is nothing about the one-flesh model which puts children in a central place. Jesus' use of the model does not suggest children. Men and women are blessed by God and commanded to 'Be fruitful and increase' (Gen. 1.28), but the blessing is not formally connected to the institution of marriage. There is no mention of marriage in the creation account of Genesis 1. The woman made from the flesh of the man is to be the man's helper or partner (Gen. 2.18), not a mother. Neither are children among the reasons Jesus gives for prohibiting divorce.

None of the minor models of marriage centre upon children. The 'dubious necessity' model incorporates children into the care which a good wife is supposed to provide for her husband. The 'worldly concession' model bluntly ignores the outcome of children in licensing marriage as a remedy for sin. Children contribute instead to the 'hardships' and 'worldly affairs' that temperate, unmarried Christians avoid. And the mutual love model emphatically celebrates the lovers' love without thought of the likely consequences of the mutual self-surrender which is the subject of the Song of Songs.

a. *Beginning with Children*

A doctrine of marriage which begins with children can be consistent with biblical models for marriage, but it cannot honestly be said to be based on them. What caused children (as a general principle) to become incorporated into Christian justifications for marriage was the need to combat a range of views outside the churches which was hostile to marriage or sexual experience altogether. The second-century Encratites (*enkrateia* means 'continence') held 'that the Christian church had to consist of men and women who were "continent" in the strict sense: they had "contained" the urge to have sexual intercourse with each other'.[2] At the same time Marcion, (*d*. c. 160) holding to a deep duality

---

1. Hos. 1.2-4, 6, 8-9; 2.2.
2. Brown, *Body and Society*, p. 92. They also abstained from meat and wine, linking these with encouragement of sexual activity.

between spirit and matter, influentially taught the necessity for complete renunciation of sexual activity within the Christian community.

> Only by rendering men and women utterly unfamiliar to each other, by demanding that they should renounce the marriages that had previously held them together, and even by dissolving the ties that bound children to their parents, could true Christians come together in a freely chosen communion, undetermined by preexisting family bonds, loyalties, and habits.[3]

The Gnostics, a widespread and diverse group of people, taught that redemption meant the conquest of matter and desire, and the absorption of female matter into male spirit.[4] For Gnostics

> To have intercourse was to open the human body to the firestorm that raged through the universe. Sexual desire was made to stand out in sharp relief as an enduring feature of the unredeemed human person: it stood for the headlong energy of a universe that was opposed to the cool tranquillity of the realm of unmoving spirit.[5]

The early church had the near impossible task of maintaining on the one hand an ethic of sexual holiness which distinguished the people of God from the pagan world, and on the other hand distinguishing the church from extremists who taught that the body, sexual desire and intercourse were too enmeshed in the fallen world ever to be redeemed. 'The continued belief in an imminent Parousia, together with the desire both to avoid the precarious burdens of childbirth and to engage in *spiritual* as opposed to physical procreation, led to the high evaluation of celibacy and virginity'[6] within the mainstream of the church's developing traditions. The second-century apologists countered by deploying the doctrine of creation. Matter was good because God had created it. But it was also 'fallen'. Marriage was also good but sexual desire was tainted with the sinfulness of the fall. The growing position that marriage was justified by its purpose of producing children emphasized the procreative purpose of sex in a context where renunciation, rather than indulgence, was the principal problem. 'We Christians', said Justin Martyr (c. 100–165), 'either marry only to produce children, or, if we

3.   Brown, *Body and Society*, p. 89
4.   Brown, *Body and Society*, pp. 115-21.
5.   Brown, *Body and Society*, p. 116.
6.   Thatcher and Stuart (eds.), *Christian Perspectives*, p. 2. For a detailed elaboration of the point, see 1.2, Richard Price, 'The Distinctiveness of Early Christian Sexual Ethics', in Thatcher and Stuart (eds.), *Christian Perspectives*, pp. 14-32.

refuse to marry, are completely continent.'[7] Christians, the Greek philosopher Athenagoras stated before the Roman Emperor in 177, 'marry only to produce children', adding that that was why they avoided sexual intercourse in pregnancy: 'as the husbandman, throwing the seed into the ground, awaits the harvest, not sowing more upon it, so the procreation of children is the measure of our indulgence in appetite'.[8]

By the beginning of the fourth century only one writer, Lactantius (c. 240–320), had sought to examine marriage in a Christian context. His analysis is remarkably close to the approval of contemporary Roman practices which were not in any case promiscuous.[9] Christians marry for the purpose of having children, he says, in the *Divine Institutes*. They support the Roman marriage law against the pagans. Uniquely among the Christian writers of the period, he sees no harm in sex during pregnancy,[10] and reserves his ire for what he regarded as an abominable but common practice, the abandonment of newborn but unwanted infants. The *Didache* in the early second century, records Christians' abhorrence of abortion.[11] A man who cannot afford to raise his children, Lactantius declares, should refrain from intercourse with his wife.[12] Lactantius's remarks about children are based more on his Christian desire to protect and nurture them, than a desire to formulate a justification for marriage that occupied the middle ground.

Such was the influence of ascetic views that Clement of Alexandria

7.   Justin Martyr, *Apology for Christians* 1.29, cited by John T. Noonan, Jr, *Contraception: A History of its Treatment by the Catholic Theologians and Canonists* (Cambridge, MA: Harvard University Press, 1986), p. 76.

8.   Athenagoras, *Legation on Behalf of Christians* 33, in Noonan, *Contraception*, p. 76.

9.   Judith Evans Grubbs, '"Pagan" and "Christian" Marriage: The State of the Question', *Journal of Early Christian Studies* 2 (1994), p. 411.

10.   Jerome argued against the practice on medical grounds, arguing that 'If a man copulates with a woman at that time, the fetuses conceived are said to carry the vice of the seed, so that lepers and gargantuans are born from this conception, and the corrupted menses makes the foul bodies too small or too big' (*Commentary on Ezechiel* 6.18: see Noonan, *Contraception*, p. 85). Noonan adds, 'It was a common belief that children conceived in menstruation were born sickly, seropurulent, or dead (Pliny, *Natural History* 7.15.67). The protection of future life became the articulated basis for the prohibition of the act as serious sin' (p. 85).

11.   *Did.*, 1.1; 2.1-2; 5.1 and 5.3, cited in Pope John Paul II, *Evangelium vitae* (Dublin: Veritas, undated), p. 97, §54.

12.   Grubbs, '"Pagan" and "Christian Marriage"', p. 398, citing Lactantius, *Divine Institutes* 6.20.25.

(c. 150–215) could ask 'whether we should marry or completely abstain from marriage'. His answer, that 'marriage should be accepted and given its proper place', was qualified by the warning that 'to have intercourse without intending children is to violate nature, which we must take as our teacher'.[13] But this poor argument, based as it is on Stoic natural law, appeals not to the Bible, or distinctively Christian considerations, but to non-Christian philosophy. It would have been possible to have appealed to Ephesians 5 which 'provided a basis for seeing marital intercourse in terms of the demands of marital love'. But, says Noonan, 'this option was generally not selected. Sexual acts and love were not associated. This dissociation was a fundamental choice made by the early Christian writers'. Such reluctance is best explained by the extent to which virginity had already become acclaimed, by the extent of the Gnostic distrust of sexuality, and by a social structure in which arranged marriages had little to do with love.[14]

Clement held that the purpose of marriage was procreation. That was why he forbade marriage to all who were incapable of having children. 'The young are not permitted to marry, the old are no longer permitted to do so. Otherwise, one may marry at any time. So marriage is the desire for procreation, but it is not the random, illicit, or irrational scattering of seed.'[15] Abortion is an evil, not least because a woman who aborts a child *also aborts the flow of human kindness*.[16] Losing sight of all the biblical models of marriage, Clement introduces new grounds for marriage which vary from civic duty to a man's private health policy. Marriage is allowed

> for the sake of our country and for the succession of children and for the completion of the world... Physical illnesses also reveal how necessary marriage is. The loving care of a wife and the depth of her faithfulness exceed the endurance of all other relatives and friends, just as she surpasses them in sympathy. Above all, she prefers to be always at his side and truly she is, as Scripture says, a necessary help (Gen. 2.18).[17]

---

13. Clement of Alexandria, *The Instructor* 2.94-95. See David Hunter, *Marriage in the Early Church* (Minneapolis: Fortress Press, 1992), pp. 43-44.

14. Noonan, *Contraception*, p. 73.

15. Clement of Alexandria, *The Instructor* 2.95. See Hunter, *Marriage*, pp. 44-45.

16. Clement of Alexandria, *The Instructor* 2.96. See Hunter, *Marriage*, p. 45.

17. Clement of Alexandria, *Miscellanies* 2.140. See Hunter, *Marriage*, p. 46.

b. *Children as a 'Good' of Marriage*

John Chrysostom (c. 347–407) found a more adequate theological argument for linking marriage to children. Taking the one-flesh model he argues that the unity of the couple in sexual intercourse embraces the offspring that result from it. He thought 'the "one flesh" is the father, the mother, and the child that is conceived from their intercourse. For the child is formed when the seeds mingle together; in this way they are three in one flesh.'[18] But it was Augustine's theology of marriage, and the role of children within it which was to influence the Western church, forever. It will be necessary to outline this and contrast its context with our own, before utilizing some of his insights in a theology of marriage which celebrates and nurtures children.

Augustine's work *On the Good of Marriage* was written as a *via media* between the two rival theological positions of Jovinian (*d.* c. 405) and Jerome (c. 342–420). Jovinian had denied the superiority of celibacy over marriage, arguing that each was equally acceptable before God. He maintained that the asceticism of Jerome was tainted with Encratism and Manichaeanism.[19] Augustine in the 370s had himself been a Manichee. The Manichees too, like the Encratites, were extreme dualists,[20] but Augustine records that Manichees sometimes had sex together while avoiding intra-vaginal ejaculation; their abhorrence, it is suggested, was (at least sometimes) directed against procreation rather than the sexual acts that led to it.[21] Jerome's intemperate response, *Adversus Jovinianum*, 'seemed to make marriage something worthy of contempt by its very nature'.[22] Augustine sought to show that celibacy was better, but that marriage and procreation were acceptable, less favourable, alternatives.

On the Good of Marriage begins by locating marriage within the

18. John Chrysostom, *Homily 20 on Ephesians* 4. See Hunter, *Marriage*, p. 83.
19. Reynolds, *Marriage in the Western Church*, p. 250.
20. Brown, *Body and Society*, pp. 197-202.
21. Noonan, *Contraception*, p. 120. Noonan notes the term 'shameful slip' in the following extract from Augustine's *Against Faustus* (22.30) as the first reference in Christian theology to the practice of *coitus interruptus* and its condemnation: 'But the perverse law of the Manichees commands that progeny above all be avoided by those having intercourse, lest their God, whom they complain is bound in every seed, should be bound more tightly in what a woman conceives. Therefore their God by a shameful slip is poured out rather than bound by a cruel connection.'
22. Reynolds, *Marriage in the Western Church*, p. 250.

created social order which promotes solidarity and friendship within and beyond the close ties of family.

> Forasmuch as each man is a part of the human race, and human nature is something social, and hath for a great and natural good, the power also of friendship; on this account God willed to create all men out of one, in order that they might be held in their society not only by likeness of kind, but also by bond of kindred. Therefore the first natural bond of human society is man and wife.[23]

Relying on the forming of the woman from the man's side (Gen. 2.15-25) Augustine notes an ontological union between them, enabling them 'to walk together, and look together whither they walk'. After the 'fellowship' of creation comes 'the connexion of fellowship in children, which is the one alone worthy fruit, not of the union of male and female, but of the sexual intercourse'. Augustine makes a distinction between the union of friendship, apart from intercourse, and the union which is sexual.[24] Leaving open the question whether the first human pair might have reproduced asexually if they had not sinned, marriage is said to be a relative good, not 'merely on account of the begetting of children, but also on account of the natural society itself in a difference of sex'.[25] The friendship which exists between husband and wife after children have come and gone is a further good of marriage. 'In good, although aged, marriage, albeit there hath withered away the glow of full age between male and female, yet there lives in full vigor the order of charity between husband and wife'.

Augustine thought all sexual desire was tainted by the fall of the human race, but that marriage was capable of converting the desire for sex into the desire for children. The thought of possible parenthood, he averred, both dampens the ardour and refines the pleasure:

> Marriages have this good also, that carnal or youthful incontinence, although it be faulty, is brought unto an honest use in the begetting of children, in order that out of the evil of lust the marriage union may

---

23. Augustine, *On the Good of Marriage* (*De Bono Conjugali*), 1. The translation used here is from Philip Schoff (ed.), *The Nicene and Post-Nicene Fathers*, II (Buffalo: Christian Literature Co., 1887), pp. 399-413.

24. While Augustine's emphasis on friendship is of particular interest in contemporary discussions, it should be noted both that friendship was understood patriarchally ('a certain friendly and true union of the one ruling, and the other obeying', 1) and that he regarded sexual union as an impediment to friendship.

25. Augustine, *On the Good of Marriage* p. 3.

bring to pass some good. Next, in that the lust of the flesh is repressed, and rages in a way more modestly, being tempered by parental affection. For there is interposed a certain gravity of glowing pleasure, when in that wherein husband and wife cleave to one another, they have in mind that they be father and mother.[26]

Even Paul's 'worldly concession' model of marriage, whereby each partner is bound to satisfy the other's moderate sexual needs, is converted into a good, that of bringing about fidelity.[27] Even if a couple live together for the purpose of having sex, they can be regarded as married if they stay together for life and seek to have children, not just intercourse. The contemporary church may be stricter even than Augustine on this point. But contraception is forbidden: they must not 'be unwilling to have children born to them, or even by some evil work to use means that they be not born'.[28] Following the strict interpretation of Jesus' sayings about divorce, Augustine believes that the marriage bond is indissoluble *for the sake of children* (below, 8.2.e): 'So strong is that bond of fellowship in married persons, that, although it be tied for the sake of begetting children, not even for the sake of begetting children is it loosed'.[29] Such an enduring bond Augustine calls 'a certain sacrament (*sacramentum*) of some greater matter from out (*sic*) this weak mortal state of men'.[30]

One further detail of *On the Good of Marriage* must briefly detain us. In seeking to say how celibacy is better than marriage the distinction is

---

26. Augustine, *On the Good of Marriage* p. 3.

27. Augustine, *On the Good of Marriage* pp. 4, 6. However, in *On Holy Virginity*, which Augustine intended as a companion volume to *On the Good of Marriage*, the anxious care involved in being a wife is made into a strong argument for virginity. 'If they were not betrothed when young, they would be despised and rejected till too old to marry; yet even if they were chosen…they either feared childlessness or were burdened by bearing and nurturing children. Their peace of mind would be disturbed by fearing false reports about themselves, or offended by false suspicions of their husbands.' See Kim Power, *Veiled Desire: Augustine's Writing on Women* (London: Darton, Longman & Todd, 1995), pp. 190-91.

28. Augustine, *On the Good of Marriage* p. 5.

29. Augustine, *On the Good of Marriage* p. 7.

30. 'By Augustine's time, the term "sacramentum" had acquired a range of powerful senses and connotations, although its meaning was still far from determined and settled. This accident of translation [from *mystèrion* in Eph. 5.32] conditioned the Christianization of marriage in the West (Reynolds, *Marriage in the Western Church*, pp. xxv-vi). Discussion of marriage as a sacrament is reserved for Chapter 7.

drawn between intrinsic and extrinsic good. Examples given of intrinsic goods are those 'which are to be sought for their own sake, such as wisdom, health, friendship'; examples of extrinsic goods are those 'which are necessary for the sake of somewhat, such as learning, meat, drink, sleep, marriage, sexual intercourse'.[31] These examples are necessary for, or contribute to, the achievement of wisdom, health and friendship, and are never ends in themselves. Now extrinsic goods are rightly used in pursuit of some intrinsic end: when they are used as ends in themselves they are used sinfully. Marriage is never an intrinsic good. Rather it exists simply and solely to promote the extrinsic goods of children and friendship, for within friendship 'subsists the propagation of the human kind, wherein friendly fellowship is a great good'. However good friendship is, marriage and sexual intercourse are not necessary to produce it for, 'such is the state of the human race now...there fails not numerous progeny, and abundant succession, out of which to procure holy friendships'. And since marriage and sex are not necessary for producing the extrinsic good of friendship, it is better not to choose them. 'It is good to marry, because it is good to beget children, to be a mother of a family: but it is better not to marry.' The goods of marriage, Augustine concludes, on account of which marriage is a good', are 'offspring, faith, sacrament'.[32] The first two are shared 'throughout all nations and men'. The third, the sacramental bond which not even separation can dissolve, is the distinction between Christian and non-Christian marriage. Pope Pius XI called these goods 'a splendid summary of the whole doctrine of Christian marriage'.[33]

These glimpses of early Christian attitudes to children may be construed to support a child-centred approach to marriage but, it will soon be argued, there are stronger reasons still for linking marriage, essentially, conceptually and definitionally, to children. Before tackling this task let us note what might be carried forward from the present discussion. Children begin to feature as a principal reason for marriage, especially as belief in the imminent return of Christ becomes less influential. The practices of infanticide and abortion are sins against the Creator, and Clement worries also about the impact of seeking an abortion *on the character of the parents*. Chrysostom further opens up the one-flesh model of marriage to include children born from and into

31. Augustine, *On the Good of Marriage* p. 9.
32. Augustine, *On the Good of Marriage* p. 32.
33. Pius XI, *Casti Connubii* (Vatican City: Vatican Press, 1930), section 2.

it. Augustine suggests that reflection on the possible procreative consequences of heterosexual love-making changes the lovers' perspective
on what they do. One of the reasons for the indissolubility of the marriage bond is for the well-being of children. Even Augustine's stern
feminist critic, Kim Power, allows that,

> in his perceptions of marital love as a sacramental bonding directed
> towards wholeness, is the possibility of a new perception of sexual rela-
> tionships, where mutual love both creates and heals the 'one flesh',
> bringing it to perfection in God... This aspect of his theology of mar-
> riage preserves his insights based on experience that loving partnerships
> bond in a deeper manner than those liaisons founded on sexual attraction
> only... His insistence on the *caritas conjugalis* that bonds husband and
> wife offers fruitful possibilities for a contemporary theology of marriage.
> When a marriage is understood as a partnership of equals, it then
> expresses the full friendship of peers who can enjoy each other.[34]

The early church's attitudes to marriage and children will influence
the contemporary church to the extent that similarities exist between its
time and our own. But there are also dissimilarities which might suggest different solutions required to be proposed today. The fourth century was a time of unparalleled confidence and expansion as the Christian faith spread across the Roman world. 'Postmodernity' suggests a
loss of faith, an incredulity towards religious explanations of the world
and of morality. The contrast here lies between the joyful embrace of a
new faith and the abandonment of an old one. For the 'Good News' of
the gospel to be heard as good news, it must speak to the present situation, not to some other one. The dialogue partners of the theologians
who were to shape the church's attitude to marriage were either other
theologians (the trilogy of Jovinian, Jerome and Augustine is a good
example), world-denying ascetics on the fringes of the church, or
beyond it altogether, or loosely-defined movements (like Gnosticism)
which were religious and heretical. The most popular philosophy of the
Roman Empire was Stoicism which urged sexual restraint and provided
strong support for marriage. Much of it was adopted by Christians such
as Clement.

In this milieu Augustine had to attempt a justification for marriage
in the face of condemnations of it from people inside and outside the
churches. Today's postmodern context represents a movement away
from the assumption of 'mandatory marriage' (Gillis's phrase: above,

34. Power, *Veiled Desire*, p. 233.

4.2.d) and is quite different. If a justification of marriage is needed now, it will not be as a second-best defence against asceticism but a rationale for it in the light of reasons why it is being abandoned. A contemporary theology of marriage cannot replicate ancient assumptions about gender hierarchy, the association between sexuality and sin, and the warfare between spirit and body. In the light of these differences it may not be the answers of a previous generation which instruct us but how they coped with the questions as we subject the horizons of our diverse thinking to the demands of the gospel.

A method for doing this might already be provided for us by the author of the Letter to the Ephesians who (above, 3.2.a), perhaps with pardonable eagerness and lack of precision, linked the experience of marriage directly to the Church's experience of Christ. We could do this a bit differently, making connections between the new, inclusive humanity or reign of God which Jesus inaugurated and our experience of marriage now. Within this reality, there is a depth of non-possessive devotion, of profound, unfailing love and solidarity in being equally in need of divine grace and in receipt of it. Marriage is able to be a *locus* where these virtues are glimpsed. The eclipse of marriage has harmed children (below, 5.2), yet children too are willed by God to be the recipients of grace through the mediation of their parents. For the sake of children the sacrament of divine-human love must be recovered and re-commended. Children were a missing feature of secular sexual ethics (above, 2.3.a); now is the time to place them centre-stage.

2. A Theology of Liberation for Children

a. Children as Victims

A vast amount of evidence has been gathered in the USA and Britain which shows that children who grow up with one parent, generally with their mother, are less likely to thrive than children who grow up with their two natural parents. This evidence is disturbing, and it is necessary to handle it without undermining the remarkable work done by single parents in raising children on their own. Some children raised by single parents turn out *better* than children with both natural parents. Some single parents make truly herculean efforts to ensure that, as far as lies in their power, their children are not disadvantaged by the absence of a parent. Single mothers in Britain have recently been scapegoated as scroungers and as a source of social evil, as if they and they only are to blame for the social crisis they are allowed to symbolize. In drawing attention to the causes of children's failure to thrive, one does so for the children's sake and for no other reason. These *caveats* can hardly be over-emphasized.

In March 1998 there were over 71 million children under 18 living in the United States, of whom 48 million, or 68%, were living with both parents. Nearly 17 million children were living with their mother only, over 5 times as many as those living with their father only.[35] In 1991 the USA's nonpartisan National Commission on Children indicated that male adolescents who are fatherless 'lack their essential mentor and role model, and suffer the consequences in higher criminal behavior, serious psychological problems, educational failure, moral debilitation, and involvement with surrogate fathers in the gang context that is now so damaging in our nation'.[36] The Commission says:

> Families formed by marriage—where two caring adults are committed to one another and to their children—provide the best environment for bringing children into the world and supporting their growth and development. Where this commitment is lacking, children are less likely to receive care and nurturing, as well as basic material support. Research on the effects of single parenthood confirms that children who grow up without the support and personal involvement of both parents are more vulnerable to problems throughout childhood and into their adult lives.[37]

The report shows that 'rising rates of divorce, out-of-wedlock child-bearing, and absent parents are not just manifestations of alternative lifestyles, they are patterns of adult behavior that increase children's risk of negative consequences'.[38] Moreover, 'following divorce, or when parents do not marry, many children experience not only financial hardship, but psychological and emotional injury as well'. Parents divorcing in the 1970s and 1980s may have been *unaware* of the harmful effects of divorce on children. However much it may appear obvious that in general children suffer adversely as a result of divorce,

35. US Census Bureau, *Current Population Survey Reports* (March 1998).

36. Stephen Post, *Spheres of Love: Toward a New Ethics of the Family* (Dallas: Southern Methodist University Press, 1994), p. 2. He cites a conclusion of the (North American) National Commission on Children, *Beyond Rhetoric: A New American Agenda for Children and Families* (Washington, DC: US Government Printing Office, 1991).

37. *Beyond Rhetoric*, p. 251, quoted in Post, *Spheres of Love*, p. 3.

38. *Beyond Rhetoric*, p. 66, quoted in Post, *Spheres of Love*, p. 53.

'divorce was thought to be a brief crisis that soon resolved itself'.[39] The Commission calls for a 'renewed commitment to children and families—to marriage, parenthood, and childhood'.[40] The 'mounting evidence', continues Stephen Post, is that,

> with exceptions, children who grow up in single-parent families do less well than those who grow up in intact nuclear families, and that this is true regardless of race, class or sex... The greatest suffering for children results from unmarried teenage pregnancy. In 1990...67.1 percent of teen births in 1990 were nonmarital, in contrast to 30 percent in 1970. 28 per cent of total births in 1990 were to unmarried women...of all births to African-American women 66.5 percent were to unmarried. An estimated half of white and greater than 90 percent of African-American teen mothers are unmarried.[41]

A later report[42] confirms the Commission's conclusions. Girls brought up by unmarried mothers are more

> likely to become unmarried mothers themselves and at increasingly young ages. Male children of unmarried mothers are not likely to become responsible husbands or fathers. The community, in turn, pays a monetary and social cost. Emotional incapacitation, aggressive behaviors, educational failure, relative poverty, need for psychological help, more delinquencies regardless of family income, depression, suicide, substance abuse, and nonmarital pregnancies are among the variables that increase when a child does not have the advantages of a loving mother and father sharing the often overwhelming responsibilities of parenthood. These realities are demonstrated by the longitudinal studies now available for the first time.[43]

Weighing all the evidence Post concludes,

> It is urgent that our culture understand this: Without the experience of parental love the child lives in resentment and anger that makes it much more difficult to love others; the more likely result of such absence of parental love is that the child will inflict wanton harms on self and others. Potential parents must then be prepared to care for the children

39.   Judith S. Wallerstein, 'Children After Divorce: Wounds That Don't Heal', in Scott and Warren (eds.), *Perspectives on Marriage*, pp. 337-46 (337).

40.   *Beyond Rhetoric*, pp. 66, 68, quoted in Post, *Spheres of Love*, p. 53.

41.   Post, *Spheres of Love*, p. 56.

42.   Sara McLanahan and Gary Sandefur, *Uncertain Childhood, Uncertain Future: Growing Up with a Single Parent* (Cambridge, MA: Harvard University Press, 1994).

43.   Quoted in Post, *Spheres of Love*, pp. 56-57.

they will bring into the world, lest a generation of children be lost to themselves and society.[44]

Studies in Britain confirm this depressing picture. The likelihood of negative consequences for children of parents born outside marriage or cared for by a single parent led the ethical socialist A.H. Halsey to write,

> No one can deny that divorce, separation, birth outside marriage and one-parent families as well as cohabitation and extra-marital sexual intercourse have increased rapidly. Many applaud these freedoms. But what should be universally acknowledged is that the children of parents who do not follow the traditional norm (i.e. taking on personal, active and long-term responsibility for the social upbringing of the children they generate) are thereby disadvantaged in many major aspects of their chances of living a successful life. On the evidence available such children tend to die earlier, to have more illness, to do less well at school, to exist at a lower level of nutrition, comfort and conviviality, to suffer more unemployment, to be more prone to deviance and crime, and finally to repeat the cycle of unstable parenting from which they themselves have suffered.[45]

Part of the evidence is produced by the National Child Development Study which has monitored all 17,000 children born in England, Scotland and Wales in the week 3-9 March 1958 on a regular basis. Six hundred of these were born outside marriage. An early study published in 1971[46] showed that 'on average the life-long socially-certified monogamous family on the pre-1960s pattern was better for children than any one of a variety of alternatives practically applicable to large urban populations'. There was 'a striking amount of downward social mobility among the mothers of the children of the uncommitted fathers'. 'The characteristics, experiences and achievements of the average child

---

44. Post, *Spheres of Love*, p. 73.

45. A.H. Halsey, 'Foreword', in Norman Dennis and George Erdos, *Families without Fatherhood* (London: Institute of Economic Affairs Health and Welfare Unit, 1993), p. xii. See also Morgan, 'Conflict and Divorce', pp. 19-20. A leading researcher in the United States draws attention to the naive and optimistic ignorance, as late as the 1970s, among parents, sociologists and the caring professions, on the effects on children of divorce. See Wallerstein, 'Children After Divorce', p. 337.

46. E. Crellin, M.L. Kellmer Pringle and P. West, *Born Illegitimate: Social and Economic Implications* (Windsor: NFER, 1971), cited by Dennis and Erdos in *Families without Fatherhood*, p. 34.

of the married father were markedly different from those of the average child of the uncommitted father.' Among children of uncommitted fathers there was a 'higher perinatal mortality'. Twice as many had some form of proteinuria connected with their mothers' smoking habits. These children had more accidents, weighed less at birth, were less likely to have a parent available to them during working hours, were three times as likely to have financial problems, lived in worse housing. Eleven per cent of children of uncommitted fathers had had to be taken into care for longer or shorter periods. They did far less well at school, and their lives were disrupted by having to move more often. When adjustments to the figures were made to take into account social class composition, '*within each class* the non-committed-father group contained a higher proportion of maladjusted children'.[47]

These depressing conclusions have been confirmed by further studies.[48] The connections between family breakdown and the huge increase in crime in the last 30 years are horrendous.[49] Halsey rightly mocks the inconsistency of many socialists in the 1980s in Britain in appearing to promote a radical individualism in the personal sphere while advocating socialist solutions to social problems elsewhere.[50] Writing in 1993 he insists,

> It is not maintained that traditionally reared children will all be healthy, intelligent and good; nor that children from parentally deprived homes will all turn out to be sickly, stupid and criminal; nor that all male youths who do not intend to marry have an appetite for destruction.

What is offered are 'multiple causes of multiple effects' which give us 'estimates of statistical association'. These provide strong support for

47.   Dennis and Erdos, *Families without Fatherhood*, pp. 37-42 (author's emphasis).

48.   E.g., the follow-up study done on 264 men and women studied in Newcastle-upon-Tyne, England, in 1979–80 whose details were known to the researchers from an earlier study when they were babies in 1947. See Dennis and Erdos, *Families without Fatherhood*, Chapter 5, pp. 48-54. See also, Jack Dominian, *et al.* (eds.), *Marital Breakdown and the Health of the Nation* (London: One Plus One: Marriage and Partnership Research, 1991); and Monica Cockett and John Tripp, *Family Breakdown and its Impact on Children: The Exeter Family Study* (Exeter: University of Exeter Press, 1994).

49.   See Norman Dennis, *Rising Crime and the Dismembered Family* (London: Institute of Economic Affairs Health and Welfare Unit, 1993).

50.   Dennis and Erdos, *Families Without Fatherhood*, p. xiii.

the conclusion, similar to the American National Commission on Children, that 'committed and stable parenting must be a priority of social policy'.[51] Dennis and Erdos speak of the 'resistible rise' of the young 'obnoxious English man', one of whose attributes is remaining 'in a state of permanent puerility'; another attribute is predictable anti-social behaviour; a third is 'progressive liberation…from the expectation that adulthood involves life-long responsibility for the well-being of their wife, and fifteen or twenty years of responsibility for the well-being of their children'.[52] Carol Smart has shown 'that it is extremely difficult for parents to form an ongoing post-divorce relationship with each other, no matter how aware they are of their children's needs'.[53]

Theologians attempting to grasp the extent of the tragedy of child neglect are likely to reflect on the causal connections made between the rampant *economic* individualism of Britain and the USA, from the 1960s onwards, and the *moral* individualism which pursues self-interest and private pleasure as a natural right, and in each case abjures the inconvenient social consequences of selfish actions. 'American liberals and European socialists' are accused of a failure 'to examine the fresh and strong free market elements that have now invaded the area of sex and sociological "fatherhood"'.[54] Jon Davies asks whether '"the market", when defined as the pursuit of individual self-interest, is now so deeply ingrained in our culture that it permeates even intra-familial relationships, hitherto seen as precisely the location of altruistic or other-regarding rather than self-regarding relationships?'[55] Individualism combines in his view with romantic love, so that,

> marriage is now the great romantic act: everything ventured on one great gesture of individualism, with no attention at all being paid to the wider kin, very little (none if that is the way it has to be) to close kin; and not very much to anything other than the most formal of religious or societal obligations. The logic of this drive to individualise the marital decision is of course the drive to individualise the marital relationship itself, with

51. Dennis and Erdos, *Families Without Fatherhood*, p. xiii.
52. Dennis and Erdos, *Families Without Fatherhood*, pp. 4-5; Chapters 7 and 8.
53. Carol Smart, 'The Ties Still Bind', *The Times Higher Education Supplement* (5 September 1997), p. 15.
54. Dennis and Erdos, *Families Without Fatherhood*, p. 68.
55. Jon Davies, 'Introduction', in *idem* (ed.), *The Family*, pp. 4-5.

both spousal and parental obligations being increasingly regarded as
matters of taste and fashion rather than of permanent social commitment'.[56]

Part of the theological critique of late capitalist societies concentrates
on the individualism Davies correctly identifies. Caution is needed in
participating in debates about child deprivation. The utmost respect for
facts is required. There is a danger that proposed corrective measures
deny women the gains they have been able to make in entering the public world by blaming them for the care deficit in the lives of many children. Whatever the ambiguities of the legacy of the sexual revolution of
the 1960s and onwards, there are unambiguous goods which have come
from it, not least gains made by sexual minorities which would not
have been possible without the confirmation of the goodness of sexual
pleasure and the separation of it from procreation which contraception
has substantially achieved. But Christians cannot both criticize the
privatization of faith in late capitalist societies while exempting from
examination the similar process of the privatization of morality. Private
decisions have public consequences with far-reaching and unantici-
pated effects.

An example of unintended effect is provided by people who insist on
making journeys by car when public transport is available or who live
in the countryside while working in the city. Public transport becomes
worse because it is under-used, the countryside becomes urbanized,
the environment polluted, congestion increases and journey times are
lengthened. Economists use the concept 'externalities' to set out the
unintended but actual consequences of private decisions.[57] The huge
cost of externalities in the area of private decisions about the use of
transport are paralleled in the area of private decisions about family
life:

> Private decisions on family structures impose costs on the rest of society.
> And these externalities are considerable. The evidence is that, on
> average, children brought up in a stable, two-parent family do better than
> in other family types... Family break-up often damages children, even
> when it makes one or both of their parents happier. In addition to the

56.   Jon Davies, 'From Household to Family to Individualism', in *idem* (ed.),
The Family: Is it Just Another Lifestyle Choice?, p. 100.
57.   Paul Ormerod and Robert Rowthorn, 'Why Family Ties Bind the Nation',
The Times Higher Education Supplement (29 August 1997), p. 16.

direct harm to children, the subsequent deviant behaviour of some of the victims creates serious costs for the rest of us.[58]

b. *Liberation for Children*

In the face of these woes, nothing less than a theology of liberation for children would be an appropriate Christian response. Davies borrows a term from liberation theology in his advocacy of 'a preferential option for the family',[59] and takes theologians to task, including me, for minimizing the importance of, and even harming, children.[60] However

58. Ormerod and Rowthorn, 'Family Ties', p. 16.

59. Jon Davies, 'A Preferential Option for the Family', in Barton (ed.), *The Family*, pp. 219-36.

60. I am said in *Liberating Sex* to be 'concerned mainly to minimise the role that children have always had in the Christian discussion of sexuality and gender'; to transmit 'the clear message that being married or not doesn't matter'; to ignore an outcome of re-thinking some forms of cohabitation that 'if you wish to increase the number of distressed children, then increase the number of children born into unmarried or cohabiting unions'; and falsely to hold that 'a strong emphasis on marriage can eclipse all other possible sexual relations' (Davies, 'A Preferential Option', pp. 221, 227, 236). These criticisms are unfortunate. The index of *Liberating Sex* records references to children on 29 different pages. The section 'Having Children' (pp. 113-14) eulogizes the place of children in Christian marriage, arguing that 'in conceiving a child, a couple may well experience their life-producing, life-bearing and life-nurturing creative powers as a surging intimation of the creative presence of God' (p. 113). The mystical idea of 'embodied knowledge' is applied to pregnancy and birth, using the theological writings of women, as a 'direct and immediate participation in God', etc. I acknowledge the children of faithful parents are more likely to thrive. I say 'Once it has been agreed that there are many thriving well-balanced children of single parents and many unthriving unbalanced children of married parents, *it is still true that marriage remains the context where children are more likely to receive the care and nurture they need* to become confident and affirming' (p. 91, emphasis added). Faithfulness is praised throughout the book. Reference to the 'complacent assumption' to which Davies takes exception comes at the end of a discussion of the Vatican's 1975 'Declarations on Certain Problems of Sexual Ethics' which, in excluding sexual intercourse for those 'who have a firm intention of marrying', also forbids them the use of contraceptives and makes assumptions about some forms of cohabitation which are simply not true. Reference to the possibility that 'a strong emphasis on marriage can eclipse all other possible sexual relations' comes at the end of a section praising marriage as a sacrament and comparing partners' commitments to each other as worship. 'The rest of the book' (p. 92) takes up these 'other possible sexual relations' including in particular lesbian and gay partnerships. Davies ignores the difference between the Christian readership of a theological book where marriage is

since he uses the term 'liberation' in a pejorative, even sarcastic way,[61] he may underestimate the power of the theology of liberation to address the situation he describes. The theology of liberation is best described in its own terms. It begins with the need to act to end oppression.

> The theology of liberation is the most 'moral' of theologies: firstly, because its methodology postulates praxis as the starting-point and goal of all theological reflection: secondly, because it requires every theologian, and so every moralist, as a Christian, to be committed, militant, as a *sine qua non* condition of undertaking moral theology.[62]

The plight of unwanted and neglected children throughout the world is the starting point of a theology of liberation for them and presupposes an absolute commitment to them.

Another good reason for speaking of a theology of liberation for children is the contrast, developed by Francisco Moreno Rejon, between a liberation ethic and a bourgeois ethic which holds as good for Europe and USA as for Latin America where it was forged. Latin American philosophy, he says,

> has produced a critical response to the ethic of the modern age as based on autonomy and typified as an ethic. It is seen as being: *progressivist* rather than new; *elitist* in the type of questions it tackles; *idealist*, in that it points to goals but ignores the means of reaching them; *privatising* not so much individualist now, but personalist, arguing about concepts such as dialogue-encounter, but not those like domination-dependence; *functionalist*: its interlocutor is the modern-bourgeois world, which it legitimises, not the world of the poor and the people, whereas an ethic centred on liberation has to start with this basic question: How can we be good while liberating ourselves?[63]

There is a striking convergence here between conservative critics of family breakdown and liberationist critics of structural injustice. It is

---

generally regarded as the sole context for full sexual experience, and the actual world, which concerns us both, where marriage is increasingly disregarded.

61.　Morality is being demolished 'in the name of liberation': 'appetitive individualism' is said to be 'so radical a liberator' of adult men from their responsibilities. See Davies, 'A Preferential Option', pp. 221, 232. Dennis and Erdos also use the term in this way, e.g., *Families Without Fatherhood*, p. 5.

62.　Francisco Moreno Rejon, 'Seeking the Kingdom and its Justice: The Development of the Ethic of Liberation', in Mieth Dietmar and Pohier Jacques (eds.), *The Ethics of Liberation*, p. 35.

63.　Rejon, 'Seeking the Kingdom', pp. 38-39.

important that they listen to each other. Autonomy is represented in the familial context by social and sexual behaviour which ignores the inconvenient consequences of the reckless pursuit of pleasure. Progressivism is represented by the discourse which depicts the worsening of life for children as merely a neutral change in circumstances. Privatization is represented by the bracketing-out of medium and long-term consequences of promiscuous heterosexual behaviour as they act negatively on children *and* parents and contribute to the huge social costs of public welfare. And functionalism is represented by the undoubted ability of Western theologians and academics, tautologously, to concern themselves with the issues which concern them, instead of issues caused by the attempt to alleviate suffering. What Antonio Moser says of the Latin American poor might be equally said of many of the children of the rich:

> Throughout the history of ethics, it has always thought *of* the poor, but never *from* them; it has thought of the poor from the point of view of the rich, thinking that touching the hearts of the rich is going to benefit the poor. The ethic of liberation, founded on a different anthropological and theological understanding, seeks to turn the process upside-down: to think from the poor, with them and in favour of them.[64]

A Christian liberation ethic, as opposed to a purely philosophical or political one, must begin, as Tony Misfud argues, 'with the person and action of Jesus Christ as the force inspiring the work of transformation at the personal and the social level'. Secondly, it will allow itself 'to be challenged by *reality*, that is not just a question of translating faith into works, but reality itself is the starting point for a reading of the signs of the times and the ethical verification of our faith'. Thirdly, it will represent '*the standpoint of marginalised humanity*, since the poor and oppressed are the most important "ethical touchstone" by which we can read reality and understand the Good News'. Fourthly, it will be an 'ethic of *solidarity* proposing the crucial values of an alternative common project formulated from the viewpoint and taking up the cause of the poor'. Fifthly, it is 'an ethic of *discernment* capable of taking on the present conflict and directing it responsibly'. And sixthly, it is 'an ethic of *wholeness*, seeking liberation in all human and social dimensions

---

64.   Antonio Moser, 'The Representation of God in the Ethic of Liberation', in Mieth and Pohier (eds.), *The Ethics of Liberation*, pp. 42-47 (46).

and a *universal* ethic calling upon us all to take up the cause of the poor and impoverished'.[65]

All six of these features of a Christian liberation ethic invite application in the context of a theology of liberation for children. The situation of children in the world today is hugely worse than the one just depicted of children in the rich countries of Europe and USA. '40,000 children die every day from malnutrition and quite common illnesses, 150 million children have to fight with damaged health and disrupted growth, and 100 million children between six and eleven do not go to school'.[66] Nonetheless, the complex of structural sin may be said to be responsible for the plight of all such children, given a theological analysis of how the rich countries of the world have manipulated the global economy for their own selfish ends. A rich country exploiting the resources of a poor country, and a male citizen of a rich country exploiting his powers of fertility by fathering unwanted children have much in common. Both act selfishly and uncaringly, with no thought for the wider implications of their actions on present and future generations. They/we are sinners awaiting liberation through 'the person and action of Jesus Christ' who remarked that 'if anyone causes the downfall of one of these little ones who believe in me, it would be better for him to have a millstone hung round his neck and be drowned in the depths of the sea' (Mt. 18.6).

The '*reality*' of children's experience cannot be detached from an adequate theology of marriage. 'Loyalty to experience', one of the methodological principles of this study (above, 1.2.d), demands that the suffering experience of children becomes determinative. Children too can be marginalized. They are often the ones with no voice, the unconsulted and sometimes undeserving victims of oppression, even if their parents are the oppressors. A 'reading of the signs of the times' from the standpoint of suffering children enables a clearer vision of just how horrible is the hedonism that puts self-interest and short-term happiness above everything else. The ethic of solidarity required for a theology of

65. Tony Misfud, 'The Development of a Liberation Ethic in the Documents of the Church since Vatican II', in Mieth and Pohier, *The Ethics of Liberation*, pp. 48-53 (53).

66. Norbert Mette, 'Not a "Century of the Child": the Situation of Children in the World in the 1990s', in Junker-Kenny and Mette (eds.), *Little Children Suffer*, pp. 3-8 (3-4).

liberation has been sketched elsewhere,[67] and rests on the empathic identification and discernment of the suffering Christ with the suffering neighbour (Mt. 25.31-46).

This study must confine itself to the immense contribution that a Christian understanding of marriage can make to the well-being of children. Partners have made unbreakable promises to each other in a covenant which is a sign of the unbreakable covenant-love of God in Christ. One of the reasons for entering into the covenant is that the partners are generally prepared to become parents, and their commitment to each other is able to provide the stability and steadfast love their children require. Their becoming one flesh in sexual union, and the provision of a home and committed parenting to their children, is God's way of sharing with them the sacred work of person-making. But having children and caring for them are part of the same continuum. A Christian heterosexual ethic must be one which safeguards children's interests and which therefore sanctions only those sexual practices which do so.

The reasons for the need to give priority to children in a heterosexual sexual ethic are found in Aquinas, and they should be able to be endorsable even by Christians who think that his view of marriage is too narrow. When Aquinas categorized fornication as a mortal sin, his reason for doing so was that the risk of having a child was against the interests of that child, should she or he be born. 'Simple fornication', he wrote, 'is contrary to the love we should bear our neighbour, for…it is an act of generation performed in a setting *disadvantageous to the good of the child to be born*.'[68] Perhaps surprisingly Aquinas compares the sin of lust with the sin of gluttony, and in themselves he finds them both trivial. Lust is a serious sin, not because it represents a loss of self-control or is a capitulation to pleasure, but because its possible consequences have the capacity to impair an entire life:

> One act of intercourse can beget a child, and therefore its inordinateness, which handicaps a child to be born, is a grave sin from the kind of act that it is, not merely because of the intemperateness of the lust. One meal does not normally upset the good of individual life taken as a whole, and therefore an act of gluttony is not of its very nature a grave

67. Stuart and Thatcher, *People of Passion*, Chapter 2, 'Passionate Ethics', pp. 25-57.

68. Aquinas, *Summa Theologiae* 2a2ae.154.2 (emphasis added).

sin. Nevertheless it would be, as was the case with Adam, if committed by someone who knew full well how it would spoil his entire life.[69]

These observations lose none of their force when reapplied in a contemporary context. Aquinas assumes that casual sex is a sin against the practice of neighbour-love, and the neighbour sinned against is the possible child. He assumes that the sexual behaviour of adults ought to be regulated by their ability to reproduce. He holds that marriage is an institution which benefits children because the commitments involved embrace them and provide a long term secure context for their upbringing. 'Obviously', he remarks (in a later comment on the betrothal of Mary and Joseph), 'the birth of children is started through sexual intercourse, but their training is carried through by other functions of the husband and wife as when they help each other to bring up their children.'[70] And marriage is the state whereby natural parents are dedicated not simply to each other and to their children but specifically to helping each other as they assume joint responsibility for their children's upbringing.

c. *Liberation for Mothers*

The reign of God is the end of oppression, and the Christian mind, attuned to the rhetoric of automatic self-sacrifice, should not leap to the conclusion that liberation for children can only be achieved at the expense of yet more selfless parental, usually maternal, devotion. Caring for children, involvement in their lives, nudging them to maturity and weaning them from total, helpless dependence to mature independence *can* be a matter of great personal fulfilment for the carers as well as the cared-for. The obvious problem with such a claim is its dangerous complacency. Relative poverty can transform the care of children into an intolerable burden. Further, in modern societies mothers are disproportionately burdened with child care (above, 2.1.c). While much progress has been made in the present century in enabling women, some of whom are also wives and mothers, to participate in the wider society, there can be no liberation for mothers without a huge change in the practice of fatherhood by husbands. This in turn, despite the efforts of individual married men who consciously set aside the models of manliness provided for them by the patriarchal societies in which they

---

69. Aquinas, *Summa Theologiae* 2a2ae.154.3.
70. Aquinas, *Summa Theologiae* 3a.29.2.

grow up, cannot be achieved without further *social* changes which individually cannot be brought about.

Feminist theology draws the important distinction

> between the potential relationship of every woman to her powers of reproduction and to children on the one hand, and motherhood as a social, cultural, and religious institution and ideology on the other. It is the institution of motherhood that keeps this potential, and women and children, under patriarchal control, and disempowers women.[71]

The institution has become so powerful it passes itself off as natural. In this respect it shares much with the mistaken belief that marriages have always begun with weddings (above, 4.2) or that female virginity has always been valued for religious reasons (above, 4.2.d). In fact 'the idealisation of the mother in looking after her children, her capacity to give birth, her care of the disadvantaged and deep religious feeling' is said to be 'an astonishingly new phenomenon' which 'arose with the nineteenth century relegation of religion and love of neighbour to the private sphere of the bourgeois family'.[72] As paid work moved increasingly outside the home, women were increasingly excluded from paid work. The home became 'the bourgeois woman's sphere'. While the husband and father becomes increasingly absent from the family, his absence means that 'the mother, whose relegation to the smaller family has made her socially powerless, becomes psychically over-dominant within it'.[73] Similar processes occurred in the United States and probably in all industrialized countries. In the seventeenth and eighteenth centuries American colonial fathers 'had primary responsibility for child care beyond the early nursing period'.[74]

The same bourgeois values which confine women to the domestic sphere also have a disastrous effect on women's sexuality and bodily

71.   Anne Carr and Elisabeth Schüssler Fiorenza (eds.), 'Editorial', *Motherhood: Experience, Institution & Theology, Concilium* 206 (6/1989), p. 3. The authors were commenting on the work of Adrienne Rich, *Of Woman Born: Motherhood as Experience and Institution* (New York: W.W. Norton, 1976), especially Chapter 10. See also Sara Ruddick, *Maternal Thinking: Toward a Politics of Peace* (Boston: Beacon Press, 1989), pp. 28-57.

72.   Johanna Kohn-Roelin, 'Mother—Daughter—God', in Carr and Schüssler-Fiorenza, *Motherhood*, pp. 64-72 (65).

73.   Kohn-Roelin, 'Mother', *Motherhood*, p. 65.

74.   Mary Francis Berry, *The Politics of Parenthood: Child Care, Women's Rights and the Myth of the Good Mother* (New York: Viking, 1993), p. 42.

self-esteem. Lawrence Stone says that in Victorian Britain 'prudery reached extraordinary heights...'

> Girls were taught by their culture to assume that they were frail and sickly, and as a result they seriously believed that they were, and in fact became so... For the first time in Western history there was a strong body of opinion which actually denied the existence of the sexual drive in the majority of women, and regarded the minority who experienced it to any marked degree as morally, mentally or physically diseased.[75]

Women's recovery in the twentieth century of their sexuality and of their rightful existence outside the home, are part of the same socio-moral process. In achieving this they are right to be suspicious of the institution of marriage, since it was used as an instrument of repression against them.

The New Familialism. Stephen Post has called for a 'new familialism that looks forward rather than backward', whose principles are '(a) children first and (b) fairness in gender roles, allowing women the same economic, social, and political opportunities as men if they wish them'.[76] Most issues facing marriage, he thinks, 'have to do with modifications of gender roles in the context of modern society and its demands, and with the removal of behavior oppressive to women'. The 'new familialism' coincides remarkably with the post-patriarchal marriage commended in this book.[77] The influential work of Susan Moller Okin on gender, justice and the family is said to be able to be used as a theological resource to 'correct' 'traditional Christian teachings on

75. Lawrence Stone, *The Family*, pp. 645, 675-76.
76. Post, *Spheres of Love*, p. 4.
77. A point of difference, however, lies in Post's advocacy of 'Dyadic Theism' in which 'The image of a mother-father God can bestow additional religious meaning on marriage. This is because under such an image, wife and husband conjoined reflect the feminine and masculine aspects of God' (see pp. 20-26). Whereas the restoration of gender-inclusive concepts and understandings of God are vital to the future of Christian theism, the postulation of a male/female dyad in God analogous to the male/female dyad of heterosexual marriage appears anthropomorphic and to do violence to the doctrine of the Trinity. The doctrine of the Trinity comes fully equipped with concepts of person, coequality, codependence, relationality and self-less love that the new familialism actually requires.

marriage'.[78] The point must be central to *any* account of marriage, religious or secular:

> women are vulnerable in gendered marriage because their social, political, and economic rights to equal opportunities are often violated. It is important that men engage in direct caregiving and nurturing of children, and that women who choose professions and other public roles be able to do so.[79]

The learning of injustice within the family leads to a tolerance of injustice in the wider society, and so has a double negative effect. We have already noted a male historian's belief (above, 2.1.f) that marriage can *never* be a matter of equality, however smooth the rhetoric. Okin also refers to 'equal sharing between the sexes of family responsibilities' as the 'great revolution that has not happened'.[80] She insists fathers and mothers must care equally for children, and that it 'is morally unacceptable to encourage family caregiving and self-denial without strongly asserting that direct caregiving roles must be as much the domain of men as of women'.[81]

The love of mothers for children has itself been a source of rich reflection in recent feminist theology. These profound analyses, which appear to be unknown outside feminist theology, begin with experience and lay theological foundations for a theology of the family grounded in the experience of its members. Sally Purvis, identifying three overlapping characteristics of mother-love and divine love posits mother-love as a 'model for *agape*'.[82] Mother-love, she says, is first 'inclusive' because 'there is a disposition on the mother's part to devote herself to the well-being of the child from birth and for its lifetime without knowing the particular talents or future achievements of that small person'. Mother-love flows equally to all the mother's children even when 'they may not be equally appealing'. Secondly, mother-love 'is both intensely involved and other-regarding', yet 'while the needs of the child may conflict with the needs of the mother, and often do, there are instances

---

78. Susan Moller Okin, *Justice, Gender and the Family* (New York: Basic Books, 1989). See also Post, *Spheres of Love*, p. 27.

79. Post, *Spheres of Love*, p. 27.

80. Okin, *Justice*, p. 4.

81. Post, *Spheres of Love*, p. 93.

82. Sally Purvis, 'Mothers, Neighbors and Strangers: Another Look at Agape', in Thatcher and Stuart (eds.), *Christian Perspectives*, pp. 232-46 (236). Subsequent references are to pp. 237-43.

when the interests of the child and the interests of the mother coincide. That is, the *mother's need* may be to feed the child, comfort her, rock, him, etc'. Thirdly, 'mother-love is unconditional. It is not dependent upon nor can it be cancelled by the behavior of the child'. While 'mothers do not manage in any sustained way' these ideal characteristics of mother-love, 'significant parallels' may be drawn between these and the love taught by Jesus in the Gospels and particularly in the parable of the good Samaritan (Lk. 10.29-37). While mother-love is by no means 'the *only* agapic model in human experience', the profound Christian experience of it may be sharply contrasted with the institution of motherhood as patriarchy has shaped it.

Shared Parenthood. Lisa Sowle Cahill's excellent and compelling study, *Sex, Gender and Christian Ethics* incorporates parenthood into the meanings given to the female body. While she welcomes the advances in sexual ethics made in particular by liberal Protestants and thinks 'Western Christian sexual ethics needs to finish cleaning its own house',[83] she is entirely right to warn against two defects in the revisionist concensus in sexual ethics now emerging in Britain and the USA. First it tends 'to neglect the social meanings of the body realized through parenthood and kinship'. Secondly, while Christian ethicists engage (disengage?) with the tradition and its emphasis on procreation, it is easy to overlook that the issues gripping people outside the churches differ enormously. In the terms used above (2.1, 2.2) the internal and external dialogues are in danger of coming apart. So while Christian ethics rightly 'engages its own procreation-focused past with a hermeneutic of suspicion', it 'fails to deal with the fact that cultural attitudes may be *at the opposite end of the spectrum from any procreative ethos*, or any requirement that sex be limited to lifelong marriage'.[84] Christians of all denominations face 'a new generation of sexual attitudes and practices in liberal democratic societies' which present 'mutual consent as practically the sole behavior-guiding norm, and hardly encourages ongoing responsibility either for one's sexual partner, or for the procreative potentials of sex'.[85]

Cahill's 'project' is 'to achieve a theory of morality in which the

---

83. Lisa Sowle Cahill, *Sex, Gender and Christian Ethics* (Cambridge: Cambridge University Press, 1996), p. 11.

84. Cahill, *Sex*, p. 10.

85. Cahill, *Sex*, pp. 10-11.

body and culture are in reasonable balance'.[86] There are 'commonalities of human experience'[87] which logically precede *any* social ordering, by means of institutions such as heterosexuality and monogamy. These commonalities include 'sexual differentiation (male–female); sexuality; kinship, both vertical and lateral...'[88] As soon as these commonalities become socially ordered, theological questions arise about the ultimate ends of human life. Two such questions involve gender and family. Is 'bodily differentiation of reproductive function, as male and female...either so clear and certain as supposed, or so indicative of social roles extending beyond conception, pregnancy, and birth?'[89] The second question 'involves the relative importance and possible interdependence of intentional commitment and biological kinship in forming families'.

A feminist treatment of these questions asks 'whether, in a non-dualist perspective, the differential embodiment of men and women must be assumed to make a difference in their way of being in the world, even if not a difference which implies hierarchy'.[90] Cahill answers affirmatively:

> Surely women's diffuse and receptive sexuality, cyclic reproductive capacity, and deeply connective relation to their children both born and unborn, contribute to women's sense of self. Women's embodied experience could not be identical to that afforded by men's sharply focused but uneasily controlled sexual response, perennial but momentaneous capacity to impregnate; the necessity to do so by means of an externally borne and hence vulnerable member; and a man's need to work out a social relation to his children without the easy and ready support of natural bodily relations (pregnancy and lactation) which place their mutual consciousness within the context of primal need fulfilment. Part of the point of feminism is that one's sense of self and relation to others does not or should not reside solely in one's sexual and reproductive experience. But to the extent that such experience is one component of one's self and one's social relations, gender infuses these realities along with many other factors.[91]

Cahill concludes that motherhood is 'a distinctive experience of

86. Cahill, *Sex*, p. 76.
87. Cahill, *Sex*, p. 80.
88. Cahill, *Sex*, p. 78.
89. Cahill, *Sex*, p. 80-81.
90. Cahill, *Sex*, p. 84.
91. Cahill, *Sex*, p. 85.

women',[92] while taking great care to acknowledge the wretchedness
that sometimes accompanies it, the inevitable ambivalent feelings
which mothers sometimes have towards their children, the fact that
women are not 'defined only or primarily by motherhood', and that the
'fundamental separability' of sexual intimacy and procreation 'has
helped make the moral defense of homosexuality possible'.[93] Motherhood is nonetheless a distinctive experience of being human.

> Insofar as it is a relation to one's children, motherhood is in many
> cultures, and perhaps universally, an avenue of fulfilment and flourishing
> for women—as fatherhood should be for men—though patriarchal con-
> trol over motherhood and economic deprivation as a condition of it are
> most certainly not.[94]

In 'the ideal family', she continues,

> both biological parents nurture children physically and emotionally, and
> educate them by example for larger social roles; in which parents and
> children are supported by a 'kin' network; and in which parents are
> fulfilled not only through sexually expressed love for each other, but
> through mutual and equal dedication to offspring, to family, and to the
> larger community'.[95]

The ideal *Christian* family not only ensures 'its own welfare, or even
that of the clan, but is able to extend altruistic identification with, and
sacrifice for, kin to include neighbors, more distant community members, and even strangers'.[96] 'The task of a Christian social ethic of sex
is to imbue sexual and reproductive behavior with the qualities of
respect, empathy, reciprocity, and mutual fidelity which would allow
sexual *and parental* love to be transforming agents in society in general.'[97]

Where, the impatient reader might demand, is liberation for mothers
in these theoretical descriptions? It is necessary to admit that, if
improvements for mothers are conditional on the cooperation of fathers,
liberation will be hard to achieve. Inasmuch as liberation depends on
the removal of injustice, such talk of liberation may be little more than
bourgeois cavil. And no matter how gender relations are reconstituted,

92. Cahill, *Sex*, p. 87.
93. Cahill, *Sex*, p. 81.
94. Cahill, *Sex*, p. 89.
95. Cahill, *Sex*, p. 107.
96. Cahill, *Sex*, p. 107. See also Post, *Spheres of Love*, Chapter 8, pp. 129-46.
97. Cahill, *Sex*, p. 119 (emphasis added).

poverty will always bring oppression in its wake. While giving these reservations their full weight, this male author tentatively puts forward four suggestions.

First, the love of mothers for their children is the principal means whereby God the Father loves their children too (but see below, 5.2.d). Mother-love *is* a poignant and excellent model of *agape*. But the question must be raised to what extent Christian mothers see mothering in this light. If the answer is 'almost never', at least two competing explanations are possible. It may be unconvincing. Or, it may be that Christian teaching, historically in the hands of men, has never made the obvious and enriching links between the outpouring of the divine love in Jesus Christ and the outpouring of maternal love for children. But a Christian theology which has overcome patriarchy and soul–body dualism, and which has no fear of the bodies of women, will be increasingly able to make connections between divine, paternal love and human, maternal love. The mother-love model of *agape* has a capacity to transform the Christian consciousness of mothering. It illuminates mothering by rendering it holy. It recognizes childcare as an icon of God's own activity of nurture. It allows the presence of God back into the darkened and mysterious corners of the *domus* beyond the historical experience of the clerical and theological mind.

Secondly, Cahill is right to affirm mothering as an 'avenue of fulfilment for women'. She is careful to affirm this in a non-oppressive way which does not create the expectation that all women will have or want to have children; or that there is anything odd about either those who do not have children or who do have children and do not find the care of children fulfilling. She has acknowledged the liberative possibilities for non-married people of the distinction between reproductive experience and sexual experience, which in late modernity has become an established fact. At the same time she has recognized that secular constructions of female heterosexual sexuality in the same period have transformed this distinction into a separation, and proceeded to rethink sexual ethics as if reproduction and therefore children have *no* part to play in interpersonal intimacy. But the separation of sexual pleasure from sexual reproduction is set to become a new secular dualism as damaging as any of the old religious dualisms between mind and body, spirit and flesh, among others. Any ethic, Christian or secular, which takes embodiment seriously, simply cannot ignore the fact that human bodies reproduce.

Thirdly, since it has been suggested that maternal care is in large measure, divine care, and so is capable of being supported by profound religious meaning, it may now be suggested that this meaning is further elucidated by the Judaeo-Christian models of marriage as covenant and one-flesh union (above, 3.2.a-b). If the marriage covenant embraces children it gives protection to the vulnerable which, in the reign of God, is an absolute priority. The one-flesh model of marriage may have considerable explanatory power in the case of the bonding between mother and child. Is not the union between mother and child also, and in a yet more obvious and literal way, a union of one flesh?

Fourthly, Christian liberation is freedom from sin and the consequences of sin. May we not say that liberation from the Victorian attitudes which denied women sexual feeling and confined their 'sphere' to the home is already a liberation from a sinful, patriarchal ideology? And that when self-giving and self-sacrifice are detached from their due place in the Christian life and made into an ideology that apportions self-giving on the basis of gender only, this too is a sinful, social situation from which Christian liberation is necessary and overdue? Is there not also Christian liberation for mothers in saying a firm 'No' to representations of female sexuality which emphasize availability and attractiveness to men without regard also for women's procreative powers?

d. *Liberation for Fathers*

How might fathers cope with Christian feminist writing about motherhood? By learning from it. An immediate problem is that motherhood, as opposed to parenthood, already assumes what it also laments—the general lack of attention given by fathers to parenting, which in a distressing and increasing number of cases has now become the problem of father-absence. Motherhood would change if fathers changed, and Christian feminists want fathers to change. On the whole fathers do not want to change. Those who do have to learn it all for themselves, for there is little encouragement from other men, and few role-models to emulate. Patterns of employment are slow to accommodate fathers wishing to devote more time to their children or provide stability for the family over time in a single home, school, neighbourhood and church. In these circumstances is liberation for fathers anything more than an empty phrase?

Fathers who do not get involved with their children impoverish themselves. They must surely be unaware of the great loss of personal satisfaction which comes from attentive parenting. Missing out on the opportunity to learn (or relearn) the virtues of tenderness, playfulness and responsiveness with one's child(ren) can result in a lack of what are now called 'social skills' which are needed in interactions with other adults. Marvelling at the gift of a new baby can enhance wonderment at the existence of anything at all and lead to a belief in God the Creator. Agonizing over a child's ill-health or misfortune or prospects can lead to a sensitivity which extends through the child much more broadly to other people, especially other children. Children are generous in what they bestow back. But the loss to uninvolved or absent fathers is nothing when compared to the loss experienced by the children themselves (above, 5.2.a). Pope John Paul II surely speaks for all Christians when he observes

> Above all where social and cultural conditions so easily encourage a father to be less concerned with his family or at any rate less involved in the work of education, efforts must be made to restore socially the conviction that the place and task of the father in and for the family is of unique and irreplaceable importance.[98]

The Pope deplores not merely father-absence but also the 'oppressive presence' of a father, especially where 'there still prevails the phenomenon of "machismo", or a wrong superiority of male prerogatives which humiliates women and inhibits the development of healthy family relationships'.

Cahill's description of non-hierarchical difference between fathers and mothers provides a constructive insight for men rethinking fatherhood, acknowledging a father's need to 'work out a social relation to his children without the easy and ready support of natural bodily relations'. Fatherhood cannot properly be disentangled from broader notions of masculinity which are themselves distortions of human, male nature.[99] Marvin Ellison's 'liberative ethic' calls on men not simply to renounce their position of social dominance over women. Men who violate their partners, he says,

---

98.   John Paul II, *Familiaris consortio*, section 25, 'Men as husbands and fathers'.

99.   See, e.g., Nelson, *The Intimate Connection*, especially Chapters 1 and 6. On the distortion of masculinity see Anthony Dyson, with Martyn Percy, 'Carnal Knowledge', in Martyn Percy (ed.), *Intimate Affairs: Sexuality and Spirituality in Perspective* (London: Darton, Longman & Todd, 1997), pp. 76-85.

operate not from a stance of being powerful and secure in themselves, but from powerlessness and fear of not being recognized as worthy. Paradoxically, a liberating ethic must therefore encourage men's *gaining power*, in the sense of enhancing their self-esteem and at the same time deepening their respect for others, especially women and children.[100]

Moral power, he contends, enables men 'to build relations that promote mutuality, not domination and exploitation'. Men's 'enculturation into dominant masculinity' damages them as much as those who are effected by them. A liberating ethic, he says,

does not ask us to deny our personal power or embrace passivity. Rather, we are called to take more honest ownership of the social power we already have *as* men and to become directly accountable to those affected by our power, especially women and children.[101]

Christian fatherhood is a self-giving to wife and children. Christian liberation is always liberation from sin. Perhaps the liberation God offers to fathers is liberation from the selfishness that puts their interests first. Since men's socialization into masculinity makes detachment and disengagement normative, the sin of self-interest is easier to commit, disguise and forget. How marriage might be a framework for mutual interest and self-giving is taken up again in Chapter 7.

e. *Children First*

In this chapter an attempt has been made to use the method of theology taught by theologies of liberation and to apply it to those children who suffer as a result of being born unwanted into the world or of becoming victims of the behaviour of their biological parents. The classical understanding of children as a good of marriage has been retrieved and restated. This position can be readily distinguished from others (mainly within Protestant theology) where children have a lesser place within marriage. A brief consideration of four of these will allow the conclusion of this chapter to emerge more clearly.

The first position is that marriage is independent of family. This was the conclusion of the General Synod Marriage Commission in 1978. The commissioners accepted that the 'love and care of children are part of the bond uniting husband and wife' but rejected the position that

---

100. Marvin M. Ellison, *Erotic Justice: A Liberating Ethic of Sexuality* (Louisville, KY: Westminster/John Knox Press, 1996), p. 98.

101. Ellison, *Erotic Justice*, p. 101.

marriage 'is best understood as "for" children'. Marriage

> is best understood as 'for' husband and wife. It is their relationship with
> each other which is the basis of marriage. On this is built their relation-
> ship with their children. Arguments, therefore, in favour of the life-long
> nature of the married relationship must be seen to stem from the char-
> acter of the husband-wife relationship itself, whether or not there are
> children.[102]

The family derives from marriage, not marriage from the family.[103]

This position is close to the one adopted here, but it leads to the diminution of the importance of marriage for the upbringing of children. That marriage is primarily for the couple and not primarily for children is self-evidently true for couples who cannot have children, or who marry when they are beyond child-bearing age. And the extreme suggestion that marriage should be confined only to couples who have children has already been rejected (above, 4.3.b). But most people who marry, at least for the first time, are capable of having children. The difficulty with the Marriage Commission's argument is its assumption that there is a *single* reason or purpose that marriage is 'for', so that a decision must be made between whether it is for the spouses or for the children. But why can it not be for both? Why not say 'both...and' instead of 'either...or'? The insistence that marriage is also for children draws on Cahill's attempt to incorporate parenthood into the meanings given to the human body, and to redress the imbalance between the body and the anti-procreative ethos of much of Western culture (above, 5.2.c). The assertion that marriage exists primarily for husband and wife is consistent with the view that heterosexual sexual *mores* are an adult matter only. While it becomes ever easier to separate pregnancy from love-making through contraception (below, 6.1-2), it becomes ever more important to recall procreation as one of the meanings of married love.

A second position is that the primary meaning of marriage can be derived from the divine order of creation which is ontologically basic to marriage, whereas the place of children within marriage is secondary. This is the well-known view of Karl Barth. The 'fundamental' truth about marriage (so he thinks) is that it is 'the special life-partnership established and maintained between a particular man and a particular

---

102. *Marriage and the Church's Task*, p. 32, §86.
103. *Marriage and the Church's Task*, p. 32, §85.

woman'.[104] As such it cannot serve any other secondary or extrinsic purpose such as

> satisfying sexual needs, or of easing the burden of man's professional work, or of meeting the instinctive need of woman to build a nest (*sic*), to create a home and maintain a household, or especially of *fulfilling the impulse for procreation and training of children and therefore the ends of a family.*[105]

If 'anything else', including 'child and family, is permitted to become a principal aim, it is disruptive of marriage'. While marriage implies 'an inner readiness for children', as a life-partnership 'it is in no way conditioned by the co-existence of children'. Marriage, Barth says, 'is necessarily *coniugium*, but not necessarily *matrimonium*'.[106] A bond it is, but parenthood it need not be. Scripture shows that in the order of creation man is superior to woman, and marriage is the loving outworking of the unequal partnership between them.[107]

The asymmetrical relationship between the sexes assumed by Barth has already been criticized (above, 3.2.a). He sees this relationship as revealed in Scripture, and marriage is a sub-relationship within the man–woman relationship which reveals the divine order. The divine order turns out to be the *patriarchal* order, but that is not the point of the present discussion. By describing marriage in such a way as to separate it from children, Barth has driven a wedge between the 'special life-partnership' and the components which together constitute it, between the relationship which mirrors the divine order, and the sexual, psychological and social elements which constitute a real marriage; between the primary, intrinsic and ontological foundation of marriage, and the secondary, extrinsic and existential practicalities of marriage. But this is to invent another dualism. Living according to the order God intends is something different from 'fulfilling the impulse for procreation'. Why can 'the impulse for procreation' not also be part of the divinely intended order, rather as the phrase 'inner readiness for children' suggests?

A third (and much more serious) position is that after Jesus Christ, the biological family has been superseded by the family of his sisters and brothers who, either in the kingdom or in the Church represent a

---

104. Barth, *Church Dogmatics*, III, 54.1, p. 186.
105. Barth, *Church Dogmatics*, III, p. 188 (emphasis added).
106. Barth, *Church Dogmatics*, III, p. 189.
107. Barth, *Church Dogmatics*, III, pp. 163-83.

new and transformed family. This family is bound by allegiance to Christ and it expresses in its relationships the divine love which Christ has made known to them. Since this position is clearly taught by the Gospels and Paul it is important to acknowledge it and to raise questions about its interpretation in postmodern times. Mark records that Jesus looked round 'at those who were sitting in the circle about him' and said '"Here are my mother and my brothers. Whoever does the will of God is my brother and sister and mother"' (Mk. 3.34). Loyalty to family members must never exceed loyalty to Jesus—'No one is worthy of me who cares more for father or mother than for me; no one is worthy of me who cares more for son or daughter' (Mt. 10.37). The happiness of 'those who hear the word of God and keep it' exceeds the happiness of the womb that carried Jesus and the breasts that suckled him (Lk. 11.27-28). The people who put their faith in Jesus are given the 'right to become children of God'; as such they are 'born not of human stock, by the physical desire of a human father, but of God' (Jn 1.12-13). Married men and women are concerned with worldly affairs and with pleasing each other. Single people can be wholly occupied with 'the Lord's business'[108] (1 Cor. 7.32-34). Barth is adamant that 'In the sphere of the New Testament message there is no necessity, no general command, to continue the human race as such and therefore to procreate children'.[109] And Rodney Clapp says the 'first family' for Christians is 'the church'.[110] Is not the emphasis on the centrality of children within marriage adopted in this chapter gravely compromised by the teaching of Jesus and (at least some) contemporary theologians?

No. Marriage can be a powerful sign of the reign of God, and is not necessarily a thwarting of it. Children are suffering preventably and culpably when they are brought into the world unwanted, and are more likely to suffer when deprived of one of their biological parents. To say this is far from defending the industrial or post-industrial nuclear family within affluent countries which appears to be collapsing into radical privacy, recreation, consumerism and, too frequently, violence. Arguments have not been offered supporting any particular type of family or household, beyond the insistence that children and marriage, like

108. I subject this argument to sustained criticism in my 'Singles and Families', pp. 11-27.

109. Barth, *Church Dogmatics*, III, p. 266.

110. Clapp, *Families at the Crossroads*, Chapter 4, 'Church as First Family', pp. 67-88.

procreation and sexual union (between women and men), finally belong together.

The clear teaching of Jesus that solidarity between people doing the will of God overrides solidarity between members of the biological family is not a comparison between types of human family, but between being members of any family and being members of the kingdom or reign of God. The reign of God is the inversion of many of the values taken for granted in postmodern societies, including individualism, competition and consumerism: where God reigns there is only generosity, the hungry are filled, the sick healed and the social outcasts welcomed. However narrow our vision of the kingdom may be, there is pride of place for children within it. Mark records the argument among the disciples about hierarchy and status in the kingdom which is settled by Jesus sitting down and telling the twelve disciples, 'If anyone wants to be first, he must make himself last of all and servant of all' (Mk 9.35). Mark connects this episode with Jesus taking the example of a child (perhaps it is part of the same incident). The child is set in front of them, Jesus puts his arm around the child and instructs the disciples. '"Whoever receives a child like this in my name", he said, "receives me; and whoever receives me, receives not me but the One who sent me"' (Mk 9.36-37). The theology of liberation for children requires putting children first as Jesus puts the child first in this episode. In a late modern context putting children first requires attending to their vulnerability and to their long-term needs, and to discover that in caring for them one cares, as this saying reminds us, also for Christ himself and for the Father. In this way marriage serves the kingdom and is not antithetical to it.

The argument that for Christians the first family is the church is also fully consistent with the inclusion of children among the purposes of marriage. While noting that the reign of God and the Church of Christ are far from being identical, and membership of one of the Christian denominations and membership of a Christian family represent widely different, albeit overlapping, responsibilities, the main problem with this position is simply to state it as good news without misrepresentation. The empirical reality of church membership is sometimes a disappointing one. However if the Church is understood beyond declining denominations still disunited over trifles, as God's spirit-filled agency that makes 'the world into a household in which all of God's creatures...find access to life',[111] then clearly it has first priority in the lives of Christians. Their families will be 'domestic churches', a term acceptable equally in the Christian East and West. That term is of course close to 'domesticity' which may send several wrong signals about cosiness, separate spheres, the place of wives, and so on. That is why the term is generally avoided in this volume. The positive signals of the term are that the presence of Christ can be experienced within a family through its network of relationships and commitments, just as that presence is discernible at the Eucharist. Perhaps it also needs to be emphasized that the family is not an end in itself, but a beginning, the preparation for mature loving relationships outside of it.

There is also a fourth, more extreme position, which says that having children represents one's preoccupation with preserving one's lineage, living on through one's progeny, or 'anxiety about posterity'.[112] Since God has redeemed us eternally in Christ we do not have to worry about our temporal preservation *post mortem* by means of memories, deeds, or more tangibly, children. Christ's resurrection guarantees our eternal destiny—nothing else matters. Clapp, arguing that celibacy is better than singleness says,

> The married Christian ultimately *should* trust that his or her survival is guaranteed in the resurrection; the single Christian ultimately *must* trust in the resurrection. The married, after all, can fall back on the passage of the family name to children, and on being remembered by children. But singles mount the high wire of faith without the net of children and their memory.[113]

This is an extraordinary argument. Leaving aside the theological premises about the resurrection, why assume that people worry about preserving themselves, whether Christian or not, and doing so through progeny? They may not care whether they are remembered by their survivors, since they will not be around to receive the admiration. They may just be more relaxed about their mortality, a state of mind and body equally consistent with Christian hope. The argument is thoroughly patriarchal[114] (and patrilineal) and worldly. It is more about

111. Meeks, *God the Economist*, p. 45.

112. Barth again! See *Church Dogmatics*, III, p. 266; and Loughlin, 'The Want of Family in Postmodernity', pp. 322-24.

113. Clapp, *Families*, p. 101 (author's emphases). While this chapter is entitled 'The Superiority of Singleness', this position is hedged with many qualifications.

114. Thatcher, 'Singles', p. 14.

handing down wealth, property and status, and it rests on a dubious psychological premise.

I think the traditional position that children are a good of marriage can be retrieved, restated through the method of the theology of liberation, and defended against a variety of theological tendencies which minimize children's importance. But children are only one of the goods of marriage. Other theological meanings are explored in Chapter 7.

Chapter 6

BETROTHAL, MARRIAGE AND CONTRACEPTION

1. *The Problem: The Place of Contraception in Betrothal and Christian Marriage*

The assumption was made in Chapter 4 that almost everyone becoming married, whether Christians or not, is already sexually active with his or her partner. The advocacy of betrothal (above, 4.3) was an attempt to restore the difference between casual sex and sex with a partner with whom commitments have been made. But the theology of liberation for children in Chapter 5 lamented the arrival of children without the love and wholehearted acceptance of both parents. Is there not a serious glitch in the argument at this point? The use of contraception need not entail the conclusion that only children who are wanted arrive. Contraception, and the discipline required for its regular use, can fail, and its use normalizes and habituates the partners into the expectation of regular penetrative sex. This chapter addresses two sets of questions, relating to contraceptive use before and after the wedding. How far can the use of contraceptive practices be advocated before the solemnization of a couple's marriage? Does the theology of liberation for children allow prospective parents in a relationship described (above, 4.1-3) as 'betrothal' to make love, albeit contraceptively, outside the binding commitment of marriage, in the knowledge that contraception cannot eliminate the possibility of pregnancy completely?[1] Secondly, is

---

1.   Linda Woodhead argues '…no contraception is so perfect that the possibility of procreation is completely precluded, and every honest sexual encounter should therefore be entered into in willing acceptance of the possibility that it may break through the context of two by engendering offspring'. See Linda Woodhead, 'Sex in a Wider Context', in Davies and Loughlin (eds.), *Sex These Days*, pp. (98-120) 108; also, Paul Ramsey, *One Flesh: A Christian View of Sex Within, Outside and Before Marriage* (Bramcote: Grove Books, 1975).

the use of contraception within marriage simply assumed nowadays, without forethought or scruple, still less *theological* reflection? What might theology usefully contribute to the discussion of the matter? Answers to these questions will be influenced by, and will contribute to, the broader theology of marriage being developed in the book.

There is nothing new about the practice of contraception, provided it is broadly enough defined. What is new is the astonishing range of contraceptive products available to affluent sexually active people, none of which is free from medical consequences or moral implications. Contraceptives have changed fundamentally and forever the meanings given to sexual experience in the late modern world. In seeking to stimulate responsible theological reflection about these changes (which are now simply taken for granted in Western societies) one comes across a strange ecclesial phenomenon. There is almost complete silence among the Protestant churches about contraception, whereas from the Roman Catholic hierarchy, there is a strident, regular condemnation of all forms of it (except for the rhythm method[2]). This chapter is a small attempt to restart positive theological thinking about contraception. The chapter laments the growth both in phallocentric sexual activity from the eighteenth century onwards and in contraceptive use which normalizes and encourages penetrative sexual intercourse as the principal act of intimacy between heterosexual couples (below, 6.1.b-1.c). It applauds the thinking done by the Church of England on contraception in the present century (below, 6.1.d). But it also rejects many of the arguments against contraception advocated by the Roman Catholic Church. These are divided into three types: those which argue that contraception is contrary to natural law (below, 6.2.a); or contrary to the 'inseparable connection' between 'procreative' and 'unitive' sexual activity (below, 6.2.b); or an expression of a decadent society, culture, or 'mentality' (below, 6.2.c). An attempt is made to learn from all three types of argument and to incorporate detail from each of them in the positive doctrine of Christian marriage developed in the book. On this basis a clear answer about the extension of contraceptive use prior to the solemnization of marriage is given (below, 6.3).

---

2.   Which, of course, for official Roman Catholic theology, is not contraception, but 'birth regulation' (below, 6.1.4, 6.2.1).

a. *'Premodern' Contraception*

According to John Noonan the term 'contraception' can 'be applied to any behaviour that prevents conception'.[3] On this view a sexually active couple who refrain from procreative sexual activity are practising contraception. That is a very broad view of contraception. On the broad view even abstinence is contraceptive. In a moment this will be called 'pre-modern contraception'. But the more usual view ('the narrow view') is that contraception prevents possible conception—it is 'contra-conception'. The near universal assumption is made that couples will be practising penetrative sexual intercourse with intravaginal male ejaculation. Contraception is supposed to prevent a possible, consequential pregnancy. Contracepted sexual intercourse is sexual intercourse accompanied by the intentional prevention of conception or impregnation through the use of various devices, agents, drugs, barriers or surgical procedures. In a moment we shall call this 'modern contraception'. We learned much from visiting premodern and early modern practice with regard to the entry into marriage: we may now be poised to learn from premodern contraception. The practice of contracepted sexual intercourse becomes more common in the nineteenth century and grows with the arrival of new contraceptive products. Penetrative sexual intercourse with contraception becomes the normative routine for all sexually active heterosexual couples, whether married or not, except for couples who are either in the early stages of a relationship, or wanting children, or being downright careless.

What has been called 'premodern contraception' must now be defined. It tells us much about contemporary sexual practices because it helps us to relativize them against alternatives. An introduction to premodern contraception is provided by the discussion (in a recent *History Workshop Journal*) of a love memoir of John Cannon, a literate Somerset farm labourer written about his relationship with his uncle's servant Mary in 1705, which lasted for 12 years. Commenting on the memoir, historian Tim Hitchcock writes,

> John and Mary...never had full penetrative sex, and throughout his memoir Cannon congratulates himself on his studious avoidance of the sins of fornication and adultery. But, he, Mary, and the two other young women John courted at the same time, did have very active sex lives. Mutual masturbation, long-drawn-out sessions of kissing and fondling,

3.   Noonan, Jr, *Contraception*, p. 1.

and sincere promises of future marriage characterised all these relationships. None of the three women involved became pregnant, and each
was, by Cannon's account at least, considered a virgin on marriage.
While unusual in being recorded, there is nothing to suggest that the
experiences of these people were other than typical of popular sexual
activity at the turn of the eighteenth century.[4]

It will be at once apparent that what John and Mary were practising
was what we call 'safe sex', and that it was a version of safe sex that
did not require condoms.[5] They used inclusive contraception. Hitchcock thinks that in the eighteenth century 'sex changed. At the beginning of the century it was an activity characterised by mutual masturbation, much kissing and fondling, and long hours spent in mutual
touching, but very little penile/vaginal penetration—at least before marriage'. By contrast,

> by the end of the century sex had become increasingly phallo-centric.
> Putting a penis in a vagina became the dominant sexual activity—all
> other forms of sex becoming literally fore-play. Indeed, it is little won-
> der that use of the word 'play' without its prefix, died out in our period.
> But, more significantly, it was the penis that became the active member.
> What the eighteenth century saw was the development of an obsession
> with the penis, and of an assumption that there was only one thing to do
> with it.[6]

While this thesis looks highly speculative, considerable evidence is
produced to support it. In particular, heightened emphasis on penetration is said to be consistent with the increase at the time in population
growth. There was 'a change in the fundamental experience of sexual
activity which owed its content to changing patterns and discourses of
consumption and production'.[7] Trends in pornography are explicable—
'while erotica may be about fondling, pornography is generally about
penetration'.[8] An increase in penetrative sex also

> fits well the story of change in gender relations and the development of
> separate spheres... Forms of sexual activity which dramatically increased
> the risk of pregnancy generally reflected the interest of men over those

4.   Tim Hitchcock, 'Redefining Sex in Eighteenth Century England', *History
Workshop Journal* 41 (1996), pp. 73-90 (73).
5.   On the different versions of safe sex and Christian attitudes to each see my
'Safe Sex', pp. 66-77.
6.   Hitchcock, 'Redefining Sex', p. 79.
7.   Hitchcock, 'Redefining Sex', p. 76.
8.   Hitchcock, 'Redefining Sex', p. 79.

of women. Mutual masturbation and anti-natal forms of sex reflected instead a set of gender relations in which women's interests were more likely to be taken into account, and in which negotiation between partners was more equal.[9]

The mistaken view that men and women both needed to reach orgasm to conceive was replaced by another mistaken view that only the emission of sperm in the vagina was necessary. Bad biology rendered women's orgasms unnecessary; bad phallocentric practice made them impossible. The thesis is consistent with the low illegitimacy rates of the Elizabethan period.[10] The perfervidly read anti-masturbatory propaganda of the time normalized penetrative sex which 'became increasingly the only form of sexual activity which could be countenanced'.[11]

Sexual intercourse did not begin in 1750. However it is very likely that an increase in penetrative sex prior to marriage did begin in the eighteenth century. This is what is intended by the contrast between 'premodern' and 'modern' contraception. Barrier methods of contraception and abortifacients were used long before this period and are also premodern. However in the present context 'modernity' stands for an increase in phallocentric activity and the eventual increase in availability of contraception which corresponds with it.

'Premodern' contraception can then be given a definite, albeit tentative, sense. Premodern sexual contacts invite speculation about gentler forms of intimacy which invite recovery and emulation. They show that, broadly understood, contraception without barriers or herbs or potions was practised, and that earlier generations possessed a knowledge that may have been largely lost among heterosexuals today, that is, the ability both to enjoy mutual sexual pleasure, and simultaneously to exercise restraint, with the result that unwanted pregnancies were much less frequent even without modern contraceptive products. Earlier generations did not require condoms to practise safe sex. Hitchcock demonstrates how a particular, phallocentric, sexual routine passes itself off as normative so that it becomes very difficult to imagine the considerable differences between premodern sexual practices and our own. Our response to the realization that premodern and premarried people were sexually active yet managed well without penetrative sex, might be similar to the recovery of the practice of betrothal. Socially

9. Hitchcock, 'Redefining Sex', p. 80.
10. See Gillis, *For Better, For Worse*, p. 37.
11. Hitchcock, 'Redefining Sex', p. 82.

constructed routines have the power quickly to pass themselves off as normative, natural, even divinely sanctioned. The joint practices of widespread penetrative sexual intercourse with contraception, create intolerable and different burdens, of expectation, of performance and of responsibility; and intolerable consequences, including health risks, abortions and unwanted children. Sexually active Christians today will want to relate to each other in *other*-centric, not phallocentric ways. In this respect they may have much to learn from premodern, pre-secular ways.[12]

b. *'Modern' Contraception*

The increase in phallocentric activity itself created demand for contraceptive products. By 1843 the vulcanization of rubber made possible the inexpensive mass production of condoms which became increasingly popular, even though throughout Europe *coitus interruptus* remained the most popular method of preventing conception.[13] Couples today have bewildering choices to make. Condoms are thinner and more reliable. There are condoms for women (made from polyurethane). There are rubber vaginal diaphragms and rubber cervical caps of different shapes and types. There are intrauterine devices (the IUD) made of plastic and copper which prevent successful implantation into the uterus wall of a fertilized egg. The 'combined pill' (or 'the pill') contains the hormones oestrogen and progestogen which prevent ovulation. A pill for men which inhibits sperm production is now in trial. There is the highly effective intrauterine system (IUS) which, when placed in the womb releases progestogen for at least three years. Progestogen thickens the mucus in the cervix and helps to stop sperm reaching an egg. It makes the lining of the womb thin and may stop ovulation. Progestogen can be injected or implanted. Conception can be permanently stopped by sterilization (blocking the fallopian tubes in women and the *vas deferens* in men). If a women uses none of these methods and has unprotected sex, a choice of emergency contraception is available: two sets of pills taken 12 hours apart ('emergency pills') or prompt fitting

---

12. Colin Hart sensibly advocates mutual masturbation for couples prior to marriage or 'who are not at present actively intending procreation'. Reluctance even to consider or discuss the practice is due, he thinks, to 'the lingering remnants of the Natural Law approach'. See his 'The "Real Thing"', *ISCS Bulletin*, 15 (1995), pp. 6-7.

13. Noonan, *Contraception*, p. 394.

of a copper IUD will normally prevent pregnancy. In Britain contraceptives and contraceptive advice are free.[14]

This panoply of contraceptive choice is a remarkable feature of late modernity. It is difficult to believe that John Cannon and his sexual partners would not have made use of some of them if they had been available in the early 1700s. Our difficulty in believing this is a useful measure of the vast changes to sexual mores which have come about, many of which Christians will want to challenge. These changes prompt an ambiguous response. Millions of couples are enabled to regulate in large measure the number of children they have and when they have them. Reliable contraception removes the immense burden of further children to families living in poverty or when the health of the mother is already at risk. It ensures that women are able to be both sexually active and able to pursue further and higher education and/or careers. Contraception separates the pleasure of love-making from the responsibilities of parenting.

These undoubted benefits appear to be balanced by the obvious deficits, which have led Pope John Paul II to describe the manufacture, development, distribution and use of contraceptives as a 'culture of death'. That is why it is necessary to point out that the joint practices of widespread penetrative sexual intercourse and exclusive contraception create intolerable burdens, which almost entirely are carried by women. It is in women that the IUS and IUD is fitted; women take the pill; women wear diaphragms and cervical caps; it is women's bodies which are injected or implanted with progestogen. Only the condom (and the vasectomy operation) is the man's responsibility. Perhaps the female condom will change all that before long. The possible negative effects on health are also born by women. Known effects include cystitis, vaginal infection, irregular, or heavy, or more painful or prolonged periods, headaches, acne, increase in weight; tender breasts, ovarian cysts, mood changes, even loss of interest in the very act that is being rendered 'safe'. It is hard to imagine men putting up with an equivalent basket of possible afflictions in order to achieve sexual freedom.

In addition to the effects on the health of individual women, there is a massive social effect on all heterosexual, sexually active women.

14.   All the information in this paragraph was taken from the free leaflets available in a local doctor's surgery, produced by the Contraceptive Education Service in association with the Family Planning Association, undated, but current in Britain in 1997.

Young males, scarcely pubescent, expect penetrative sex, and young women are under great social pressure to provide it. Contraception normalizes the expectation. As Sally Cline has pointed out modern sexual mores provide a strong argument for women's celibacy. The regularization of sexual intercourse outside committed relationships represents the extension of 'sexual consumerism' into the most intimate areas of our lives.[15] 'A big disadvantage of reliable contraception was that women no longer had a justifiable excuse to refuse unwanted sexual advances. The removal of the threat of pregnancy meant coercive sex became more frequent.'[16]

c. *Lambeth and Rome: 'Christian Principles' or 'Criminal Abuse'?*
In 1930 the Lambeth Conference representing Anglican churches throughout the world, approved of the use of contraception in particular circumstances. It was the first statement of approval of contraception of any major Christian church. Resolution 15 stated,

> Where there is a clearly felt moral obligation to limit or avoid parenthood, the method must be decided on Christian principles. The primary and obvious method is complete abstinence from intercourse (as far as may be necessary) in a life of discipline and self-control lived in the power of the Holy Spirit. Nevertheless in those cases where there is such a clearly felt moral obligation to limit or avoid parenthood, and where there is a morally sound reason for avoiding complete abstinence, the conference agrees that other methods may be used, provided that this is done in the light of the same Christian principles. The Conference records its strong condemnation of the use of any methods of conception control from motives of selfishness, luxury, or mere convenience.[17]

The text of this resolution repays careful study. First, couples must be married. Any extension of the use of contraception outside of marriage would have been unthinkable. Secondly, couples must be under an obligation 'to limit or avoid parenthood'. It was not enough merely to wish to have few or no children or to postpone their arrival. Moral obligations are stronger, verifiable reasons, such as belief in parental inability to provide for children, or for further children; or risk to the health of the mother, or likelihood of a child seriously deformed being born.

15.   Sally Cline, *Women, Celibacy and Passion* (London: André Deutsch, 1993), p. 1.
16.   Cline, *Women*, p. 27.
17.   *The Lambeth Conference 1930* (London: SPCK, 1930), p. 43.

Thirdly, in emphasizing obligation, the Conference uses strong language (reminiscent of ancient anathemas?) to exclude 'motives of selfishness, luxury, or mere convenience'. Couples may not contracept because they wish to separate procreation from pleasure; or because children are likely to lower their parents' standard of living, or (almost unthinkably) because married women might wish to pursue a career. The Conference had affirmed in an earlier resolution the teaching of Aquinas that the 'primary end' of marriage was 'the procreation of children', and this could not be superseded by any secondary end to do with making love.

Fourthly, couples acting under an obligation to limit births and considering contraception have the choice between abstinence from sexual intercourse and other methods. The rhythm method of contraception was insufficiently well known in 1930 for the Conference to take it into account. Fifthly, couples should first attempt to limit births by not having sex. The influence of St Paul (1 Cor. 7.5) is obvious here in two ways. Paul approved of the practice of abstinence from sexual intercourse for short periods, and was aware of the dangers of abstinence for longer ones. His 'concession' (v. 6) becomes the chief unspoken reason why other methods than abstinence, principally the condom, are permitted. Nonetheless the Conference is clear that abstinence is better than indulgence, and that the former is an appropriate expectation within an ordered and disciplined Christian life. Sixthly, there must be a 'morally sound reason' why complete abstinence is impossible. This, presumably, is the honest admission that managing without sex is too difficult or unnecessarily demanding (Paul would have been happy with these reasons), or that it would lead to sexual temptation elsewhere. Only when all these criteria are satisfied, can contraceptive use be sanctioned.

Lambeth delegates in 1930 would be astonished and dismayed at the widespread use of contraception now, inside and outside marriage, and for the very reasons they excluded. They affirmed sex outside marriage to be a 'grievous sin', noted contraceptives increasing in use among the unmarried, and resolved to press for legislation 'forbidding the exposure for sale and the unrestricted advertisement of contraceptives, and placing definite restrictions upon their purchase'.[18] Striking a different note more likely to be heard today they also resolved that 'Fear of consequences can never, for the Christian, be the ultimately effective

18. *The Lambeth Conference 1930*, p. 44 (resolution 18).

motive for the maintenance of chastity before marriage. This can only be found in the love of God and reverence for His laws'.[19]

Anglican heart-searching about contraception continued, and an influential Anglican report nearly 30 years later was still grappling with 'the vexed question whether contraception is admissible or, if it is admissible, in what circumstances it may rightly be used'.[20] There was still an 'urgent need to establish, if possible, an Anglican attitude' towards the 'question of family planning and consequently the question of using contraceptives to that end'.[21] On the one hand, this report suggested 'it would be very unwise at this juncture for the Church to endorse in any way the opinion that contraception is a positive good needing no special circumstances to justify it'. On the other hand it rejected natural law arguments against contraceptive practice on the familiar ground that 'man' is 'at once a child of nature, and a spirit standing outside nature'.[22] Human sexuality is 'demonstrably supranatural', and 'the fact that man in his freedom stands above nature' leads the report writers to conclude that 'contraception is morally right in certain circumstances'.[23] They pointed out that since natural coitus could still be immoral, and since 'contraception appears to promote the highest personal ends of sexual union', it was 'pertinent, therefore, to ask whether "natural" *coitus*...is not simply an arbitrary *a priori* concept to which there is no correspondence in reality'. Their report took the approach of trying to be a 'spiritual adviser'[24] to married couples, and concluded, after examining contrary arguments, 'that a Christian marriage may justifiably include the use of contraceptives'.[25]

The 'Criminal Abuse' of Contraception. The Roman Catholic response, *Casti connubii*, depicted contraception as the first of the 'vices opposed to Christian marriage'.[26] Contraception was said to frustrate 'the marriage act' and to constitute a 'criminal abuse'. All possible grounds for using contraception were summarily rejected, whether a sufficiency of

19. *The Lambeth Conference 1930*, p. 44 (resolution 19).
20. *The Family in Contemporary Society* (London: SPCK, 1958), p. 123.
21. *The Family in Contemporary Society*, p. 129.
22. *The Family in Contemporary Society*, p. 144 (based on an argument of Reinhold Niebuhr in *The Nature and Destiny of Man*).
23. *The Family in Contemporary Society*, p. 145.
24. *The Family in Contemporary Society*, p. 130.
25. *The Family in Contemporary Society*, p. 154.
26. Pius XI, *Casti connubii*, section 4, 'Vices Opposed to Christian Marriage'.

children, desire for one's spouse without the 'consequent burden', inability to achieve continence or other severe difficulties based on the mother's health or the family's poverty. Pope Pius XI's principal argument was that nothing which is 'intrinsically against nature may become conformable to nature and morally good'. Both he and Lambeth accepted the distinction between the primary and secondary ends of marriage. Restating the traditional position which Vatican II was to modify, he argued that 'since...the conjugal act is destined primarily by nature for the begetting of children, those who in exercising it deliberately frustrate its natural power and purpose, sin against nature, and commit a deed which is shameful and intrinsically vicious'. Contraception is still identified with the sin of Onan which the 'Divine Majesty' punished with death.[27] With specific reference to the Lambeth decision, the Pope declared,

> Since, therefore, openly departing from the uninterrupted Christian tradition, some recently have adjudged it possible solemnly to declare another doctrine regarding this question, the Catholic Church, to whom God has entrusted the defense of the integrity and the purity of morals, standing erect in the midst of the moral ruin which surrounds her, in order that she may preserve the chastity of the nuptial union from being defiled by this foul stain, raises her voice in token of her divine ambassadorship and through Our mouth proclaims anew: any use whatsoever of matrimony exercised in such a way that the act is deliberately frustrated in its natural power to generate life is an offense against the law of God and of nature, and those who indulge in such are branded with the guilt of a grave sin.

Recourse to Rhythm. While contraception of any kind was absolutely proscribed, the use of infertile periods for sexual intercourse was considered a permitted exception. Those 'who, in the married state, use their right [to sexual intercourse] in the proper manner, although on account of natural reasons either of time or of certain defects, new life cannot be brought forth' are not to be 'considered as acting against nature'. Permission for sex in infertile periods was justified by the very distinction which condemned sex in fertile ones, that between the primary end of marriage, children, and the secondary end, the needs of the couple themselves.

27.   Gen. 38.6-10. For the issues raised see, e.g., Stuart and Thatcher, *People of Passion*, p. 100.

For in matrimony as well as in the use of matrimonial rights there are also secondary ends, such as mutual aid, the cultivation of mutual love, and the quieting of concupiscence which husband and wife are not forbidden to consider, so long as they are subordinated to the primary end and so long as the intrinsic nature of the act is preserved.[28]

2. Three Types of Argument against Contraception, and their Transformation

a. Natural Law and the 'Sin against Nature'

The approval of the rhythm method of 'birth limitation' or 'family planning', first issued in *Casti connubii* in 1930 has become increasingly important to Roman Catholic moral theology,[29] especially since the opportunity to permit contraceptive use was emphatically foreclosed by *Humanae vitae* in 1968. 'God has wisely arranged that the natural laws and times of fertility so that successive births are naturally spaced ... ' Based on natural law, the church teaches 'that it is necessary that each conjugal act remain ordained in itself to the procreating of human life'.[30] 'Today', says the Pontifical Council for the Family, writing in 1996, 'the scientific basis of the natural methods for the regulation of fertility are recognized',[31] and abstinence from intercourse during fertile periods is to be 'inserted into the pedagogy and process of the growth of love', thereby leading spouses to 'practice periodic continence'.[32] They must ensure that their desire to 'space the births of their children' is not 'motivated by selfishness but is in conformity with the

28. Pius XI, *Casti connubii*, section 4.

29. See, e.g., Paul VI, *Humanae vitae* (English text in Janet Smith, *Why Humanae Vitae Was Right: A Reader* [San Francisco: Ignatius Press, 1993], Appendix, 'Paul VI, Encyclical Letter on the Regulation of Births, *Humanae vitae*' [trans. Janet E. Smith], pp. 533-67), section 16; John Paul II, *Familiaris consortio* (John Paul II, Apostolic Exhortation, *On the Family*, to the Episcopate, to the Clergy and to the Faithful of the Whole Catholic Church Regarding the Role of the Christian Family in the Modern World, 1981), sections 31-32.

30. Paul VI, *Humanae vitae*, section 10. Ralph McInery defends this position in '*Humanae vitae* and the Principle of Totality', cited in Smith, *Why Humanae Vitae Was Right*, p. 332.

31. Pontifical Council for the Family, *Preparation For The Sacrament Of Marriage* (Vatican City: Vatican Press, 1994), section 35.

32. John Paul II, *Evangelium vitae*, 97 and *Catechism of the Catholic Church*, §§2366-2371 are also cited.

generosity appropriate to responsible parenthood'.[33]

Humanae vitae began with the statement 'God has entrusted spouses with the extremely important mission of transmitting human life', and spouses are told that 'in fulfilling this mission' they 'freely and deliberately render a service to God, the Creator'.[34] The encyclical reminds readers that 'Today's society calls for responsible parenthood'.[35] This is said to be 'rooted in the objective moral order established by God—and only an upright conscience can be a true interpreter of this order'. The consciences of the couple are unequipped to decide whether to use contraceptives, for

> in regard to the mission of transmitting human life, it is not right for spouses to act in accord with their own arbitrary judgment, as if it were permissible for them to define together subjectively and willfully what is right for them to do.

Arguments against Natural Law. There appear to be various difficulties in the advocacy of the 'spacing of births' for Christians inside and outside Catholicism. First, the physiological knowledge on which it is based is extremely modern. The scientific basis of the rhythm method was certainly not known when Pope Pius XI approved it in the encyclical *Casti connubii.* The original accommodation of the rhythm method was *not* based on the reliable discoveries of Ogino (Japan, 1924) and Knaus (1929) that 'ovulation occurred sixteen to twelve days before the anticipated first day of the next menstrual period'.[36] It was based on the earlier claim of Pouchet (in 1845) 'that conception could take place *only during menstruation and a period of from one to twelve days after menstruation'.*[37] As a 'law of nature' or 'law of generation' it has been available only for the last two thirds of the twentieth century, and many Christians spacing births in accordance with the version known to Pius XI presumably became pregnant. However, provided the 'natural

33.   *Catechism of the Catholic Church* (London: Geoffrey Chapman, 1994), §2368.

34.   Paul VI, *Humanae vitae*, 1. See also *Catechism of the Catholic Church*, para. 2367.

35.   Paul VI, *Humanae vitae*, 10.

36.   Noonan, *Contraception*, p. 443.

37.   Uta Ranke-Heinemann, *Eunuchs for the Kingdom of Heaven: The Catholic Church and Sexuality* (Harmondsworth: Penguin Books, 1990), p. 293 (emphasis added).

method' is properly taught and carefully implemented, it is effective.[38]

Secondly, the Anglican argument that the spiritual nature of women and men enables them both to stand outside 'nature' while firmly belonging to it, appears to be successful with regard to the observance of natural law. Nature includes humanity, and there are countless instances of medical and technological intervention in natural processes which are taken for granted.[39] (The Roman Catholic theologian Victor Steininger ridicules the claim that all sexual acts must be open to life can be derived from natural law.[40]) Thirdly, the issue remains whether couples who deliberately abstain from love-making during fertile periods but who make love at other times are practising 'birth regulation', the 'spacing of births', family planning', and so on, or whether they are practising contraception. This is because not having sex at certain times is not just not doing anything, and so not doing anything wrong. As Gareth Moore points out 'They do not just not have intercourse; they actively avoid intercourse, as part of their plan to avoid children', and this practice, although allowed by *Casti connubii*, is clearly inconsistent with that encyclical's portentous proscription of 'any use whatsoever of matrimony exercised in such a way that the act is deliberately frustrated

38.   It is important to be precise. 'Natural methods' means the 'sympto-thermal method' which 'combines the temperature method, cervical mucus method and calendar method with some other signs. These signs include the position, softness or firmness of your cervix and whether its entrance is slightly open or tightly closed, ovulation pain and breast discomfort'. If it is used according to instructions it is '98% effective'. Leaflet 'Contraception: Choosing and Using Natural Methods', Contraceptive Education Service and Family Planning Association, undated (but in circulation in 1997).

39.   For a forceful exposition of this point in the nineteenth century, see John Stuart Mill's 'Nature', in *Nature, the Utility of Religion, and Theism* (written 1850–58), text in Alasdair Clayre (ed.), *Nature and Industrialization* (Oxford: Oxford University Press, 1977), pp. 303-12.

40.   He finds similarities between the claim 'We may not use contraceptives, since God made man without such aids' and the following absurdities: '1. Since God has created only black and white sheep, we should not dye woollen clothes blue and red. 2. Since God sends rain, we should not open an umbrella. 3. Since God created day and night, we should not use artificial light to illuminate the night. 4. Although it would have been very useful for the economy if the Tajo had been made navigable, a specially appointed royal commission decided against it on the ground that God would have made it navigable from the beginning if he had wanted it to be so.' See Victor Steininger, *Divorce: Arguments for a Change in the Church's Discipline* (London: Sheed & Ward, 1969), pp. 125-26.

in its natural power to generate life'.[41] The broader definition of contraception (above, 6.1.b) clearly covers it. They intend not to have children and to separate love-making from baby-making. The secondary literature emphasizes that couples even abstaining from sexual intercourse during fertile periods (practising 'Natural Family Planning' or 'NFP' is now the preferred term) may still be doing so immorally because they display an evil intention or 'contra-life will'.[42]

Fourthly, there is a theological problem about the mission of transmitting human life. While God may 'plan' to perpetuate the human race through the uncontracepted love-making of spouses, it does not follow from this rather anthropomorphic depiction of God's intention that *every* act of love-making must be uncontracepted. What is actually involved in stating that conception is a mission at all? Since God is Creator, it is legitimate to claim that sheep, pied fly-catchers (which are by human standards, promiscuous) and sticklebacks have been entrusted with the mission to 'transmit' life, but all that such a claim would amount to is that, given a favourable environment, God has made provision for the reproduction of species, including the human species. The papal inference is, of course, far stronger. In the human case there is a divine plan or mission over and above the natural fecundity of couples and the social institution of marriage which legitimizes it. This is known by a dubious insight into natural law, supported by divine revelation. Any personal decision to have, to postpone having, or not to have children is soon submerged and negated in the overall divine plan to transmit human life. This plan belongs to a different scale entirely. Any reservation about having children is then depictable as failing to cooperate with God's plan for the propagation of human life, and the accusation of sin automatically follows.

41. Gareth Moore, *The Body in Context: Sex and Catholicism* (London: SCM Press, 1992), p. 165.

42. Germain Grisez, Joseph Boyle, John Finnis and William E. May, *The Teaching of Humanae vitae: A Defense* (San Francisco: Ignatius Press, 1988), p. 44. For a convincing criticism of this highly conservative position, see Moore, *The Body in Context*, pp. 166-73. A slight but important modification of the defence of the official Vatican position is advanced by W.H. Marshner, who argues on the basis of 'act-classification' that 'no couple choosing to abstain periodically, regardless of their reason for doing so, is ever practicing contraception'. See his 'Can a Couple Practicing NFP Be Practicing Contraception?', *Greg* 77.4 (1996), pp. 677-704 (677). Nonetheless they still display a 'contra-life resolve' (p. 678).

Finally, there is a difficulty surrounding 'responsible parenthood' as Paul VI understands it. It seems to require a theological erudition few mothers and fathers can match, for responsible parents are 'required to recognize their duties toward God, toward themselves, toward the family, and toward human society'. In fulfilling these duties they are *not* free to decide for themselves.

> It is not right for spouses to act in accord with their own arbitrary judgment, as if it were permissible for them to define altogether subjectively and willfully what is right for them to do. On the contrary, they must accommodate their behaviour to the plan of God the Creator...

Thus qualified, decisions to limit births (except by abstinence from sex or use of the rhythm method), are *a priori* irresponsible. There can be few matters more important than parental responsibility, yet in the encyclical it is predefined by means of a dubious theological orthodoxy.

Securing God's Will for the Monthly Cycle. These arguments, aside from appeals to divine authority, convince very few. Critics of NFP who wish to remain within Catholic teaching may ask exactly what God has allegedly willed by means of the monthly cycle. John Noonan has shown that the natural law argument can also be used to protect periods of infertility, even by medical means. 'If God intends the human sexual act to be fruitful, He does not intend it to be fruitful thirty days a month.'[43] Since a woman's egg lives outside the ovary for less than a single day, and sperm lives for up to five days,[44] God has designed that pregnancy is possible on at the most, five days a month, and impossible for 25 days a month. These are God's laws of generation. Since God has provided a natural rhythm of five fertile days and 25 infertile days, women with irregular periods may receive treatment to regularize them. *Humanae vitae* allows 'the use of medical treatment necessary for curing diseases of the body although this treatment may thwart one's ability to procreate'.[45] Hormonal treatment to secure the infertile period is equally in accord with God's laws. 'When steps are taken to assure that intercourse is not fertile in a period not intended by

43. Noonan, *Contraception*, p. 547.

44. Noonan says two days (*Contraception*, p. 548). The British Contraception Education Service leaflet, 'Contraception: Choosing and Using Natural Methods' says 'Sperm can live in a woman for up to five days'.

45. Paul VI, *Humanae vitae*, 15.

nature to be fertile, man acts in subordination to the divine plan.'[46] The reliable securing of infertility is a 'liberating' achievement equally in accordance with natural law. It follows from this clarification of the encyclical that loyal Catholic wives are entitled to secure regular rhythm by medical means. If, by securing the one, regular rhythm, the sterilizing of intercourse is also secured, then by the principle of double effect[47] the latter is legitimate provided it is not directly willed. For wives with regular rhythms, contraception may assist the securing of infertile periods, but may not interfere with fertile periods. Only at such times is the link between procreation and union to be maintained.

Contraception as a Heresy? A further blow against natural law arguments against contraception, is based on the claim that *the historical development of opposition to contraception is shaped by doctrinal considerations which no longer apply.*

Noonan has observed that disagreements with particular groups of people at different times have been influential in shaping the Church's opposition to contraception. The three most important groups were the Gnostics, the Manichees and the Cathars. Some Gnostics opposed the creation of children for religious or theological reasons, that is, they objected to bringing children into a world that was unbearably sinful, and into the realm of matter that was inescapably evil.[48] Manichees too were *theologically* opposed to the creation of children. Christians believed (whether truthfully we do not know) that Manichees thought 'procreation is the result of eating and concupiscence. Intercourse is plainly treated as fornication. The King of Darkness is seen as the author of generation'.[49] It did not however follow from the Manichees' opposition to having babies they were opposed to having sex. On the contrary, Bishop Titus declared, sometime after 363, that they 'contemptuously vituperate the procreation of children and desire that there be bodily intercourse without procreation'. Perhaps they were having sex like John Cannon and Mary. Titus confirms,

---

46.   Noonan, *Contraception*, p. 551.

47.   The principle that where an action is likely to have different effects, one licit and the other illicit, it is morally permissible to take the action, intending the one effect but not the other.

48.   Noonan, *Contraception*, pp. 81-85.

49.   Noonan, *Contraception*, p. 113.

> indulging in pleasure more frequently, they [the Manichees] hate the
> fruit that necessarily comes from their acts; and they command that
> bodies be joined beyond what is lawful and restrict and expel what is
> conceived and do not await births at their proper times, as if birth alone
> were dangerous and difficult.[50]

Augustine (above, 5.1.b) was to confirm that the Manichees were
practising *coitus interruptus*.[51]

The Cathars in the twelfth and thirteenth centuries (also called Albigensians) had similar theological views which led once more to the
irresolvable clash between the denial, on theological grounds, of the
goodness of sexual intercourse and marriage, and the permissibility of
sexual experience as long as it excluded sexual intercourse and marriage. The Cathars agreed not to have children. This was the root of
their heretical opposition to marriage. Their avoidance of children in
marriage was condemned in canons promulgated against them, as fornication and, less precisely, as adultery or homicide. Linking all three
groups together across a thousand years of Church history, Noonan
observes that in dealings with the Cathars,

> the orthodox *relived the experience of the Fathers facing the Gnostics,
> the Fathers facing the Manichees.* The orthodox commitment to mar-
> riage was reaffirmed by the assertion that procreation was an absolute
> value in intercourse; contraception was once more condemned without
> exception.[52]

Thereafter the practice of contraception was described as homicide.[53]

The suggestion to be developed is based on the obvious disappear-
ance of the theological convictions of these three groups among the
hundreds of millions of contemporaries practising contraception today.
Contemporary users of contraception, whatever their reasons or motives
may be, do not resemble Gnostics, Manichees or Cathars. They do not
consciously believe that matter is evil or that procreation is evil or
wrong. They just do not want, or yet want, to get pregnant. They do not
hold heretical religious beliefs; they are quite likely not to hold overt

---

50.   Noonan, *Contraception*, p. 114.

51.   Noonan, *Contraception*, p. 121.

52.   Noonan, *Contraception*, p. 179.

53.   The text of the decretal *Si aliquis* said 'If someone to satisfy his lust or in
deliberate hatred does something to a man or woman so that no children be born of
him or her, or gives them to drink, so that he cannot generate or she conceive, let it
be held as homicide'. See Noonan, *Contraception*, p. 169.

religious beliefs at all. If they hold a metaphysical view about material reality, it is likely to be the opposite of the Gnostic view. It is the view rather that the material world is good; that sexual pleasure is to be enjoyed and unwanted children are best avoided. It can be readily conceded that the Catholic Church had little alternative but to oppose these weird teachings and their sexual outcomes. But the absence of these strange teachings among users of contraception ought to result in the cessation of arguments based on such teachings against them. It is of course open to opponents of contraception to claim that all or some contraceptive users are, after all, the modern day equivalents of, say, Albigensians or Manichees. That would be a formidable task.[54]

So the fear of any sexual experience or act which does not result in an attempt at procreation is based in orthodox doctrine and the fight against heresy. Any departure from procreative routines was inescapably linked with false doctrine. Since *the connection between sexual intercourse and the expression of love had not by then been generally established*, no orthodox theologian could have countenanced the separation between the act and the only reason which permitted it.

> If pleasure in intercourse was, in the view of important authorities, always sinful, if the seeking of pleasure in intercourse could be mortal or, at best, venial sin, if love had no relation at all to acts of intercourse, then the notion of deliberately separating coitus from its one justification could not have been considered by any theologian.[55]

By the time of Aquinas the 'vice against nature' covered almost *any* sexual act except heterosexual penetrative sexual intercourse, and even that had a 'natural' position from which no deviation was allowed.[56] The absolute prohibition against contraception has been located in and largely produced by a trio of influences which have no place in contemporary discussions: the fear of heresy, the fear of pleasure and (despite Eph. 5.22-31) the failure to connect the making of babies with the

---

54. Pope John Paul II uses the term 'new Manichaeanism' to describe the social processes whereby sexuality is separated from religious meaning, the human body is separated from the human spirit 'which gives it life', and the human person, 'ever a subject, becomes an object'. See John Paul II, *Letter to Families*, section 19. While casual and promiscuous sex may be described in this way, it is hard to see how the 'new Manichaeanism' can be applied to contraception within marriage.

55. Noonan, *Contraception*, p. 198.

56. Noonan, *Contraception*, p. 225.

making of love. If contraceptives are to be discouraged today, a different case has to be made out.

Learning from 'Nature'. The natural law arguments which have been considered in this section should convince no-one. The theological assertions that God has a plan which contraception frustrates, or has designed a series of laws of generation which are beyond human modification, are weak, and their weakness is undisguised by appeals to papal or divine authority. Decisions about when couples get pregnant must be returned to the couples themselves. It is unfortunate that they are deemed irresponsible if they plan their pregnancies by methods other than rhythm. However, criticisms aside, what positive contributions might these arguments make to an understanding of Christian marriage and the place of contraception within it? Here are three suggestions.

First, any appeal to natural law encourages us to look for basic considerations which are fundamental to being human, discoverable by human reason, and logically prior to historical change or social construction. One such consideration is that heterosexual sexuality cannot be finally separated from reproductive capacity and so from prospective parenthood. Contraception is therefore best understood as a temporary measure. This is not to say married Christian couples might choose to remain childless. But they would be unusual, and would be likely to have unusual reasons for doing so. Everyone has parents. While sexuality and fecundity can be separated they also belong together. That is why the second Vatican Council stated 'By its very nature the institution of marriage and married love is ordered to the procreation and education of the offspring and it is in them that it finds its crowning glory'.[57]

Secondly, natural methods of contraception are commendable. There are several reasons for their unpopularity. The rhythm method was commended before its scientific basis was properly understood. It is unreliable when only a single indicator is used (above, 6.2.a), for example, the calendar method,. There have been many failures. It has been commended by a celibate male hierarchy with little understanding of the rhythms of women's bodies. It is disassociated from contraception among Roman Catholics (because it is always called something

---

57. *Gaudium et spes*, §48, 'Holiness of Marriage and the Family'.

else), and the elimination of the possibility of choosing other methods than natural ones may well cause resentment. Despite these negative features, and contrary to widespread expectation, it works. There are reasons other than prudential ones for commending it. Natural methods make a couple more aware of their fertility. It provides a self-knowledge that comes about through heightened body-awareness, through listening, observing, touching, sensing. Natural methods can be used to plan pregnancies as well as prevent them.

Thirdly, there are several connections to be established between 'natural' and 'premodern' contraception (above, 6.1.b). Natural methods proclaim that none of the modern paraphernalia of chemicals, hormones, implants, bits of copper, plastic or rubber, and so on, are needed to make love without making babies. Natural methods require 'periodic continence' (above, 6.2.a). But there may be different ways whereby continence can contribute to the 'conjugal spirituality'[58] of the couple. Continence may be the means whereby the set of modern assumptions about phallocentric behaviour, the normativity of penetration as standard sexual activity, the continuous availability of women's bodies (above, 6.1.b) are deliberately subverted in the name of a mutual tenderness and joint responsibility.

b. *Sex and Love: An 'Unbreakable Connection'?*
A principal argument of *Humanae vitae* is based on 'the characteristics of married love', a papal analysis unthinkable in any other century, including the first quarter of the twentieth. The strategy here is to claim that procreative and unitive acts, that is, baby-making and love-making, are inseparable, and then to show that the practice of contraception is a sinful attempt to separate them. Since God has arranged an unbreakable connection between procreation and union, the attempt to separate them is a grave sin against God. Conjugal love 'is a very special form of personal friendship whereby the spouses generously share *everything* with each other'.[59] Granted the totality of 'everything', contraception is then able to be interpreted as a withholding of each partner from the other, a failure to share the God-given power of fecundity. Conjugal love is said

---

58.   See Mary Anne McPherson Oliver, *Conjugal Spirituality: The Primacy of Mutual Love in Christian Tradition* (Kansas City: Sheed & Ward, 1994); and below, 7.1.b.

59.   Paul VI, *Humanae vitae*, 9, emphasis added.

to be 'both *faithful and exclusive* to the end of life'.[60] Although this passage is about fidelity, more is built into fidelity than faithfulness to each other. Rather, joint faithfulness 'to the end of life' is asserted, before coming to be understood as constant openness to fertility which the practice of contraception wilfully subverts. This is to insert a whole new series of meanings into 'fidelity'. In a similar way, conjugal love is said to be 'fruitful', but children are the particular fruit the Pope has in mind. 'The whole of the love is not contained in the communion of the spouses; it also looks beyond itself and seeks to raise up new lives.' Thus qualified, contraception may be depicted as compromising the fruitfulness of marital love. 'God has wisely arranged the natural laws and times of fertility.'[61] But the church's teaching about the operation of this natural law is that 'it is necessary that *each* conjugal act remain ordained in itself to the procreating of human life' (above, 6.2.a).[62] However the grounds offered for the view that each act must be open to life are based *a priori* on the doctrine of marriage revised as recently as the Second Vatican Council, and not on natural law at all. Just as marriage has two ends, 'the procreation and education of children' and the 'mutual love of the partners',[63] so sexual intercourse conveys these meanings simultaneously, and in such a way that they are inseparable.

A comparison between the developing Anglican and Roman Catholic positions on contraception between 1930 and 1970 can now be made. It is well to begin with agreements. First, the unbreakable connection between the procreative and unitive meanings of marriage was affirmed by the 1958 Lambeth Conference albeit in different terms. A Committee Report endorsed by the Conference defined the 'three great purposes' served by the institutions of marriage and family to be 'the procreation of children, the fulfilment and completion of husband and wife in each other, and the establishment of a stable environment within which the deepest truths about human relationships can be expressed

---

60.   Paul VI, *Humanae vitae*, 9 (translator's emphasis).

61.   Paul VI, *Humanae vitae*, 11. Since *Humanae vitae* allows knowingly making love during infertile times, it is a pity that God did not wisely arrange to tell earlier generations what these laws and times were. The hypothesis that 'ovulation occurred sixteen to twelve days before the anticipated first day of the next menstrual period' was first stated and supported by evidence as recently as 1924. See Noonan, *Contraception*, p. 443.

62.   Emphasis added. Ralph McInery defends this position in '*Humanae vitae* and the Principle of Totality', p. 332.

63.   *Gaudium et spes*, §50.

and communicated'.[64] These three purposes form a unity and the 'commanding problem...which every husband and wife faces' is 'maintaining a right relationship' between them.[65] After *Humanae Vitae* was published the 1968 Lambeth Conference recorded its 'appreciation of the Pope's deep concern for the institution of marriage and the integrity of married life'.[66] But the Conference quickly moved on to state its disagreement with *Humanae Vitae*'s conclusions about contraception, giving as its reasons the resolutions which it had passed previously. Anglicans were warned in 1958, as they had been in 1930, that 'sexual love is not an end in itself nor a means to self-gratification, and that self-discipline and restraint are essential conditions of the responsible freedom of marriage and family planning'. But the gulf between Lambeth and Rome was widening, for the Conference resolved

> the responsibility for deciding upon the number and frequency of children has been laid by God upon the consciences of parents everywhere: that this planning, in such ways as are mutually acceptable to husband and wife in Christian conscience, is a right and important factor in Christian family life and should be the result of positive choice before God.[67]

If the procreative and unitive meanings of sex had been applied to sexual activity as a whole, and not to every sex act in particular, the widening gulf could have been avoided.

According to the new fledgling orthodoxy of *Humanae vitae*,

> There is an unbreakable connection between the unitive meaning and the procreative meaning [of the conjugal act], and both are inherent in the conjugal act. This connection was established by God, and Man is not permitted to break it through his own volition.

> Therefore, because of its intrinsic nature the conjugal act, which unites husband and wife with the closest of bonds, also makes them capable of bringing forth new life according to the laws written into their very natures as male and female. And if both essential meanings are preserved, that of union and procreation, the conjugal act fully maintains its

64. *The Lambeth Conference 1958* (London: SPCK; New York: Seabury Press, 1958), p. 144.

65. *The Lambeth Conference 1958*, p. 146.

66. *The Lambeth Conference 1968; Resolutions and Reports* (London: SPCK; New York: Seabury Press, 1968), p. 36, resolution 22.

67. Resolution 115 of the 1958 Conference was quoted in full and reaffirmed at the 1968 Conference. See *The Lambeth Conference 1968*, p. 36, resolution 23.

capacity for [fostering] true mutual love and its ordination to the highest
mission of parenthood, to which Man is called.[68]

Since 1968 the 'unbreakable connection' has been confidently
repeated as settled moral doctrine. It is now depicted as 'the constant
teaching of the church'.[69] A couple breaking the connection is said to
'degrade human sexuality and with it themselves and their married
partner by altering its value of "total" self-giving'.[70] The 'sincere gift of
self' has its own 'logic'. Without this logic, 'marriage would be empty;
whereas a communion of persons, built on this logic, becomes a communion of parents'. The unitive and procreative dimensions of marriage '*cannot be artificially separated* without damaging the deepest
truth of the conjugal act itself'.[71] As a consequence even contraceptive
practice which avoids penetration altogether is absolutely proscribed. It
cannot be an expression of love because a true expression of love has to
be capable of producing life.

> There must be a rejection of all acts that attempt to impede procreation,
> both those chosen as means to an end and those chosen as ends. This
> includes acts that precede intercourse, acts that accompany intercourse,
> and acts that are directed to the natural consequences of intercourse.[72]

Beneath the dark opacity of these proscriptions lurks the fear of all
forms of sexual intimacy except for the one which conforms to God's
plan. It is a remarkable high risk strategy. Only full unprotected vaginal
intercourse can express real human love.[73]

Breaking with the Unbreakable Connection. The inseparability of unitive and procreative meanings of sexual intercourse looks remarkably
like a new doctrine of indissolubility (above, 2.1.b). The 'unbreakable

---

68.   Paul VI, *Humanae vitae*, 12 (emphasis added: brackets in translator's text).
69.   Pope John Paul II, *Letter to Families* (1994), section 12.
70.   John Paul II, *Familiaris consortio*, section 32. See also, *Catechism*, §2366.
71.   Pope John Paul II, *Letter to Families*, section 10.
72.   Paul VI, *Humanae vitae*, 14.
73.   Dietrich von Hildebrand defends the Vatican position by invoking the
distinction between instrumental and superabundant finality. Superabundant finality
'has a meaning and value independently of the end to which it leads'. 'The God-
given, essential link between love of man and woman and its fulfillment in the
marital union, on the one hand, and the creation of a new person, on the other hand,
has precisely the character of superabundance, which is a much deeper connection
than would be one of merely instrumental finality'.

connection' between openness to life and mutual self-giving has more than a passing metaphysical resemblance to the doctrine of the indissolubility of the marriage bond between husband and wife (below, 8.2.e). Unfortunately the arguments supporting the unbreakable connection have little power to convince. First, there has to be a suspicious ring about the centrality of mutual love in the doctrine of marriage. However welcome the emphasis, it is a very late development in Catholicism,[74] as recent as the advocacy of the rhythm method for the 'spacing of births'. It is an island of innovation in a sea of conservatism.

Secondly, one might want to ask *why* it is that the link between procreation and union cannot be broken. If it is a metaphysical bond then it is prone to all the difficulties the doctrine of the indissolubility of marriage runs into in the face of marriages that have clearly ended (below, Chapter 8). What is it worth to say the bond remains? Married partners may wish, as an *expression* of mutual love, to separate union from procreation, something 'nature' in any case may be said to achieve for them most of the time (above, 6.2.a). Why should they believe that this cannot validly be done or that it is contrary to God's order? Whether an act of love represents total self-giving is presumably better assessed on existential, not metaphysical grounds.

Thirdly, we might reopen the question why all love-making a married couple ever makes must fall under the joint rubrics of mutual self-donation and potential openness to the creation of new life? Why could not the couple cooperate with God in the mission of procreation by *sometimes* being open to new life? That every act of love-making be subjected to these stringent criteria of meaning is said by one positive Catholic writer to combine 'a preposterous…harmful and even oppressive suggestion' with 'an unreal idealization of sex acts' which 'can demean married persons' positive experiences of sexuality'.[75]

The assertion that *every* conjugal act must be open to procreation leads, fourthly, to the fundamental issue which *Humanae vitae* foreclosed. It is well known that the Commission set up by Pope Paul VI to consider contraception produced a 'majority' and a 'minority' report. A 'key argument' of the majority report was 'that it is not necessary for

---

74. Pius XI, *Casti connubii*, 1, 'Love of Husband and Wife'. For the historical details see Noonan, *Contraception*, pp. 494-500.

75. Cahill, *Sex*, p. 204.

each marital act to remain open to procreation so long as the "totality"
of the acts are so open'. It also asserted that 'Infertile conjugal acts constitute a totality with fertile acts and have a single moral specification'.[76] This advice would have maintained the obligation on fertile
married couples to seek to become pregnant at some time during their
marriages, but not to require them to be open to it at all times. But the
advice was discarded. Instead, the minority report (which 'reportedly
carried the signatures of only three theologians') 'stressed the con-
stancy of Church teaching on contraception and argued that a change
would be disastrous for Church authority', and that it would 'warrant a
change in other teachings about sexuality, such as masturbation'.[77]
Overwhelming advice in favour of change was rejected, and the principal reasons for rejection may have been the difficulty of reconciling
contraceptive practice with earlier teaching, and the fear of further
doctrinal development in the area of sexual morality. Ironically, perhaps no decision has undermined the teaching authority of the Roman
Catholic Church more than that announced in *Humanae vitae*.

Sixthly, what might be called 'the argument from obsolescence' is
applicable here. Noonan's long-concealed impatience with the post-
Humanae vitae refusal of contraception finally surfaces at the end of his
long book. He avers,

> That intercourse must be only for a procreative purpose, that intercourse
> in menstruation is mortal sin, that intercourse in pregnancy is forbidden,
> that intercourse has a natural position—all these were once common
> opinions of the theologians and are so no more. Was the commitment to
> an absolute prohibition of contraception more conscious, more universal,
> more complete, than to these now obsolete rules? These opinions, now
> superseded, could be regarded as attempts to preserve basic values in the
> light of biological data then available and in the context of the chal-
> lenges then made to the Christian view of man.[78]

Learning from the Unbreakable Connection. How might the unbreakable connection contribute to a developing doctrine of Christian marriage? One suggestion, made by the otherwise conservative Roman
Catholic theologian Margaret Monahan Hogan, is a simple relocation

---

76.   Janet Smith, '*Humanae Vitae* at Twenty', in Smith (ed.), *Why Humanae
Vitae Was Right*, pp. 499-518 (505-506).
77.   Smith, '*Humanae Vitae*', p. 506 (emphasis added).
78.   Noonan, *Contraception*, p. 532.

of the unbreakable connection from each act of intercourse of a married couple to the marriage or union itself.[79] It is the marriage itself which establishes the connection between sex and love, between procreation and union, not each act of intercourse within it. Welcoming the development in papal teaching about the meaning of marriage from *Casti connubii* on, she notes that the teaching has failed to acknowledge that 'Reproduction is known by contemporary science to be distant in space and time from the act of conjugal intercourse'.[80] Official teaching is based on the assumption, common until the nineteenth century, that reproduction was 'an immediate effect of intercourse'. The teaching does not take sufficiently into account that 'the marital union is nourished by conjugal intercourse', and it has yet to accommodate the 'participation in the ethical discussion of men *and women*', which has at last brought '*the lived experience of the generation of the marital union*'[81] into theology. Retaining the scholastic language of ends, Hogan increases the number of the ends of marriage from two to three, to take account of the renewed emphasis on union. Outlining a position to which she believes the developing teaching of the Magisterium will inevitably lead, she argues that the ends of marriage are 'the union itself, the children, and the flourishing of the individual partners', and 'the subjects who constitute the marriage have specific identities as spouses, as parents, and as individuals'.[82] So, corresponding to the three ends of marriage now redescribed, are the three roles each partner plays within the marriage as husband or wife, mother or father, man or woman.

Retaining teleological language Hogan argues that the union between husband and wife is a 'necessary' end of marriage, whereas the end of children is 'contingent'. 'The conjugal act is always unitive' but only 'sometimes reproductive'.[83] In the light of this priority of the union over its possible procreative function, 'the claim that there is an inseparable nexus between the procreative meaning and the unitive meaning in every act of conjugal intercourse can no longer be maintained'.[84] The

79. Margaret Monahan Hogan, *Finality and Marriage* (Marquette Studies in Philosophy; Marquette: Marquette University Press, 1993).

80. Hogan, *Finality and Marriage*, p. 89.

81. Hogan, *Finality and Marriage*, p. 89 (emphasis added).

82. Hogan, *Finality and Marriage*, p. 102.

83. Hogan, *Finality and Marriage*, p. 103.

84. Hogan, *Finality and Marriage*, p. 104.

union rather serves as 'the matrix of conditions for specific procreative and personalist ends. 'Both physically and psychologically' these ends 'are separate as ends of the act of intercourse.'[85] This, thinks Hogan, is 'the emerging position' of the tradition.

The position that marriage itself provides the inseparable connection between sex and love is a positive way of reading the direction of recent Catholic teaching, although traditionalists will find in it the emergence of a new doctrine of totality expressly excluded by Paul VI. One would need to add that the connection between sex and love cannot be *a priori* guaranteed, that it depends on the continual realization of the marriage as a reciprocal covenant (above, 3.1, 3.2.a), and that sex within marriage does not always carry with it loving, unifying, sentiments. Concentration upon the union which is the marriage itself shifts theological attention away from sex and towards the quality of the marriage itself. It reaffirms that children are part of the meaning of marriage but not the whole meaning of it. It coincides with what was urged as the 'new familialism' and 'shared parenthood' (above, 5.2.c).

c. *Moral Deficit Arguments*

The third type of argument against contraception is the moral deficit argument, according to which the evil of contraceptive use is either its contribution to a culture of death, or already a consequence of such a culture. Pope Paul VI held contraception would 'justify behavior leading to marital infidelity or to a gradual weakening in the discipline of morals'.[86] 'The young', he warned, are 'so susceptible to temptation that they need to be encouraged to keep the moral law'. Contraception is a disincentive. Husbands using contraceptives 'will lose respect for their wives'. Rulers who 'care little about the moral law' will be able to effect birth-limitation policies.[87] Finally, people will think they have limitless power over their bodies, whereas 'there are some limits to the power of Man over his own body and over the natural operations of the body, which ought not to be transgressed'. Since all these predictions

85.   Hogan, *Finality and Marriage*, p. 105. The analysis continues by assigning to each of the ends of marriage a level of 'finality', whether 'horizontal', 'vertical' or 'transcendental'. I am wary of these abstractions and their very limited communication currency.

86.   Paul VI, *Humanae vitae*, p. 17.

87.   And see John Paul II, *Familiaris consortio*, 30.

are said to have come true, Paul VI has been declared a 'prophet'.[88]

Four Sinful 'Mentalities'. Subsequent Vatican teachings on the family, sexuality and marriage would denounce various 'mentalities' which contribute to, or express, the culture of death. A decade or so after *Humanae vitae*, *Familiaris consortio* warned against a 'contraceptive mentality', a term which would appear more frequently in forthcoming Vatican documents. It was associated with

> a corruption of the idea and the experience of freedom, conceived not as a capacity for realizing the truth of God's plan for marriage and the family, but as an autonomous power of self-affirmation, often against others, for one's own selfish well-being.[89]

Contraception, then, is direct evidence of selfishness. The Pontifical Council For The Family document *Preparation For The Sacrament Of Marriage* associates the contraceptive mentality with 'widespread, permissive laws' and 'all they imply in terms of contempt for life from the moment of conception to death'.[90] The 'prevailing mentality' is to be sharply rejected. In *Evangelium vitae* contraception and abortion are linked with a 'culture of death', a 'conspiracy against life',[91] and another negative mentality, hedonism.

> In very many...instances such practices are rooted in a hedonistic mentality unwilling to accept responsibility in matters of sexuality, and they imply a self-centered concept of freedom, which regards procreation as an obstacle to personal fulfilment. The life which could result from a sexual encounter thus becomes an enemy to be avoided at all costs, and abortion follows on from failed contraception.[92]

Investment in both contraception and abortion is evidence of a 'veritable *structure of sin*', a '*war of the powerful against the weak*', and a '*conspiracy against life*'.[93]

Alternatively contraception is associated with *consumer* and *anti-life* mentalities. Couples 'imprisoned in a consumer mentality' value

88.   Smith, *Why Humanae Vitae Was Right*, Chapter 22.

89.   John Paul II, *Familiaris consortio*, 6, 'The Situation of the Family in the World Today'.

90.   Pontifical Council For The Family, *Preparation For The Sacrament Of Marriage* (1996), section 49.

91.   John Paul II, *Evangelium vitae*, p. 22.

92.   John Paul II, *Evangelium vitae*, p. 24.

93.   John Paul II, *Evangelium vitae*, p. 22.

money more than babies. Their 'sole concern is to bring about a continual growth of material goods', and they 'finish by ceasing to understand, and thus by refusing, the spiritual riches of a new human life. The ultimate reason for these mentalities is the absence in people's hearts of God'.[94] An all-pervasive 'anti-life mentality is born'. Over-anxiety about the need to limit the world's population is cited as an example of this mentality. Such anxiety is an 'example of a certain panic deriving from the studies of ecologists and futurologists on population growth, which sometimes exaggerates the danger of demographic increase to the quality of life'. There are two cultures, the 'culture of life' and 'the culture of death'.[95] 'The church stands for life.'[96] 'Today', complains the Vatican, 'we see with alarm the spread of a "culture" or a mentality that has lost heart with regard to the family as a necessary value for spouses, children and society.' This is due to 'a secularized atmosphere' which

> especially affects young people and subjects them to the pressure of a secularized environment in which one ends up losing the meaning of God and consequently the deep meaning of spousal love and the family as well... In countries where the process of de-Christianization is more prevalent, the disturbing crisis of moral values stands out, in particular, the loss of the identity of marriage and the Christian family and hence the meaning of engagement.[97]

Criticisms of Moral Deficit Arguments: A 'New Life Mentality'? These arguments combine deeply-held convictions held by almost all Christians with highly contentious claims which detract from the extent of agreement which may already exist. The most recent statement from the Anglican–Roman Catholic International Commission says the two churches 'share the same spectrum of moral and theological considerations' while disagreeing about the arguments and conclusions derived from them.[98] Beginning with the contentious elements of the moral

94.   John Paul II, *Familiaris consortio*, section 30.

95.   John Paul II, *Evangelium vitae*, p. 37.

96.   The title of section 30 of *Familiaris consortio*.

97.   Pontifical Council For The Family, *Preparation For The Sacrament Of Marriage* (1996), sections 11-12.

98.   Second Anglican–Roman Catholic International Commission, *Life in Christ: Morals, Communion and the Church* (London: Church House Publishing; London: Catholic Truth Society, 1994), p. 30, §82.

deficit arguments, one might ask whether the absolutist and increasingly strident position taken over all contraceptive use achieves anything, or is theologically unsustainable. Contraceptives cannot be disinvented; their use, however, is able to be modified, and this appears to be the more urgent problem, confining procreative sexual activity to marriage, and enjoying less phallocentric sexual activity on the way.

An analogous case might be provided by another product of modernity, the motor car. Few people doubt the damage it does to the environment: the remedy in the first instance relies not on its elimination but on incentives to make fewer journeys, in smaller cars, burning cleaner fuels, on existing roads, while gaining the political will to deal with the motor manufacturing and petroleum industries and promoting affordable public transport. Modification, not elimination, is the way forward. In the same way the prohibition of the sale of alcohol is not the best way of controlling the problem of drunken drivers.

Couples having sex in relationships which do not have the approval of Christians may nonetheless be exercising responsibility in safeguarding against pregnancy. It may be true that contraceptives make adultery more likely because they make pregnancy less likely, but that claim would sanction an argument to confine contraceptives within marriage, not to eliminate them altogether. Fidelity has always needed to be encouraged whether or not condoms are on sale or wives are on the pill. Do husbands lose respect for their wives because of contraception? If so, is it because they will forget the natural fertility of their wives' bodies, and come to see them only as pleasure-giving? Is it obviously true that in marriages where there has been no contraception, husbands' respect for wives was maintained. The so-called rendering of the marital debt (above, 3.1.d) was just such an arrangement, and it contributes little to an adequate theology of marriage. If contraception is mutually agreed, for reasons mutually accepted, it is difficult to think that it will lead to loss of respect by either for the other.

While some concern about the projected increase in the world's population may be a 'panic', concern about the world's growing population cannot be dismissed by dismissing the panic accompanying some predictions of its rise. A principled argument exists that in some poor countries it would be better for fewer children to be born. There are also unexamined problems in the unqualified support for 'life'. Between 1950 and 1990 child mortality declined by two-thirds from around 300 births to 100 births per thousand, an improvement 'to a greater degree than in the whole of previous world history'.[99] This is a remarkable achievement, but is it not noteworthy as a contribution to a culture of *life*? The culture of life seems to be narrowly contrasted with the practices of contraception, abortion and euthanasia. It is not extended, for example, to experimentation on animals, or the factory-farming of chickens or calves, or the shooting of migrating birds or wild animals for sport. Catholic theology has not, generally speaking, been a friend to animals.[100] More reflection may be needed on the necessity for the elimination of some forms of life (e.g. certain viruses, rats in sewers) for human life to be promoted. 'Serving life' might carry more conviction if it were environmentally as well as foetally worked out. One wonders whether the teaching against all forms of contraception itself deserves the designation of a 'mentality', like those it picks out as contrasts. All Christians should surely and broadly be 'pro-life', but a 'pro-life mentality' which over-simplifies complex issues and extends moral absolutes into areas where responsible theological and moral diversity exists has already become an unhelpful ideology.

There are further doubts about these moral deficit arguments. Medical science has a panoply of ways of prolonging human life. Are these parts of the culture of life, or an evasion of death (which might also be explained by an absence of God in people's hearts)? It is difficult to see how the temporary suspension of fertility contributes to an unwholesome transgression of the body's natural limits, since these limits are being extended by the medical profession in the name of research, not by patients whose expectations of transforming or postponing mortality have been sinfully fuelled by contraceptive practices. Couples who postpone the advent of children in order to establish careers, or to pay off their university tuition fees, or afford the down payment on a house and the enormous interest on a mortgage, may be offended by the suggestion that consumerism drives and ultimately corrupts their intentions.[101] And while couples in late modern societies may have lost the

99.   Mette, 'Not a "Century of the Child"', pp. 5-6. Mette uses the World Bank 1993 annual report as her source.

100.   See Andrew Linzey, *Animal Theology* (London: SCM Press, 1994).

101.   The document *Preparation for the Sacrament Of Marriage* (1996), in its description of 'an accentuated deterioration of the family and a certain corrosion of the values of marriage' includes marriage 'usually contracted at a later age'. See Introduction, p. 1. The Council has not taken into account that the rising age of marriage is in fact a return to Elizabethan levels (above, 4.2.e).

meaning of engagement, the argument of this book has identified betrothal as a more promising way of returning to a Christian entry into marriage (above, 4.3).

Learning from the Moral Deficit Arguments. The Pope also expresses deeply-held convictions shared by Christians throughout the world. More people are probably having more penetrative sex, inside and outside marriage, with and without contraceptives.[102] One consequence is extensive recourse to abortion, a fact deplored by almost all Christians including non-Roman Catholics who nonetheless reject the 'absolutist' position of that church.[103] The argument that yet more contraceptive education and provision is needed in order to reduce unwanted pregnancies may be unsafe. The availability of contraceptives may normalize the expectation of penetrative sexual intercourse whether or not it is properly used on particular occasions of having sex. Chastity is safer and cheaper. The Pope is right to point out that much sexual behaviour is driven by selfishness, by the desire for pleasure, often without responsibility. His critique of culture is similar to those authors descrying the cultures of narcissism and cynicism.[104] His reference to a 'structure of sin' analyses promiscuity as liberation theologians analyse poverty—it is there, prior to reflection upon it, passing itself off as natural, and fuelled by impersonal forces. The link between consumer choice and moral choice, which tempts us to treat people as replaceable things, is widely made. Very few Christians will disagree with the Pope's analysis that the ultimate reason for irresponsible sexual relations is 'the absence in people's hearts of God'. The Pope is surely right to condemn the hedonistic mentality, provided he is not condemning pleasure as such. But the assumption that all recourse to contraception is an instance of it removes the distinction between outright promiscuity and responsible use of contraception by Christian couples, and ends up by degrading them.

102. Stone, *The Family*, p. 485.

103. See, e.g., Board for Social Responsibility of the Church of England, *Abortion and the Church: What Are the issues?* (GS Misc 40B; London: Church House Publishing, 1993), p. 27.

104. E.g., Christopher Lasch, *The Culture of Narcissism: American Life in an Age of Diminishing Expectations* (New York: W.W. Norton, 1978); Richard Stivers, *The Culture of Cynicism: American Morality in Decline* (Oxford: Basil Blackwell, 1994); and Robert Bellah, *Habits of the Heart* (New York: Harper & Row, 1985).

3. Conclusion: Contraception in Christian Marriage

While dissenting from the ban on contraception it was possible to be positive about many of the insights in the papal arguments. In particular it was suggested that within the unity of a married couple's life together, sex and love cannot finally be separated, that natural methods of contraception can combine a return to premodern ways of lovemaking while providing subversive reasons for the periodic continence which accompanies them. Borrowing from Hogan, the shift in Vatican thought towards concentration on the union which is marriage was given further impetus, and much of the description of the sinful mentalities was endorsed. But no reasons were found in the literature from *Humanae vitae* on for revising the Anglican judgment of 1958 'that a Christian marriage may justifiably include the use of contraceptives'.

The 1930 Lambeth Conference permitted contraception provided the choice of any other method than abstinence was 'decided on Christian principles'. It may be useful to borrow that Conference's method for dealing with the problem by evoking its appeal to Christian principles while widening that appeal to take advantage of the changes both in theology and in society which have occurred since then. Theology is more aware than in 1930 of how marriage was distorted by patriarchal assumptions, rigid gender roles and a lack of equality. The Christian principles that might govern contraceptive choice are the ten contrasts between secular and Christian understandings of marriage (above, 2.3.b), the two principal biblical models of 'covenant' and 'union' (above, 3.2.a-b) and the understanding (yet to be developed) that marriage is a sacrament (below, 7.1-2). Among the social changes since 1930 are that men and women marry later; nearly as many married women work outside the home as married men (though not necessarily in fulltime work); that the school leaving age has been raised for everyone, that between 20 per cent and 50 per cent of all young people in developed countries go on to university or college before embarking on a career. These far-reaching changes provide far more demanding conditions for the exercise of chastity.[105]

---

105. For a discussion of what chastity is in these changed circumstances see my 'Postmodernity and Chastity', in Davies and Loughlin (eds.), *Sex These Days*, pp. 122-40.

The 1958 Anglican report took the approach of trying to be a 'spiritual adviser'[106] to married couples. Advisory clinics and centres are common throughout most of the Western world. What advice might the churches give? First, it will need to be advice—informed counsel which may be freely set aside, and does not take the form of directives which, when unheeded, constitute grave sins. Within the framework of life-long commitment Christian marriage devolves responsibility to couples and does not derogate it. Remarkably the text of the 1930 Lambeth conference resolution (above, 6.1.d) still provides a good starting point. The pursuance of a career for women, whether married or not, can clearly count as a 'moral obligation' to postpone parenthood. Preparation for careers, including higher education, training and apprenticeship, can be protracted and exhausting. That women should eventually receive the same career opportunities as men is a social obligation as such ('the new familialism', above, 5.2.c). Since the means of almost ensuring infertility are available, the deliberate postponement of parenthood cannot be classified as merely selfish. There may be financial reasons which make it advantageous for children that their parents should have postpone having them. Couples may wish to grow in their intimacy before becoming parents, to the benefit of themselves and their children. In doing so they might wisely delay the 'conclusion of the passage into marriage',[107] not frustrating one of its sacred purposes. Postponement of the changes parenthood brings to the marriage may result in better preparedness to face them.

The warnings provided by the Conference resolution are equally salutary. There may well be specific instances of a general mentality under the rubric of 'motives of selfishness, luxury, or mere convenience'. If children are to be avoided merely because they are seen as an obstacle to selfish ambition, or as an avoidable expense, or as a threat to an immaculately ordered household, then the Lambeth warning is applicable. However, it is rarely observed that *having* children may be equally selfish. It is unquestionably wrong to assume that, merely because a couple choose to have children they are 'choosing life'. They might see a new baby as a *chic* fashion accessory, or think of parenthood as a new project to encourage their own self-development, as a large distraction in an otherwise empty life, the fulfilment of

---

106. *The Family in Contemporary Society*, p. 130.
107. Whitehead and Whitehead, 'The Passage into Marriage', p. 143.

a desire to feel needed, and so on.[108] Motives *are* essential to contraceptive use, but it should not be assumed that having children is always unselfish.

The expectation of 'complete abstinence from intercourse (as far as may be necessary)' also remains pertinent. How far abstinence *was* necessary, was uncertain in 1930. A couple today who avoided intercourse at all times when they wished to avoid having children would seem to be under the thraldom of a theology which regards all sexual intercourse as regrettable, and justifiable only when desiring children. Fortunately few Christians advocate such views today. Since regular sex (assuming full consensuality) is likely to contribute to the well-being of the union, abstinence for its own sake is unlikely to be virtuous or effective. But abstinence from penetrative sex (i.e. intimacy but without intercourse) is essential in the early stages of a heterosexual relationship, and indeed there is evidence (above, 6.1.b) of contentment with such experience prior to and during betrothal. Now that there are reliable scientific information about the cycle of fertility and experienced teachers of natural methods of contraception, abstinence from sexual intercourse at times known to be fertile represents an option which bypasses modern methods and their side-effects, and employs abstinence in a more focussed and spiritually positive way. But natural methods remain an option only. As the Conference agreed, 'other methods may be used'.

In direct response to the question how far the use of contraception may be advocated before the solemnization of a couple's marriage, the method of the Lambeth Conference in dealing with contraception within marriage is again a pertinent one. There is a strong argument for an honest recognition of the practice of sexual intercourse prior to the wedding ceremony, just as there was a strong argument in 1930 for an honest recognition of the use of contraception inside and outside marriage. In approving the marital context for contraception the Conference took a brave step which is no longer questioned in the Anglican church. Equally the Conference, in approving contraception, was careful to hedge about its permission with careful qualifications. There seems no good reason why the recognition of contraception prior to the solemnization of marriage may not also be recognized, provided a similar set of qualifications is also made.

108. See Beck and Beck-Gersheim, *Chaos*, Chapter 4, 'All For Love of a Child'; and see above, 2.2.d.

It is disappointing that few theologians and church leaders show much enthusiasm even for a reopening of the question. A case for the honest recognition of contracepted sexual intercourse prior to the wedding ceremony might contain the following (and doubtless other) reservations. First, all sexually active couples need to rediscover the pleasures, responsibilities and genuine freedoms of non-penetrative intimacy. Secondly, as the House of Bishops noted in their 1991 *Statement*, the principle of proportion applies to the deepening intimacy of sexually active couples.

> It may be put this way: the greater the degree of personal intimacy, the greater should be the degree of personal commitment... Often it is only because a relationship has advanced to a point of deep trust, valuing and commitment that inhibitions and privateness are surrendered, and intercourse becomes a welcomed possibility.[109]

Utilizing the controlling emphasis (above, Chapter 5) of children on heterosexual practice, one might proffer the strong suggestion, thirdly, that 'the point of deep trust' is by itself insufficiently determinative for sexual intercourse to begin. Rather, if there is to be a point, it should be when a couple are sufficiently committed to each other that in the future they are willing to become partners in parenthood. If, prior to that future time they become pregnant, their commitments to the child are paramount. From that point sexual intercourse using any available method of contraception would be an honourable intention to postpone, rather than to avoid, having children.

Fourthly, undergirding this position is the argument of Chapter 4 regarding the precedent for, and the desirability of returning to, a phased entry into the permanent state of marriage. Couples having sex after this point would not be having 'sex before marriage' because they would have already begun the entry into marriage. (A processive view of the entry into marriage allows, of course, for its 'consummation' to be years after first intercourse [above, 4.3.a].) Their commitment to each other and to possible children would be analogous to, if not a contemporary reclamation of, the premodern condition of betrothal. Fifthly, the acknowledgment that complete sexual intimacy prior to a service of wedding is more a permission than a recommendation (like Paul's permission to marry). Sixthly, many of the denunciations of

109. *Issues in Human Sexuality: A Statement by the House of Bishops* (London: Church House Publishing, 1991), p. 19, §3.2.

contraception expressed by Pope John Paul II, provided they are understood as warnings against its easy misuse and overuse, its contribution to sexual selfishness, irresponsibility, and so on, remain valuable. Contraception has produced the casualization of sex rather as capitalism has produced the casualization of labour. There is no doubt that the casualization of sex remains a great evil. Even on a purely consequentialist view too many people are permanently hurt by it. For Christians there are very powerful arguments for avoiding it (above, 2.3).

Finally the expectation that a married couple should live their life together 'in a life of discipline and self-control in the power of the Holy Spirit' need not be compromised in any manner by the use of contraceptives. It is prurient to associate discipline and self-control solely with abstinence from particular opportunities for married intercourse. The preparation for children, which may involve several years of a couple's shared life, is likely also to require discipline and self-control, expressed in a different way, even if the pill or the coil is part of it. Instead of advising couples that every 'marriage act' must be open to life, it might be better to emphasize that children generally bring enormous joy into marriages and so it might be advisable for them not to deprive themselves of the blessings they bring for too long before having them. Nonetheless when partners become parents the union of marriage changes forever[110] and some couples may need to save for years to afford a home. There is good unselfish reason then for husband and wife to enjoy each other and their union before the children arrive, and at the same time to prepare for the changes when their union includes vulnerable, dependent offspring and marital love is extended to embrace them. When the roles of mother and father are added to the roles of wife and husband, the new roles change the old ones (above, 5.2.c), and the gifts of discipline and self-control will increasingly be required.

110. See Christopher Clulow (ed.), *Partners Becoming Parents: Talks from the Tavistock Marital Studies Institute* (London: Sheldon Press, 1996).

Chapter 7

Marriage: Communal Partnership, Mutually Administered Sacrament

This chapter is an attempt to provide a cumulative, theological picture of Christian marriage, first as a state of communion or communal partnership between two persons, and secondly as a Christian sacrament, unique among sacraments because it is the only one which is administered by laypeople to each other without a priest. The first part of the chapter exposes the present lack of attention to marital spirituality and draws on the Christian accounts of the person, of friendship, of love and of communion, culminating in the life of the Trinity, and relating each to the hiatus which is the absence of a spirituality for married couples. The second part of the chapter grounds the reception of the sacrament precisely in the ministry of the spouses to each other, and offers an account of sacramentality which both incorporates Protestant reservations about sacramental language and opens the sacrament out so that the generous grace of Christ may be found in faithful and mutual marriages beyond the bounds of Christian confession.

The chapter prepares the way for the two remaining chapters, since the vision for marriage sketched in it will enable the doctrine of indissolubility to be reformulated (in Chapter 8) so as to make provision, within the developing theology of Christian marriage, for divorce and for the remarriage of divorced people. It will also become obvious that much of the theological language necessary for the description of marriage is readily applicable to the loving unions between lesbian and gay people. The extent to which, if at all, it is desirable to offer an inclusive understanding of Christian marriage, available to straight and to lesbian and gay couples, is a subject of Chapter 9.

1. *Marriage as Communal Partnership*

The term 'partnership' is meant to affirm the end of hierarchical and patriarchal accounts of marriage. Such a partnership can be 'the queen of friendships' (below, 7.1.c), a covenant (below, 7.1.d) that becomes unbreakable, embraces family and spills beyond it into the wider society. It assumes partnership in earning, housekeeping and parenting, in advance of the negotiated outworkings of these shared responsibilities, and it refuses fixed gender assumptions about who does what (below, 7.2). It should be noted however, that there is nothing intrinsic to the concept 'partnership' which requires equality among partners. 'Communal' is meant to convey the sense that the partners' love is able to be a sharing in that communion which is the life of the triune God (below 7.1.g). That love, pouring itself out in creation and self-gift, always tumbles out beyond itself to embrace what is other than it. It is the kind of love that 'will never come to an end' (1 Cor. 13.8). Care will be taken to put experience first (above, 1.2.d). The absence of the experience of the married in the development of marital theology at the Vatican has been called by the Catholic church's leading writer on marriage an 'invalidating gap'.[1] This warning will be taken very seriously, and theological descriptions of marriage will be taken as referring to possibilities, not to assumed realities. It will be assumed that if in a marriage there is love, then there is the basis for theological reflection. If there is love, then there is already a lens pointing into the transcendent, a point of contact between human and divine love, between a couple's love for each other, and God's love for both of them.

a. *The Christian Understanding of the Person*

We have found reason earlier to criticize modern notions of the individual, and particularly their distortive effects on marriage. Postmodern philosophy and premodern theology converge in affirming the social character of the individual person. Seyla Benhabib unwittingly concurs with Christian social anthropology when she affirms, against Enlightenment philosophy, that,

> the subject of reason is a human infant whose body can only be kept alive, whose needs can only be satisfied, and whose self can only develop *with the human community* into which it is born. The human infant

---

1.   Mackin, *The Marital Sacrament*, p. 665.

becomes a 'self', a being capable of speech and action, only by learning to interact in a human community. The self becomes an individual in that it becomes *a 'social' being capable of language, interaction and cognition.* The identity of the self is constituted by a *narrative unity...*[2]

A.M. Allchin, speaking from the Orthodox perspective, says,

for most Orthodox writers in contact with the West the distinction between individual and person is of vital importance. *Individual*, in this perspective, is a way of speaking of a human being as a unit, separate from others, but strictly comparable with them, a replaceable part of a much larger whole. *Person*, on the other hand, speaks of the human being in relationship with his fellows but sees him as unique and irreplaceable, regards him not as part of a larger whole, but as one in whom the whole is mysteriously present.[3]

Prior to any consideration of marriage Christians hold that human beings are created for each other, that everyone becomes a person through relationships with other persons, and that human personal being is capable of sharing in God's own being as a communion of divine Persons. As McFadyen writes, such a concept of the human person

is both dialogical (formed through social interaction, through address and response) and dialectical (never coming to rest in a final unity, if only because one is never removed from relation). In dialogue the partners are simultaneously independent (otherwise the listening and speaking of both would be unnecessary) and inseparably bound together in a search for a mutuality of understanding. The basis of a dialogical understanding of personhood is that we are what we are in ourselves only through relation to others.[4]

It may be a fallacy to assume that built into the concept of person there is a presumption of equality of treatment. Recognizing someone as a person has not always led to recognition of their equal rights. The theological beliefs that all women and men are children of God, and

---

2.   Benhabib, *Situating the Self*, p. 5 (emphases added).

3.   A.M. Allchin, 'The Sacrament of Marriage in Eastern Christianity', Appendix 3 of *Marriage, Divorce and the Church*, The Report of a Commission appointed by the Archbishop of Canterbury to prepare a statement on the Christian Doctrine of Marriage (London: SPCK, 1971), p. 115.

4.   Alistair I. McFadyen, *The Call to Personhood: A Christian Theory of the Individual in Social Relationships* (Cambridge: Cambridge University Press, 1990), p. 9.

that Christian women and men are brothers and sisters in Christ are more promising. As we shall see *divine* Persons are equal (below, 7.1.e-f). For the moment it is sufficient to note that it is impossible to speak, in Christian faith, about being or becoming a person without simultaneously speaking about other persons. Relationality is a veritable structure of human being.

b. *Spirituality for Spouses*
Human being then, prior to marriage is social and relational in character, dialogical and dialectical, independent and dependent. The marriage relationship thus represents a striking intensification of created normality. John Stuart Mill reminds us that historically marriage has probably never been like this, that the wife, her body, property, rights and privacy, have historically been incorporated into her husband.[5] Canon law recognized a single, juridical entity, the marriage, but the subordination of the wife made it clear that the union was represented by the husband.[6] When a recent writer attempted to write a book about conjugal spirituality, she came across the remarkable fact that nothing had ever been written about it before![7] It had simply been assumed that marital intimacy would work against spirituality; that celibacy was better; and that the celibate male's experience of spirituality was normative. A very recent Vatican document on marriage preparation says of 'spousal spirituality' only that 'by involving human experience which is never separated from moral life', it 'has its roots in Baptism and

5.   John Stuart Mill, *The Subjection of Women* (1869), especially Chapter 2.
6.   Hogan, *Finality and Marriage*, p. 87. See Pius XI, *Casti connubii*, where Pope Pius XI explains that the 'order of love' between husband and wife 'includes both the primacy of the husband with regard to the wife and children', and 'the ready subjection of the wife and her willing obedience' (p. 7).
7.   Mary Anne McPherson Oliver, *Conjugal Spirituality*, e.g., p. 18 (and throughout). There is now a Roman Catholic journal devoted to the promotion of marital spirituality, the *International Journal for Married Spirituality* (INTAMS). There is much official alarm about the 'general experience among Church members' which shows 'that even committed couples do not develop a vital consciousness' of the sacrament, and that their understanding of it 'does not come up to the standard of present-day sacramental theology'. See Klaus Demmer, 'The Origin of an Idea', *International Journal for Married Spirituality* 1.1 (1995), p. 22, and Chapter 1 of Klaus Demmer and Aldegonde Brenninkmeijer-Werhahn (eds.), *Christian Marriage Today* (Washington: Catholic University of America Press, 1997).

Confirmation'.[8] It thereby passes up the opportunity to enlarge on the human experience necessary for a sacramental marriage and to suggest how a couple might deepen their life with God as they deepen it with each other. The absence of attention to the spiritual needs of married people, coupled with the obvious, often insuperable, difficulties, that people encounter in their marriages makes the creation of married spirituality an urgent theological and pastoral task. In order to encourage this task, five suggestions for fostering conjugal spirituality are made next.

Five Suggestions for Conjugal Spirituality. First, married couples may find it helpful to apply the symbols of covenant and union to their marriage simultaneously, and to counterbalance each with the other, for 'covenant' clearly maintains the separate identities of the spouses as they undertake a common project, whereas the one-flesh union clearly maintains their oneness, 'a union of hearts and lives'. Ironically the term 'contract' which is rightly criticized as a description of marriage (above, 3.2.a) successfully maintained the separateness of the contracting parties and in one matter at least (sexual access to each others' bodies), full (albeit theoretical) equality.[9] It may be helpful for spouses to see themselves as simultaneously separate persons and united partners, and to regard their separateness and togetherness as dialectically related, that is, one polarity cannot function properly unless the other one does, and that is a rule that applies equally to both. Nearly 50 years ago Derrick Sherwin Bailey warned against couples regarding their union as an 'amalgamation in which the identity of the constituents is swallowed up and lost in an undifferentiated unity', or as 'a mere conjunction in which no real union is involved'.[10] Or, drawing on Hogan's convincing argument that 'the subjects who constitute the marriage

---

8.   Pontifical Council For The Family, *Preparation For The Sacrament of Marriage* (1996), section 41.

9.   'This equality of rights which is so much exaggerated and distorted, must indeed be recognized in those rights which belong to the dignity of the human soul and which are proper to the marriage contract and inseparably bound up with wedlock. In such things undoubtedly both parties enjoy the same rights and are bound by the same obligations; in other things there must be a certain inequality and due accommodation, which is demanded by the good of the family and the right ordering and unity and stability of family life', Pius XI, *Casti connubii*, p. 22.

10.   Bailey, *Mystery*, p. 44.

have specific identities as spouses, as parents, and as individuals',[11] we might say that a marriage is more likely to flourish when each of these three roles is attended to and nurtured. A husband and a wife are simultaneously a person, a partner, and (probably at some time) a parent. Attending to one another's needs in all three roles might constitute the first basic task of marital spirituality.

Secondly, couples may wish to distinguish for themselves between oppressive and non-oppressive elements which together comprise their marital union. A married union which creates dependence or assumes a fusion of individuals into a single synthesis, is a distortion of marriage:[12] conversely a union which exists through mutual presence, intimate communication and reciprocal love may be said, with *Familiaris consortio*, to represent 'the mystery of Christ's incarnation and the mystery of his covenant'.[13] André Guindon warns against wives 'falling prey to an ideology (which macho males will inevitably encourage) of pseudo-intimacy, a sort of "togetherness" which sacrifices healthy autonomy and self-care to the illusory security of continuing dependence'.[14] A beginning to the project of union may be discerned in a couple's discovery, across the sexes, of their *common humanity*. 'When a man and a women leave their parents and start living together they will find *the same humanity* in each other. Together they will face existence, sharing the same life conditions, running the same risks.'[15]

Guindon's understanding of the dialectic between wives and husbands as persons and as spouses sets an agenda for the development of conjugal spirituality. Any arrangement whereby a spouse abandoned his or her freedom or was required to surrender it would compromise the spouse as a person—'nothing of worth would be left for the other to love. The very basis for human otherness would be lacking'. Equally, 'any dissolution of oneself into a kind of two-in-one being would amount to a moral suicide'. What is needed, rather, is

> an interchange of intimate communication between the spouses which gradually makes them uniquely present to each other—to each other's

11. Hogan, *Finality and Marriage*, p. 102. See above, 6.2.b.
12. John Paul II, *Familiaris consortio*, comes dangerously near to this position. 'Conjugal love...aims at a deeply personal unity, the unity that, *beyond union in one flesh, leads to forming one heart and soul*' (section 13, emphasis added).
13. John Paul II, *Familiaris consortio*, section 13.
14. Guindon, *The Sexual Creators*, p. 97.
15. Guindon, *The Sexual Creators*, p. 97.

bodies, minds, needs, feelings, hearts, desires, fears, hurts, joys, and dreams. From the new vantage point which this conjugal presence and sharing gives them, spouses acquire an original insight into the nature and the fecundity of human affiliations.[16]

One might add to these remarkable intuitions that insofar as married couples realize a divine presence in their being present for each other, they acquire an experiential insight into the fecundity of the divine love made present in Christ.

Thirdly, any attempt to practice a conjugal spirituality has first to stare into the hiatus that confronts it. Traditional spirituality 'sees discrete individuals as the locus of spiritual value and the couple as two individuals on separate journeys to spiritual growth'. Conjugal spirituality is the loving *ethos* of a marriage, each trying to love the other as God loves them in Christ and recognizing Christ in each other. It empowers the couple to grow together and each partner to grow separately, each enabled by the other. It

points to the possibility of a shift of the center of spiritual attention from within individuals to the spaces between them, to their encounters and to the interpenetration which sometimes results. It is a spirituality which looks for the presence and action of God in relationships and in their impact, and which affirms the couple as a spiritually and theologically significant unit.[17]

This is surely an area where the experience of married couples is vital. It ought to be possible for innovative and exciting investigations to be carried out among Christian people (preferably thousands of them, worldwide) to measure the hiatus in conjugal spirituality, to find out whether couples even think of finding and serving Christ in and through one another, and so on. While sociological and psychological research into marital difficulties is pervasive, marital spirituality, and especially the blocks that prevent it from happening, is a genuinely new field.

16. Guindon, *The Sexual Creators*, p. 98. 'Fecundity' in all of Guindon's work is a term broader than the capacity to produce children. 'It is a creative power of meaningful and loving relational life, the use of which must be regulated by the truth of the historical becoming of persons in the community to which they belong. In short, human sexuality is fecund when it promotes humanly *tender/sensuous life, self identity, personal worth, and community*' (p. 78, author's emphasis).

17. Oliver, *Conjugal Spirituality*, p. 21.

Fourthly, Oliver's vision of conjugal spirituality is a breakthrough from a spirituality of celibacy, individuality and bodily anxiety to one which takes seriously the partnership of marriage as a *locus* for spiritual growth. Oliver's terms 'conjugal soul' and 'conjugal body' convey a remarkably fresh approach to the dynamics of *henosis* or one-flesh unity. The 'conjugal soul' of a couple is born:

> When the outward pull of attraction becomes strong enough to cause interaction and to create relationship, a new density of being becomes necessary to reestablish the individual's stability in the face of the continual and progressive 'de-centering' which is taking place... The inner core of the individual who persists in relationship becomes subtly and over time substantially different from its previous self. In this sense, every soul is a conjugal soul, one which links a person affected by relation.[18]

While the term 'conjugal soul' has its application early in the life of a couple, and may be predicated in different degrees, to all close human ties, the 'conjugal body' is 'the basis for "conjugal soul" in its most fully developed, archetypal form. Each, neither absorbing nor being absorbed, becomes more and more permeable to the other. A substantial interpenetration of being takes place'. Using the familiar geometrical figure of two overlapping circles, she says

> The circles actually begin to overlap, creating a spiritual reality which is both 'I' and 'not I', 'Thou' and 'not Thou', significantly and recognizably both two and one. When a pair goes from closeness to commitment, each comes to be partly other as well as self. It is no longer spiritually accurate to consider one alone, in isolation from the conjugal dimension which pervades it.[19]

Finally the difference between traditional and conjugal spirituality can be illustrated by the contrast between centrifugal and centripetal forces. Traditional spirituality emphasizes centrifugal movement, away from the self as the centre of the world. Conjugal spirituality emphasizes centripetal movement, 'revolving around the axis created by its own being, the axis defining two as standing in relation'. That is why 'the primary spiritual task of conjugal love is the creation, maintenance, and growth of that unique reality which is each new relation, the necessary foundation for joint outward-looking service'.[20] The hope is

18. Oliver, *Conjugal Spirituality*, pp. 44-45.
19. Oliver, *Conjugal Spirituality*, p. 45.
20. Oliver, *Conjugal Spirituality*, p. 53. I am more suspicious about the

maintained that 'loving relationship of itself produces anti-bodies against egotism and provides a training ground for creating wider and wider circles of love'.[21] Further support for conjugal spirituality will be given (below, 7.1.d) in the discussion of love as *relation*.

Since there are few precedents, Oliver's version of conjugal spirituality is valuable. 'Conjugal' is clearly intended more broadly than formal marriage and so the analysis may be more broadly applied. While conscious of the havoc caused by exploitative relationships she affirms that 'attraction, desire and longing are spiritually worth the risk, for they force us continually outward to learn the lessons of unity'. Love and longing are good for us, for 'they break down our ego boundaries, allowing the self to be enlarged and enriched by knowing others, by learning from them and interacting with them'.[22] The psychological content of her writing is closely linked to theology and closely informed by it. Conjugal love, she says, is itself a 'spiritual discipline' because it 'can pleasurably tempt one toward self-forgetfulness and self-transcendence'. What moves us in the other may be nothing less than a revelation of God—'The recognition of "God" in another, our attraction to this revelation, and the affinity it brings into being are the basis for spiritual friendship as well as for the more intimate conjugal relations.'

c. *The 'Queen of Friendships'*
Marriage is a special kind of friendship. To speak this way is to concede that the category of friendship is broader than marriage. Friends, in Oliver's term, may be said to share a conjugal soul. Some feminist theologians have rightly pressed the question whether marriage should be *defined* in terms of friendship. Rosemary Haughton who writes as a feminist theologian and a worker with homeless women, many of them victims of marital violence, thinks,

> There is one thing which makes it possible for couples now to survive the pressures of conflicting opinion about sex and marriage, Church controversy around and over them, economic stress and all the great public anxieties of our time, and to create through all that a relationship which

description of the developmental stages of the couple's life (Chapter 5), partly because all developmental theories appear to impose generalities on highly particular people and situations. But the whole book is innovative and deserves positive discussion.

21. Oliver, *Conjugal Spirituality*, p. 105.
22. Oliver, *Conjugal Spirituality*, p. 52.

is flexible, realistic, compassionate and hopeful. That one thing is most
named as friendship. Marital friendship is not an extra. It is the thing that
can make marriage possible, when the patriarchal systems no longer
work, as it has in the past often made love and mutuality possible within
a patriarchal system. If I am right, the presence of divine reality in the
relationship has its basis in the quality of friendship, and not in any
definitions based on sexual intimacy as such. If this is so we have to
deal, as suggested, with the fact that such friendship also exists in relationships between people of the same sex, sexual or not; in that case the
whole business of defining relationships in terms of their degree or kind
of sexual expression immediately begins to look rather primitive, if not
downright silly.[23]

Friendship on this view is the preserver and enabler of marriages,
generating its own dynamism which is especially effective when the
social environment is hostile and official church attitudes uncomprehending. Friendship subverts patriarchy and provides an alternative to it
because it is based on equality and mutuality, and not on dominance
and hierarchy. It is the means whereby the presence of God is known
within the marriage. And it is inclusive, because it operates in the
relationships of lesbian, gay and straight people, single and married
people alike—they all have friendship in common—whether or not
they are sexually active. But despite the promise which friendship has
as a model for, or an alternative to, marriage, there are good reasons for
claiming that marriage demands, and offers, more.

That marriage is, among other definitions, a special friendship, has
been repeatedly stated by traditional and patriarchal thought, pre-
Christian and Christian, philosophical and theological. This might,
prima facie, be thought to qualify considerably the hope invested in
friendship by feminist theology as the meaning of marriage, should
marriage remain at all. There is a full discussion of friendship between
husband and wife in Aristotle, who based it in pleasure, utility and
sometimes in virtue.[24] Both Robert Grosseteste (*d*. 1253) and Thomas
Aquinas were influenced by Aristotle's account of friendship, and
married friendship in particular. All three authors, together with Augustine, see friendship as a 'natural' or universal human good, which in the
particular case of marriage becomes intensified, because each partner is

23.   Haughton, 'The Meaning of Marriage', p. 152; and see Stuart, *Just Good
Friends*, p. 117.

24.   Aristotle, *Nichomachean Ethics*, books 8–9: see in particular 1162a15-27.
For a theological comment, see Hogan, *Finality and Marriage*, p. 91.

'a source of delight to the other' and 'if children are procreated their presence will increase that natural friendship'.[25] Aquinas, in a passage which was positively to influence the Puritans' approach to marriage as friendship, and which drew heavily from Aristotle, observed,

> The greater the friendship is, the more solid and long-lasting will it be. Now there seems to be the greatest friendship between husband and wife, for they are united not only in the act of fleshly union, which produces a certain gentle association even among beasts, but also in the partnership of the whole range of domestic activity. Consequently, as an indication of this, man must even 'leave his father and mother' for the sake of his wife, as is said in Genesis [2.24].[26]

We have seen a glimpse of the role of friendship in Augustine's theology of marriage, (above, 5.1.b) noting its compatibility with the domination and submission assumed to be crucial to its order. Aelred of Rievaulx (*d.* 1167), commenting on the creation of woman from the side of man, (Gen. 2.21-22), exclaims,

> How beautiful it is that the second human being was taken from the side of the first, so that nature might teach that human beings are equal and, as it were, collateral, and that there is in human affairs neither a superior nor an inferior, a characteristic of true friendship.[27]

Bishop Jeremy Taylor (*d.* 1667) devoted a work to the topic friendship, noting that 'nearness of friendship' is impossible 'where there is not mutual love'.[28] Marriage, he says, is the

> queen of friendships, in which there is a communication of all that can be communicated by friendship: and it being made sacred by vows and love, by bodies and souls, by interest and custom, by religion and by laws, by common counsels and common fortunes; it is the principal in the kind of friendship, and the measure of all the rest.[29]

25.   H.P. Mercken (ed.), *The Greek Commentaries on the Nicomachean Ethics of Aristotle in the Latin Translation of Robert Grosseteste* (2 vols.; Leuven, 1992), 1162a 24-28 (Text and reference in James McEvoy, 'Friendship Within Marriage: A Philosophical Essay', in Luke Gormally [ed.], *Moral Truth and Moral Tradition: Essays in Honour of Peter Geach and Elizabeth Anscombe* [Dublin: Four Courts Press, 1994], pp. 194-202 [198]).

26.   Aquinas, *Summa contra gentiles* 3.123.6.

27.   Aelred of Rievaulx, *Spiritual Friendship* 1.57-58 (quotation from McEvoy, 'Friendship Within Marriage', p. 197).

28.   Jeremy Taylor, *A Discourse of the Nature, Offices, and Measures of Friendship*, in *Works XI* (London: Longmans, 1839), p. 308.

29.   Taylor, *Discourse*, p. 325.

It is sometimes overlooked that *Humanae vitae* speaks of marriage as 'a very special form of personal friendship whereby the spouses generously share everything with each other'.[30]

The conviction that a purpose of marriage is the mutual companionship of each of the partners with the other is also based in early canon law and liturgy, even if the term 'friendship' is not used. Martin Bucer (*d*. 1551) held that companionship was the most important part of marriage.[31] Homily 18 of the second Book of Homilies (said in Article 35 of the 39 Articles of the Church of England, with the other homilies, to 'contain a godly and wholesome Doctrine') says marriage was instituted that 'man and woman should live lawfully in a perpetual friendship',[32] while the marriage service says marriage 'was ordained for the mutual society, help, and comfort, that the one ought to have of the other, both in prosperity and adversity'. There seems to have been a clear incompatibility in Puritan thought between the renewed emphasis on friendship and the patriarchal form of domination and submission, which was to have a lasting effect. If the couple were to love each other and care for each other, take mutual delight in sensual and sexual pleasure, the submission of wives was increasingly going to be seen as counterproductive to the accomplishment of these ends.[33]

Friendship in most of these theologians is a matter of degree, culminating in the highest friendship of all, which is the friendship of marriage. There is confidence among these male authors that this picture of marital friendship reflects actual states of affairs, not merely possible ones, irrespective of how things turn out or are perceived by wives. Spouses who are friends may be a constant delight and tenderness to each other, and close lasting friendship must be central to any Christian theology of marriage. The Catholic priest James McEvoy thinks 'marriages that do not grow along the lines of friendship are likely to fail, and to be dissolved'.[34] Friendship is also central to the experience of lesbian and gay people in their partnerships. But the further question

30. Paul VI, *Humanae vitae*, 9.

31. Kenneth Stevenson, *Nuptial Blessing: A Study of Christian Marriage Rites* (New York: Oxford University Press, 1983), p. 190.

32. Homily 18, 'On the State of Matrimony'.

33. Edmund Leites, 'The Duty to Desire: Love, Friendship and Sexuality in Some Puritan Theories of Marriage', *Journal of Social History* 13 (1985), pp. 391-95.

34. McEvoy, 'Friendship Within Marriage', p. 201.

arises: when married heterosexual partners speak of friendship, are they speaking of the same thing as lesbian and gay partners? Elizabeth Stuart has called for a 'redefining' of marriage as a 'relationship in which two friends of the opposite sex enter into a covenant of passionate radical vulnerability'.[35] How far is such a redefinition of marriage justified?

Friendship, Marriage and Children. There is no single definition of friendship. Aristotle and Cicero set Western attitudes to friendship, and Taylor's lengthy and impassioned letter on the subject remains remarkable reading. The radical friendship which is advocated in much feminist and lesbian writing[36] clearly 'highlight[s] the value of relationship between women in a society which ignores and denigrates such relationships, and emphasizes the transformative power of horizonal relationships in a faith which emphasizes the value of the vertical'.[37] Mary Hunt means by friendship 'those voluntary human relationships that are entered into by people who intend one another's well-being and who intend that their love relationship is part of a justice-seeking community'.[38] This friendship is rooted in particular experience, and is defined against domination by men. Marriage as advocated here is friendship, and married partners have much to learn from lesbian and gay partnerships about what mutuality may mean in practice.

Nonetheless it is not possible to define marriage wholly in terms of friendship. The stance taken over a theology of liberation for children (above, 5.1-2) forbids it. Fertile, sexually active, heterosexual couples, whether married or not, are likely at some stage to produce children: lesbian and gay couples are not. This is a crucial difference which must be honoured (below, 9.2.b). A sexual ethic for everyone must provide the highest place for commitment and fidelity implicit in the notion of covenant: but a heterosexual sexual ethic cannot avoid the possibility of

---

35. Stuart, *Just Good Friends*, p. 234.

36. E.g., Janice G. Raymond, *A Passion for Friends: Towards a Philosophy of Female Affection* (Boston: Beacon Press, 1986); Mary Hunt, *Fierce Tenderness: A Feminist Theology of Friendship* (New York: Crossroad, 1991); Stuart, *Just Good Friends*.

37. Jennifer L. Rike, 'The Lion and the Unicorn: Feminist Perspectives on Christian Love as Care', in Thatcher and Stuart (eds.), *Christian Perspectives*, pp. 247-62 (254.)

38. Hunt, *Fierce Tenderness*, p. 29.

the birth of children, and consequently a third of one's adult life partly devoted to their nurture. Faced with these additional and formidable commitments, 'intending one another's well-being', is an insufficiently strong indicator of resolve, and does not in any case address the experience of heterosexual couples that children may arrive unexpectedly or be passionately wanted. Living together with one's partner and one's children requires great patience and perseverance which the institution of Christian marriage exists to support. While the best marriages are friendships, there is more to marriage than friendship.

Stuart may acknowledge this when she speaks of the support children need when they are conceived or adopted. She writes,

> A parent's relationship with a child is a *de facto* life-long one, and when two people enter into an agreement to have children together (by whatever means) they have a right to expect of each other life-long commitment to and responsibility towards that child. Parenting is a full-time co-operative job.[39]

Well, this looks remarkably like an informal marriage awaiting solemnization (even if the child has been adopted). There is an 'agreement', 'life-long commitment', 'responsibility' for the child and acknowledgment that parenting is a shared job. Such an arrangement is certainly more than friendship since friendships do not, normally at least, require these extraordinary commitments. Yet marriage exists to promote them. The category of friendship has become too broad,[40] and cannot be an alternative for the institution of marriage, despite its lived imperfections.

d. *Covenanted Love*

Any contemporary theology of marriage is likely to start with the experience of human love. However such a starting point is far from obvious, and so several caveats will first need to be made. First, up to *Casti connubii* in 1930 the association between love and marriage has been avoided in Roman Catholic thought.[41] Secondly, the perils of

---

39.   Stuart, *Just Good Friends*, p. 222.

40.   Lisa Sowle Cahill criticizes what she sees as an over-emphasis on friendship in contemporary theological accounts of marriage. Like the category of love in Christian ethics, she says 'it is a norm that nobody can disagree with', and that Christian discipleship requires more than friendship. See her comments at the end of Haughton, 'The Meaning of Marriage', pp. 156-57.

41.   Even passages of Scripture such as Eph. 5 which are commonly understood

romantic love are well known: when in the seventeenth and eighteenth centuries, romantic love was popularized, it was regarded as a form of madness.[42] Thirdly, any attempt to define love into the marriage relation runs the risk of ignoring or masking how power works within it. As Stanley Hauerwas observes, when this happens,

> the fact that marriage involves power is unacknowledged, so that the language of love often becomes the way coercive relations are legitimized... Power, however, must be understood not simply as physical force, but the ability to impose on the other one's understanding of the relation.[43]

Here is a timely warning against oppressive and asymmetrical self-giving. Fourthly, expectations of how men and women express their love are highly gendered, and are likely to require rescue from ingrained patriarchal assumptions. A jarring example of gendered expectation was found (above, 3.2.a) in Ephesians 5 where husbands were expected to embody the love of Christ for the Church by giving themselves up for their wives and treating them as their own bodies, while wives were expected to show subjection to (v. 22) and reverence for (v. 33), their husbands.

The point that married love is able to be a living representation not simply of divine love, but of the central mysteries of the faith is variously expressed in official documents. In *Familiaris consortio*,

> the communion of love between God and people...finds a meaningful expression in the marriage covenant which is established between a man and a woman.

> For this reason the central word of revelation, 'God loves his people', is likewise proclaimed through the living and concrete word whereby a man and a woman express their conjugal love. Their bond of love becomes the image and the symbol of the covenant which unites God and his people.[44]

to establish analogies between divine and married love, were either generally ignored in the Western tradition or used in the liturgy for the consecration of virgins who were married to Christ.

42. Stone, *The Family*, p. 181.

43. Stanley Hauerwas, 'The Family as a School for Character', in Scott and Warren (eds.), *Perspectives on Marriage*, pp. 146-57 (156 n. 2).

44. John Paul II, *Familiaris consortio*, 12, 'Marriage and Communion Between God and People'.

There is little doubt about the order of the disclosure of the divine
love and the divine covenant in these words. The sense of them is
clearly empirical. Inasmuch as there may be lived out in everyday life a
human covenant, the fabric of this covenant, its weave and woof,
becomes also the texture of the divine covenant. The 'expression' of
conjugal love is an expression of God's love. The use of the terms
'image' and 'symbol' to describe the relation between the human
covenant of marriage and the divine covenant between God and God's
people bears an ontological reference. The couple participate in the
divine covenant. One comes to expression in the other. When Christ is
spoken of as the 'Bridegroom of the Church',[45] nuptial imagery borrowed from Eph. 5.25-27 is used as a way of achieving experiential
continuity between the two covenants. The openness of one to be the
expression of the other is why the failure of a Christian marriage is a
disaster not simply for the couple and their children, but also for the
church, because that marriage is no longer able to represent the divine
love. 'The churches have a serious stake in ministering to married
Christians because the break up of a marriage means the failure of an
icon to perdure in its iconic function.'[46]

Marriage then is in Catholic thought a primary means of evangelism.
People wanting to find out about the central mysteries of the faith will
find them set out in the covenant of Christian marriage. The central
doctrines of incarnation and atonement are re-enacted by it. The
'original truth of marriage' is said to reach its 'definitive fullness in the
gift of love which the word of God makes to humanity in assuming a
human nature, and in the sacrifice which Jesus Christ makes of himself
on the cross for his bride, the church'.[47] The marriage of baptized persons is said to become 'a real symbol of that new and eternal covenant
sanctioned in the blood of Christ'. The married couple are not expected
to achieve that transparency of love which reveals God's love unas-
sisted, for 'The Spirit which the Lord pours forth gives a new heart, and
renders man and woman capable of loving one another as Christ has
loved us'. 'Conjugal charity' is proclaimed as 'the proper and specific

45.   The title of section 13 of *Familiaris consortio* is 'Jesus Christ, Bridegroom
of the Church, and the Sacrament of Matrimony'.
46.   Timothy D. Lincoln, 'Sacramental Marriage: A Possibility for Protestant
Theology', *Proceedings of the American Theological Library Association* 49
(1995), pp. 205-216 (215).
47.   John Paul II, *Familiaris Consortio*, 12.

way in which the spouses participate in and are called to live the very charity of Christ, who gave himself on the cross'.[48]

Marriage is therefore an icon, what Guroian calls 'a material embodiment of the truth that the church has agreed upon'.[49] The icon is, however, uniquely appropriate to express the divine love, for its 'material embodiment' is a living, loving, human couple, and what it embodies is the divine love manifested in the gift of Jesus Christ and the giving of his life for the Church and for the world. That is why spouses are said to be 'the permanent reminder to the church of what happened on the cross; they are for one another and for the children witnesses to the salvation in which the sacrament makes them sharers'. Their bond 'represents the mystery of Christ's incarnation and the mystery of his covenant'.[50]

e. *The Big Shift: From Love as Attitude to Love as Relation*

The required work on the concept of love, to prepare it for use in a Christian theology of marriage, is extensive. A major shift is required from the understanding of love as an attitude to love as a relation. The dominant understanding of love is that it is an *attitude*. As such it has a subject, the human agent who expresses the attitude, and an object of the attitude, which may or may not be another person. As an attitude it is a property of an agent who displays it in his or her actions. Love is the supreme Christian attitude, a virtue which we realize only with the help of God. The objection raised here against love as an attitude is not that it is wrong but that it is one-sided, and that the other side is rarely put. The alternative approach to love is as a relation, where both lover and beloved are equally subject, and love is the relation between them. This is an approach to love which should enrich conjugal spirituality (above, 7.1.b).

Balance may be restored to the concept of love by understanding it as *a property of the relation between the lover and who or what is loved*. An anonymous act of love towards a beneficiary may be capable of being understood as embracing donor and recipient; more importantly and simply, loving partnerships between people require to be treated as a relation. When marital breakdown occurs, both accounts of love may be needed to make phenomenological sense of the breakdown, that is,

---

48. John Paul II, *Familiaris consortio*, section 13.
49. Guroian, *Ethics After Christendom*, p. 50.
50. John Paul II, *Familiaris consortio*, section 13.

one partner may continue to love the other, but since the other no longer loves, love continues as an attitude (of one of the partners) and terminates as a relation (between them both). This double description of love, as an attitude and as a relation, is a basic premise of a theology of married love, and will greatly assist in examining divorce in the next chapter (below, 8.2.f).

As with the case of marital spirituality, there is little explicitly to be found in the tradition which sees love as a property ('quality' is a better word) of a relationship between people, instead of a property of one person toward another (which may or may not be reciprocated). An obvious suggestion to make is that, in the case of a couple permanently committed to each other, love is clearly a property, indeed the essence, of the relationship. Insofar as a property must logically belong to a subject, the subject would be, using Oliver's innovative term, the 'conjugal body' of the couple in their permeation, but not absorption, of each other. Love on this view is both an attribute of each of the separate partners to each other and an attribute of the relationship or union between them.

One of the few contemporary theologians to have argued for the shift in the understanding of love from attitude to relation is Vincent Brümmer, though his reluctance to deploy the social model of the Trinity prevents him from developing it as the traditional Trinitarian doctrine might have encouraged him to do. His name for relational love is 'fellowship'.[51] In a relation of love, 'personal value and identity are *bestowed* on me by the fact that others consider me irreplaceable to them'.[52] 'In an agreement it is the value of my services to you which is at stake, whereas in fellowship my value as a person is at stake.'[53] Applied to the theology of marriage, we might justifiably say the contrast between agreement and fellowship mirrors the contrast which has been noted and developed (above, 3.2.a) between contract and covenant. There are several senses in which relational love is a risk. One is vulnerability to the possible lack of reciprocation. 'If I openly declare my love to you, I take responsibility for what I say. I therefore cannot

51. Vincent Brümmer, *The Model of Love* (Cambridge: Cambridge University Press, 1994). Section 7.3, 'Agreements and Fellowship' (pp. 164-73), provides a similar sort of contrast to that developed between contract and covenant (above, 3.2.1).

52. Brümmer, *The Model of Love*, p. 166 (author's emphasis).

53. Brümmer, *The Model of Love*, p. 167.

easily disavow my declaration in order to save face if you should spurn me.'[54] One is also vulnerable to change in oneself, one's beloved, and in the relationship. This is because 'Such relationships depend on the partners remaining faithful to each and to the identity which they adopt in identifying with each other'. But, as Brümmer explains,

> As human persons, however, we are not only able to become unfaithful to each other and thus to the identity which we adopt for ourselves, but the circumstances of our lives could give rise to changes in our identity which make it difficult for us to continue to identify with each other. Our identity as persons is not immutably stable.[55]

Faithfulness, then, is both a commitment and a risk, and in societies where adultery is common and faithfulness undermined, the risk is greater, and some people are put off entering into marriage for fear the risk is too great. An original meaning of 'sacrament' was 'fidelity', the only 'good' of marriage which Augustine believed to be uniquely Christian (above, 5.1.d). Since human love exists *between* lovers and is a cooperative, relational venture, it is beyond one's own power as a single person to control. There are no guarantees about its perpetuity or quality. It is always prospective.

The experience of loving and being loved provides a beginning for the reflection on and the experience of divine love. Reciprocal human love is one of the ways by which divine love is known. The central belief about God, that 'God is love' (1 Jn 4.8, 16) is taken for granted. The content of this concept of love is derived from Jesus Christ (1 Jn 4.9-10). The life, death and resurrection of Jesus is the criterion for what is to count as love, in Christian faith.[56] The doctrines of atonement and incarnation are complementary ways of describing the extent of divine love, and Christian marriage is one way whereby it is possible to share in divine love directly (below, 7.1.e-f).

Being loved is a great good, not least because we are thereby affirmed and valued. The message of the gospel is that the divine love has reached out to us and accepted us, whatever our state of heart and mind, and however unacceptable we are to ourselves. Indeed the experience of being loved was the foundation of the Puritan marriage

54. Brümmer, *The Model of Love*, p. 168.
55. Brümmer, *The Model of Love*, p. 171.
56. Adrian Thatcher, *Truly a Person, Truly God* (London: SPCK, 1990), p. 141, and see Chapter 11, 'Personal Knowledge and Divine Love'.

ethic.[57] It may be an overwhelming disclosure of the being and work of God. The experience of the care, companionship and passion of one's partner may be the clue to the experience of the caring, companionate, passionate God. André Guindon was right to claim the experience of 'covenant love' within marriage was *simultaneously* an experience of the divine love expressed in the covenants of God with God's people. He held that,

> covenant love becomes experientially instructive of Who God is. By a loving and faithful covenant with this mysterious 'other' (i.e., this 'who I am not': man for woman and woman for man), one acknowledges that one becomes who one is mainly through the other's redemptive care. This constitutes a privileged way of discovering the mystery of redemptive Truth and transcendence. The Mystery of God's otherness combined with her loving concern for her creature is one which authentic witnesses of conjugal loving fecundity can help us all intuit.[58]

Love which becomes a total commitment to one's partner can become a sharing in the greater reality of God's covenant love for God's people: the otherness of our partner in his or her being which is also a being-for-us, is a representation of the divine Otherness and divine caring for us. Conjugal loving, mixed as it is with divine loving, becomes redemptive. Insofar as the love of husband and wife is realized in their partnership, that partnership is a 'witness' to the divine love.

f. *Communion of Persons*

What was said earlier about the social nature of the person in Christian faith, marital spirituality, the mutuality of friendship, and love as a relation, can now receive further elucidation through the Christian doctrine of the Trinity. Analogies may legitimately be devised between the relation between human persons and the divine Persons of the Trinity, provided that it is remembered there are at least as many dissimilarities as similarities between human and divine Persons. Although there has been a recent (and mainly Protestant?) revival of interest in that doctrine, there has been an unwavering emphasis on the Trinity in official Roman Catholic thought and particularly in its relation to marriage. Divine love is revealed in the incarnation of God in Christ and in the atonement brought about by Christ's suffering love. It is also revealed at the very heart of the divine essence, since God's essence is to be a

57. Leites, 'The Duty to Desire', p. 392.
58. Guindon, *The Sexual Creators*, p. 105.

loving communion of Persons. The shift from an individual to a relational account of human love has just been described. A similar shift may now be discerned in the meaning of what it is to be made in the image of God. Individualistic accounts of the *imago dei* regard the human being as a finite reflection of the monotheistic God, although the earliest biblical text on which the doctrine of the divine image is based (Gen. 1.27) allows a relational understanding of the divine image as shared between male and female. However, crucial to the theology of marriage is the *Trinitarian* understanding of the divine image, whereby what is imaged in humanity is the loving communion of coequal Persons in the Trinity. While this is undoubtedly a recent recovery of emphasis in approach to the Trinity (and humanity) among Protestants, it is in fact a common feature of Catholic and Orthodox thought. What is needed is a clearer vision of what human communion, which is at the same time a sharing in the communion of the Trinity, might mean.

Familiaris consortio has no hesitation in developing the meaning of the statement that 'God is love' by means of a fully developed Trinitarian theology which was obviously not in the mind of St John:

> 'God is love' and in himself he lives a mystery of personal loving communion. Creating the human race in his own image and continually keeping it in being, God inscribed in the humanity of man and woman the vocation, and thus the capacity and responsibility, of love and communion. Love is therefore the fundamental and innate vocation of every human being.[59]

While marriage is not necessary to the purposes for which God created us, communion is. Communion is an inclusive human vocation: marriage is a particular and intense form of communion. Marriage is a lesser vocation than the vocation to communion. The very particularity and intensity of it may well provide the grounds for many people deciding they do *not* have a vocation to it.

The *Catechism of the Catholic Church* described the Christian family as 'a communion of persons, a sign and image of the communion of the Father and the Son in the Holy Spirit. In the procreation and education of children it reflects the Father's work of creation'.[60] In the later *Letter to Families* the family is said to be

---

59. John Paul II, *Familiaris consortio*, section 11, 'Man, the Image of the God Who Is Love'.

60. *Catechism of the Catholic Church*, §2205.

in fact a community of persons whose proper way of existing and living together is communion: *communio personarum*. Here too, while always acknowledging the absolute transcendence of the Creator with regard to his creatures, we can see the family's ultimate relationship to the divine 'We'. *Only persons are capable of living 'in communion'*. The family originates in a marital communion described by the Second Vatican Council as a 'covenant', *in which man and woman 'give themselves to each other and accept each other'*.[61]

Orthodox writers have generally affirmed the social Trinity, but its association with marriage in contemporary Orthodox thought is striking. Kallistos Ware says that in Orthodoxy 'Marriage, the "sacrament of love", is a direct expression of our human personhood according to the image and likeness of the Holy Trinity. Formed as an icon of the Trinitarian God, the human person is made for mutual love'. Commenting on Gen. 1.27, Ware remarks, 'The image of God is given, not to the man alone or to the woman alone, but to the two of them together. It comes to its fulfilment only in the "between" that unites them to each other'. In language similar to that used by the Vatican he affirms,

> Personhood is a mutual gift; there is no true human (*sic*) unless there are at least two humans in communion with each other. To say 'I am made in God's image' is to affirm: 'I need you in order to be myself'. The divine image is in this way a relational image, manifested not in isolation but in community—and above all, in the primordial bond between husband and wife that is the foundation of all other forms of social life. Monastics and lay people not called to matrimony, if they are to be authentically human, need to realize in some other way the capacity for mutual love which finds its primary expression through the man-woman relationship within marriage.[62]

g. *Marriage as Perichoresis*

It has already been suggested that the language of interpersonal communion derived from the doctrine of the Trinity may help to fill the hiatus (above, 7.1.b) with regard to conjugal spirituality. There are good reasons for adopting and refining the suggestion of Michael

---

61. John Paul II, *Letter to Families*, section 7 (author's emphases), 'The Marital Covenant'. The quotation is from *The Pastoral Constitution on the Church in the Modern World—Gaudium et spes*, §48.

62. Ware, 'The Sacrament of Love', p. 79; see also, Allchin, 'Sacrament of Marriage', pp. 115-17.

Lawler that marriage be understood as a form of *perichoresis*, the term used (from the sixth century onwards) for the relations between the divine Persons of the Trinity and the two natures of God the Son.[63] The word derives from *chorein*, 'to make room for another', and from *peri*, 'round about'.[64] It is defined as 'the dynamic process of making room for another around oneself'. We have seen how Trinitarian thought has been used by Orthodox and Roman Catholic thought to explicate the meaning of Christian marriage. Perichoresis helps us to visualize what it is to be a person-in-relation on the basis of the communion of the Persons within the Trinity. It prompts us towards affirming our own identity as a person while recognizing that other persons make us who we are and we help make other persons what they are. Marriage is of course unnecessary to experience finitely the infinite communion of the Trinity, since, as bearers of the divine image, our destiny is communion with others and with God. But marriage is an intensification of relationship at its most personal and enduring.

Perichoresis depicts persons as made for communion with each other: with persons love can be a relation. It embraces both. While official theology affirms that the communion which is marriage and the communion which is God participate in each other, attention to

63. Michael Lawler, '*Perichoresis*: New Theological Wine in an Old Theological Wineskin', *Horizons* 22.1 (1995), pp. 49-66. However Lawler extends perichoresis into two further areas which unacceptably stretch the application of the term to marriage. He thinks that, like the Person of Christ, marriage has two natures, social and religious, and that these natures are also 'fully mutual and equal' (p. 55); that 'God and God's Christ are present as third partners' in the marriage (p. 56); and that the spouses become 'one marital person' (p. 58) by perichoresis. But Trinitarian perichoresis allows the persons to be both distinct and one in their communion. The subjects of the perichoresis are the persons, and in the Trinity persons do *not* become one. If the subject is marriage, then an abstract noun replaces the personal subjects. Marriage is then said to possess two natures, but these natures are better understood as properties, as in double-aspect theories of persons. Persons can be 'fully mutual and equal', but it is hard to see how natures can. Making God a third partner in the marriage is at least a bad category mistake. God cannot be a partner in a marriage—one is married to a spouse, not to God, and the single term 'partner' cannot cover both without doing violation to language. In Trinitarian perichoresis relations between coequal persons provide the material for the downward extension to marriage. For these reasons I think Lawler overplays the application of perichoresis to marriage and loses its subtlety.

64. Lawler, '*Perichoresis*', p. 49. Other theologians derive the term from *perichoreuein*, 'to dance around' (see Lawler, p. 53, for examples).

particular details of the perichoresis is likely to have a radicalizing effect on the meaning of marriage, perhaps not noticed. For example, perichoresis as a model for marital communion subverts patriarchal marriage completely, for just as the model of friendship was finally incompatible with ruling and obeying, so the model of perichoresis is incompatible with theories and practices of gender which announce masculine superiority (e.g., the theory which says 'a woman's head is man' [1 Cor. 11.3]). The Persons who together make up the one God are in every respect coequal. Subordination of the Son and/or the Spirit to the Father is expressly ruled out in the Church's doctrine and by the Church's great statement about the Trinity, the Athanasian creed or *Quicunque vult*. Perichoresis does not allow one Person power over the other. In marriage understood as perichoresis, partners do not exercise power over each other, but give themselves *to* each other. Domination impairs communion and so is a form of sinfulness. Spouses share in Christian redemption when loving communion is realized between them. 'Making room for one another' is particularly appropriate to partners who are constantly in each other's company, and often in each other's way. It is an art which requires attentiveness, intuitiveness, indeed, nothing less than divine grace. Just as the divine communion goes beyond itself to create a world and share its being, so the communion of marriage may empower each partner in turning their love for each other outwards to the wider community, to children and to God.

Perichoresis is an appropriate term to describe a relation to another person in whose care we place ourselves and for whom we care. Perichoresis may imply a continuity of presence that friendship does not. Language which has been historically reserved for reverent musings about the holy mystery of God is especially appropriate for filling the hiatus in compiling a theology and spirituality of marriage.

2. *Marriage as a Sacrament*

The difficulties in speaking of marriage as a sacrament within the internal dialogue between and within the churches has already been noted (above, 2.1.d). Having explored the theology of marriage as a communal partnership, it is now possible to map some of the meanings of marriage explored there onto marriage understood as a sacrament. It will be necessary to begin with standard Protestant objections to marriage as a sacrament, and work through some contemporary understandings of the term in order to commend (and extend) a sacramental theology of marriage.

a. *Towards an Ecumenical Theology of Sacrament*
Protestant Objections. Three standard objections to marriage as a sacrament are, that it converts a human arrangement into a divine institution; that it ignores the empirical reality of actual marriages; and that it wrongly confuses and conflates the two orders of creation and redemption. Karl Barth is an influential spokesperson for the first objection. He rejected marriage as a sacrament on the grounds that marriage was a human relationship which was wrongly 'divinized' by the weight of sacramental theology. He thought this theology was 'an attempt to remove from the relationship of man and woman as completed in marriage its character as a relationship which is simply and genuinely creaturely'. The marital sacrament is, on this view, 'an exaggeration or apotheosis of the relationship of male and female', and that 'it does no good to this relationship if under any title it is removed from the creaturely sphere'.[65]

The second and third objections are expressed by the Archbishop of Canterbury's 1971 Commission on *Marriage, Divorce and the Church.* The commissioners found 'good reasons' why Anglicans should not accept marriage as a sacrament 'in the Tridentine sense'. One of them is that while 'Christians may be assisted by grace towards the perfection of life to which their marriage tends', it 'is not always possible by empirical observation to discriminate *in kind* between the marriages of those who are baptized and those of the unbaptized. Marriage stands in the order of nature: grace perfects it'.[66] The commissioners at this point appear to put experience before doctrine and let the former determine the latter. On empirical grounds they separate the baptism of spouses from the quality of their marriages, noting that Christian marriage 'does not necessarily imply that mutual consent in the marriage of the baptized effects something which is wholly lacking for the unbaptized'. Their sound insistence on marriage as a human, as well as a Christian institution, leads them to affirm (doubtless influenced by Emil Brunner[67]) that

---

65. Barth, *Church Dogmatics*, III, IV, pp. 124-25.
66. *Marriage, Divorce and the Church*, pp. 36-37 (authors' emphasis).
67. 'In Protestantism also the Sacrament belongs…to the order of redemption, not to the order of creation…To make marriage into a sacrament means to connect

Marriage belongs to the order of creation rather than that of redemption. Acceptance of marriage as a sacramental reality, welcome because of the verities which this language can imply, has been accompanied among many Anglicans by a very profound unease about its definition as one of the seven sacraments.[68]

Barth's insistence on the human frailty of marriage is ironic. While he introduces a note of realism into the theology of marriage (by emphasizing the mess that sinners tend to make of it) he himself has done perhaps more than any other theologian in the twentieth century to divinize, not marriage but, heterosexuality as a God-given absolute. Barth has attempted to essentialize the relations between men and women, claiming divine authority for his insistence on female subordination, so his worry about loading up marriage with a theological weight it is unable to bear might be more consistently directed. The commissioners' observation that the status of spouses with regard to baptism is no predictor of the quality of their relationship is a valuable one, likely to be confirmed by the observations of every reader of this page. Reference to the orders of creation and redemption reminds Christians not to be parochial about marriage, since it is a pre-Christian and a global institution. But there is another approach to marriage as a sacrament which actually incorporates these difficulties and utilizes them in its commendation of the Faith. It is to say that God's grace should not and finally cannot be confined to professing Christians but may be active in any committed, loving relationship. The very abundance of grace entails that it will spill out where it is not expected. Just as the order of baptized and unbaptized is subverted by the sheer generosity of God, so the two orders of creation and redemption are subverted, this time by the work of God in Christ who has reconciled everything and everyone to Godself, irrespective of the human ability to acknowledge it, the vacillating credibility of the churches, the ingrained habit of dividing up the human race in accordance with religious difference, and so on. These thoughts lead to what has been called 'natural sacramentality' and are developed later (below, 7.2.e).

Marriage was not designated a sacrament of the Church, equal in

it with the Church in the way in which Baptism and the Eucharist are connected with the Church, as a sign and a means of communicating the Divine grace of Redemption'. Emil Brunner, *The Divine Imperative* (trans. Olive Wyon; Philadelphia: Westminster Press, 1947), p. 649.

68. *Marriage, Divorce and the Church*, p. 37.

status to all the others until the Council of Verona in 1184. The Vulgate translation of the phrase 'This is a great mystery' (*mustèrion mega*) in Eph. 5.32 was *sacramentum*, and this word undoubtedly led twelfth-century theologians to read into the 'great mystery' sacramental meanings then current, which neither the author of Ephesians nor Augustine (2.1.d) could have understood. The 'pledge' or 'loyalty oath', together with the behaviour which showed its worth, transferred from military enlistment to marital fidelity, became something else. Calvin and Luther understood sacraments as 'comprised of signs tied ineluctably to God's grace in Christ'.[69] Since they also held that grace was 'God's unmerited forgiveness, the rescue from sin', they were in no doubt that marriage could not be sacramental. There was an obvious reason: it did not confer forgiveness of sins. It belonged to the order of creation, not redemption. This distinction has just been noted in a near contemporary Protestant work. Paradoxically as marriage lost its sacramental status in Protestantism, it was invested with sacral, but non-sacramental, dignity as a divine 'ordinance', essential for stable families and societies.

'Sacrament' is understood today more loosely and inclusively than at the time of the Reformation. Some Protestant theologians admit that the loss of sacramental status may have fatally undermined the doctrine of indissolubility which since the time of Augustine was supported by it. A sacrament may simply be said to be a means by which God is uniquely present in the material, human world. For Christians, Christ is the ultimate sacrament, for it is through Christ that God became and becomes present in the material, human world, and in bringing grace into our lives, the sacraments bring the grace *of Christ*.[70] Resolution 13 of the 1930 Lambeth Conference acknowledged 'that intercourse between husband and wife as the consummation of marriage has a value of its own *within that sacrament*, and that thereby married love is enhanced and its character strengthened'.[71]

At the outset of Theodore Mackin's compendious third volume of his

69. Lincoln, 'Sacramental Marriage', p. 206.

70. John Macquarrie, *A Guide to the Sacraments* (London: SCM Press, 1997), pp. 35-36; Edward Schillebeeckx, *Christ the Sacrament* (London: Sheed & Ward, 1963), p. 13.

71. *The Lambeth Conference 1930*, resolution 13. The Encyclical Letter after the Conference called marriage 'sacramental' without qualification (p. 22). And the Conference Committee on The Life and Witness of the Christian Community even assigned 'a sacramental value' to the sex act (p. 92).

trilogy on marriage in the Catholic church, an 'interactionist' view of the sacrament is outlined. Sacraments are 'situated' not simply in ceremonies but in people's lives and God interacts sacramentally with us in both. 'As a situation a sacrament is a setting for interaction between God and human beings: as a relationship the substance thereof is this interaction. God takes the initiative in this interaction.' With regard to the particular sacrament of marriage, Mackin says

> in entering men's and women's lives thus sacramentally God does so with double and interlocking intent: to draw men and women to himself, and to draw them to one another. In drawing them to himself in faith, trust and love, he would also draw them to one another in the same believing, trusting and caring attitude.[72]

Many Protestants should find themselves able to affirm a sacramental sense of marriage in this sense. If a sacrament mediates God's presence, the confinement of marriage to the order of redemption unacceptably restricts the omnipresence of God. Sacraments make visible the reality of God's love. 'In the sacraments, God continues in present visibility what God has already done in self giving in the historical visibility of Jesus Christ.'[73]

b. *Communal Partnership as the Matrix of the Sacrament*
The question for Protestants is 'In Christian marriage is God at work communicating divine love?'[74] If the answer is a qualified 'Yes', then marriage can be called a sacrament, with the proviso that divine love is communicated in many other ways and other relationships than marriage, and the institution of marriage whether or not between Christian spouses does not by itself guarantee the experience of God's love at all. Rather, in calling marriage a sacrament one consciously links the sacramental traditions of the churches with the experience of loving relationships. The content of a married couple's sacrament is what they share with each other. In order to make this claim good it is necessary to introduce the semi-technical term 'matrix' and speak of 'the matrix of the sacrament'. A matrix in ordinary language is a situation or surrounding substance within which something else originates, develops or is contained. Examples of a matrix are the womb, the formative cells or

72. Mackin, *The Marital Sacrament*, pp. 7-8.

73. James F. White, *Introduction to Christian Worship* (Nashville: Abingdon Press, rev. edn, 1990), p. 189.

74. Lincoln, 'Sacramental Marriage', p. 211.

tissue of a part of the body, the solid matter in which a fossil or crystal is embedded, and a binding substance, as cement in concrete. The term has a long history in sacramental theology. As Mackin explains,

> The matrix of a sacrament is the human conduct, conduct perhaps formed into a ritual, that is taken and made into the sacrament, or into which the sacrament is grafted and whence it draws its substance and its meaning. The matrix consists not merely of the physical ingredients of the pre-existent conduct or ritual; it is the latter, including their meaning that common use has given them to date. Thus not water alone is the matrix of baptism, nor is it alone the bathing with water prescinding from the cultural meaning or bathing. For baptism the matrix is water the source of life, the environment of new life, used in cleansing away the old and beginning the new.[75]

There is thus a kaleidoscopic convergence of meanings that provides the matrix for the marital sacrament. Without the matrix there is no sacrament, and the matrix clearly affects how the sacramental grace is received. Now within some Roman Catholic theology there is an understandable reaction to Tridentine thought (which was itself in part a reaction to the extreme of Reformed theology). In contradistinction to the reformed churches, the Council of Trent emphasized the reception of grace through the performance of the sacrament (the *opus operatum*), declaring that 'if anyone says that grace is not conferred *ex opere operato* through the sacraments of the New Law, but that faith alone in the divine promises is sufficient to obtain grace: let him be anathema'.[76] Whereas Protestants are more willing to speak of marriage as a sacrament, Catholics are more willing to emphasize the role of faith in receiving the sacraments, including marriage.

Emerging from theologies of marriage in the different churches is the conviction that God works through what the partners bring to their marriage and through their ministry of their sacrament to each other (below, 7.2.c). In other words, the matrix of the sacrament is the relationship of each to the other. This meagre-looking gain has the far from meagre outcome of ushering all that has been said about marriage as communal partnership (above, 7.1) into the space of sacramental marriage, of accounting for the sacrament in these terms, and of course

75. Mackin, *The Marital Sacrament*, p. 11.
76. Denzinger-Schönmetzer, *Enchiridion Symbolorum: Definitionum et Declarationum de Rebus Fidei et Morum* (33rd edn, 1965 [1608]). See also Lawler, 'Mutual Love', pp. 339-61.

accounting for marital breakdown by means of the absence of them.

Specifically what was said (above, 7.1.a) about how, in Christian anthropology, persons are 'made for each other', may be reread in the light of marriage as a sacrament. When both partners love each other as they love themselves, or grow as persons because of the love of the other for them, then their interchange of love may be sacramental for them. Their *communio* makes the divine *communio* present to them. Their *communio* includes their separateness, for in a committed partnership, loving respect for the other requires recognition of their individuality within the shared experience of Molloy's 'conjugal soul' (above, 7.1.b). If a married couple are bound by friendship, the meaning of their friendship is that they are equal partners in their marriage. If there is friendship and inequality within a marriage, there is likely also to be self-deception, for psychological realism compels an examination of how the dynamics of power and influence are distributed in the relationship. In seizing on the doctrine of perichoresis in an effort to think about conjugal spirituality, it is hardly an accident of analogy that the Persons in eternal communion with each other are coequal, and that in their communion their identities remain distinct.

The shift signalled in the doctrine of love, from an attitude towards another, to a relationship with an other, has consequences for the marital sacrament. A loving relationship is incarnated in the endless give and take which is life with a life-partner. It is, by its own character, reciprocal, since when it is unbalanced or one-sided it is impaired and imposes burdens on the partner who gives the most and receives back the least. The Trinity is a relational understanding of God, and Christians may experience their loving relationships as sharing in the personal communion which is the heart and nature of God. The experience of being unconditionally affirmed by one's partner, as the male Puritan writers understood, is able to be a sign pointing to the unconditional affirmation and redemption of sinners through God's action in Christ.

There is a further, albeit speculative, element within the broad understanding of the matrix of the sacrament. Societies with high levels of poverty and/or patriarchal control, or which provide little social support for marriage as a lifelong commitment, are not able to provide a stable matrix for the sacrament of marriage to grow. It has more than once been necessary to point out that personalism has scant regard for economic and social contexts, and that without these, persons, whether married or not, cannot flourish. The broad scope of the sacrament's matrix adds a new dimension to marital theology.

Some recent Roman Catholic theology has emphasized the Church as the 'sacrament of the Spirit'. The Spirit is understood as the bringer of the new community of equals, and marriage as a sign of the new sacramental community contains in itself mutuality, equality and community. Francis Schüssler Fiorenza, suspecting that covenant language will ever privilege men, suggests that Spirit-language be used instead to unlock the sacramental mystery of marriage. Every time there is a marriage there is a new community of life. By stressing that 'the sacramental and symbolic function of marriage relates primarily to the church as the emergent post-Easter community of disciples rather than to the covenantal relation between Christ and the church', the way is open to

> emphasise the fundamental equality of husband and wife in the role of forming a new community. Their equality in discipleship and in the formation of a new community of marriage and their hope for that community can symbolize the equality and hope of discipleship in the post-Easter Christian community.[77]

c. *Mutuality in Ministry*

The role of God the Spirit in promoting and deepening communion within the marriage, is likely to be operative through the intentions and actions of the partners—confirming, encouraging some; discouraging, dissuading others. The experience of God the Spirit through the mutual ministry of married partners to each other in deepening love is a great insight of theology. It is a deliberate contrast to the depiction of the Spirit as extrinsic to the marriage, directing the married couple to purely spiritual ends.[78] The grace of God, however generous, will not be forced upon us. An almost forgotten feature of marriage in the Western church is that the state of marriage is not conferred upon a

---

77.   Schüssler Fiorenza, 'Marriage', p. 332.

78.   This position is taken by Geoffrey W. Bromiley, *God and Marriage* (T. & T. Clark: Edinburgh, 1981). In the chapter 'God the Holy Spirit and Marriage' he sees the Spirit's function as providing guidance to couples in fulfilling biblical norms. 'Applied to marriage this objective reality takes the form of biblical directions or injunctions for Christians by which the will of the Spirit is known and for the implementing of which the power of the Spirit is available' (p. 54). Do not these emphases need to be counterbalanced by the location of the Spirit as intrinsic to the marriage, sharing the couple's life even as she shares the life of Father and Son?

marrying couple by anyone except themselves. The priest or minister may officiate, declare them married, pronounce a blessing on the married pair, but the marriage is achieved and carried out by the public declaration of consent. Marriage is therefore unique among the sacraments in that it is the only one that the participants administer to each other. Indeed Catholic priests have recently been reminded of their 'duty' to 'highlight the role of the ministers of the sacrament who, for Christians of the Latin Rite, are *the spouses themselves*, as well as the sacramental value of the community celebration'.[79] But this detail has great significance for the life together which follows. In order for marriage to unlock its potential there must be a mutuality of sacramental ministry. Using Mackin's terms of conduct and ritual, the ritual of administering the sacrament to one another during the marriage service already expresses the conduct whereby each is already administering the sacrament to each other by being there for each other, giving to and receiving from each other. The matrix of the sacrament *is* this conduct, and through the conduct the appearance of grace may be discerned.

This is the matrix of the couple's sacrament, which they minister to each other, and which the Spirit is able to touch and empower. Pope John Paul II, with fine theological language but perhaps little inkling of the actual processes involved, has taught that the communion of spouses

> is nurtured through the personal willingness of the spouses to share their entire life project, what they have and what they are: for this reason such communion is the fruit and the sign of a profoundly human need. But in the Lord Christ God takes up this human need, confirms it, purifies it and elevates it, *leading it to perfection through the sacrament of matrimony*: the Holy Spirit who is poured out in the sacramental celebration offers Christian couples the gift of a new communion of love that is the living and real image of that unique unity which makes of the church the indivisible mystical body of the Lord Jesus.[80]

The Christian life has long been understood as a striving with God's help for perfection, and detrimental to the achievement of it have been unrealistic models of perfection, forged out of the spiritual struggles of

---

79. Pontifical Council For The Family, *Preparation For The Sacrament Of Marriage* (1996), §63.

80. John Paul II, *Familiaris consortio*, 19, 'The Indivisible Unity of Conjugal Communion'.

single, celibate men. However an advantage of the language of perfection is that it assumes the possibility of growth towards it, and the likelihood of struggle and effort in the attainment. The needs of married Christians, rarely articulated, are especially complex because they have separate roles as spouses, persons and often as parents, and the combination of these roles within each spouse, together with the combination of both sets of roles in the one 'conjugal body' will necessarily entail conflict, endless negotiation, give-and-take and compromise. In these circumstances maintaining the relationship at all may appear an achievement—Christian growth through the joys and sorrows, anger and frustration of family life is indeed a matter of grace. Out of this grace, strikingly different models of perfection can be expected.

Despite the obviously 'top-down' nature of the description of the Spirit's work in *Familiaris consortio*, it is a valuable one, provided it assumes the matrix of, for example, earning money, doing chores, choosing and enjoying holidays, celebrating birthdays, shopping, balancing responsibilities of home and work, caring for one another while sick, making up quickly after rows, making love, making meals and washing up after them, making separate spaces as well as forging joint activities, and enlarging their mutual love in order to embody it more widely in church and community and probably children. Their communal partnership is simultaneously their sacrament.

d. *Betrothal as a Sacramental Beginning*

Marriage as a sacrament has been opened up in these pages, but an insistent question remains whether is has been opened sufficiently. Catholic writers have recently been exercised by the problem whether it is possible for unbaptized persons to experience the grace of the sacrament; and whether baptized but non-practising Christians *do* receive the sacrament. There is also an authoritative ruling that the relationship between engaged couples is not sacramental. Perhaps by utilizing the arguments advanced in this book, progress may be made on both counts.

The growth of married partners in mutual love is assumed before and after their marriage, and an impressive programme of marriage preparation has been commended by the Pontifical Council For The Family in their document *Preparation for the Sacrament of Marriage*

(1996). However a key sentence confirms the modern expectation that a marriage begins with a ceremony together with the inescapable logical inference that the experience of being betrothed cannot be sacramental. 'Although *still not in a sacramental way*, Christ sustains and accompanies the journey of grace and growth of the engaged toward the participation in his mystery of union with the Church'.[81] There are many reasons why this position is untenable. First, it has been shown (above, 4.2) that the assumption that marriages have always begun with weddings is historically and theologically inaccurate. The demand for truthfulness and fidelity to past traditions requires theologies of marriage at least to note the diversity of premodern practice together with its creative possibilities. Secondly, almost everyone who thinks and writes about marriage nowadays, wisely takes for granted that marriages are processes, not events. Occurrences, like betrothals, wedding ceremonies, becoming pregnant, becoming a parent are momentous events within an overall shared process which is the marriage. The Vatican also shares this view in its acknowledgment of the need for growth prior to marriage, and further growth after the ceremony, indeed to perfection. Once grace is located and expected through the process, it is increasingly difficult to confine its entry to particular events, the more so since the sheer ordinariness, routine and maintenance of the marriage is where that grace is likely to become available.

Thirdly, the exclusion of sacramentality from engagement seems to have disastrous pastoral consequences. The early flowering and blossoming of mutual love is potentially one of the most graced times in people's lives. It conveys hope, joy and promise, and is itself a powerful 'sign' of the God who is love. The celebration of passionate love between the lovers in the Song of Songs may be a surer guide than the inhibited caution of celibate theologians to the transcending joy of erotic love between two people who treat each other as equals in partnership and desire (above, 3.2.e). Fourthly, we have had reason to note the inadequacy of the 'event mentality' which officially identifies the consummation of a marriage with the first act of sexual intercourse. But just as a processive view of consummation leads to the honest admission of the difficulty of pin-pointing precisely when a marriage is deemed to be completed or fulfilled, so a processive view of marriage

---

81. Pontifical Council For the Family, *Preparation for the Sacrament of Marriage* (1996), §47 (emphasis added).

should lead to the honest admission of the difficulty of pin-pointing precisely when a non-sacramental relationship takes on a sacramental character. Finally, a further unfortunate implication of the official view is that grace comes to the couple only *after* the momentous decision to offer their marriage to the church for solemnization and ratification. Are they on their own when coming to the most momentous decision of their lives?

e. *Towards 'Natural Sacramentality'*
There is a decisive refutation of most of the theological claims in these pages. It is the number of broken marriages. Christian marriages are not notably more successful than any others. The difference between Christian and non-Christian, Church and world, religious and civil, is no predictor of how marriages turn out. One possible response to this dilemma is to abandon the theological superstructure which has attached itself to marriage and which has been partially reaffirmed in this chapter. It is hard to see how this response can be consistent with a developing tradition. A more satisfactory response rejoices in the presence of God in all marriages which exemplify the mutual devotion and communal partnership which are necessarily part of the Christian vision for marriage. In other words, it is liberating to begin to take a non-possessive approach to the dispensing of God's grace, and to delight in its healing power outside the mediating structures of the churches. Since marriage is the only sacrament which is administered by women and men to each other without priestly intervention, marriage may also be the sacrament which helps Christians to realign their thinking about how God the Spirit moves within the world.

What further theological justification is available to support the view that God's grace is able to be experienced by married couples whether they are Christians or not? The official teaching of the Roman Catholic Church is based on the juridical understanding that both parties must be baptized for the marriage to be a sacrament. The sacrament is 'either there or not there'. Conversely, 'although the couple may be genuinely holy and receive enormous gifts from God, their marriage cannot be regarded publicly as a sacrament if one or both have not been baptised'.[82] The official teaching of the Anglican Church is that the sacramentality of marriage 'transcends the boundaries of the Church'.[83]

82. Brown, *Marriage Annulment*, p. 27.
83. *Life in Christ*, p. 22, §62.

Anglicans 'do not make an absolute distinction between marriages of the baptised and other marriages, regarding all marriages as in some sense sacramental'.[84] They are said by their official representatives to 'recognise a sacramentality in all valid marriages'.[85] Two other official Anglican documents affirm 'God is generous in bestowing grace, and he does not confine his gifts within the Christian dispensation, and so what matrimony is may sometimes be as clearly seen in a non-Christian marriage as in a Christian one'.[86] But there are problems with both positions. In the Roman case is it not contradictory for the couple to be said to receive 'enormous gifts' from God, yet to receive them without sacramental grace? The Roman position fails to address the universal pastoral problem in that church of baptized couples with no profession of faith seeking to be married. Such people have been called 'baptized nonbelievers'.[87] Is not faith also required for the sacrament to be received?[88] In the Anglican official document no theological reason is given for affirming the 'natural sacramentality' of marriages. Instead the *de facto* historical explanation is offered that

> For many years in England after the Reformation, marriages could be solemnised only in church. When civil marriages became possible, Anglicans recognised such marriages, too, as sacramental and graced by God, since the state of matrimony had itself been 'adorned and beautified' by Christ by his presence at the marriage at Cana of Galilee.[89]

As with betrothal (above, 4.3), the Anglicans adopt a bold theological position without adequate theological reasons which could easily have been found. Ironically it is within the rich tradition of Roman Catholic thought about marriage that support for natural sacramentality, something that official teaching cannot bring itself to acknowledge, is found.

A major source is Karl Rahner's famous essay 'Marriage as a Sacra-

84. *Life in Christ*, p. 27, §74.

85. *Life in Christ*, p. 28, §77.

86. *Marriage, Divorce and the Church*, p. 24: General Synod, *An Honourable Estate*, p. 64, §162. The latter report 'has only the authority of the Working Party which prepared it'.

87. Susan Wood, SCL, 'The Marriage of Baptized Nonbelievers: Faith, Contract, and Sacrament', *TS* 48 (1987), pp. 279-301.

88. The problem of 'automatic sacramentality' and the distinction between the sacramental status of a marriage and its fruitfulness is discussed by Wood. See 'The Marriage of Baptized Nonbelievers', pp. 284-86.

89. *Life in Christ*, pp. 22, §62. The 1662 Book of Common Prayer is cited.

ment'.[90] Here is a theological analysis of divine and human love and of the mingling of each with the other which allows the sheer generosity of divine love to disrupt any categories of limitation that might be imposed upon it. Since his argument is vital for the developing theology of marriage but is also difficult and protracted, I have broken it down into sections. Beginning with the great commandments of Jesus to love God and to love our neighbours as ourselves, Rahner argues first that the love of God and the love of neighbour cannot be separated. That is because the 'Love of neighbour...is the means without which love of God, a right knowledge of God and of our true and total commitment to him, is quite impossible'.[91] It follows that personal relationships provide the medium for the relationship with God. 'For the "world" in and through which, according to Christian philosophy and theology, God can be "recognized" is precisely in its ultimate depths, not merely our material environment, but first and last the world of personal relationships.'[92] It follows that God is the basis of all loving relationships, irrespective of the religious allegiances of the lovers. In loving her neighbour a person 'can make real to himself and freely accept that transcendental orientation of the spirit...the ultimate basis and absolute goal of which is that Mystery upholding all and upheld by none which we call "God"'.[93] God is encountered and known in the movement of the human person towards another in openness, commitment and care.

It follows from these premises that atheists therefore can experience and know the love of God. Rahner says so explicitly:

> Even the atheist who truly loves makes experience in his love (provided only that it is what it must be) of God, *whether or not he can express this to himself in his conscious thoughts or words.* Even in his case the absolute quality of personal love for the 'thou' of his fellow man utters a silent 'yes' to God.[94]

That God's love is not so confined should occasion no surprise. It does, however, wreck the supposition that baptism or explicit Christian faith is a requirement for the reception of sacramental grace. A couple who share the depths of human love also experience God.

90. Rahner, 'Marriage as a Sacrament', pp. 199-221.
91. Rahner, 'Marriage as a Sacrament', p. 204.
92. Rahner, 'Marriage as a Sacrament', p. 204.
93. Rahner, 'Marriage as a Sacrament', p. 204.
94. Rahner, 'Marriage as a Sacrament', p. 204 (emphasis added).

There is a hope of the two beings *as they actually exist* arriving at what is ultimate and definitive in the existence of them both, and in a love of this kind this hope is positively affirmed. This too has its basis in the ultimate orientation to God as also has the basic faithfulness which such love involves.[95]

Rahner affirms that mutual love is always endowed by God's grace. The personal love

which creates the state of marriage as the mode in which to manifest itself, is in fact in the present order of salvation sustained by the grace of God which *always* imbues this love with its salvific power, exalts it and opens it to the immediacy of God himself.[96]

God is thought to be active in this love prior to the acknowledgment of God in faith, if it happens. God is active in human love 'even before this love encounters the message of the gospel proclaimed and made known as such in explicit words'.[97] Divine love permeates human love. But why? Because there is a 'more general theological principle' which is derived from basic Christian convictions about God's presence in the world. The principle is

in the present order of salvation a moral act that is truly positive ('actus honestus') is in fact also a salvific act ('actus salutaris') in the proper sense in virtue of the grace which always exalts it and which is offered always to every man by the universal salvific will of God.[98]

Theologians unhappy with the principle have failed to realize the conditions needed for faith and for salvation . They

were incapable of rightly appreciating how it is possible, outside the sphere of the *explicit* preaching of the gospel, for that true faith to exist which is necessary for salvation, and also for a salvific act in the true sense to be posited.[99]

A simpler statement of the principle is that

in the order of salvation as it *de facto* exists there are no merely 'natural' moral acts on man's part. These acts are *de facto*, when they are posited at all, also upheld by grace and supernaturally orientated to God in his direct act of self-bestowal.

95. Rahner, 'Marriage as a Sacrament', p. 205 (emphasis added).
96. Rahner, 'Marriage as a Sacrament', p. 205 (author's emphasis).
97. Rahner, 'Marriage as a Sacrament', p. 205.
98. Rahner, 'Marriage as a Sacrament', p. 205 (author's emphasis).
99. Rahner, 'Marriage as a Sacrament', pp. 205-206 (author's emphasis).

Rahner thought that this principle 'applies primarily' to marriage, but was not confined to it. '*Genuine love is* de facto *always that theological virtue of* caritas *which is sustained by God himself through his grace.*'[100] God imparts God's self to the couple through their mutual love. This love

> attains to God in that absolute proximity in which he imparts his own self—and not in the form of any merely creaturely gift—as the inner-most mystery and life of man. In virtue of the fact that it is *caritas*, therefore, this love is also the event of the loving self-bestowal of God upon us which alone empowers us to love God and man. *Caritas*, therefore, is the event of the love of God for us and of our love for God taken as a unity.[101]

What then is the difference between a marriage between two baptized individuals and a 'secular marriage'? Rahner has another first-class answer: a marriage in which a couple express their whole commitment to each other is a 'sign'; the Church itself is a 'sign'; and in a speci-fically Christian marriage, both signs are brought together and empower each other. When the Church acts as a sign, she 'fulfils her own nature because she is the community of love bearing witness to Christ'.[102] Christ is what the Church signifies. But even a worldly marriage is a sign. Since

> married love has the character of a pointer and a sign, marriage itself is never a merely 'worldly affair'. For this love itself is no worldly affair, but rather the event of grace and love which unites God and men. When a marriage of *this* kind, therefore, takes place in the Church, it is an element in the process by which the Church fulfils her own nature as such, one which is brought into being by two baptised Christians who, through their baptism, have been empowered to play an active part in this self-realisation.[103]

Rahner's account of the divine love, over 30 years old, is able to advance the theological reasons for extending the sacramentality of official Roman teaching beyond the administration of the church and grounding the official Anglican teaching in profound Christian theol-ogy. The essay reflects very much the personalism of the 1960s, prob-ably to the detriment of social and political considerations. Sexist

100. Rahner, 'Marriage as a Sacrament', p. 206 (author's emphases).
101. Rahner, 'Marriage as a Sacrament', p. 206.
102. Rahner, 'Marriage as a Sacrament', p. 212.
103. Rahner, 'Marriage as a Sacrament', p. 213.

language was not then an issue. Atheists may dislike being assured that their commitments are made possible by the presence of the divine within them. But none of these considerations detracts from the essential message of the essay that God's generous love is available everywhere, whether or not it is acknowledged: that this love is no respecter of distinctions between creation and redemption, or between sacred and secular realms.[104] Other writers warm to Rahner's denial that there can be a natural order or realm of action separate from God. 'There is no other, no alternative order human beings can choose for themselves, no order literally secular because God is not active in it, because human beings have designed it and manage it independently of him.'[105] 'Even in the case of the unbaptized', claims Susan Wood, 'the personal love which creates the state of marriage is in the present order of salvation graced and salvific.'[106]

God's grace is available to everyone, and people far from formal allegiance to Jesus Christ experience it in their lives. The difference between Christian marriage and other marriages may be that within the Christian faith the communion of marriage is named, understood and celebrated in the light of the communion of the Trinity and the covenant between God and God's people. The naming of these realities will of course influence the way they are experienced, but their availability to be experienced cannot be seriously doubted. If the move away from the 'automatic sacramentality' of marriages, the assumption that sacramental grace is objectively bestowed if certain conditions pertain, is helpful, another move towards the automatic sacramentality of all marriages whether Christian or not, would not be helpful. Indeed it would be as mechanical as the view it replaced. Rather, a Christian understanding of God's generous love and its outpouring all over the world requires Christians to say, with Rahner, that where there is generous, committed, human love, there also God is.

---

104. Cathy Molloy wisely speculates: 'It may be that future theologians will return again and again to Rahner in trying to come to the truth of love in many human relationships that are not marriage and are yet waiting to be included in the human view of God's saving love.' See Molloy, *Marriage*, p. 46.

105. Mackin, *The Marital Sacrament*, p. 672.

106. Wood, 'The Marriage of Baptized Nonbelievers', p. 299.

Chapter 8

THE PARTING OF THE WAYS

When married partners divorce, they 'go different ways'. The English word 'divorce' derives from the Latin *divortium* which comes from the verb *divertere*, 'to go different ways'. Is Christian faith able to bring Good News to people whose marriages are in peril, or which have failed completely? Have the churches been too closely identified with rigorous and insensitive moral teaching to be able to minister to such people? Or have they capitulated to the overwhelming demand for divorce throughout the world in the second half of the twentieth century? Some of the historical changes to marriage which have come about within Christianity have already been charted; now it is appropriate to consider changes which are happening to divorce at the present time. This is done in three parts. Section 8.1 analyses the main New Testament passages about marriage and divorce. It does so from what will be called a 'conventional perspective', finding in them hard teachings forbidding divorce and identifying remarriage with adultery. The further historical hardening of Christian marriage doctrine is briefly described. Section 8.2 returns to the same passages bringing to them the benefits of contemporary but constructive biblical scholarship. Different conclusions are now drawn from the same passages, which, it will be argued, do not merely capitulate to distressing social trends, but offer a more hopeful view of divorce and remarriage in at least some cases. In 8.3 Christian teaching is tested in the face of arguments from inside and outside the churches which deplore the liberalization of divorce laws. The practice of annulment, increasingly widespread in Roman Catholicism, is rejected on theological grounds. The conclusion is reached that, while extensive recourse to divorce in many societies is in many cases a misuse of the hard-won freedom of married people to exit from loveless and frequently violent marriages, there are overwhelming theological grounds on the basis of which Christians may, as a last resort, divorce and remarry.

1. *Divorce and Remarriage: A Conventional Perspective*

a. *The Conventional View*

The earliest reference to the teaching of Jesus apparently forbidding divorce is found in 1 Corinthians 7, where Paul distinguishes between a 'ruling' of 'the Lord' and his own teaching (1 Cor. 7.10). As reference is made throughout the present chapter to this passage, it is quoted extensively (so will be three other passages when we get to them). Paul says,

> [8]To the unmarried and to widows I say this: it is a good thing if like me they stay as they are; [9]but if they do not have self-control, they should marry. It is better to be married than burn with desire.

> [10]To the married I give this ruling, which is not mine but the Lord's: a wife must not separate herself from her husband—[11]if she does, she must either remain unmarried or be reconciled to her husband—and the husband must not divorce his wife.

> [12]To the rest I say this, as my own word, not as the Lord's: if a Christian has a wife who is not a believer, and she is willing to live with him, he must not divorce her; [13]and if a woman has a husband who is not a believer, and he is willing to live with her, she must not divorce him (1 Cor. 7.8-13).

According to the Lord's ruling a wife must not separate herself from her husband, and a husband must not divorce his wife. If the wife becomes separated she should remain unmarried or become reconciled (10-11). However a particular problem at Corinth addressed by Paul was whether a separation was allowable in the case of a mixed marriage between a Christian and an unbeliever (12-16). Paul's own teaching was permissive. The believing partner must not initiate the separation, but if the unbelieving partner wants one it should be allowed. The believing partner 'is not bound by the marriage' (15). There is a further reason why the believing partner must not initiate the separation. Probably under the influence of the teaching of Jesus that a married couple become 'one flesh', the believing partner is said to be the means whereby the unbelieving partner and their children belong to God (14). The mixed marriage is presumably one in which the Christian party is a convert to the faith after the marriage. In Paul's view, conversion after the wedding releases the believing spouse from a marriage the unbelieving spouse no longer wants. The state of no longer being bound by the marriage leaves the Christian partner free, but not encouraged, to remarry. This became known as the 'Pauline privilege'. It has been invoked countless times when a married person becomes a convert. But it has no application to married people who have received a Christian wedding. It applies to 'mixed marriages' only.

In Mk 10.1-12, the teaching of Jesus about divorce is given as a response to a trick question from unnamed people in the crowd. The narrative reads:

> [1]On leaving there he came into the regions of Judaea and Transjordan. Once again crowds gathered round him, and he taught them as was his practice. [2]He was asked: 'Is it lawful for a man to divorce his wife?' This question was put to test him. [3]He responded by asking, 'What did Moses command you?' [4]They answered, 'Moses permitted a man to divorce his wife by a certificate of dismissal.' [5]Jesus said to them, 'It was because of your stubbornness that he made this rule for you. [6]But in the beginning, at the creation, "God made them male and female". [7]"That is why a man leaves his father and mother, and is united to his wife, [8]and the two become one flesh." It follows that they are no longer two individuals: they are one flesh. [9]Therefore what God has joined together, man must not separate.'
>
> [10]When they were indoors again, the disciples questioned him about this. [11]He said to them, 'Whoever divorces his wife and remarries commits adultery against her; [12]so too, if she divorces her husband and remarries, she commits adultery' (Mk 10.1-12).

The question 'Is it lawful for a man to divorce his wife?' is designed to highlight conflict between Jesus and the interpreters of Jewish Law. Deuteronomy 24.1-4, which is quoted by Jesus' interlocutors (Mk 10.4), assumes the normative practice of the divorce of a wife for 'something offensive in her', and the teaching of Jesus conflicts with this assumption (above, 3.1.b). Jesus explains the provision of the Law of Moses for divorce as a concession to male 'stubbornness' (10.5), and appeals to the Genesis creation narratives (10.6), to a time before the Law when divorce was not permitted. The making of people as male and female, the leaving home of the husband to establish a new household with the wife, their unity, and their becoming 'one flesh' (10.7-8) constitute an institution of marriage which is intended to be permanent, created by God at the time of the creation of the world. God joins together men and women in marriage, and 'what God has joined together, man must not separate' (10.9). Mark depicts the disciples as perplexed by this radical, uncompromising teaching, so they question him further (10.10).

The clarification sought is equally unambiguous. 'Whoever divorces his wife and remarries commits adultery against her; so too, if she divorces her husband and remarries, she commits adultery.' A similar saying is preserved by Luke—'A man who divorces his wife and marries another commits adultery; and anyone who marries a woman divorced from her husband commits adultery' (Lk. 16.18).

Assuming that Mark's Gospel was written in Rome, the reference to a wife divorcing her husband may be explained by the attempt to apply the teaching of Jesus to the Roman context where it was open to women as well as men, to apply for divorce. The uncompromising teaching of Jesus remains unaltered. According to the conventional interpretation, then, God joins the partners together in marriage. No one must separate what God has joined. They have no authority to perform the action, and since God has joined them they are inseparable. If either party divorces the other and remarries, they have not merely thwarted the purpose of God who in joining them, wills that they should have stayed together. Because God still regards them as married to their former partner, any further marriage adds the sin of adultery to the sin of divorce.

Matthew (19.1-12) alters Mark's version in several ways. This is his account:

> [1]When Jesus had finished this discourse he left Galilee and came into the region of Judaea on the other side of the Jordan. [2]Great crowds followed him, and he healed them there.
>
> [3]Some Pharisees came and tested him by asking, 'Is it lawful for a man to divorce his wife for any cause he pleases?' [4]He responded by asking, 'Have you never read that in the beginning the Creator made them male and female?' [5]and he added, 'That is why a man leaves his father and mother, and is united to his wife, and the two become one flesh. [6]It follows that they are no longer two individuals: they are one flesh. Therefore what God has joined together, man must not separate.' [7]'Then why', they objected, 'did Moses lay it down that a man might divorce his wife by a certificate of dismissal?' [8]He answered, 'It was because of your stubbornness that Moses gave you permission to divorce your wives; but it was not like that at the beginning. [9]I tell you, if a man divorces his wife for any cause other than unchastity, and marries another, he commits adultery.'
>
> [10]The disciples said to him, 'If that is how things stand for a man with a wife, it is better not to marry.' [11]To this he replied, 'That is a course not everyone can accept but only those for whom God has appointed it.

[12]For while some are incapable of marriage because they were born so, or were made so by men, there are others who have renounced marriage for the sake of the kingdom of heaven. Let those accept who can' (Mt. 19.1-12).

Jesus' questioners are named as Pharisees (Mt. 14.3), and their question, 'Is it lawful for a man to divorce his wife for any cause he pleases?' (3) locates his answer firmly within the current controversy between the followers of Shammai and the followers of Hillel. Both groups, following established Jewish custom, allowed divorce, only by husbands of wives, and for the reason given in Deut. 24.1, 'because he finds something offensive in her'. But the Shammaites allowed divorce only for a wife's infidelity, whereas the Hillelites allowed divorce for any minor misdemeanour. Among the Hillelites Rabbi Akiba allowed divorce for husbands who merely preferred another woman.[1] Matthew's insertion of the words 'for any cause he pleases', absent from Mark's account, relates the question to the current controversy. The answer of Jesus in Matthew is similar in content, but spread across two questions from the Pharisees, not one. Divorce and remarriage are condemned on the same grounds as in Mark (Mt. 19.9). With Matthew, however, there is a huge complication, for Jesus answers 'I tell you, if a man divorces his wife for any cause other than unchastity, and marries another, he commits adultery' (19.9). An exception to the 'no divorce' teaching, *porneia* or unchastity, is allowed (below 8.1.c) which is not found in Mark and Luke.

In Matthew the disciples respond to both the teaching and the clarification by observing that 'it is better not to marry' at all (19.10). Jesus again confirms the uncompromising nature of his teaching, admitting no further exceptions. He tells them marriage is not for everyone: it is a calling from God (19.11). Some people are born or made incapable of marriage, and some who are capable of marriage renounce it 'for the sake of the kingdom of heaven' (12). Most commentators think Matthew has added the exception clause (*mè epi porneia* 'for any cause other than unchastity') to his sources. The further confirmation of the 'no divorce' teaching in Mt. 19.11-12 would make better sense if the exception clause was inserted later. But there is a second exception clause, in Matthew's 'Sermon on the Mount':

1. Ken Crispin, *Divorce: The Forgivable Sin?* (London: Hodder & Stoughton, 1988), p. 26.

[27]'You have heard that they were told, "Do not commit adultery". [28]But what I tell you is this: If a man looks at a woman with a lustful eye, he has already committed adultery with her in his heart.'[31]

'They were told, "A man who divorces his wife must give her a certificate of dismissal". [32]But what I tell you is this: If a man divorces his wife for any cause other than unchastity he involves her in adultery; and whoever marries her commits adultery' (Mt. 5.27-28; 31-32).

Matthew has arranged his material in 5.17-48 in order to show that the standards of conduct and attitude required in 'the kingdom of heaven' fulfil and exceed the standards of conduct and attitude required by the Jewish Law. This is done by a series of contrasts between the teaching of the Law and the teaching of Jesus, and the topics of two such contrasts are adultery (5.27-30) and divorce (5.31-32). The 'no divorce' position, but with the solitary exception for the wife's unchastity (*parektos logou porneias*), also occurs here.

On a conventional view the teaching of Jesus is again sharply contrasted with the practice of the Hillelite Jews. God joins married couples together, and no human being is to separate them. Divorce and remarriage are tantamount to adultery, presumably on the grounds that God does not recognize the separation of the partners of the former marriage. A divorced man who remarries is an adulterer, and a divorced woman, whether or not she marries again, is somehow involved in adultery. Matthew on all these points agrees with Mark. Matthew does not discuss the divorce of a husband by a wife. But Matthew's exception clauses make a huge difference (below, 8.2.c). On the conventional view, a wife's adultery gives a husband a ground for a separation (but no remarriage).

The Shepherd, a curious work composed by Hermas during the first half of the second century confirms the position that there can be separation and no remarriage in the unique case of a wife's infidelity (but see below, 8.2.e). An angel is asked what a husband is to do with a persistently adulterous wife:

'What then', I said, 'sir, shall the husband do if his wife persists in this passion?' 'Let him send her away', he said, 'and let the husband remain single. But if after sending away his wife he marries another, he also commits adultery himself'. 'If then', I said, 'sir, after the wife is sent away the woman repents, and she wishes to return to her own husband, she will be taken back won't she?' 'Indeed', he said, 'if her husband will not take her back he sins and brings upon himself a great sin...'[2]

Separation for infidelity is a requirement, according to Hermas, not an option, for either partner, and a further reason for forbidding remarriage is to make possible reconciliation with a repentant spouse. Augustine believed that 'divine law forbids remarriage even when a valid divorce has dissolved the life-sharing union...a bond (a *vinculum*) survives despite the divorce'.[3] As we have noted (above, 5.1.b) Augustine thought the difference between a Christian and a pagan marriage lay in the indissoluble bond or *sacramentum* between the parties. Augustine's teaching was adopted by the mediaeval church. Separation ('from board and bed'—*a mensa et a thoro*) was allowed for cases of serious sexual sin, but no remarriage. 'Divorce' meant separation only. This was the view in the Western church for most of its history. The Eastern churches allow divorce and remarriage (below, 8.2.f). The Roman Catholic Church continues to affirm that a valid consummated marriage cannot be dissolved. The grounds however, for seeking annulment have greatly multiplied in the last quarter of the twentieth century. The Protestant churches of the Reformation allowed divorce on the honest ground that the marriage was spiritually dead:

> Protestant reformers simply argued that crimes such as adultery rendered the guilty party spiritually dead. Thus, as in physical death, the marriage bond was dissolved and the innocent spouse was free to remarry and avoid the temptations of life alone.[4]

Contemporary Protestant practice varies alarmingly. And the Church of England has an anomalous official position. It recognizes divorce and civil remarriage. At the same time clergy have discretion to bless civil marriages involving divorced persons while being unable to perform them. There is therefore much diversity of practice among the churches. Divorce and remarriage is another area where it is necessary to pursue the internal dialogue between the churches and the external dialogue with post-traditional societies simultaneously (above, 2.3). How best can theology help the churches to interpret the mind of Christ to those

2. Hermas, *The Shepherd*, Mandate 4.1.6-8. See William A. Heth and Gordon J. Wenham, *Jesus and Divorce* (London: Hodder & Stoughton, 1984), p. 22: and Hunter, *Marriage*, pp. 9-10, 29-30.
3. Reynolds, *Marriage in the Western Church*, p. 211.
4. Harrington, *Reordering Marriage*, p. 88.

people, inside and outside the churches, who are struggling with difficult marriages and contemplating the ending of them?

2. *Divorce and Remarriage: A 'Revisionary Perspective'*

We have now considered a 'conventional' approach to the main New
Testament texts on marriage and divorce. Let us now return to these
texts, employing more of the theological insights derived from contemporary scholarship. There are textual, historical and theological grounds
for thinking the teaching of Jesus to be considerably more permissive
than the conventional view allows. Some of these grounds are discussed in this section.

a. *Is Remarriage Adultery?*

Many of the sayings of Jesus about marriage and divorce have been
preserved in different forms, thereby indicating that controversy about
the meaning of the teaching is actually older than the biblical manu-
scripts themselves. David Parker has analysed several of these sayings.[5]
The meaning of the saying of Jesus in Mt. 5.32 forbidding the remarriage of a woman divorced may be clarified by the version of it preserved in the fifth–sixth century manuscript, D (and three early Latin
texts). Here Jesus says, 'If a man divorces his wife for any cause other
than unchastity he involves her in adultery'. The remaining words 'and
whoever marries her commits adultery' which are found in various
translations in all English Bibles, are absent from these texts. Once the
practice of divorce is separated from the issue of remarriage, as it is in
these early texts, it becomes clear, says Parker, that 'it is the cruelty of
putting off the wife that Jesus is criticizing—divorce makes the wife
into an adulteress, one guilty of *porneia*, even though she is not'.[6]

The longer text, which appears to consign the divorced wife to permanent singleness, contaminating by adultery anyone who has sexual
relations with her, may mean nothing of the kind. It may be aimed at

> protecting a rejected wife from further ignominy, by establishing her
> right to remain single: her loyalty to her husband has not, from her side,
> been broken. From her point of view, it is as though she were married
> still, and this is to be respected. She is not disposable property.

5.   David Parker, 'The Early Traditions of Jesus' Sayings on Divorce', *Theology*, 96.773 (1993), pp. 372-83.
6.   Parker, 'The Early Traditions', p. 374.

The saying 'If a man divorces his wife he involves her in adultery' (Mt. 5.32), 'condemns the cruel and arbitrary dismissal of a faithful wife'. As Parker says, 'the problem addressed is the opposite of the use to which the passage is often put. It is employed to hinder divorced people who wish to remarry. It was intended to protect vulnerable people who wished not to remarry'.[7]

Involving a divorced wife in adultery may therefore be plausibly understood as dishonouring an innocent woman divorced at the whim of a patriarchal husband through no fault of her own. She would be unjustly assumed by her community to have been unfaithful to her husband.[8] But this is very different from the conventional view which identifies the status of a divorced woman with an adulteress. Involving someone in adultery is different from the accusatory 'causeth her to commit adultery' of the Authorized Version version of Mt. 5.32. Instead of being stigmatized as an adulteress just for being divorced, she is protected from this stigma because the words of Jesus address the unjust male practice that would put her in such a position. A revisionary interpretation of the saying parts company with the assumption that the remarriage of a divorced woman is excluded by identifying her as an adulterer. It recognizes her possible plight as a victim of male power, of 'hardness of heart', and honours her fidelity by continuing to regard her as married.

b. *A New Law?*

It is at least likely, therefore, that the sayings of Jesus which protect marriage and make divorce more difficult, were never intended to prevent the remarriage of people who were separated, nor to compel women to remain in marriages where their physical and mental health is threatened, by sealing off escape routes. Jesus *does* protect marriages from being broken up, and one of the ways he does so is both to seek to protect women from trivial divorces and to protect the married status of divorced women who did not wish their marriages to end. But is the teaching of Jesus to be regarded as a new law, one which supercedes the law of Moses and which requires obedience as the only appropriate response? Or is there again an alternative reading of the texts which is more responsive to the tragic complexities of failing marriages?

7.   Parker, 'The Early Traditions', p. 379.

8.   See Crispin, *Divorce*, p. 42, also citing B. Ward Powers and John Wade, *Divorce, the Bible and the Law* (Sydney: AFES Graduates Fellowship, 1978), p. 17.

The question whether Jesus intended marital legislation is discussed by A.E. Harvey.[9] Reasons for thinking that Jesus *did* intend a new law of marriage include the legal form of some of his sayings; the precedent in the Dead Sea Scrolls where a community, similar to the followers of Jesus, had its own rules about marriage; and the contrast in the Sermon on the Mount between the Mosaic Law and the teaching of Jesus (Mt. 5.17-48), prefaced by the warning of Jesus, 'Do not suppose that I have come to abolish the law and the prophets; I did not come to abolish, but to complete' (17-18). The exception clauses in Matthew's Gospel may also be thought to presuppose that the 'no divorce' teaching was understood in at least a quasi-legal way. Exceptions may be thought to establish rules. The early church understood the sayings of Jesus to have the *force* of law.

Nevertheless there are strong countervailing reasons supporting the view that Jesus is to be understood as a religious and moral teacher rather than a lawyer. If Jesus was proposing laws it is necessary now to ask how they might have been implemented, who would implement them, whether the Mosaic system was being replaced, and so on. The Church never sought to treat other parts of Matthew 5 as laws, for example, the forbidding of oath-taking (33-38),[10] self-defence (39), walking the extra mile (41) and giving to anyone who asks (42). Harvey observes it is difficult to imagine Jesus 'laying down rules which would have excluded many of his hearers from following him' because divorce was 'by no means uncommon'.[11] There is precedent for moral teachers to convey their message 'by adopting the style of a law-giver'.[12] Harvey thinks Jesus pressed home his teaching by deliberate exaggeration, and that 'there is a case' for thinking the hard sayings of Jesus about divorce are 'not a law or a rule, but a moral injunction, fully in Jesus' characteristic style and causing some amazement among his contemporaries who took divorce for granted: divorce is equivalent to adultery'.[13]

---

9.   A.E. Harvey, *Promise or Pretence? A Christian's Guide to Sexual Morals* (London: SCM Press, 1994), pp. 18-28.

10.   For the proposal that the teaching of Jesus on remarriage is to be treated as similar to his teaching on swearing, see Hugh Montefiore, *Remarriage and Mixed Marriage: A Plea for Dual Reform* (London: SPCK, 1967), p. 8.

11.   Harvey, *Promise or Pretence?*, p. 20.

12.   Harvey, *Promise or Pretence?*, p. 22.

13.   Harvey, *Promise or Pretence?*, p. 22.

The vital point to be carried over to contemporary discussion about divorce and remarriage is that the assumption that the law of Christ forbids it *is* an assumption. Jesus is against divorce. Easy recourse to it by men betokens a failure of what is expected in the reign of God, and of the peculiar intensity of neighbour-love which the covenant of marriage enjoins upon the parties. The practice of the followers of Hillel is condemned by Jesus on the grounds of their defective attitude to women, their 'stubbornness' which is also responsible for their mis-use of Scripture. On this account, Jesus is rightly understood to be intent on preserving marriages and making divorces more difficult.

There are also wider questions which cannot be addressed here, in particular, whether a legal interpretation of the teachings can be recon-ciled with the broad insistence in the theology of Paul that faith in Christ brings freedom from law and bestowal of new life graced by God the Spirit.[14] It does not need to be shown that the teaching of Jesus is not a law. It needs to be shown that the teaching of Jesus may not be a law, and so the assumption that it is a law is radically questionable.[15] It will be said that any weakening of the force of Jesus' teaching on divorce and remarriage is an accommodation to secular morality, a 'watering down' of God's will to human caprice, a misuse of Scripture, and so on.[16] But there are exegetical and theological grounds for thinking this kind of 'defence' of Christian teaching is mistaken.

The view that Jesus proclaims an ideal about the permanence of mar-riage which cannot be departed from without sorrow and hurt is not

14. See Stanley B. Marrow, 'Marriage and Divorce in the New Testament', *ATR*, 70.1 (1988), p. 14.

15. The minority report for the Convocations of Canterbury and York in 1935 contained the interesting suggestion that, just because Jesus was divine, he omni-sciently refrained from identifying his teaching with any human, temporal legisla-tion. 'He implicitly asserted His claim to be the Son of God by his refusal at all times to speak as a human legislator, or to give His sanction to any rule of life which was other than the ultimate ideal, the perfect law of God.' See Convocations of Canterbury and York, *The Church and Marriage* (London: SPCK, 1935), p. 35.

16. This is the usual conservative (as opposed to liberal) evangelical response to the suggestion that divorce and remarriage may be consistent with the teaching of Jesus. See Andrew Cornes, *Divorce and Remarriage (Biblical Principles and Pastoral Practice)* (London: Hodder & Stoughton, 1993). Cornes holds that the contention that 'Christ's instructions are not laws' is one of six ways of neutralizing the hard sayings of Jesus about divorce which Christians who are not conservative evangelicals are prone to adopt (pp. 34-39).

compromised by the likelihood that the ideal is more a vision of faith than a new law. The view that Jesus did not intend to legislate was in any case a common one among the churches of the Reformation. It has been given a new impetus by Parker who reminds us of our exegetical advantage over earlier generations of Christians in having available more manuscript evidence of diversity of interpretation of the sayings of Jesus. This very diversity leads him to conclude that

> the quest for a law in the teaching of Jesus cannot be pursued in the face of the evidence that, for those early Christians who passed the tradition to us, *there was no law*, but an idea to be explored, a tradition whose meaning had to be kept alive by a reflection and reinterpretation.[17]

This, a textual, conclusion, is supported by a different, but still evangelical, judgment that Jesus was not interested in making laws: rather he wished to protect the vulnerable and the weak and so spoke out about the impact of unjust divorce laws on vulnerable women and children. Greg Forster's resolution of the problem of the apparent legal character of the teaching of Jesus is based on the deep, compassionate understanding which Jesus, thinks Forster, displayed towards the victims of divorce. Jesus was not interested in making new laws:

> Instead he listened to the hurts people left as a result of divorce and shaped his moral teaching to redress those hurts within the Law. Thus we see a concern for individuals who fell foul of the way the Law was applied. He was also concerned for the 'weightier matters' of the Law. One of these principles was the protection of those in a weak position because of the nature of society. The widow and orphan were typically 'weak' in Old Testament society. One of the reasons Jesus opposed divorce was that he saw how women could be exploited by it.[18]

c. *The 'Exception Clauses': How is 'Unchastity' to be Understood?'*
As we have seen, Matthew alone of the Gospel writers allows an exception to the 'no divorce' rule. A man may not divorce his wife 'for any cause other than unchastity' (5.32, 19.9). This repeated exception potentially transforms the 'conventional view' of the teaching of Jesus. There are two prior questions to be settled first: does the exception derive from Jesus himself or is it an interpolation, probably by Matthew

---

17. Parker, 'The Early Traditions', p. 380 (emphasis added). (Does he mean to say 'by a *process of* reflection and reinterpretation'? If so, there is another textual variant here of which he is unaware!)

18. Forster, *Healing Love's Wounds*, p. 159.

himself? And what is the meaning of 'unchastity' (*porneia*)?

Most commentators think that Matthew added the clauses.[19] I accept this view. If it is correct it may show that Matthew and his church were developing the general rule of Jesus, and (just as important) that they felt free to do so. If the clauses are additions, they may be evidence for a developing understanding of Jesus' teaching in the light of pastoral needs. The meaning of *porneia* is much more difficult to establish. The issue has attracted a large literature.[20] It may mean marriages between believer and unbeliever within the prohibited degrees described in Lev. 18.6-18. Deriving from the Jewish practice that unfaithful wives were automatically divorced, the exception clause may be intended to continue to authorize this practice in the church.[21] The majority of commentators believe *porneia* should be associated with sexual sin, disagreeing over whether it serves as a synonym for adultery[22] or has a wider, more indefinite meaning.

This problem has a particular bearing on contemporary divorce practice, because its resolution will throw light on whether the exception is limited to adultery or can, with textual support, be more broadly understood. An interesting case for the wider interpretation has been put forward by Ken Crispin. Matthew, he says, does not mean 'adultery' in 5.32. The word for adultery, *moicheia*, has already been used in 5.27-28 in the saying about the commandment forbidding it, and it is likely that if Matthew had meant to identify adultery as the sole reason justifying divorce, he would have used *moicheia* again. However, a newer argument is based on the theological considerations found in Ezra 9 and 10. Here the men of Israel returning from exile are required to end their marriages with non-Jews contracted during the exile and divorce their wives and children. Their sin is clear: it compromises Jewish racial purity. The relevance of the episode for understanding the background to Jesus' teaching on divorce is that divorce in the Hebrew Scriptures is not confined to adultery or to the notorious fault of 'something offensive' (Deut. 24.1) in the wife or her behaviour which led to the issuing of a 'certificate of dismissal' (Mk 10.4; Mt. 5.31).

Jesus would certainly have known about divorce in the book of Ezra.

---

19. For an example of the contrary view see William A. Heth, 'The Meaning of Divorce in Matthew 19.3-9', *Churchman* 98.2 (1984), pp. 136-52 (147).

20. Some of it is listed by Marrow, 'Marriage and Divorce', p. 11.

21. So, Heth, 'The Meaning of Divorce', p. 147.

22. So, Parker, 'The Early Traditions', p. 379.

In Judaism, the grounds for divorce are broader than adultery, and have to do at least with racial or sexual purity.[23] But to say this is already to broaden out the semi-technical meaning of adultery as the sole ground for divorce to a more general meaning, as when someone, something, some relationship, even a whole people, is rendered ceremonially spoiled and dirty by an action of some kind. *Porneia*, Crispin concludes, 'may be taken to include any kind of misconduct or immorality which is so serious that it pollutes or perverts the marital relationship'.[24] He speculates that, in speaking of *porneia*, 'Jesus was not really creating an exception permitting the termination of a marital relationship, but merely recognising that such conduct may itself destroy the relationship'.[25]

This conclusion, that *porneia* is *any* sort of conduct which destroys the marriage, greatly enlarges the scope of the exceptive clauses. The problem of the meaning of *porneia* is probably intractable. If, however, the broader meaning is acceptable, other conclusions follow. First, if divorce is allowed only for conduct that wrecks a marriage, then a Christian should still not consider it unless and until that point is reached. The exception, although broadened, does not weaken the demanding responsibilities which marriage imposes. Secondly, this interpretation of *porneia* would mean that, to give an obvious example, 'a wife need not feel locked into a marital relationship with a man who was repeatedly guilty of gross violence towards her and/or their children merely because he had not committed adultery'.[26] Thirdly, this interpretation removes the theological incongruity of supposing that the mind of God, in apparently allowing divorce for adultery and no other reason, is also consistent and just.

The exception clauses, then, may provide an *a fortiori* argument in favour of divorce in cases where the conduct of either party destroys the marriage. The early church allowed divorce only for adultery.[27] If

---

23.   See Countryman, *Dirt, Greed and Sex*, Part 1, pp. 11-143 for the complexities of purity laws and their treatment in the New Testament.

24.   Crispin, *Divorce*, p. 29.

25.   Crispin, *Divorce*, p. 34.

26.   Crispin, *Divorce*, p. 29.

27.   Three different answers were given to the question whether remarriage was permitted to the innocent party in a divorce when the other was still alive. One position allowed remarriage for men only. In the East it was allowed for both. In the West, after Jerome and Augustine, it was allowed to neither. See Reynolds,

Crispin's interpretation of *porneia* is right then that argument is more powerful. If divorce is allowable for adultery only, then at least it is allowable for something. But if it is allowable at all, and for the serious damage that adultery is likely to do to a marriage, then it is presumably equally allowable for the serious or very serious damage done by, say, desertion or marital rape or other abuse.[28] The broader interpretation of *porneia* allows for additional grounds to those provided by adultery alone. The exception clauses, understood this way, also provide evidence of development in the early church's understanding of the mind of Christ. Paul allowed a different exception. Our handling of the exception clauses is better expedited by the conviction not that we have here a new law, but that Christ gives us a new freedom to interpret his teaching in new ways.[29]

Again there are marked differences between the conventional and the revisionary approaches to the exception clauses and their meaning. The first approach regards the no divorce principle as a divine law instituted by Jesus. It then admits a single exception, the unchastity of a wife, which provides the sole ground for a husband initiating divorce (but not necessarily remarriage). On the revisionary view *porneia* may be seen as a general category of destructive behaviour, not confined to a single, sexual offence. Since marriages can be wrecked by either partner, the *porneia* of either gives grounds for divorce to the other. While every effort should be made to achieve the healing of a broken marriage where hope of reunion remains, the saying is fully consistent with the

Marriage in the Western Church, pp. 175-76. On the growing severity of the Western Church's teaching on remarriage, Reynolds says 'the interpretation of Jesus' prohibition of remarriage that eventually prevailed in the West was not an inevitable deduction from Jesus' teachings. The Fathers could, in good faith, have treated Jesus' prohibition of divorce as they treated his prohibition of oaths: namely (if I may put this bluntly), as an impractical ideal. Moreover, one does not always prohibit by law what one admits to be morally wrong. For example, few societies have laws against telling lies. The regime was partly a consequence of a certain strictness as far as sexual and marital matters were concerned (what Jerome called "the severity of the gospel"). By applying the prohibition of remarriage strictly, the Latin Fathers made Jesus' teaching into a law antithetical to that of Rome' (pp. 147-48).

28. On this point, see my *Liberating Sex*, p. 121: and Gary Liaboe, 'The Place of Wife Battering in Considering Divorce', *Journal of Psychology and Theology* 13 (1985), pp. 129-38.

29. Marrow, *Marriage and Divorce*, pp. 14-15.

view, generally assumed in the time of Jesus, that the law should recognize that marriages end.

d. *Separation but no Remarriage?*

'What God has joined together man must not separate' (Mk 10.9; Mt. 19.6). These words of Jesus clinch his 'no divorce' teaching. However, as with the disciples who first heard them, they leave us with several problems which have been aired already (above, 2.1.b).The traditional position about remarriage in the Western church from Jerome to the Reformation is that it is impossible, since when one is validly married, and the marriage has been consummated by sexual intercourse, the marriage is indissoluble, and one is not free to remarry, at least for as long as one's former partner is alive. Separation, however, is permitted, but not remarriage, and the marriage bond or *vinculum* remains. Whether intact or in tatters, it is indestructible.

Roman Catholic and conservative evangelical Christians agree in holding that married, separated Christians are not free to marry again. Heth and Wenham regard it as 'certain that Jesus did not permit remarriage for any reason'. They think 'it seems safest to say that Jesus gave an absolute prohibition of divorce *and* remarriage'.[30] They hold that 'Jesus said that a man may have one wife or no wife, and if someone puts away their partner for whatever reason they must remain single'.[31] This position assumes that marriages are indissoluble (below, 8.2.e), because God joins the parties together, and (a different point) that remarriage is in any case excluded by the teaching of Jesus. However both of these assumptions are contentious (and their pastoral consequences sometimes disastrous). There are at least four reasons for thinking that this extreme 'rigorist' approach does not reflect the mind or the spirit of Jesus.

First, when the disciples of Jesus suggest that marriage is better avoided altogether, Jesus replies that renunciation of marriage 'is a course not everyone can accept, but only those for whom God has appointed it' (Mt. 19.13). Jesus clearly acknowledges the obvious point that celibacy is impossible for at least some people, a thought also made explicit by Paul (1 Cor. 7.1-2, 8-9). Once this point is firmly established, the further question arises: does the ending of a marriage

---

30.   Heth and Wenham, *Jesus and Divorce*, p. 198.

31.   Heth and Wenham, *Jesus and Divorce*, p. 199; and see Cornes, *Divorce and Remarriage*, pp. 291, 296, 307-308.

through divorce invalidate it? Is it not incongruous to suppose that on the one hand, some people *cannot* live without marriage, and on the other hand, that these same people, should their marriages break down, *must* live without marriage? This is an impossible theological and pastoral position because it assumes God requires us to exercise the very gifts that God has not given us.[32] Hugh Montefiore thinks admission of the necessity of marriage for some people is itself a principle which justifies remarriage without further qualification. Since Jesus allows that not everyone can remain single, this concession is thought to apply to individuals *whether or not they have been married*. Why should a divorced person remain single, if he or she is a person who cannot live without marriage? 'Not all men can possibly live celibate lives, such as a divorced person who remains single has to lead. He is worse off than a celibate proper, for he has had celibacy forced upon him without its attendant compensations.'[33]

Secondly, Paul also allows remarriage, and for similar reasons. This is a conclusion which has not been generally accepted and may still elicit surprise from some theologians. However, the arguments are strong and it is time they were given serious attention. They are based on three passages all in 1 Corinthians 7. Paul tells 'the unmarried' and 'widows' that 'it is a good thing if like me they stay as they are; but if they do not have self-control, they should marry' (8-9). However, according to Crispin, the word for 'unmarried' (*agamos*) also 'refers to a person who is no longer married but who may have been married in the past'.[34] This interpretation is thought to be established by comparing it with *parthenos*, the word used by Paul when he refers to single, not yet married people (7.25). Paul's contrast between them is deliberate. The link between the unmarried and widows confirms that Paul is talking here about postmarried people as well as premarried people. The advice is clear: remain unmarried, but marry if you lack self-control. The position of divorced men is also specifically addressed later in the chapter (27-28). 'Has your marriage been dissolved? Do not seek a wife. But if you do marry, you are not doing anything wrong...' On this interpretation, marrying again is a definite option (though not a recommendation).

32. Marrow, *Marriage and Divorce*, p. 14.
33. Montefiore, *Remarriage*, p. 10.
34. Crispin, *Divorce*, pp. 44-45.

The conclusion that Paul approves of (but does not commend) remarriage would seem to be inconsistent with the clear teaching elsewhere in the chapter where Paul, in obedience to 'the Lord', rules 'a wife must not separate herself from her husband—if she does, she must either remain unmarried or be reconciled to her husband—and the husband must not divorce his wife' (10-11). These verses have undoubtedly helped to establish the conventional Christian view that divorce and remarriage are not even to be considered as practical possibilities. But again there is a sound exegetical position running counter to the usual interpretation. It relies on understanding the distinction between *apoluò* and *aphiemi* in a particular way. *Apoluò* means 'divorce' whereas *aphiemi* means 'remove' or 'abandon'.[35] Now when Paul says 'the husband must not divorce his wife', the verb used is *aphiemi* [*mè aphievai*]. The English translation is misleading, for a less final meaning is intended. Paul is not talking about divorce but about separation: 'A wife must not separate herself from her husband.' Nonetheless Paul allows that a wife *may*, for whatever reason, separate from him. His advice *then* is to remain unmarried or be reconciled. 'Clearly what Paul has in mind was *a short-term situation immediately following separation*.'[36] Paul, thinks Crispin,

> was contemplating a period immediately following separation when the prospect of a reconciliation existed and it had not become clear that the marital relationship had terminated. If, despite the wife's efforts, the relationship was finally extinguished then without any further step being taken both the husband and the wife would be regarded as *agamos*, that is, unmarried.

Paul, then, on this interpretation, allows remarriage, but only as a last resort, and after efforts at reconciliation have been made in the light of the teaching of Jesus that marriage is for life. There are two more reasons for thinking the conventional interpretation 'no remarriage' is wrong.

Thirdly, the wrongness of a man divorcing his wife and marrying again is, according to Mt. 5.32 that 'he involves her in adultery' and 'whoever marries her commits adultery'. But why is the wife involved in adultery if she is divorced? The conventional answer is that she would be bound to seek remarriage, while in the eyes of God she remains married to her former husband. But it is by no means certain

35. So, Crispin, *Divorce*, p. 46.
36. Crispin, *Divorce*, p. 46.

that she would need to remarry. Since dowries were returnable she might wish to, and be able to, remain single. And we have already seen that the ire of Jesus may be directed against the cruelty of the husband in divorcing her. She is involved in adultery because her divorce makes her look as if she has been unfaithful. The argument that remarriage is equivalent to adultery is circular. 'Jesus did not say the woman would be made an adulteress by the act of remarriage. What he said was that her husband, by divorcing her, made her an adulteress.'[37]

Fourthly, the state of affairs which the conventional interpretation of the 'no remarriage' teaching assumes, that separation is permitted but remarriage is not, is not found in the New Testament or its background. The men Jesus was criticizing were divorcing in order to remarry. 'Divorce and remarriage went together: Jesus could hardly have targeted one without the other.'[38] There is no intermediate position between marriage and divorce which allows for separation but not remarriage. The contrary position depends upon a reading back into the texts of the mediaeval idea of divorce, separation *a mensa et thoro*, from board and bed. The conventional view has even relied on a view which is unbiblical (that separation but with no possibility of remarriage makes sense).These four important considerations, taken cumulatively, allow divorced Christians to affirm with some confidence that remarriage *may* be an option for them.

e. *An Indissoluble Bond?*
A minimal conclusion to be derived from the discussion so far is that the official Roman Catholic and hardline evangelical positions excluding the possibility of divorce and remarriage, are far from obvious. The next suggestion to be considered is whether the assumption that marriage *cannot* be dissolved rests on a series of mistakes. A surface reading of the saying 'What God has joined together, man must not separate' (Mk 10.11; Mt. 19.6) does not tell us that God *does* join every couple together. Nor does it say that God does not or cannot separate what God once joined together. Rupert of Deutz (d. 1129–30) expressly allows that, in the case of husband and wife separating in order to enter the religious life, God *does* separate what God has joined.[39] But once the admission is established that God separates what God has joined,

37. Crispin, *Divorce*, p. 42.
38. Harvey, *Promise or Pretence?*, p. 25; and see Crispin, *Divorce*, pp. 11, 16.
39. See Reynolds, *Marriage in the Western Church*, pp. 227-28.

who are we to limit the reasons for or occasions on which God might do this? Neither does the text exclude the possibility that while 'man must not separate', the Church may separate on behalf of God. This is of course Orthodox doctrine. Kallistos Ware says the 'basic principle' underlying Orthodox practice is

> our conviction that Christ has entrusted to the Church full power to regulate the administration of the sacraments. If each sacrament is a divine action, effected by Christ *within the Church*, then the Church, as steward of the sacraments and by virtue of the authority to bind and loose conferred upon it by Christ himself (Mt. 16.19; 18.18; Jn 20.23), has the right to release the couple from the marriage bond and to permit a remarriage. This is done by the Church, not arbitrarily, nor as a weak and easy concession to the *mores* of contempory secular society, but in the name of Christ's own continuing compassion and loving kindness for humanity.[40]

The saying 'What God has joined together, man must not separate' is not obviously derived from, or an inference from, the texts from Genesis which precede it. It may derive from the indefinite Jewish belief that 'marriages are made in heaven'. Harvey thinks it would have been

> absolutely characteristic of him [Jesus] to have taken the *possibility* that a marriage was 'made in heaven' as the basis for a radical position about divorce. Of any given marriage it *might* be the case that God had ordained it. In case that was so—in case this was one that God had 'joined together'—no one should take the risk of flying against God's will by having a divorce.[41]

This is of course little more than surmise, but the surmise indicates that the weighty interpretation placed on the saying that God makes *all* marriages, so none of them can be unmade, is scarcely justified.

The conviction that a marriage *cannot*, not merely that it *should not*, be dissolved derives from Jerome and Augustine, and the underlying reasons for this development are described in detail by Philip Reynolds. A key factor in the development was the growing conviction that the Church in the now Christianized Roman Empire, has the power to make her own laws, especially in those areas where biblical teaching was obviously at stake. To the human law or *lex humana*, the Church wished to add divine law or *lex divina*.[42] As the Church assumed

---

40. Ware, 'The Sacrament of Love', p. 87.
41. Harvey, *Promise or Pretence?*, p. 26 (author's emphases).
42. Reynolds, *Marriage in the Western Church*, p. 121.

legislative powers, it used the penalties of excommunication and penance as means of enforcement. Since the crime of adultery was punished by excommunication,[43] the words of Jesus dealing with divorce and remarriage came to assume a new significance as grounds for punishment. Until the fourth century only Hermas had forbidden remarriage to husbands divorcing their wives for *porneia*.[44] Augustine, in *On Adulterous Marriages*, 'reaffirms that remarriage after a valid divorce on the ground of fornication is adultery, and he deduces from this that divorce cannot dissolve the bond (*vinculum*) of marriage'.[45] A comparison is made between the status of a baptized excommunicated Christian and a divorced person. Just as the sacrament of baptism is said to remain in an excommunicated Christian so the bond of marriage remains in a divorced person even after divorce.[46] On this view divorce is not merely inadvisable; it becomes impossible.

The growing conviction that a valid marriage is *unable to be dissolved* was supported by the belief that one of the goods of marriage, the *sacramentum*, was what rendered the marriage indissoluble. It was the good that distinguished a Christian from a pagan marriage. But the question remained and remains unanswered,

> If marriage is a life-sharing union, how can spouses who are *de iure* separated remain married? If marriage entails the obligation to live together and to render the conjugal debt, how can persons whom the Church has entirely and permanently absolved from these obligations remain married?[47]

Hensley Henson caustically observed (in 1910) that the prohibitive marriage law of the Western church

---

43. Reynolds, *Marriage in the Western Church*, p. 145.

44. There is no space for the controversy whether the early Church allowed remarriage to men who divorced their wives for adultery. According to Henri Crouzel, all theologians except one in the first five centuries 'agree that remarriage following divorce for any reason is adulterous'. See Heth and Wenham, *Jesus and Divorce*, p. 22, based on a reading of Crouzel's *L'église primitive face au divorce du premier au cinquième siècle*. Reynolds (*Marriage in the Western Church*, p. 189) says that, with the exception of Hermas (quoted above, 8.1.a), 'We have to wait until the fourth century to find other sources stating explicitly that a man who has divorced his wife for fornication must not remarry'.

45. Reynolds, *Marriage in the Western Church*, p. 210.

46. Augustine, *Ad pollentium de adulterinis coniugiis* 2.4. See Reynolds, *Marriage in the Western Church*, pp. 210-11.

47. Reynolds, *Marriage in the Western Church*, p. 225.

was conditioned by so large and liberal a system of dispensations, and admitted such strange applications of the doctrine of nullity, that in practice marriages were cancelled with scandalous frequency, and the Law of the Church, in spite of its theoretical severity, appeared in the judgment of serious men to have become a potent influence of moral confusion and laxity.[48]

This system of prohibited degrees covered not merely consanguinity. Ties of 'spiritual affinity' were also thought to be created between those who acted as godparents or sponsors of a child at baptism or confirmation and the family of the child.[49] Such prohibited degrees in many cases did not prevent marriages but were used to annul them subsequently.

The Protestant churches at the Reformation denied that marriage was a sacrament, and thereby removed the principal reason for thinking that a marriage was *unable* to be dissolved.[50] Anglicans thereafter have been consistently divided, 'indissolubilists' siding with the earlier view, and 'dissolubilists' holding that divorce and remarriage was justified on the grounds of a former partner's adultery, according to the strict interpretation of Matthew's exception clauses.[51] The view therefore that a marriage cannot be dissolved can only with difficulty be derived from Scripture. It is a forced interpretation of the teaching of Jesus. Its theological outworking is tied to a particular historical context, and later

48. H. Hensley Henson, *Marriage and Divorce* (London: Hugh Rees, 1910), p. 8. See also Brooke, *The Medieval Idea of Marriage*, pp. 133-34. Brooke notes that by the late eleventh century the prohibited degrees of marriage extended to sixth cousins.

49. Cosgrove, 'Consent', p. 95. And see *Marriage, Divorce and the Church*, p. 9.

50. Henson marshalled impressive sources to argue that once the doctrine of marriage as a sacrament is 'explicitly repudiated', 'the conceit of the absolute indissolubleness of marriage will fall with it'. He held any difference in practice between separation and divorce was 'merely chimerical and fancy' (*Marriage and Divorce*, p. 16).

51. See A.R. Winnett, *Divorce and Remarriage in Anglicanism* (London: Macmillan, 1958), and his conclusion on pp. 272-76. Bishop Edward King of Lincoln in 1895 declared indissolubility 'only declares what God's original antecedent Will is with regard to marriage; of which there can be no doubt'. With regard to dissolubility 'We are not saying what ought to be the normal conditions of married life, but what may be done under head of equity and mercy to save man from the worse results of his own folly' (cited in *Marriage, Divorce and the Church*, p. 6).

reinforced by a sacramental theory which is not recognized by Protestants, some Anglicans, and (for different reasons) the Orthodox. While the Roman Catholic position on indissolubility has hardened considerably since Vatican II that church's stance on annulment has in fact become notoriously liberal (below, 8.3).

f. *'Spiritual Death' as Release from Marriage?*

The Orthodox Church and most Protestant churches allow divorce on the basis of the spiritual death of the marriage. However the Orthodox do not accept that the character of marriage as a sacrament renders dissolution impossible. Indeed since the Orthodox do not believe that marriage ends at death but lasts for eternity, the belief that a marriage can die spiritually has added force. Justifying the Orthodox position on the granting of divorce, Kallistos Ware explains

> The total breakdown of personal relationships, the extinction of reciprocal love, abolishes the marriage bond just as much as, indeed much more than, the occurrence of physical death. In permitting a divorce when the partners have become irrevocably alienated, the Church does not bring the marriage to an end but simply recognizes a *fait accompli*.[52]

The marriage has already ceased to exist.

The situation described here as spiritual death may perhaps be more poignantly expressed in the language of conjugal spirituality (above, 7.1.b). The 'conjugal soul' of the partners may be said to die. The 'de-centring' which has taken place in the course of coming together to live a common life remains, but no longer supports the couple. Instead there may be a yearning for 're-centredness' away from the alienating partner. The difference between centrifugal and centripetal forces is especially relevant in articulating the spiritual pain of a marriage breakdown. If one is spiritually enriched through the centripetal movement to one's partner and through one's partner to God, and if this movement is curtailed or blocked, a crisis which may terminate in 'spiritual death' has already loomed. Another way of describing spiritual death is to use the language of relational love (above, 7.1.e). It was noted that in reciprocal human love, love is not merely an attitude of each in respect of the other, but is the quality of the total relationship which unites them both. When a marriage is precipitated into crisis, the relational love which defines the couple is at risk. Whereas love may continue as an

---

52. Ware, 'The Sacrament of Love', p. 90.

attitude of one of the partners, the other may not reciprocate, and the conjugal soul may be in mortal danger. Spiritual death may be imminent. In circumstances such as these every effort must be made to examine whether reconciliation is possible and, if it is, to seek to achieve it. It has already been suggested that the words of Paul in 1 Cor. 7.10-11 refer precisely to this vulnerable period of a marriage.

The belief that marriage is a sacrament is ultimately irrelevant to its permanence. This is acknowledged by the Orthodox.

> While the sacrament of marriage is indeed a divine action, it is not a piece of magic, but also requires human co-operation. The sacramental gift of Christian marriage needs to be accepted and lived on the human side, and it can eventually be rejected. When this has happened, the Church does not insist on the permanent continuation of a lifeless outward form, which has ceased to be grace-giving and has become mutually destructive.[53]

The descriptions of communal partnership as the 'matrix' of the sacrament (above, 7.2.b), of the mutual ministry of the sacrament (above, 7.2.c) and of 'natural sacramentality' (above, 7.2.e) assume that grace is received through the sacrament of marriage, not prior to it, or in spite of it. A marriage which is spiritually dead cannot be artificially kept alive by a dubious sacramental theory.

A 'revisionary perspective' upon the New Testament texts and the conventional interpretation of them has now been attempted. This has been part of the 'internal dialogue' among Christians and the churches (above, 2.1). Its conclusions must now be assessed in the light of the external dialogue with the world the churches serve.

3. *Divorce, Annulment and Remarriage*

Three features of the external dialogue are of particular concern: the sheer *extent* of divorce, its unintended consequences, and justified anxiety about the impact of divorce on the future of marriage.

a. *The 'Downward Spiral' of Divorce?*
In the USA the divorce rate peaked in 1983, at 5.2 for every thousand of the population. In 1996, the rate had fallen to 4.3, but this figure nonetheless represents 1,150,000 divorces.[54] An official commentary on

---

53. Ware, 'The Sacrament of Love', p. 90.
54. Centre for Disease Control and Prevention (CDC), 1998.

these statistics in 1997 notes 'The marital institution has been modified substantially in one regard: *in the incorporation of divorce as a normatively-acceptable mode of transition from one marriage to another*'.[55]

In 1992 in Britain, there were 160,000 divorces, compared with just under 24,000 in 1960.[56] The anxiety about the irreparable damage done to the institution of marriage, thereby changing for the worse its character for future generations, is powerfully expressed inside and outside the churches. I share this anxiety. However arguments based on the misery of divorce and the damage to the future of marriage are often mixed with a frankly reactionary view within which a resurgence of patriarchal power is evident, leading to the advocacy of new legal restrictions on divorce and to the inevitable diminution of the newly-won freedoms, in particular for married women. Some disentanglement is required, of a concern for the future well-being of children and their parents from assumptions that some of the social patterns and practices of premodern and early modern societies and the beliefs that informed them, were self-evidently better, and that they can be or ought to be resurrected. It is necessary to consider these arguments and to separate concern for the future of marriage from advocacy of particular forms of marriage together with restrictions on the exit from it.

The term 'divorce spiral' was used in the 1950s to counter the growing demand for the liberalization of divorce laws in the United Kingdom. In 1958 A.R. Winnett warned all the Anglican churches worldwide that

> The State in nearly every country where the Anglican Communion is represented has so enlarged the grounds and multiplied the facilities for divorce that the institution of marriage, as a lifelong and exclusive union, is in jeopardy, with grave consequences to the stability of society and to the well-being of children.[57]

Opportunity for divorce, he averred, inevitably plants the thought in the minds of marrying couples 'that if the marriage does not turn out happily there is always a way of escape'. A consequence of any liberalization of the law would be that 'the will is weakened to make the marriage happy by the exercise of unselfishness, patience and forgiveness,

55. *Statistical Abstract*, p. 112 (emphasis added).
56. Robert Whelan, 'Editor's Introduction', in *idem* (ed.), *Just a Piece of Paper?*, p. 1.
57. Winnett, *Divorce*, p. 273.

and thus the marriage is impaired from the start'. The worldwide Church 'is entrusted with the task of upholding the Christian standard of indissoluble marriage, and in this she stands almost alone'.[58] Winnett held that any weakening of the Church's witness would betray 'the steadfastness and heroism of those men and women who through difficulties and suffering are remaining faithful to their marriage vows, and would bring yet more marriages into peril'. He regarded it as 'unthinkable' that Anglicans 'should go back upon the almost universally recognised rule that no marriage of any divorced person should take place with the Church's rites so long as the other partner lives'.[59] Similar arguments are regularly made by the Vatican and by Roman Catholic theologians.

Many of the arguments against liberal divorce laws are stated in *Just a Piece of Paper?* Law is said to have a 'tutelary role' in bringing about good behaviour among citizens. Any permissiveness encourages further permissiveness to develop.[60] Divorce law is 'the means by which a society signals [or fails to signal] its support for the special importance of adults devoting themselves to the upkeep and nurture of their own children'. The liberalization of the law 'alters the nature of the contract it terminates', and 'divorce becomes the first option rather than the last'.[61] All marriages are now 'provisional' and 'on a makeshift footing' because 'People are under less pressure to restrain, resolve or conceal their disagreements, misdemeanours and complaints'.[62] The status of marriage is reduced, not merely to a derogatory 'piece of paper', but to something even worse, for legal contracts, which *are* pieces of paper, are enforceable, whereas marriage contracts have become 'unenforced and unenforceable'.[63] The sheer numbers of 'isolated men, either divorced or never married, and consequently not bound into the social fabric by the ties of family responsibilities' may constitute an emerging 'warrior class'.[64] The elimination of the need to establish the blame for divorce proceedings by proving who is responsible and what fault was

58. Winnett, *Divorce*, p. 274.
59. Winnett, *Divorce*, pp. 274-75.
60. David G. Green, 'Foreword', in Whelan (ed.), *Just a Piece of Paper?*, p. iv.
61. Whelan, 'Editor's Introduction', p. 2; and Morgan, 'Conflict and Divorce', in Whelan, *Piece of Paper?*, pp. 19-36.
62. Morgan, 'Conflict and Divorce', p. 23.
63. Whelan, 'Editor's Introduction', p. 3.
64. Whelan, 'Editor's Introduction', p. 6, citing also R. Deech, *Divorce Dissent: Dangers in Divorce Reform* (London: Centre for Policy Studies, 1994), p. 10.

involved, has badly backfired. 'Abolishing fault abolishes the concept of personal responsibility... Marital breakdown becomes instead something that just happens to unfortunate individuals, like meningitis or an earthquake.'[65] No-fault divorce is a positive incentive to committing adultery.[66] Marriage as the 'basis of the social order' has already been 'dissolved'. There has been a 'marked decline in the quality of life' in the last 25 years due to 'the collapse of the traditional family'.[67] United Kingdom law has a 'no pain, no blame, no shame justice system'. This system is deceitful and even contrary to natural justice since 'Denying a wronged party the opportunity to say their spouse behaved badly is inimical to justice'.[68] Divorce law reforms have fostered the 'cruel illusion' that 'divorce can be achieved with the barest minimum of pain for all concerned'.[69] The effects on children of divorce have already been discussed (above, 5.1.b). Research on the causes of divorce reveals that neither conflict nor marital violence is generally one of them.[70] Stressful experiences which may have little to do with the marriage, boredom with marriage, poor legal, medical or therapeutic advice, vague notions of incompatibility or love for someone else are common causes. Half of divorced men and at least one quarter of divorced women are believed to regret their divorces.[71] Divorce is 'rarely a mutual decision'.[72] The welfare bill for support for non-traditional families is 'staggering' and diverts welfare funds from other people in need of them.[73]

There is considerable truth in these arguments. But they do not tell the whole story. There are also strong counter arguments. From a Christian point of view there cannot be a single divorce without there also being regret or hurt, often extending beyond the parting spouses. Much was claimed for marriage in the last chapter, including the need for divine help in staying together. Those Christians who affirm the need

65. Melanie Phillips, 'Death Blow to Marriage', in Whelan, *Just a Piece of Paper?*, pp. (13-18) 14.

66. Norman Barry, 'Justice and Liberty in Marriage and Divorce', in Whelan (ed.), *Just a Piece of Paper?*, p. 48.

67. Whelan, 'Editor's Introduction', pp. 1-12 (8-9).

68. Phillips, 'Death Blow', p. 15.

69. Phillips, 'Death Blow', p. 17.

70. Morgan, 'Conflict and Divorce', p. 22. See sources cited there.

71. Morgan, 'Conflict and Divorce', p. 23.

72. Morgan, 'Conflict and Divorce', p. 27.

73. Barry, 'Justice', pp. 37-38.

for divorce and allow for remarriage are no less saddened than those who do not, whenever a marriage comes to an end. It is certain that some partners divorce for trivial reasons; that children are, in general, worse off as a result of divorce; and that the meaning of marriage, at least in the popular consciousness, is continuing to change. The question for Christians is whether opposition and condemnation is the only or even the right response to the contemporary situation.

Winnett has forgotten that Orthodox and Protestant churches alike admit that spiritual death is a valid, albeit regrettable reason for the acknowledgment of the ending of marriage. He did not have before him the interpretation of the exception clauses just examined (above, 8.2.c). If he had had this, it may well have influenced his judgment. He is concerned to stifle the provision of a 'way of escape' from unhappy marriages. Forty years on this seems an unfortunate phrase to have used, since an escape is a breaking loose from confinement, an avoidance of danger. A means of escape from a violent marriage is a moral and political imperative in any society. Much more legal protection is needed for women who seek the protection of police from violent husbands or partners. Winnett also forgot that the mediaeval church *did* provide a way of escape from intolerable marriages. A contemporary of his, Reginald Haw, had just written,

> Far from upholding the pure and simple teachings of Christ, as he proclaimed the divine law of marriage for all time, the medieval Church caused men to think lightly of a law of indissolubility which they could circumvent by pleading a manufactured nullity, an artificial affinity or a bogus questioning of the reality of consent.[74]

Both writers were critical of mediaeval solutions. An issue for them is that while the grounds for annulment in the mediaeval church may have been to some extent contrived, even bizarre, that church found a way of releasing partners from broken marriages, and there was a welcome realism about this practice which neither writer was prepared to own in their own time.

Winnett was right to insist on the task of upholding the Christian standard of indissoluble marriage. But this task raises further questions about what is meant and how the task is to be done. The recognition that some marriages are intolerable is fully consistent with maintaining a Christian vision of marriage as an indissoluble union. It is the will of

74. Reginald Haw, *The State of Matrimony* (London: SPCK, 1952), p. 18.

God that every marriage should succeed, but human behaviour does not always conform to the will of God. If we cannot know finally whether God has joined a couple together (above, 8.2.e) we lack the basis for the assertion that they cannot be unjoined. In any case the conviction that a marriage *cannot* (in contrast to the conviction that it *should* not) be dissolved is a highly contingent development (above, 8.2.e). Unfortunately even the fine sentiment that liberalization will betray the steadfastness and heroism of spouses in difficult marriages has to be challenged. Are there marriages with *no* difficulties? Cannot Christians both encourage partners in failing marriages if one or both of them is resolved to keep the marriage together, *and* recognize that some marriages are beyond saving? Does the gospel really require wives who have been victims of marital violence perhaps for years, to remain within their marriages out of loyalty to Christ? Should Christ really be understood to love the institution more than the person?

With regard to the unthinkable possibility of remarriage, Orthodox, Protestant and Roman Catholic (via the process of annulment) churches permit it, although the incidences of it in 1958 were but a fraction of present numbers. The Anglican Lichfield Report (1978) proposed 'a system whereby, without conceding a general right of remarriage in church, divorced persons were in certain cases permitted to be married in church following a pastoral enquiry'.[75] The problems generated by the possibility of a system of pastoral enquiry were never resolved. Against the practice of general remarriage on application, the commissioners posited the 'discarded spouse'

> who had put up with much ill-treatment on the part of her husband because she believed it her Christian duty to do her utmost to salvage her marriage, and who was finally supplanted by another woman, would get a very clear message on what the Church really thought about the sanctity of marriage and how much it really cared for her, if she saw it celebrating their new attachment by a solemn ceremony in church.[76]

The example is a convincing one. A married man divorced on the basis of his adultery and seeking remarriage in his local church with his former partner in adultery represents a hard case. But, leaving aside the complex motivations that may have lain behind the man's behaviour, let us suppose his former wife, several years later, wishes to remarry while her ex-husband is still alive. The same rule would also operate

75. *Marriage and the Church's Task*, p. 84, §233.
76. *Marriage and the Church's Task*, p. 95, §260.

against her doing so. And this would be unfair. We have already found reason to argue that the state of being divorced and not free to remarry is not merely unfair: it is unbiblical.

The arguments of *Just a Piece of Paper?* also leave aside, and beg, many questions. The tutelary role of law in optimizing right conduct has fairly obvious limits. Does not good law provide for the exercise of moral choice and protect the weak? There are very strong moral arguments for a married couple staying together, but since it is love which binds people together, staying together is an act of personal freedom and commitment which must be endlessly renewed. A legal framework for this renewal exists despite more liberal divorce laws. There are plenty of disincentives still in place again hasty divorce. One will be poorer; one's physical and mental health is likely to deteriorate in the short and medium term. It is not clear what the conservatives want. It would be theoretically possible to adopt the laws of some countries (and once of Calvin's Geneva) and make adultery a crime, perhaps a capital one. This would undoubtedly have a tutelary effect on the institution of marriage: one would need to ask whether there was not a better way of avoiding adultery, for example, renewing one's vow to remain faithful to one's partner whatever the civil law allowed. In fact those who argue for the tutelary role of law in relation to the institution of marriage would have a stronger argument if they extended it to the protection of wives and partners some of whom have a life-threatening tutelary need for protection which the law manifestly does *not* provide.

It is probably true to say that permissive laws encourage further permissiveness to develop, and that permissive divorce laws have had a deleterious effect on marriage that none of their advocates intended. What is an appropriate response? Not moral panic. Perhaps there is some comfort in the 'social eversion' hypothesis of Lawrence Stone, according to which 'both sexual repression and sexual permissiveness eventually generate extremist features, which in turn set in motion counterforces'.[77] It is very likely that it was a lack of permissiveness which led to the clamour for (highly popular) reforms to the law. Divorce law reform has provided a radically new freedom to end unhappy marriages. There will be no retreat on this hard-won freedom. In very many

---

77. Stone, *The Family*, p. 545. But Stone notes 'There is no reason to believe that there is a cyclical law in operation, for the swings can be accounted for by specific changes in religious enthusiasm, and by the time it takes for excesses to generate their own opposites'.

cases however, that freedom has been misused. Those who would seek to withdraw the freedom have to ask whether there is a better way, a more responsible use of freedom which enables distressing and painful marriages to end while providing encouragement to couples to remain in marriages at the times when they are disinclined to do so. Many people divorcing in the 1970s simply *did not know* about the prolonged and verifiable negative impact of divorce on children. There are many other cases where whole societies need to learn how to use new freedoms. There is a clear need for moral education programmes which deal with these matters. And, it must be said, these are unlikely (at least in Britain) since teachers are highly reluctant to appear to make overt moral judgments of any kind (especially if a majority of children in the classroom come from 'non-traditional' family backgrounds).

Christians will want to re-emphasize their understanding of marriage as a covenant, a conjugal union and a mutually administered sacrament in the present situation. The micro-politics of mutual love have never been more important. There is a widespread rejection of patriarchal marriage. I worry as a Christian that the growing number of people who reject patriarchal marriage are unaware that there may be another kind of marriage, non-patriarchal marriage. What this is like and how it is to be worked out is not immediately apparent. It is here that the churches might give a strong lead. The overcoming of patriarchy is the latest change in the institution and theology of marriage. I think it is an over-whelmingly positive one. But beginning with children (above, 5.2) and receiving the grace of God in conjugal spirituality offer an alternative to easy divorce in very many cases. If Christian marriage offers a sacra-mental experience, people will continue to want it. It is best com-mended by being lived. There is an unwarranted pessimism among the arguments considered in this section. Even the abolition of fault in divorce law need not be understood as the abolition of blame. The reluctance to apportion blame need not mean that no one *is* to blame. It may mean only that the practice of apportioning blame can heighten the potential for destructiveness and be counterproductive. There is an absence of reference to the quality of marriages, especially for women, among the critics of liberalization.

b. *Arguments over Annulment*
The argument of this chapter has sanctioned divorce and remarriage as a combined possibility. The Roman Catholic Church will not allow the

dissolution of valid, consummated marriages, but under certain circumstances it will annul them. The practice of annulment is not well understood in the rest of Christendom, and outside the churches it is much
more common to speak of divorce than annulment. Can non-Catholic
churches learn from annulment? Are there not sound reasons, both
logical and historical, for thinking that a marriage which is 'dead' was
never a true marriage in the first place?

As Ralph Brown explains, there are two main aspects of consent:
consent *to* (i.e., the object of consent) and consent *with* (i.e., 'those
powers and requirements which allow one to consent to the object').[78]
So, people under marriagable age are deemed to lack the necessary
powers and requirements. People who consent to something but are
constrained 'by means of physical or moral force or fear exerted', may
be deemed retrospectively not to have given consent.[79] So in order to
consent to marriage, a person has to be 'sane and possessed of a degree
of judgemental ability to decide upon marriage; as well as to have at
least a minimal ability to form and sustain the partnership'. There are
two types of grounds for annulment in contemporary Catholic practice:
'if there was no consent given to the marriage, or if the consent was in
some way defective'.[80]

The category of defective consent has grown to huge proportions and
spawned several sub-categories. A person may 'simulate' consent. So
coercion to undertake a marriage, or admission of cowardice in resisting pressure to marry, would count as simulated consent (or 'total simu-
lation'). But a person may simulate consent when under no pressure
at all. An example of this is the 'Exclusion of the Right to Conjugal
Acts'.[81] A spouse may, on marrying, intend to refuse sexual intercourse
with his or her partner. More probably, there may be 'an intention to
remove the other person's right to those conjugal acts of themselves
suitable for the procreation of children'.[82] For example a husband, after
a wedding, may insist on wearing a condom or require his wife to take
the contraceptive pill. Any husband who did this could be deemed to
have simulated consent at the time of the marriage because consent to a
marriage as understood in the Roman Catholic tradition is to consent to

78. Brown, *Marriage Annulment*, p. 26.
79. Brown, *Marriage Annulment*, p. 27.
80. Brown, *Marriage Annulment*, p. 37.
81. Brown, *Marriage Annulment*, p. 44.
82. Brown, *Marriage Annulment*, p. 49.

the principle that every act of sexual intercourse should be open to procreation. Subsequent behaviour proves that no such consent was in fact given.

This widening out of defective consent potentially licenses the dissolution of literally millions of marriages. It has however been widened even further. A person may enter into marriage believing it to be, as the authors of *Just a Piece of Paper?* warned, 'provisional'. This is a widespread secular understanding of the limited obligations of marriage. He or she only has to 'enter into a union with the deliberate intention of terminating it in certain circumstances'. Since Christian marriage is indissoluble it can be deduced from any intention of dissolving it that it was not Christian marriage to which consent was given. This is the 'Intention to Exclude Indissolubility'.[83] If a person is *unaware* that in consenting to marriage she or he is consenting to a permanent arrangement, an annulment may be obtained on the grounds of 'The Hypothetical Exclusion of Permanence'.[84] Similarly if a spouse did not intend to remain faithful to his or her partner, an annulment may be obtained on the grounds of the 'Intention to Exclude Fidelity'.[85] A further lack which is a ground of annulment is the 'inability to assume the obligations of marriage'. This ground is based directly on canon law which indicates that 'no-one who is unable, for causes of psychological nature, to assume the essential obligations of marriage can validly contract marriage'.[86] A spouse whose conduct wrecks a marriage may be deemed unable on psychological grounds to keep the vows he or she has made. 'With regard to the application of jurisprudential considerations to these psychiatric problems', tribunal judges should ask 'whether the condition makes it *impossible* for the person to assume the essential obligations of marriage'.[87]

In the light of these somewhat amazing enlargements of the grounds for annulment, the negative judgment (of an Eastern Orthodox theologian) that 'hideous abuses' have been heaped on the institution of marriage by the Roman 'system of annulments', is understandable.[88] What, we might wonder, is the doctrine of indissolubility worth, when the

83. Brown, *Marriage Annulment*, p. 51.
84. Brown, *Marriage Annulment*, p. 56.
85. Brown, *Marriage Annulment*, pp. 57-58.
86. Brown, *Marriage Annulment*, p. 100. Canon 1095 n. 3, is cited.
87. Brown, *Marriage Annulment*, p. 102 (author's emphasis).
88. Zion, *Eros and Transformation*, p. 119. And see above, 2.1.b.

practice of annulment has moved so far? The issue is no longer the indissolubility of the union, but the union itself, since the practice of annulment assumes, not that there was once a valid marriage and now there no longer is, but that the marriage was no marriage in the first place. One may surmise that the issue has not become a major source of disagreement in the churches because the extent of the practice is still not generally known. These generous grounds of annulment contribute to the very state of affairs which is officially and rightly deplored—the provisionality of marriage.

The retrospective nature of annulment together with its ever expanding application must unwittingly cast a shadow of doubt over marriage itself. One Catholic critic criticizes the extent of the juridical character of the process. Annulment, he says, is 'very appealing to the legal, Western mind, for it is only in Western culture that we receive a printed-out receipt for a tube of toothpaste'. Annulment is 'for the sophisticated and the educated. It demands a gathering of documents to properly decipher the shades of meaning in the legal terminology. People from the Third World and minority groups have trouble thinking in these terms'.[89] In 1978 the Anglican Lichfield commissioners focused their criticisms on the use of 'psychological immaturity' as a ground for annulment. They acidly observed,

> We know of no general agreement...among theologians, psychologists or the general public about what constitutes psychological maturity or immaturity in people of any age. In a fundamental sense all of us are engaged in a process of growing towards maturity throughout our lives and are necessarily immature at the outset of a relationship which makes such a significant contribution to that growth.[90]

There was a muted sense (even in 1971) that contemporary annulment practice mirrors the corrupt excesses of mediaeval times, based on the prohibited (and inflated) degrees of kindred and affinity. It exceeds mediaeval practice in its sheer scale.[91] Zion's objection to the practice

---

89. Barry Brunsman, *New Hope for Divorced Catholics* (San Francisco: Harper & Row, 1985), pp. 59-60.

90. *Marriage and the Church's Task*, p. 81, §224. The earlier Root Commission signalled their discomfort with Catholic annulment practice by observing 'Others deduce from a failure to grow in matrimonial union an incapacity to do so from the beginning; this is an extension from the notion of physical incapacity to consummate into the psychological'. See *Marriage, Divorce and the Church*, p. 63.

91. Brunsman, *New Hope*, pp. 60-61.

lies in its ability to cover up 'the evils attendant upon marital break-down and the acknowledgement of sin in such instances'.[92] Validity, he says, 'has no place in the Orthodox assessment of marital reality'.

For these reasons there is unlikely to be any take-up of annulment practice outside the Catholic communion: indeed within the tribunals of that church a tighter interpretation of the grounds for annulment is to be expected. The question asked at the beginning of this section has a negative answer: the special pleading that a dead marriage was never really a marriage in the first place flies in the face of too many difficul-ties. Annulments provide a way out of marriages that have failed: there is honesty and precedent in acknowledging this. But the refusal to admit that a marriage which has ended was still a marriage is a 'new pretence'.[93] The error lies in the uncritical acceptance of the principle of the indissolubility of marriage.

c. *A Sacramental, but not an Indissoluble Bond*
It has already been suggested that the doctrine that marriage *cannot* be dissolved rests on a mistake (above, 8.2.e). Reynolds describes this development concisely—it is a 'shift from deontological matters (rules and prohibitions) to ontological ones (bonds and states)', which, in rul-ing out divorce and remarriage only '*appears* to be causal and explana-tory: remarriage is invalid *because* the bond remains'.[94] The Western church took this unfortunate step in the time of Jerome and Augustine and it has had an ambiguous influence ever since. 'Augustine's prob-lem', says Reynolds, 'is that he is conflating an *existential* bond (a relationship, in other words) with the *indissoluble* bond (whatever that may be). The premise that it is conjugal charity that makes marriage ought to entail that marriage is dissoluble.'[95] These shifts are echoed throughout contemporary theological writing on marriage, even though many authors do not appear to be aware of their historical grounding. When the classical and contemporary accounts are brought together they provide a very strong case for believing the bond of marriage is sacramental, but not indissoluble. Since this position appears to reverse

92. Zion, *Eros and Transformation*, p. 119.
93. Harvey, *Promise or Pretence?*, p. 133.
94. Reynolds, *Marriage in the Western Church*, p. 221 (*'appears'* is an added emphasis).
95. Reynolds, *Marriage in the Western Church*, p. 307 (emphases added).

standard teaching that the sacrament is what *makes* a marriage indissoluble, some further clarification is necessary.

Indissolubility is widely interpreted as a process of growth, as a consequence of mutual love, as a mutual *task* and as a relational bond. None of these designations presume that the bond *cannot* be dissolved. Bernard Cooke explains,

> Men and women are gradually initiated into marriage as a human relationship and a Christian sacrament; the initiation is never completed in this life—no more than is a person's lifelong initiation into Christianity, for becoming married is for most Christians a major element in the broader initiation into Christ.[96]

On this view a marriage becomes 'increasingly indissoluble as it becomes increasingly Christian'. Cooke holds that

> the more profoundly Christian a marriage relationship becomes, the more inseparable are the two persons as loving human beings, and the more does their relationship sacramentalize the absolute indissolubility of the divine-human relationship as it finds expression in the crucified and risen Christ.[97]

The view that indissolubility is a fruit of mutual human love, mingled with the divine love of Christ for the Church, has recently been restated by Kevin Kelly. In the Catholic teaching of earlier periods, 'Indissolubility was considered to be one of the essential properties of marriage, rather than something flowing from the very nature of the couple's love for each other'.[98] Now indissolubility is to be understood not as a property externally conferred, but one which can be realized in the growth of the partners' mutual love for each other. When a couple marry, they

> do not suddenly find themselves tied by an indissoluble bond which has an existence independent of them. When they marry, they give their pledge that they will form an indissoluble union of persons through their love for each other. The indissolubility of their marriage is *a task to be undertaken.*[99]

This restatement of the meaning of the indissoluble bond of marriage was affirmed by the majority of the Lichfield commissioners in 1978.

96. Bernard Cooke, 'Indissolubility', p. 71.

97. Cooke, 'Indissolubility', p. 71.

98. Kevin T. Kelly, *Divorce and Second Marriage: Facing the Challenge* (London: Geoffrey Chapman, new and expanded edn, 1996), p. 15.

99. Kelly, *Divorce*, p. 16 (author's emphasis).

The commissioners agreed that because the marriage bond 'unites two persons at the centre of their being', it should be called an 'ontological' or a 'relational bond'. They also agreed that 'there actually occur such ontological unions between man and wife, unions which, as a matter of fact, nothing can dissolve'.[100] But they could not agree how 'to describe those unions which, to all outward appearances, have broken down'. A majority affirmed the 'dissolubilist position', that is, they rejected the view that 'even when a marriage had broken down and reconciliation was, at least humanly speaking, no longer possible, some bond between husband and wife still existed'.[101]

Finally the obvious looking assumption that marriage is able to be dissolved surrenders nothing of theological significance. It is not a capitulation to modern trends. Remarriage for the innocent partner in an adulterous marriage was permitted by the *Reformatio Legum Ecclesiasticarum*, much of which was produced by Thomas Cranmer.[102] The indissolubilist position founders on Augustine's problem of the inability to say what binds couples who have come apart. It relies on a concept of sacramental grace which is quasi-magical. Grace does not override freedom: if it did its recipients would be compromised as personal subjects who would not need to 'work' at their marriages. God's grace is realized in freedom, not against it.

d. *Pastoral Consequences*

There is merit in a 'third way' between the hard evangelical interpretation of the teaching of Jesus and the 'indissolubilist' position of Catholicism. It can claim to be the most pastorally sensitive of various positions on divorce. First, there is a real danger that hard evangelical teaching compounds the pastoral pain of a broken marriage. We have already met the contention of Heth and Wenham (above, 8.2.d) that Jesus did not permit remarriage for any reason. At the end of their book they consider what pastoral advice Christian ministers who agree with

100. *Marriage and the Church's Task*, p. 37, §97.

101. *Marriage and the Church's Task*, p. 37, §98. However the attempt to infer the existence of *two* bonds, the first established by consent and commitment; the second, the relational bond still waiting to be realized, seems confused and unnecessary. See p. 38, §99.

102. The *Reformatio Legum Ecclesiasticarum* was a collection of proposed canons which were published in 1553 and never adopted. See, e.g., David Atkinson, *To Have and To Hold: The Marriage Covenant and the Discipline of Divorce* (London: Collins, 1979), pp. 58-62.

their version of the indissolubilist position would give to Christians
who have divorced and remarried. They say,

> Those couples who have already remarried after divorce may be won-
> dering how their situation fits into all of this. We believe that you should
> see that your present marriage is God's will for you. You should seek to
> be the best husband or wife you can be, rendering to each other your full
> marital duty. If you come to the realisation that Jesus calls remarriage
> after divorce the sin of adultery, then call sin 'sin' rather than seek to
> justify what you have done. We believe this will bring great freedom to
> your marriage and will break down barriers to ministry you may have
> encountered before.[103]

There appear to be grave problems with this advice. On their view,
remarriage is objectively and certainly a sin. Nonetheless in particular
cases it turns out that it is not a sin at all because it may be the will of
God that some people remarry. Surely it is not suggested that as long as
the sin of remarriage is committed in ignorance, it is not only pardonable, but no sin? Since a second marriage is capable of conformity to
God's will, why is God depicted as forbidding it? Unfortunately the
problems do not end here. Since a second marriage is tantamount to
adultery and so sinfully constituted, how can it be a fulfilling relationship? Suppose the partners in a happy second marriage become convinced, after exposure to the indissolubilist position, that they are still
married to their former partners and living in adultery. What are they to
do? They are 'to call their sin "sin"'. But what do they do then? Do
they, in obedience to the will of God, separate again and remain single?
Such advice is bad advice. Impossible doctrinal positions collide unpre-
dictably with real situations, leading to shallow theological compromises which turn out to be contradictions.

The position just described deserves the name '*biblical* indissolubility'. The Catholic counterpart is '*sacramental* indissolubility'. Theodore Mackin exposes the pastorally disastrous impact of this teaching.
He considers the case of a devout Roman Catholic married woman who
is abandoned by her husband after 29 years of marriage. She believes
she has the gift of marriage. Her husband divorces her and enters into a
civil marriage with someone else. After two years she enters into a
loving relationship with another man and they wish to marry. 'A retrospective examination' of the early years of her marriage 'has turned up
no flaw in character of either herself or her husband, no impediment

---

103. Heth and Wenham, *Jesus and Divorce*, p. 200.

that could constitute grounds for finding nullity'.[104] She cannot marry the man she loves because she remains married to the man who left her and married someone else. Her 'former' marriage is deemed still to be a sign of the self-giving and sacramental love of Christ for his Church. Her question, observes Mackin, is 'Why such a theory of marriage's indissolubility has been designed, installed and kept, since there is no internal logic demanding its keeping, and the keeping of it cannot have fidelity to Christ's command as its reason?' It does not (in any empirical sense) protect marriage, because the rate of failure of Catholic marriages is no different from other marriages. The doctrine is finally incoherent, produces misery, and awaits reform.

The third way differs, not in its refusal to acknowledge the tragedy involved in marital breakdown, but in its offering of Christian hope to the postmarried who wish to remarry. Jesus' way of dealing with people was to offer them hope for the future, and not to resort to the law to entrap them in the past. Greg Forster comments on Jesus' pastoral strategy in his interaction with the woman at the well (Jn 4.1-30) and the woman taken in adultery (Jn 7.53–8.11). Noting how Jesus knew the woman at the well had been married five times and was living with a man to whom she was not married, and that Jesus wished to meet this man, Forster has a profound insight into the attitude of Jesus:

> Whether divorce is part of this story or not, what we see here is Jesus working towards a better future for a person whom circumstances or sin have left socially weak and emotionally vulnerable. For her 'salvation' meant not only meeting and trusting the Messiah, but seeing her family life set by him on firm foundations... Jesus' approach was pastoral rather than legalistic when he was dealing with the needs of an individual whom he met. This approach looked forward rather than back.[105]

Forster observes a similar strategy in Jesus' intervention in the case of the woman about to be stoned to death for adultery. Jesus, he observes, forced

> powerful men to realize that they were just as much sinners as a weakly-placed woman. He did not pronounce a legal judgement against her, but he did not condone her action either. She was to carry on her life and from then on not sin again. What she had done was wrong, Jesus states gently, but what was important was what happened from then on. Once

104. Theodore Mackin, SJ, *Divorce and Remarriage* (New York: Paulist Press, 1984), p. 545.
105. Forster, *Healing Love's Wound*, p. 59.

again, Jesus' practice was pastoral in a face-to-face situation. He looked
to getting the future right rather than enforcing a law and he defended
those whom society picked on in the way it used its laws.[106]

This description of the attitude of Jesus is what is meant here by a third
way. It indicates the limitless compassion and grace of God and the
transforming power of both in the renewal of broken lives.

106. Forster, *Healing Love's Wounds*, p. 60.

Chapter 9

CHRISTIAN MARRIAGE AFTER MODERNITY

'Postmodernity' has been used in this book to convey the opportunity that exists for Christian theology to engage with thought forms and practices which have lost or are in danger of losing contact with it. The location of ourselves at or towards the end of modernity has also enabled the developing theology of Christian marriage to be linked with wider social, cultural and intellectual upheavals. The vision of marriage after modernity has not abandoned its premodern roots; on the contrary, as it has tried to listen and respond to the postmodern crisis, it has been able to appreciate its historic rootedness in different ways. A new context generates new questions, which in turn make new discoveries possible. The new questions have been frequently awkward to handle, and the answers have frequently incorporated premodern practices.

There have been plenty of 'awkward questions'. Findings on the more likely plight of children who are brought up by one parent or who are hurt by divorce have led to a renewed concentration on the centrality of children to the institution of marriage. The renewed emphasis on procreation is very much a premodern theme, a stark contrast to the 'pure relationship' of late modernity. The widespread practice of cohabitation at the end of modernity led to the rediscovery of betrothal which is also premodern in theology and practice. The modern panoply of contraception led to the suggestion that non-penetrative sexual experience could be an appropriate form of sexual expression outside marriage and that use of natural methods of contraception was particularly commendable for couples who wished to postpone having children. Those who, in Christian terms, do not have a 'vocation to marriage' have much to learn from the ancient advocates of celibacy. The unprecedented demand for divorce in the late modern era prompted neither a liberal condonement nor a conservative reaction, but rather a thanksgiving that the ancient permission for divorce had been reclaimed, together with a prayer that recourse to it would become less common. Critics wishing to argue that the vision of marriage commended in this book is merely a capitulation to late modern forms of it will need to deal with the fact that it can claim to be grounded in Scripture and history. Marriage 'after modernity' does not imply a smooth linear progression towards the present *status quo* but rather a more complex vision of marriage arrived at through the interplay of clashing loyalties (above, 1.2) to which all Christian theologians should subscribe.

1. *Christian Marriage after Patriarchy*

A further advantage of situating the inquiry undertaken by this book at the end of modernity is that it relativizes our own time, and requires both an appreciation of the past and an openness to God's future. The treatment of marriage 'after modernity' provides a sufficiently broad canvas for wide, far-reaching social changes to be brought into the frame. Two of these are the overcoming of patriarchy and heterosexuality as institutions. This book assumes there *can* be non-patriarchal, Christian marriage, and indeed, there must be, if the understanding of marriage as a lifelong covenant is to survive. It has also been admitted (above, 2.1.f) that non-patriarchal marriage will be difficult to achieve. Christian traditions of marriage have been carriers of patriarchy—that much is sadly obvious. However, there are grounds for hope that the understanding of marriage within the churches will continue to grow in the direction of non-patriarchal mutuality. Nonetheless non-patriarchal marriage by itself is not enough.

The writers advocating a post-Christian understanding of sexual relationships in Chapter 2, assumed, however misleadingly, that the battle waged against patriarchy by the warriors of the new sexual freedoms had been won. The frequent termination of the pure relationships which characterize the new equality suggests that patriarchy in its more insidious private forms of male behaviour and attitude is far from dead. Plastic sexuality, reinvented humanism, pragmatic sexual ethics, and the secular religion of love all assume the grand narratives of the religious past to have been bad for us. But what do they offer in return? There are two crucial points here. The first is that these self-consciously late modern and post-Christian writers describe real achievements in the conquest of patriarchy and these should be welcomed by Christians. It is part of a lively Christian faith to be constantly surprised by the traces of the work of God the Spirit outside the churches but within the wider body of humanity where the Son of God has his permanent home (Jn 1.14). The second point is that the relationships envisaged by these writers are individualistic, provisional and endlessly revisable. Christian marriage offers an alternative where commitments entered into are lifelong, and where sacramental grace is available to sustain and nurture the marriage as a permanent project of partners, persons and (very likely) parents.

Put bluntly, plastic sexuality is not yet redeemed! Reinvented humanism arrives at profound insights into that equality of worth of human beings which a hierarchical view of human relationships inevitably loses sight of, while it dismisses the transcendent source of love which may yet be found to be the guarantor of the very equalities the new humanism celebrates. The pragmatic ethic needs something more than vague appeals to 'responsibility', when the chosen complexities of sexual experience engulf the individual. What happens when the proclaimers and practitioners of the 'secular religion' of romantic love move on to *their own* post-religious phase, much as contemporary people are assumed by these writers to have done, in evacuating themselves from the formal requirements and disciplines of faith?

The post-Christian writers announce sexual relationships which celebrate mutuality and equality. While there is undoubtedly room for a critical examination of what these concepts entail, where they come from, and how theology is able to contribute to them, Christians should welcome these achievements. But while post-Christian writers proclaim also a post-patriarchal present, Christians can justifiably point out that these social arrangements have so far done little to foster commitments that empower couples to arrive at a deepening love for each other which thrives on mutual acceptance and forgiveness of each other, and on the spiritual growth which works to remove the need for forgiveness in the first place. While the churches from a contemporary perspective have been slow to proclaim the equality of partners within marriage, they have always proclaimed the enduring nature of marriage through felicity and adversity. While post-Christians (at least those considered in Chapter 2) appear to have removed Christian marriage from among the various forms of being-with-another currently on offer, marriage is able to provide precisely what the new provisionality conspicuously lacks.

Postmodern, yet Christian, marriage, offers the vital prospect of marriage which is post-patriarchal yet enduring. The crisis for marriage is that its patriarchal form is outmoded and rightly rejected while non-patriarchal versions of marriage either remain in infancy or are simply unacknowledged as a real possibility. Marriage has generated its own transformations in the past: the present transformation from patriarchy to equality remains an imperative for all the churches. The removal of patriarchy from marriage may also dislodge many of the factors contributing to marital breakdown and to the reluctance to make permanent, open-ended commitments to a single partner. But the end of patriarchy does not mean the end of unprovisional commitment: it merely removes the main obstacle in the way of exercising it. The obligation on husbands to love their wives 'as Christ loved the church and gave himself up for it' (Eph. 5.22) remains undiminished by the admission that the obligation is based on an offensive patriarchal theory which requires the submission of women to men, and the assumption that such heroic other-regarding acts could only be performed by men. The removal of the theory is a wholly positive development. The obligation is not diminished, but rather, intensified, because, after patriarchy, it becomes a shared one, and consequently one that is likely to have a higher chance of being carried out (above, 3.2.a).

The handling of the Ephesian marriage text to eliminate ancient assumptions about male superiority remains instructive in indicating what is involved in advocating a non-patriarchal form of Christian marriage. Patriarchy has to be faced, not evaded. Since the theology of Christian marriage has been in the hands of men since the letter to the Ephesians was written (and still largely remains so), it is not surprising that it is proving difficult to dislodge. The disowning of the patriarchal premises in this text is essential for husbands' sake, for wives' sake, for Christ's sake, indeed for everyone's sake. In a non-patriarchal marriage the husband has an equal partner in giving and receiving married love as Christ loves the Church. The love the husband has for his wife will be deeper because she will be his equal, but not a dependent being capable only of obedience, submission and reverence in relation to him. Because she turns out, after patriarchy, to be able to love reciprocally and thereby exercise freedom, his love can be more genuine. If she loves her husband as Christ loves the Church she becomes an equal partner in the joint project of the marital covenant and the androcentric calling into question of her abilities is removed. Non-patriarchal marriage makes the couple jointly subject to Christ, thereby intensifying the place of Christ in the marriage. Under patriarchy the wife submits to Christ through her husband; after patriarchy each submits to each other and Christ is the 'head' of both of them. This does not tamper or jeopardize the place of Christ within a couple's marriage: it gives it the possibility of greater realization because the authority of Christ in the marriage is given a higher status by not being mediated through maleness.

What happens in reading the Ephesian text 'after patriarchy' is able to illustrate a different kind of reading—the 'reading' of the contemporary con*text* of marriage also as a breaking away from patriarchy. But there is much that Christian marriage can never be 'post-' because the loving communion on which it is founded is the communion of the Trinitarian God, and the invitation to share in it is given by the self-giving of the Trinitarian God in the Person of Christ. The tragedy for postmodern marriage is that while patriarchal versions of marriage are rejected, marriage itself has been gravely weakened and taken on forms which, while stressing equality, also incorporate elements which are inimical to the preservation of marriage in any form. A version of marriage which is emphatically post-patriarchal, while emphatically not post-Christian, will alone meet the demand *both* for genuine equality between partners *and* for a deepening and enduring relationship between them.

This is the hope for Christian marriage after modernity. If it is to become a reality it is likely that Christians practising it will need increasingly to become critical of postmodern trends which seem to marginalize marriage completely: in short they will become increasingly 'counter cultural' in respect of marriage. This will be no new matter. Christian attitudes cannot fail to be influenced by the wider social attitudes to marriage. That is, the temptation to regard marriage (and the having or not having of children) merely as a private matter must be resisted, since there are public influences, expectations and consequences surrounding a couple's supposedly private decisions. The ever-increasing demands of employers (especially in the overworked countries of Britain) easily militate against the cultivation of successful marriages. The undislodged (but nonetheless recent) expectation that mothers ought to be responsible, not merely for breast feeding babies, but for almost all the care of children needs to be addressed with a vigour not yet seen. The assumption that women do it actually contributes to the problem of father-absence because the role of the father as an active care-provider is still sometimes suspiciously regarded. The practices of work-sharing and job-sharing remain undeveloped. Arrangements for childcare which increase the role of fathers and which do not diminish the role of both parents are clearly desirable. Motherhood is an undoubted disadvantage in many jobs. The reorganization of work in ways which favour inclusive parenthood has scarcely begun. There are wider social changes which are necessary for post-patriarchal marriage to thrive. Christians should be working for these while, if they are married, at the same time practising a conjugal spirituality (above, 7.1.b) which deepens their marriage by deepening their joint relationship with God.

2. *Christian Marriage 'after Heterosexuality'?*

Another benefit of locating marriage at the end of modernity is that it cannot be separated, in some parts of the world at least, from the wider acceptance, recognition and re-evaluation of the relationships between lesbian women and gay men. In the USA there are more than 1.6 million households consisting of partners of the same sex.[1] The churches are deeply divided about homosexuality. What, if anything, can the vision of marriage outlined in this book, contribute to the ongoing discussion?

The phrase 'after heterosexuality' does not, of course, imply that in the postmodern world heterosexual people will find their attraction to the sex which is not their own will become outmoded. What then, does it mean? It means that heterosexuality has hitherto operated as an exclusive social institution, which together with marriage, has regulated all sexual contact. Heterosexuality has confined sexual expression between people of different sexes: marriage has limited sexual expression to persons married to each other. Heterosexuality became compulsory. It was believed to have been ordained by God. Any homosexual expression could not therefore please God. Heterosexuality enforces itself by marginalizing lesbian, gay and bisexual people. 'After heterosexuality' means once heterosexuality was *compulsory*: now it no longer is. To utter the words 'after heterosexuality' is to be able to relativize another hitherto unquestioned institution; perhaps it is to see that the term itself belongs to the medical terminology of the late

---

1.   US Census Bureau, *Current Population Survey Reports* (March 1998).

nineteenth century; that its purpose has been to enforce, to marginalize, to stigmatize. It is to entertain the possibility that the diversity of sexual orientation found among human beings is due to our having been wonderfully made by God. It is the possibility of straight, lesbian, bisexual and gay people being able to join together in worship and proclaim together in praise:

> You it was who fashioned my inward parts; you knitted me together in my mother's womb.
>
> I praise you, for you fill me with awe; wonderful you are, and wonderful your works.
>
> You know me through and through: my body was no mystery to you, when I was formed in secret, woven in the depths of the earth.
>
> Your eyes foresaw my deeds, and they were all recorded in your book; my life was fashioned before it had come into being' (Ps. 139.13-16).

a. *Do Same-Sex Couples Want to be Married?*

In order to keep the discussion within bounds,[2] three questions will be briefly addressed. First, what do lesbian and gay people want for their relationships? Secondly, is marriage a heterosexual institution anyway? Thirdly, are there obvious elements within Christian marriage which overlap with lesbian and gay partnerships? The first question is necessary because it is often addressed by straight theologians in a downright patronizing way. Lesbian and gay people often provide the means for straight people to define their own sexual identity. They are what straight people are not. Thus designated as other, 'they' can be endlessly discussed as a peculiar theological (i.e., straight) problem. Divisions are then allowed to arise between those heterosexuals who are prepared to regard homosexuals as honorary heterosexuals who can therefore be married, and those who are confident that no such accommodation is able to be given. There must be a better way of thinking our differences.

Do lesbian and gay people, and particularly Christian people, want to be married? No single answer to this question is able yet to be given, and there may in any case be a difference between what lesbians and gay men want. When I wrote *Liberating Sex* I was swayed by the

---

2. I have discussed marriage in the context of lesbian and gay relationships in my *Liberating Sex*, Chapters 9 and 10, pp. 127-59. See also Stuart and Thatcher, *People of Passion*, Chapters 7, pp. 167-200.

arguments of the late Robert Williams that any socio-legal arrangement which was not marriage would be regarded in the wider society as 'substandard' or 'abnormal'.[3] Williams's worry about the lack of recognition of legally registered partnerships seems to have been confirmed by the partnership laws which have recently been introduced in several European countries. Since they apply (except for the Netherlands) to same-sex couples only, and the rules governing citizenship, recognition and custody are different from those governing married couples, some lesbian and gay partners still find the new partnership laws discriminatory.[4] There are powerful arguments for regarding lesbian and gay marriage as 'a civil right'.[5] In particular the legalization of same-sex marriages would provide protection for adopted children who are vulnerable to being torn away from the non-biological parent(s) when those parents lack the protections of legalized marriage. On the other hand Elizabeth Stuart says she has 'yet to find a lesbian' who 'wants to define their relationship in terms of marriage'.[6] As she says, there is widespread dissatisfaction with marriage, especially from wives, and the failure of the churches to recognize or criticize its shortcomings has elevated marriage into an 'idol' (the 'idolatry of the ideal').[7] Given that marriage is in trouble, Stuart thinks lesbian and gay people would be making a tactical and existential mistake to make it a model for their own relationships. The model of friendship is more promising.

While there may be no single view among lesbian and gay partners about the desirability of marriage, inside and outside the churches, there is a clear unanimity in favour of the removal of obvious forms of discrimination in such areas as pensions, the right to public housing, intestacy and (in Britain) assessment for inheritance tax. There may also be stronger support for marriage among same-sex partners in the USA than in Europe. The lack of agreement about the appropriateness of marriage for lesbian and gay people is explicable partly by deeper questions about what marriage is. If marriage is exclusively a

3. Thatcher, *Liberating Sex*, p. 147. See Robert Williams, 'Towards a Theology for Lesbian and Gay Marriage', in Thatcher and Stewart, *Perspectives*, pp. 279-300 (281).

4. Stonewall Factsheet, 'Same Sex Couples and the Law' (March 1998).

5. Craig R. Dean, 'Gay Marriage: A Civil Right', *Journal of Homosexuality*, 27.3 (1994), pp. 111-15.

6. Stuart, *Just Good Friends*, p. 117.

7. Stuart, *Just Good Friends*, p. 109.

heterosexual institution, then gay and lesbian partners are not free to avail themselves of it even if some of them want to. But is it?

b. *Is Marriage a Heterosexual Institution?*
This book has linked Christian marriage very strongly with having and caring for children. In this respect marriage *is* a heterosexual institution.[8] Straight conservative Christians and lesbian and gay Christians critical of marriage are in ironic agreement about the point. But the observation that marriage is a heterosexual institution is based on the historical truism that marriages have hitherto been confined to heterosexual couples and the biological truism that conception requires a contribution from both sexes. Neither truism provides sufficient reason for preventing the extension of marriage to committed lesbian and gay couples in lifelong unions or for confining marriage *in perpetuo* to straight people. It is surely obvious that marriage historically has changed and will continue to change. Why should it not change in order to encompass those lesbian and gay couples who wish it for themselves? It is equally obvious that there are *de facto* many thousands of gay and lesbian parents all over the world, some with children of former heterosexual marriages, some with children by artificial insemination, and some who have fostered and adopted children as their own (where the law and the absence of homophobia allow). There are no good reasons for thinking that lesbian and gay parents are not good parents, or that sexual orientation disqualifies a person from being a parent. British courts have recently accepted that children growing up in lesbian and gay families 'do not suffer at school nor are they confused about their gender or sexual orientation'.[9] But the fact remains: only straight couples can be the biological parents of their children. Is this a sufficiently strong consideration to confine marriage to straights?

The arguments pursued in Chapters 5 and 6 have a bearing on this question. The 'theology of liberation for children' was based on children as oppressed by parents who have them but do not want them, or

8.   Pam Lunn thinks the heterosexual emphasis on the consummation of marriage through sexual intercourse is not transferable to same-sex partnerships. It follows, she thinks, 'that lesbian and gay partnerships are not, and cannot be, marriages'. See her 'Anatomy and Theology of Marriage: Is Gay Marriage an Oxymoron?', *TheolSex*, 7 (1997), pp. 10-26 (17).

9.   Stonewall Pamphlet, *Equality 2000* (1998). (Golomok and Tasker, City University, 1995 is [incompletely] cited.)

abandon them, or coerce them into domestic arrangements they do not wish for themselves. In these senses children are *victims*. But they are clearly victims of the behaviour of their heterosexual parents. Liberation for these children is about being undisruptedly wanted and loved by their natural parents, from conception to adult life. Children, including unborn children, come first in the sexual and social behaviour of the men and women who conceive them. But children who are fostered and/or adopted by lesbian and gay parents are not victims. The marriage of their adoptive parents may make their futures more secure.

The argument from the 'unbreakable connection' between sex and love (above, 6.2.b-c) establishes a further point. The bond between children and their biological parents is not merely a biological bond. Pope John Paul II was applauded for observing that children are sometimes in danger of being regarded merely as an undesirable outcome of sexual intercourse, 'an enemy to be avoided at all costs'. The 'contraceptive mentality' was thought not merely to postpone having children but to avoid them altogether. It is often overlooked that millions of couples desire children intensely and feel a sense of deep fulfilment in being parents. Having children is also a joy, not simply a mistake. Since children generally flourish better when they are brought up by two parents who are committed to them, it is necessary to confirm the ancient view that procreation is one of the purposes of marriage, perhaps the main one.

There are good theological arguments for restating this position. The Old Testament assumes children are a blessing from God. Children require the same love, protection and faithfulness which their parents promise to each other. They are included in their parents' vows. These vows are as much for their sake as they are for their parents' sake. The union of 'one flesh' between married heterosexual partners has an additional possible consequence: children. That is the enormous and obvious difference between actual heterosexual and possible homosexual marriages. A danger of extending the purpose or scope of marriage to lesbian and gay couples is that it may weaken further the strong connection between marriage and children urged in this book. When thinking about and seeking to accommodate this absolute difference between different-sex and same-sex marriages, the context of postmodernity itself prompts a recognition (if not a celebration) of difference, whereas the extension of marriage to cover both types of union would seem to go in for the discredited tactic of minimizing difference for the sake of imposing on it a higher order or unity. In this case, it might be urged, marriage remains the 'hegemonic discourse'. It retains its hegemonic position by incorporating into it those whose experience of it is certain to be different.

I arrive therefore at two tentative conclusions. The first is that children are inseparably and not merely contingently connected to the purposes of marriage. This is a conclusion based not on an essentialism which dictates that the connection exists, as it were, in advance of the evidence; nor (God forbid) on an (unacknowledged) desire to exclude lesbian and gay partners from the same rights and privileges that married, straight partners enjoy. It is based on the difference between the two types of union which manifests itself biologically, and, just because it is biological, it exists at the most basic level of our being. To this extent marriage *is* a heterosexual institution. The second conclusion is that marriage is able to be extended theologically to lesbian and gay couples. I do not believe these conclusions are incompatible. The uncertainty among lesbian and gay people about whether marriage is to be shunned as a heterosexual institution or campaigned for as a legal right is entirely understandable and is to be respected, especially given the legal and social discrimination of the past and the present. Those who argue for the extension of marriage beyond heterosexual couples as lifelong covenants (below, 9.2.c) ought to find the arguments in this book support them. The emphasis on children is intended to protect children, not to add to discrimination against lesbians and gays by emphasizing a criterion for marriage which they are unable to satisfy. The Church has never insisted that the intention to have children is a condition of marriage, and couples who are known to be infertile or are no longer fertile are not forbidden to marry. 'Procreation is unnecessary to the success of marriage.'[10]

c. *The Solution: 'Covenanted Love'?*
Whether marriage should continue to be confined to straight people may be answered additionally by raising our third question, whether there are obvious elements within Christian marriage which overlap with lesbian and gay partnerships. The answer, of course, is a resounding 'Yes'. Accepting the difference that straight people have children, most of the descriptions of marriage as communal partnership (above, 7.1) and mutually administered sacrament (above, 7.2) are readily and

10. Thatcher, *Liberating Sex*, p. 145.

happily applicable to enduring lesbian and gay relationships. This is not to say, of course, that lesbian and gay Christians *ought* to adopt the language used there for themselves. 'Partnership' suggested equality; 'communal' a sharing in the communal life of God. Do lesbians and gays not so share in the communion of the Trinity? The Christian understanding of the human person (above, 7.1.a, 7.1.e), according to which we are made for relation with each other, does not depend on heterosexuality for its fulfilment—fidelity to the experience of lesbian and gay people is conclusive proof of that. The dynamics of conjugal spirituality (above, 7.1.b) clearly apply more broadly than to the married ('every soul is a conjugal soul...').

It was suggested that heterosexual marriage could not be wholly described in terms of friendship (above, 7.1.c) because the commitments made in marriage included children. But married people have much to learn from the way friendship is understood in lesbian and gay communities. Elizabeth Stuart says,

> In my experience, most gay and lesbian people use the language of friendship when speaking about their primary relationships. 'Friendship' suggests a relationship of equals who delight in each other's company and have concern for each other's well-being. 'Friendship' also conjures up images of inclusivity rather than exclusivity... The concept of friendship also admits diversity, and gay and lesbian relationships are nothing if not diverse.[11]

Straight Christians looking for convincing models of marriage after patriarchy will do well to look here. The friendship of marriage is bound to be enriched by it.

Similar connections may be made between heterosexual and homosexual partnerships with regard to the sacramentality of each. Lesbian and gay people find God in their mutual love. Are they deluded? The sacramental understanding expressed in this book deliberately adopted the term 'communal partnership' as the 'matrix' of the sacrament (above, 7.2.b). Indeed 'mutuality in ministry' (above, 7.2.c) is more likely, in fact, to be expressed in avowed egalitarian relationships than in hierarchical ones (as marriage has been for most of its history). The strongest connection between heterosexual and homosexual partnerships is provided by Rahner's essay (above, 7.2.e). God is the source and substance of all loving relationships without restriction. Since God

11. Stuart, *Daring To Speak Love's Name*, p. 19.

has so made the human world that all human love is infused with divine love, there cannot be two orders, a sacramental order where grace is dispensed to the baptized, and a non-sacramental order which awaits redemption. God is not so illiberal. The commitments of lesbian and gay people in their partnerships are no less sacramental, no less able to be (using Rahner's term) a 'sign' of that divine love which is Jesus Christ.

Anglicans are in an especially good position to understand 'natural sacramentality' since, as we have noted, on their own admission they 'do not make an absolute distinction between marriages of the baptised and other marriages, regarding all marriages as in some sense sacramental'.[12] There may be a deep incongruity here. The official position is that sacramental grace is available to married atheists as long as they are straight, and unavailable to Christians in lifelong partnerships as long as they are lesbian or gay. Of course if lesbian and gay partnerships are not marriages, the incongruity does not arise, but if sacramental love spills over and out of its containment in official categories, and if in very many respects lesbian and gay partnerships *do* resemble marriages, then the incongruity re-emerges. Once sacramentality is loosed from its ecclesially administered confinements why continue to confine it to straights?

I have suggested both that marriage is a heterosexual institution and that lesbian and gay partnerships have many features in common with it. The extent of common features can be registered by reading the prayers which are used by lesbians and gays at blessing ceremonies. In the lesbian and gay prayer book, *Daring To Speak Love's Name*, couples describe their relationship as a 'loving union', a 'holy relationship', a 'holy union', a 'covenant', 'our friendship', a 'covenant of friendship and loyalty'.[13] They choose to be 'life-companions'. They 'bear witness to the union of Christ and his Church'. They give themselves wholly to each other; they make 'life-long commitments' to each other.[14] These are profoundly moving blessings, prayers, professions, promises. What straight person could look these partners in the face and say they lack God's grace? An Anglican priest who has provided services of blessing for lesbian and gay couples for many years,

---

12. Above, 7.2.e. The quotation is from Second Anglican–Roman Catholic International Commission, *Life in Christ*, §62, p. 22.

13. Stuart, *Daring To Speak Love's Name*, pp. 31, 32, 33, 37, 38, 53.

14. Stuart, *Daring To Speak Love's Name*, pp. 34, 35, 42.

testifies: 'In my experience everyone has asked to make a life-long commitment despite my suggesting they follow the example of monks and nuns and make a one-, three- or five-year commitment.'[15] How could it be that these lifelong commitments are less worthy signs of the love of Christ for the Church than those of the legally married?

A mediating position between the reservation of marriage for straight couples (because they have children) and the extension of marriage to include lesbian and gay partnerships may be to utilize the notion of 'covenanted love' for all three kinds of relationship. There are two same-sex friendships in the Bible (David and Jonathan, Ruth and Naomi) which are also covenants (above, 7.1.d). Perhaps some of the criticism of covenant might be more accurately directed against asymmetrical versions of it (above, 3.2.a). I think the conviction that sacramental grace cannot be confined to Christians sets in motion a dynamic, rooted in God's omnipresent, redeeming love which will not accept the confining of sacramental grace to straight couples. Theologically, there *is* 'marriage after heterosexuality'. That commits me *both* to the view that marriage is a straight institution because children belong to it, *and* to the view that lifelong commitments are sacramental whether they are between people of the opposite or same sex. The argument of this book moves in a firmly inclusive direction. I do not ask that it be accepted by all lesbian and gay Christian couples. But I hope that the vision of marriage I have outlined is a vision more congruent with lesbian and gay experience, and that one day lesbian, straight and gay will rejoice without reserve in each other's partnerships, whether they are called 'marriages' or not, because they are mutually administered sacraments of God's grace and signs of Christ's covenanted love.

3. *Christian Marriage after Modernity*

Ten contrasts between Christian and post-Christian approaches to marriage were outlined (above, 2.3.b), and the argument of subsequent chapters has sought to expound and celebrate the Christian alternative to those voices which proclaim that whatever is postmodern must also be post-Christian. I am content that this book be judged on the extent to which it has commended Christian marriage as part of an alternative to the post-Christian approaches to sexual relations sketched earlier.

15. Malcolm Johnson, in Stuart, *Daring To Speak Love's Name*, pp. 65-66.

In accordance with the 10 contrasts, Christian marriage 'after modernity' was expected to exhibit at least the following traits: (1) Marriage would remain central, not peripheral, to the Christian understanding of sex and love. It would be an institution of mutual self-giving. (2) There would be no abandonment, but rather a recovery of many of the traditional meanings of marriage, including children, fidelity, sacramentality. (3) Children would be regarded as evidence of the blessing of God on marriage. (4) In contrast to modern individualism a social view of the human person as a person-in-relation was commended. (5) The primary model of love suggested for Christian marriage was the divine-human love rooted in the divine Trinity. (6) One's identity as a Christian and as a person was not simply a lifelong project but was conferred by being with others in relationship. Marriage was considered as the exemplar of what being with another actually means. (7) The depth of the Christian 'passionate ethic' was contrasted with the superficiality of some post-traditional ethics. (8) A positive developmental assessment of Christian tradition (not merely the Christian marriage tradition) was urged. Tradition, combined with a modicum of reverent imagination, liberates by showering us with new possibilities which are forever old, forever new. (9) The model of a lifelong covenant with one person was commended as a core meaning of marriage; and (10) the claim was made that while patriarchy was redundant in marriage after modernity, religious faith was a positive necessity in providing the ethos of permanent commitment and deepening love. Perhaps the vision of marriage as a communal partnership (above, 7.1) and as a mutually administered sacrament (above, 7.2) has indicated the extent of the neglected wealth of the Christian traditions of marriage which are yet to be fully appropriated. Have these traits been amplified and commended in the book?

Readers must judge for themselves. It is sometimes hard when advocating a particular point of view to avoid giving the impression of rejecting other points of view as inferior. I hope people who have never married or who have been wounded by marriage have not themselves felt marginalized by my enthusiasm for it. The theology of love and of natural sacramentality are intentionally inclusive. No one is beyond God's grace because they are outside the various bounds that constitute ecclesiastical or social norms. That is not to claim a certain cleverness in manipulating the discourse of marriage in such a way that everyone, whether married or not, can be conveniently positioned in relation to it.

Not even inclusive language is free from considerations of power, in particular the power of those proposing it and the priority accorded to *their* experience and position, whether overt or not. Married couples are able to experience God's grace in a particular way: it is not the only way. In the postmodern context where Christian marriage may be little understood, and for many untried, this book is offered as a celebration and commendation of a living tradition which is alike, premodern, modern and postmodern. Its joyful bias lies, not in an attempt to define as worse people who live outside marriage, but rather in the belief that it is one of the ways of living in relationship whereby we may 'in company with all God's people, be strong to grasp what is the breadth and length and height and depth of Christ's love, and to know it, though it is beyond knowledge' (Eph. 3.18).

BIBLIOGRAPHY

Alderman, G., *Modern Britain 1700–1983* (London: Croom Helm, 1986).

Allchin, A.M., 'The Sacrament of Marriage in Eastern Christianity', Appendix 3 of *Marriage, Divorce and the Church*, The Report of a Commission appointed by the Archbishop of Canterbury to prepare a statement on the Christian Doctrine of Marriage (London: SPCK, 1971).

Allen, Diogenes, *Christian Belief in a Postmodern World: The Full Wealth of Conviction* (Louisville, KY: Westminster/John Knox Press, 1989).

Anderson, Bernhard A., 'Covenant', in Bruce M. Metzger and Michael D. Coogan (eds.), *The Oxford Companion to the Bible* (Oxford: Oxford University Press, 1993), p. 139.

Atkinson, David, *To Have and To Hold: The Marriage Covenant and the Discipline of Divorce* (London: Collins, 1979).

Bailey, Derrick Sherwin, *The Mystery of Love and Marriage* (London: Camelot Press, 1952).

Baker, J.H., *An Introduction to English Legal History* (London: Butterworth, 1979).

Barry, Norman, 'Justice and Liberty in Marriage and Divorce', in Whelan (ed.), *Just a Piece of Paper?*.

Barth, Karl, *Church Dogmatics. III. Doctrine of Creation*, Part 4 (Edinburgh: T. & T. Clark, 1961).

Barton, C., *Cohabitation Contracts* (Gower: Aldershot, 1985).

Barton, Stephen C. (ed.), *The Family in Theological Perspective* (Edinburgh: T. & T. Clark, 1996).

—'Is the Bible Good News for Human Sexuality? Reflections on Method in Biblical Interpretation', in Adrian Thatcher and Elizabeth Stuart (eds.), *Christian Perspectives on Sexuality and Gender* (Leominster: Gracewing; Grand Rapids: Eerdmans, 1996), pp. 4-13.

—'Biblical Hermeneutics and the Family', in Stephen C. Barton, (ed.), *The Family in Theological Perspective*, pp. 3-24.

Beck, Ulrich, and Elizabeth Beck-Gernsheim, *The Normal Chaos of Love* (trans. Mark Ritter and Jane Wiebel; Cambridge: Polity Press, 1995).

Bellah, Robert, *Habits of the Heart* (New York: Harper & Row, 1985).

Benhabib, Seyla, *Situating the Self: Gender, Community and Postmodernism in Contemporary Ethics* (Cambridge: Polity Press, 1992).

Bernard, Jessie, *The Future of Marriage* (New Haven: Yale University Press, 1973).

Berry, Mary Francis, *The Politics of Parenthood: Child Care, Women's Rights and the Myth of the Good Mother* (New York: Viking, 1993).

Bromiley, Geoffrey W., *God and Marriage* (Edinburgh: T. & T. Clark, 1981).

Brooke, Christopher, *The Medieval Idea of Marriage* (Oxford: Clarendon Press, 1989).

Brown, G., and T. Harris, *The Social Origins of Depression* (London: Tavistock, 1978).

Brown, Peter, *The Body and Society: Men, Women and Sexual Renunciation in Early Christianity* (London: Faber & Faber, 1989).

Brown, Ralph, *Marriage Annulment in the Catholic Church* (Bury St Edmunds: Kevin Mayhew, 3rd edn, 1990).

Brümmer, Vincent, *The Model of Love* (Cambridge: Cambridge University Press, 1994).

Brundage, James A., *Sex, Law and Marriage in the Middle Ages* (Aldershot: Variorum, Ashgate Publishing, 1993).

Brunner, Emil, *The Divine Imperative* (trans. Olive Wyon; Philadelphia: Westminster Press, 1947).

Brunsman, Barry, *New Hope for Divorced Catholics* (San Francisco: Harper & Row, 1985).

Cahill, Lisa Sowle, *Sex, Gender and Christian Ethics* (Cambridge: Cambridge University Press, 1996).

Carey, John J. (ed.), *The Sexuality Debate in North American Churches 1988–1995* (Lewiston: Edwin Mellen Press, 1995).

Carlson, Eric Josef, *Marriage and the English Reformation* (Oxford: Basil Blackwell, 1994).

Carr, Anne, *Transforming Grace: Christian Tradition and Women's Experience* (New York: Harper & Row, 1988).

Carr, Anne, and Elisabeth Schüssler Fiorenza (eds.), *Motherhood: Experience, Institution & Theology, Concilium* 206 (6/1989).

Catechism of the Catholic Church (London: Geoffrey Chapman, 1994).

Childress, James F., *Who Should Decide?: Paternalism in Health Care* (New York: Oxford University Press, 1982).

Clapp, Rodney, *Families at the Crossroads: Beyond Traditional and Modern Options* (Leicester: Inter-Varsity Press, 1993).

Clark, David, and Douglas, Haldane, *Wedlocked? Intervention and Research in Marriage* (Cambridge: Polity Press, 1990).

Cline, Sally, *Women, Celibacy and Passion* (London: André Deutsch, 1993).

Clulow, Christopher (ed.), *Partners Becoming Parents: Talks from the Tavistock Manual Studies Institute* (London: Sheldon Press, 1996).

Clulow, Christopher, and Janet Mattinson, *Marriage Inside Out: Understanding Problems of Intimacy* (Harmondsworth: Penguin Books, 1989).

Cockett, Monica, and John Tripp, *Family Breakdown and its Impact on Children: The Exeter Family Study* (Exeter: University of Exeter Press, 1994).

Codex Iuris Canonici (1983).

Commission Théologique Internationale, *Problèmes doctrinaux du mariage chrétien* (Louvain-la-Neuve: Centre Cerfaux-Lefort, 1979).

Convocations of Canterbury and York, *The Church and Marriage* (London: SPCK, 1935).

Cooey, P., S.A. Farmer, and M.E. Ross (eds.), *Embodied Love: Sensuality and Relationship as Feminist Values* (San Francisco: Harper & Row, 1987).

Cooke, Bernard, 'Indissolubility: Guiding Ideal or Existential Reality?', in Roberts (ed.), *Commitment to Partnership*, pp. 64-78.

Cooper-White, Pamela, *The Cry of Tamar: Violence Against Women and the Church's Response* (Minneapolis: Fortress Press, 1995).

Copley, Anthony, *Sexual Moralities in France, 1780–1980* (London: Routledge, 1989).

Cornes, Andrew, *Divorce and Remarriage: Biblical Principles and Pastoral Practice* (London: Hodder & Stoughton, 1993).

Cosgrove, Art, 'Consent, Consummation and Indissolubility: Some Evidence from Medieval Ecclesiastical Courts', *Downside Review* 109 (1991), pp. 94-104.

Countryman, William, *Dirt, Greed and Sex: Sexual Ethics in the New Testament and their Implications for Today* (London: SCM Press, 1989).

Crellin, E., M.L. Kellmer Pringle and P. West, *Born Illegitimate: Social and Economic Implications* (Windsor: NFER, 1971).

Crispin, Ken, *Divorce: The Forgivable Sin?* (London: Hodder & Stoughton, 1988).

D'Costa, Gavin, 'Christ, the Trinity, and Religious Plurality', in *idem* (ed.), *Christian Uniqueness Reconsidered*, pp. 16-29.

D'Costa, Gavin (ed.), *Christian Uniqueness Reconsidered: The Myth of a Pluralistic Theology of Religions* (Maryknoll, NY: Orbis Books, 1990).

Davies, Jon, 'A Preferential Option for the Family', in Barton (ed.), *The Family*, pp. 219-36.

—'Introduction', in *idem* (ed.), *The Family: Is It Just Another Lifestyle Choice?*, pp. 1-7.

—'Neither Seen Nor Heard Nor Wanted: The Child as Problematic. Towards an Actuarial Theology of Generation', in Michael A. Hayes, Wendy Porter and David Tombs (eds.), *Religion and Sexuality* (Sheffield: Sheffield Academic Press, 1998), pp. 326-47.

Davies, Jon (ed.), *The Family: Is it Just another Lifestyle Choice?* (London: Institute of Economic Affairs, Health and Welfare Unit, 1993).

Davies, Jon, and Gerard Loughlin (eds.), *Sex These Days: Essays on Theology, Sexuality and Society* (Sheffield: Sheffield Academic Press, 1997).

Dean, Craig R., 'Gay Marriage: A Civil Right', *Journal of Homosexuality*, 27.3 (1994), pp. 111-15.

Deech, R., *Divorce Dissent: Dangers in Divorce Reform* (London: Centre for Policy Studies, 1994).

Delhaye, Phillippe, Mgr, 'Propositions on the Doctrine of Christian Marriage', in Malone and Connery, *Contemporary Perspectives on Christian Marriage*, pp. ??.

Demmer, Klaus, 'The Origin of an Idea', *International Journal for Married Spirituality* 1.1 (1995).

Demmer, Klaus, and Aldegonde Brenninkmeijer-Werhahn (eds.), *Christian Marriage Today* (Washington: Catholic University of America Press, 1997).

Dennis, Norman, *Rising Crime and the Dismembered Family* (London: Institute of Economic Affairs Health and Welfare Unit, 1993).

Dennis, Norman, and George Erdos, *Families Without Fatherhood* (London: Institute of Economic Affairs Health and Welfare Unit, 1993).

Denzinger-Schönmetzer, *Enchiridion Symbolorum: Definitionum et Declarationum de Rebus Fidei et Morum* (33rd edn, 1965 [1608]).

Dobash, R.P., and R.E. Dobash, *Violence Against Wives* (Shepton Mallett: Open Books, 1980).

Dominian, Jack, *et al.* (eds.), *Marital Breakdown and the Health of the Nation* (London: One Plus One: Marriage and Partnership Research, 1991).

Dunn, James D.G., 'The Household Rules in the New Testament', in Barton (ed.), *The Family in Theological Perspective*, pp. 43-64.

Dyson, Anthony, with Martyn, Percy, 'Carnal Knowledge', in Percy (ed.), *Intimate Affairs*, pp. 76-85.

Eichenbaum, L., and S. Orbach, *What Do Women Want?* (New York: Berkeley, 1984).

308 *Marriage after Modernity*

Elliott, Peter J., *What God Has Joined: The Sacramentality of Marriage* (New York: Alba House, 1989).

Ellison, Marvin M., *Erotic Justice: A Liberating Ethic of Sexuality* (Louisville, KY: West-minster/John Knox Press, 1996).

The Family in Contemporary Society (London: SPCK, 1958).

Farley, Margaret A., *Personal Commitments* (San Francisco: Harper & Row, 1990).

Flanagan, Kieran, *The Enchantment of Sociology* (London: Macmillan, 1996).

Flandrin, J.L., *Families in Former Times* (Cambridge, 1976).

Flannery, Austin OP, *Vatican Council II: The Conciliar and Post Conciliar Documents* (Leominster: Fowler Wright, rev. edn, 1988).

Forster, Greg, *Cohabitation and Marriage: A Pastoral Response* (London: Marshall Pickering, 1994).

—*Healing Love's Wounds: A Pastoral Approach to Divorce and to Remarriage* (London: Marshall Pickering, 1995).

—*Marriage Before Marriage?: The Moral Validity of 'Common Law' Marriage* (Bram-cote: Grove Books, 1988).

Gardella, Peter, *Innocent Ecstasy* (New York: Oxford University Press, 1985).

General Assembly Special Committeee on Human Sexuality, Presbyterian Church (USA), *Keeping Body and Soul Together: Sexuality, Spirituality and Social Justice* (1991).

General Synod, *An Honourable Estate* (London: Church House Publishing, 1989).

General Synod Board for Social Responsibility of the Church of England, *Abortion and the Church: What Are the Issues?* (GS Misc 408; London: Church House Publishing, 1993).

General Synod Board for Social Responsibility, *Something to Celebrate: Valuing Families in Church and Society* (London: Church House Publishing, 1995).

General Synod Marriage Commission, *Marriage and the Church's Task* (The Lichfield Report; London: CIO Publishing, 1978).

Giddens, Anthony, *The Transformation of Intimacy: Sexuality, Love and Eroticism in Modern Societies* (Cambridge: Polity Press, 1992).

Gillis, John, *For Better, For Worse: British Marriages, 1600 to the Present* (Oxford: Oxford University Press, 1985).

Gledhill, Tom, *The Message of the Song of Songs* (Leicester: Inter-Varsity Press, 1994).

Golby, J.M., and A.W. Purdue, *The Civilization of the Crowd: Popular Culture in England 1750–1900* (London: Batsford, 1984).

Gormally, Luke (ed.), *Moral Truth and Moral Tradition: Essays in Honour of Peter Geach and Elizabeth Anscombe* (Dublin: Four Courts Press, 1994).

Greeley, Andrew (ed.), *The Family in Crisis or Transition*, Concilium 121 (1/1979).

Green, David G., 'Foreword', in Whelan (ed.), *Just a Piece of Paper?*.

Grisez, Germain, Joseph Boyle, John Finnis and William E. May, *The Teaching of Humanae vitae: A Defense* (San Francisco: Ignatius Press, 1988).

Grubbs, Judith Evans, '"Pagan" and "Christian" Marriage: The State of the Question', *Journal of Early Christian Studies* 2 (1994), pp. 361-412.

Guindon, André, 'Case for a "Consummated" Sexual Bond before a "Ratified" Marriage', *Eglise et Théologie* 8 (1977), pp. 137-81.

—*The Sexual Creators: An Ethical Proposal for Concerned Christians* (Lanham, MD: University Press of America, 1986).

—*The Sexual Language: An Essay in Moral Theology* (Ottawa: University of Ottawa Press, 1976).

Guroian, Vigen, *Ethics After Christendom: Toward an Ecclesial Christian Ethic* (Grand Rapids: Eerdmans, 1994).

Hall, D.R., 'Marriage as a Pure Relationship: Exploring the Link between Premarital Cohabitation and Divorce in Canada', *Journal of Comparative Family Studies* 27.1 (1996), pp. 1-12.

Halperin, David J., *Seeking Ezekiel* (Pennsylvania: Pennsylvania State University Press, 1993).

Halsey, A.H., 'Foreword', in Dennis and Erdos, *Families Without Fatherhood.*

Harrington, Joel. F., *Reordering Marriage and Society in Reformation Germany* (Cambridge: Cambridge University Press, 1995).

Hart, Colin, 'The "Real Thing"', *ISCS Bulletin* 15 (1995), pp. 6-7.

Hart, Mark D., 'Reconciliation of Body and Soul: Gregory of Nyssa's Deeper Theology of Marriage', *TS* 51.3 (1990).

Harvey, A.E., *Promise or Pretence? A Christian's Guide to Sexual Morals* (London: SCM Press, 1994).

Haskey, John, 'Pre-marital Cohabitation and the Probability of Subsequent Divorce: Analyses Using New Data from the General Household Survey' (Population Trends, 68; London: HMSO, 1992), pp. 10-19.

Hauerwas, Stanley, 'The Family as a School for Character', in Scott and Warren (eds.), *Perspectives on Marriage*, pp. 146-57.

Haughton, Rosemary, 'The Meaning of Marriage in Women's New Consciousness', in Roberts (ed.), *Commitment to Partnership*, pp. 141-54.

Haw, Reginald, *The State of Matrimony* (London: SPCK, 1952).

Hayes, Michael A., Wendy Porter, and David Tombs (eds.), *Religion and Sexuality* (Sheffield: Sheffield Academic Press, 1998).

Heller, A., and F. Fehér, *The Postmodern Political Condition* (Cambridge: Polity Press, 1988).

Hensley, H., *Marriage and Divorce* (London: Hugh Rees, 1910).

Heth, William A., 'The Meaning of Divorce in Matthew 19.3-9', *Churchman* 98.2 (1984), pp. 136-52.

Heth, William A., and Gordon J. Wenham, *Jesus and Divorce* (London: Hodder & Stoughton, 1984).

Hitchcock, Tim, 'Redefining Sex in Eighteenth Century England', *History Workshop Journal* 41 (1996), pp. 73-90.

Hodgson, Peter, *Winds of the Spirit: A Constructive Christian Theology* (London: SCM Press, 1994).

Hogan, Margaret Monahan, *Finality and Marriage* (Marquette Studies in Philosophy; Marquette: Marquette University Press, 1993).

Hornsby-Smith, Michael P., *Roman Catholic Beliefs in England* (Cambridge: Cambridge University Press, 1991).

Hugenberger, Gordon Paul, *Marriage as a Covenant: A Study of Biblical Law and Ethics Governing Marriage Developed from the Perspective of Malachi* (VTSup, 52; Leiden: E.J. Brill, 1994).

Hunt, Mary, *Fierce Tenderness: A Feminist Theology of Friendship* (New York: Crossroad, 1991).

Hunter, David, *Marriage in the Early Church* (Minneapolis: Fortress Press, 1992).

Jamieson, Lynn, *Intimacy: Personal Relationships in Modern Societies* (Cambridge: Polity Press, 1998).

Jarrett, D., *England in the Age of Hogarth* (St Albans: Paladin, 1976).

Jenkins, Gary, *Cohabitation: A Biblical Perspective* (Nottingham: Grove Books, 1992).

John Paul II, *On the Family* (Apostolic Exhortation: Vatican Press, 1981).

—*Evangelium vitae* (Dublin: Venius, n.d.).

—*Familiaris consortio* (Vatican City: Vatican Press, 1981).

—*Letter to Families* (Vatican City: Vatican Press, 1994).

Junker-Kenny, Maureen, and Norbert Mette (eds.), *Little Children Suffer*, *Concilium* 1996/2.

Kasper, Walter, *Theology of Christian Marriage* (London: Burns & Oates, 1980).

Kaye, Bruce, '"One Flesh" and Marriage', *Colloquium* 22 (1990), pp. 46-57.

Kelly, Kevin T., *Divorce and Second Marriage: Facing the Challenge* (London: Geoffrey Chapman, new and expanded edn, 1996).

Kohn-Roelin, Johanna, 'Mother-Daughter-God', in Carr and Schüssler Fiorenza, *Motherhood*, pp. 64-72.

Küng, Hans, *Christianity: The Religious Situation of Our Time* (London: SCM Press, 1995).

Kurz, Demie, *For Richer, For Poorer: Mothers Confront Divorce* (London: Routledge, 1995).

Lambeth Conference 1930 (London: SPCK, 1930).

Lambeth Conference 1958 (London: SPCK; New York: Seabury Press, 1958).

Lambeth Conference 1968: Resolutions and Reports (London: SPCK; New York: Seabury Press, 1968).

Lasch, Christopher, *The Culture of Narcissism: American Life in an Age of Diminishing Expectations* (New York: W.W. Norton, 1978).

Lash, Nicholas, *Change in Focus: A Study of Doctrinal Change and Continuity* (London: Sheed & Ward, 1973).

Laslett, Peter, *The World We Have Lost* (London: Methuen, 1965).

Lawler, Michael G., 'Faith, Contract, and Sacrament in Christian Marriage: A Theological Approach', *TS* 52 (1991), pp. 712-31.

—*Marriage and Sacrament: A Theology of Christian Marriage* (Collegeville, MN: Liturgical Press, 1993).

—'The Mutual Love and Personal Faith of the Spouses as the Matrix of the Sacrament of Marriage', *Worship*, 65 (1991), pp. 339-61.

—'Perichoresis: New Theological Wine in an Old Theological Wineskin', *Horizons* 22.1 (1995), pp. 49-66.

Lehmann, Karl, 'The Sacramentality of Christian Marriage: The Bond between Baptism and Marriage', in Malone and Connery (eds.), *Contemporary Perspectives*, pp. 91-116.

Leites, Edmund, 'The Duty to Desire: Love, Friendship and Sexuality in some Puritan Theories of Marriage', *Journal of Social History* 15 (1982), pp. 391-95.

Liaboe, Gary, 'The Place of Wife Battering in Considering Divorce', *Journal of Psychology and Theology* 13 (1985), pp. 129-38.

Lincoln, Timothy D., 'Sacramental Marriage: A Possibility for Protestant Theology', *Proceedings of the American Theological Library Association* 49 (1995), pp. 205-216

Lindsey, William D., 'Crossing the Postmodern Divide: Some Implications for Academic Theology', *TheolSex* 7 (1997), pp. 53-69.

Linzey, Andrew, *Animal Theology* (London: SCM Press, 1994).

Loughlin, Gerard, 'The Want of Family in Postmodernity', in Barton (ed.), *The Family in Theological Perspective*, pp. 307-28.

Lunn, Pam, 'Anatomy and Theology of Marriage: Is Gay Marriage an Oxymoron?', *TheolSex* 7 (1997), pp. 10-26.

Lyon, David, *Postmodernity* (Buckingham: Open University Press, 1994),

Lyons, William, *Approaches to Intentionality* (Oxford: Oxford University Press, 1997).

Macfarlane, Alan, *Marriage and Love in England: Modes of Reproduction 1300–1840* (Oxford: Basil Blackwell, 1987).

MacIntyre, Alasdair, *Whose Justice? Which Rationality?* (London: Gerald Duckworth, 1988).

Mackin, Theodore, SJ, *Divorce and Remarriage* (New York: Paulist Press, 1984).

—*The Marital Sacrament* (Mahwah, NJ: Paulist Press, 1989).

—*What is Marriage?* (New York: Paulist Press, 1982).

Macquarrie, John, *A Guide to the Sacraments* (London: SCM Press, 1997).

—*Principles of Christian Theology* (London: SCM Press, 1966).

Malina, Bruce J., *The New Testament World: Insights from Cultural Anthropology* (Atlanta: John Knox Press, 1981).

Malone, Richard, Mgr., and John R. Connery, SJ (eds.), *Contemporary Perspectives on Christian Marriage: Propositions and Papers from the International Theological Commission* (Chicago: Loyola University Press, 1984).

Marrow, Stanley B., 'Marriage and Divorce in the New Testament', *ATR*, 70.1 (1988), pp. 3-15.

Marshner, W.H., 'Can a Couple Practicing NFP Be Practicing Contraception?', *Greg* 77.4 (1996), pp. 677-704.

McEvoy, James, 'Friendship Within Marriage: A Philosophical Essay', in Gormally (ed.), *Moral Truth and Moral Tradition*, pp. 194-202.

McFadyen, Alistair I., *The Call to Personhood: A Christian Theory of the Individual in Relationships* (Cambridge: Cambridge University Press, 1990).

McGowan, Jo, 'Marriage versus Living Together', in Scott and Warren (eds.), *Perspectives on Marriage*, pp. 125-29.

McLanahan, Sara, and Gary Sandefur, *Uncertain Childhood, Uncertain Future: Growing Up with a Single Parent* (Cambridge, MA: Harvard University Press, 1994).

McPherson, Mary Anne Oliver, *Conjugal Spirituality: The Primacy of Mutual Love in Christian Tradition* (Kansas City: Sheed & Ward, 1994).

Meeks, M. Douglas, *God the Economist: The Doctrine of God and Political Economy* (Minneapolis: Fortress Press, 1989).

Mellor, Phillip A., and Chris Shilling, 'Confluent Love and the Cult of the Dyad: The Pre-contractual Foundations of Contractarian Relationships', in Davies and Loughlin (eds.), *Sex These Days*, pp. 51-78.

Mercken, H.P (ed.), *The Greek Commentaries on the Nicomachean Ethics of Aristotle in the Latin Translation of Robert Grosseteste* (2 vols.; Leuven, 1992).

Mette, Norbert, 'Not a "Century of the Child": The Situation of Children in the World in the 1990s', in Junker-Kenny and Mette (eds.), *Little Children Suffer*, pp. 3-8.

Meyendorff, John, *Marriage: An Orthodox Perspective* (St. Vladimir's Seminary Press, 1975).

Middleton, J. Richard, and Brian J. Walsh, *Truth is Stranger Than It Used To Be: Biblical Faith in a Postmodern Age* (London: SPCK, 1995).

Mieth, Dietmar, and Pohier, Jacques (eds.), *The Ethics of Liberation: The Liberation of Ethics, Concilium* (1984).

Mill, John Stuart, 'Nature', in *Nature, the Utility of Religion, and Theism* (written 1850-58), text in Alasdair Clayre (ed.), *Nature and Industrialization* (Oxford: Oxford University Press, 1977), pp. 76-85.

—*The Subjection of Women* (1869).

Mills, John Orme, OP (ed.), 'The Sociologist and God: Facing the Issues Raised by Kieran Flanagan's *The Enchantment of Sociology*', *New Blackfriars* 78.913 (1997), pp. 102-52.

Misfud, Tony, 'The Development of a Liberation Ethic in the Documents of the Church since Vatican II', in Mieth and Pohier (eds.), *The Ethics of Liberation*, pp. 48-53.

Molin, Jean-Baptiste and Protais Mutembe, *Le rituel du mariage en France du XIIème au XVIème siècle* (Paris, 1974).

Molloy, Cathy, *Marriage: Theology and Reality* (Blackrock, Ireland: Columba Press; Toronto: Novalis, 1996).

Montefiore, Hugh, *Remarriage and Mixed Marriage: A Plea for Dual Reform* (London: SPCK, 1967).

Moore, Gareth, *The Body in Context: Sex and Catholicism* (London: SCM Press, 1992).

Morgan, Patricia, 'Conflict and Divorce: Like a Horse and Carriage?', in Whelan (ed.), *Just a Piece of Paper?*, pp. 19-36.

Moser, Antonio, 'The Representation of God in the Ethic of Liberation', in Mieth and Pohier (eds.), *The Ethics of Liberation*, pp. 42-47.

Murphy, Roland E., *A Commentary on the Book of Canticles or Song of Songs* (Minneapolis: Fortress Press, 1990).

National Commission on Children, *Beyond Rhetoric: A New American Agenda for Children and Families* (Washington, DC: US Government Printing Office, 1991).

Nelson, James B., *Body Theology* (Louisville, KY: Westminster/John Knox Press, 1992).

—*The Intimate Connection: Male Sexuality, Masculine Spirituality* (Philadelphia: Westminster Press, 1988; London: SPCK, 1992).

Noonan, John T., Jr, *Contraception: A History of its Treatment by the Catholic Theologians and Canonists* (Cambridge, MA: Harvard University Press, 1986).

Ntakarutimana, Emmanuel, 'Being a Child in Central Africa Today', in Junker-Kenny and Mette (eds.), *Little Children Suffer*.

Okin, Susan Moller, *Justice, Gender and the Family* (New York: Basic Books, 1989).

Ormerod, Paul, and Robert Rowthorn, 'Why Family Ties Bind the Nation', *The Times Higher Education Supplement* (29 August 1997).

Outhwaite, R.B., *Clandestine Marriage in England, 1500–1800* (London: Hambledon Press, 1995).

Palmer, Paul F., SJ, 'Christian Marriage: Contract or Covenant?', *TS* 33 (1972), pp. 617-65.

Parker, David, 'The Early Traditions of Jesus' Sayings on Divorce', *Theology* 96.773 (1993).

Parker, Stephen, *Informal Marriage, Cohabitation and the Law, 1750: 1989* (New York: St Martin's Press, 1990).

Paul VI, *Humanae vitae* (English text in Smith, *Why Humanae Vitae Was Right*).

Percy, Martyn (ed.), *Intimate Affairs: Sexuality and Spirituality in Perspective* (London: Darton, Longman & Todd, 1997).

Phillips, Melanie, 'Death Blow to Marriage', in Whelan (ed.), *Just a Piece of Paper?*, pp. 13-18.

Piper, John, and Wayne Grudem, *Recovering Biblical Manhood and Womanhood: A Response to Evangelical Feminism* (Illinois: Wheaton, 1991).

Pius XI, *Casti connubii*, Vatican Text of the Encyclical Letter of Pope Pius XI on Christian Marriage (Vatican City: Vatican Press, 1930).

Pontifical Council for the Family, *Preparation For The Sacrament Of Marriage* (Vatican City: Vatican Press, 1996).

Post, Stephen, *Spheres of Love: Toward a New Ethics of the Family* (Dallas: Southern Methodist University Press, 1994).

Power, Kim, *Veiled Desire: Augustine's Writing on Women* (London: Darton, Longman & Todd, 1995).

Powers, B. Ward, and John Wade, *Divorce, the Bible and the Law* (Sydney: AFES Graduates Fellowship, 1978).

Price, Richard, 'The Distinctiveness of Early Christian Ethics', in Thatcher and Stuart (eds.), *Christian Perspectives*, pp. 14-32.

Purvis, Sally, 'Mothers, Neighbors and Strangers: Another Look at Agape', in Thatcher and Stuart (eds.), *Christian Perspectives*, pp. 232-46.

Quaife, G.R., *Wanton Wives and Wayward Wenches: Peasants and Illicit Sex in Early Seventeenth Century England* (London: Croom Helm, 1979).

Rahner, Karl, 'Marriage as a Sacrament', *Theological Investigations* (23 vols.; London: Darton, Longman & Todd, 1967), X, pp. 199-221.

Ramsey, Paul, *One Flesh: A Christian View of Sex Within, Outside and Before Marriage* (Bramcote: Grove Books, 1975).

Ranke-Heinemann, Uta, *Eunuchs for the Kingdom of Heaven: The Catholic Church and Sexuality* (Harmondsworth: Penguin Books, 1990).

Raymond, Janice G., *A Passion for Friends: Towards a Philosophy of Female Affection* (Boston: Beacon Press, 1986).

Rejon, Francisco Moreno, 'Seeking the Kingdom and its Justice: the Development of the Ethic of Liberation', in Mieth and Pohier (eds.), *The Ethics of Liberation*.

Rémy, Jean, 'The Family: Contemporary Models and Historical Persective', in Greeley (ed.), *The Family in Crisis or Transition*.

Report of a Commission appointed by the Archbishop of Canterbury to prepare a statement on the Christian Doctrine of Marriage (The Root Commission) (London: SPCK, 1971).

Reynolds, Phillip Lyndon, *Marriage in the Western Church: The Christianization of Marriage During the Patristic and Early Medieval Periods* (Leiden: E.J. Brill, 1994).

Rich, Adrienne, *Of Woman Born: Motherhood as Experience and Institution* (New York: W.W. Norton, 1976).

Rike, Jennifer. L., 'The Lion and the Unicorn: Feminist Perspectives on Christian Love as Care', in Thatcher and Stuart (eds.), *Christian Perspectives on Sexuality and Gender*, pp. 247-62.

Roberts William P. (ed.), *Commitment to Partnership: Explorations of the Theology of Marriage* (New York: Paulist Press, 1987).

Ruddick, Sara, *Maternal Thinking: Toward a Politics of Peace* (Boston: Beacon Press, 1989).

Ruether, Rosemary Radford, 'Church and Family V: Church and Family in the 1980s', *New Blackfriars* 65 (1984).

—*Gaia and God: An Ecofeminist Theology of Earth Healing* (London: SCM Press, 1993).

—'Spirit and Matter, Public and Private: The Challenge of Feminism to Traditional Dualisms', in P. Cooey, S.A. Farmer and M.E. Ross (eds.), *Embodied Love: Sensuality and Relationship as Feminist Values*.

Schillebeeckx, Edward, *Christ the Sacrament* (London: Sheed & Ward, 1963).

—*Marriage: Human Reality and Saving Mystery* (London: Sheed & Ward, 1965).

Schoff, Phillip (ed.), *The Nicene and Post-Nicene Fathers*, III (Buffalo: Christian Literature Co., 1887).

Schüssler Fiorenza, Francis, 'Marriage', in Fiorenza and Galvin (eds.), *Systematic Theology: Roman Catholic Perspectives*, pp. 305-46.

Schüssler Fiorenza, Francis, and John P. Galvin (eds.), *Systematic Theology: Roman Catholic Perspectives* (2 vols.; Minneapolis: Fortress Press, 1991).

Scott, Kieran, and Michael Warren (eds.), *Perspectives on Marriage: A Reader* (New York: Oxford University Press, 1993).

Second Anglican–Roman Catholic International Commission, *Life in Christ: Morals, Communion and the Church* (London: Church House Publishing; London: Catholic Truth Society, 1994).

Seidman, Steven, *Embattled Eros: Sexual Politics and Ethics in Contemporary America* (London: Routledge, 1992).

Smart, Carol, 'The Ties Still Bind', *The Times Higher Education Supplement* (5 September 1997), p. 15.

Smith, Janet, '*Humanae Vitae* at Twenty', in *idem* (ed.), *Why Humanae Vitae Was Right*, pp. 499-518.

—*Why Humanae Vitae Was Right: A Reader* (San Francisco: Ignatius Press, 1993).

Shelby, John Spong, *Living in Sin? A Bishop Rethinks Human Sexuality* (San Francisco: Harper & Row, 1988).

Steininger, Victor, *Divorce: Arguments for a Change in the Church's Discipline* (London: Sheed & Ward, 1969).

Stevenson, Kenneth, *Nuptial Blessing: A Study of Christian Marriage Rites* (New York: Oxford University Press, 1983).

Stivers, Richard, *The Culture of Cynicism: American Morality in Decline* (Oxford: Basil Blackwell, 1994).

Stone, Lawrence, *The Family, Sex and Marriage in England 1500–1800* (London, Weidenfeld & Nicolson, 1979).

—'Passionate Attachments in the West in Historical Perspective', in Scott and Warren (eds.), *Perspectives on Marriage*, pp. 171-79.

Stonewall Factsheet, 'Same Sex Couples and the Law' (March 1998).

Stonewall Pamphlet, *Equality 2000* (1998).

Storkey, Alan, *Marriage and its Modern Crisis: Repairing Married Life* (London: Hodder & Stoughton, 1996).

Stuart, Elizabeth, *Daring To Speak Love's Name: A Gay and Lesbian Prayer Book* (London: Hamish Hamilton, 1992).

—*Just Good Friends: Towards a Lesbian and Gay Theology of Relationships* (London: Mowbray, 1994).

Stuart, Elizabeth, and Thatcher, Adrian, *People of Passion: What the Churches Teach About Sex* (London: Cassell, 1997).

Taylor, Jeremy, *A Discourse of the Nature, Offices, and Measures of Friendship*, in *idem*, *Works XI* (London: Longmans, 1839).

Thatcher, Adrian, *Liberating Sex: A Christian Sexual Theology* (London: SPCK, 1993).

—'Safe Sex, Unsafe Arguments', *Studies in Christian Ethics* 92 (1996), pp. 66-77.

—'Postmodernity and Chastity', in Davies and Loughlin (eds.), *Sex These Days*, pp. 122-40.

—'Singles and Families', *TheolSex* 4 (1996), pp. 11-27.

—*Truly a Person, Truly God* (London: SPCK, 1990).

Thatcher, Adrian, and Elizabeth Stuart (eds.), *Christian Perspectives on Sexuality and Gender* (Leominster: Gracewing; and Grand Rapids: Eerdmans, 1996).

—*The Family in Contemporary Society* (London: SPCK, 1958).

Thiselton, Anthony, *Interpreting God and the Postmodern Self: On Meaning, Manipulation and Promise* (Edinburgh: T. & T. Clark, 1995).

Tilley, Terrence W., *Postmodern Theologies: The Challenge of Religious Diversity* (New York: Orbis Books, 1995).

Tillich, Paul, *Systematic Theology*, II (3 vols.; Digswell Place: Nisbet, 1957).

US Census Bureau, *Current Population Survey Reports* (March 1998).

US Census Bureau, *Monthly Vital Statistics Report*, 43.12 (supp.) (July 1995).

US Census Bureau, *Statistical Abstract of the United States 1997* (Washington DC: Hoover's Business Press, 1997).

Wallerstein, Judith S., 'Children After Divorce: Wounds That Don't Heal', in Scott and Warren (eds.), *Perspectives on Marriage*, pp. 337-46.

Walton, Heather, 'Theology of Desire', *TheolSex* 1 (1994), pp. 13-41.

Ware, Kallistos, 'The Sacrament of Love: The Orthodox Understanding of Marriage and its Breakdown', *Downside Review* 109 (1991), pp. 79-93.

Weeks, Jeffery, *Invented Moralities: Sexual Values in an Age of Uncertainty* (Cambridge: Polity Press, 1995).

Weems, Renita J., *Battered Love: Marriage, Sex and Violence in the Hebrew Prophets* (Minneapolis: Augsburg–Fortress, 1995).

—'Gomer: Victim of Violence or Victim of Metaphor?', *Semeia* 47 (1989), pp. 87-104.

Wellings, Kaye, Julia Field, Anne M. Johnson and Jane Wadsworth, *Sexual Behaviour in Britain: The National Survey of Sexual Attitudes and Lifestyles* (Harmondsworth: Penguin Books, 1994).

Whelan, Robert (ed.), *Just a Piece of Paper? Divorce Reform and the Undermining of Marriage* (London: Institute of Economic Affairs Health and Welfare Unit, 1995).

White, James F., *Introduction to Christian Worship* (Nashville: Abingdon Press, rev. edn, 1990).

White, S.K., *Political Theory and Postmodernism* (Cambridge: Cambridge University Press, 1991).

Whitehead, Evelyn Eaton, and James D. Whitehead, *Marrying Well: Stages on the Journey of Christian Marriage* (New York: Image Books, 1983).

—'The Passage into Marriage', in Scott and Warren (eds.), *Perspectives on Marriage*, pp. 136-45.

Williams, Robert, 'Towards a Theology for Lesbian and Gay Marriage', *ATR* 72 (1990).

Williams, Rowan, review of *Liberating Sex* by Adrian Thatcher (London: SPCK, 1993), in *Theology* 98.781 (1995).

Winnett, A.R., *Divorce and Remarriage in Anglicanism* (London: Macmillan, 1958).

Witte, John, Jr, *From Sacrament to Contract: Marriage, Religion, and Laws in the Western Tradition* (Louisville, KY: Westminster/John Knox Press, 1997).

Wood, Susan, SCL, 'The Marriage of Baptized Nonbelievers: Faith, Contract, and Sacrament', *TS* 48 (1987), pp. 279-301.

Woodhead, Linda, 'Sex in a Wider Context', in Davies and Loughlin (eds.), *Sex These Days*, pp. 98-120.

Zion, William Basil, *Eros and Transformation: Sexuality and Marriage: An Eastern Orthodox Perspective* (Lanham, MD: University Press of America, 1992).

INDEXES

INDEX OF REFERENCES

OLD TESTAMENT

INDEX OF SUBJECTS

INDEX OF AUTHORS